MW01012173

Spaces of Treblinka

Spaces of Treblinka

Retracing a Death Camp

JACOB FLAWS

University of Nebraska Press

LINCOLN

Chapter 5, "A Sensory Space," is derived in part from the article "Sensory Witnessing at Treblinka," *Journal of Holocaust Research*, January 2021, available at http://www.tandfonline.com/doi.org/10.1080/25785648.2020.1858583.

The University of Nebraska Press is part of a land-grant institution with campuses and programs on the past, present, and future homelands of the Pawnee, Ponca, Otoe-Missouria, Omaha, Dakota, Lakota, Kaw, Cheyenne, and Arapaho Peoples, as well as those of the relocated Ho-Chunk, Sac and Fox, and Iowa Peoples.

Library of Congress Cataloging-in-Publication Data

Names: Flaws, Jacob, author.

Title: Spaces of Treblinka: retracing a death camp / Jacob Flaws.

Description: Lincoln: University of Nebraska Press, [2024] | Includes bibliographical references and index.

Identifiers: LCCN 2024020316

ISBN 9781496239730 (hardcover)

ISBN 9781496241153 (epub)

ISBN 9781496241160 (pdf)

Subjects: LCSH: Treblinka (Concentration camp) | Holocaust, Jewish (1939–1945)—Poland. | Holocaust, Jewish (1939–1945)—Psychological aspects. | Holocaust, Jewish (1939–1945)—Personal narratives. | Holocaust survivors. | BISAC: HISTORY / Modern / 20th Century / Holocaust | HISTORY / Wars & Conflicts / World War II / European Theater

Classification: LCC D805.5.T74 F53 2024 | DDC 940.53/185384—dc23/eng/20240620

LC record available at https://lccn.loc.gov/2024020316

Designed and set in Minion Pro by Scribe Inc.

Dedicated to David Shneer z"l

My faith has been tempered in Hell. My faith
has emerged from the flames of the crematoria,
from the concrete of the gas chamber. I have seen
that it is not man who is impotent in the struggle
against evil, but the power of evil that is impotent
in the struggle against man. The powerlessness of
kindness, of senseless kindness, is the secret of its
immortality. It can never be conquered. The more
stupid, the more senseless, the more helpless it may
seem, the vaster it is. . . . This dumb, blind love
is man's meaning. Human history is not a battle
of good struggling to overcome evil. It is a battle
fought by a great evil struggling to crush a small
kernel of human kindness. But if what is human in
human beings has not been destroyed even now,
then evil will never conquer.

—Vasily Grossman, *Life and Fate*

CONTENTS

ILLUSTRATIONS

ACKNOWLEDGMENTS

Any book is impossible without the help of many. The deepest gratitude I have and ever could have is for my family. To my incredible wife, Theresa, thank you for always being my rock in the waves, my light in the darkness, and my shelter from the storm. And to my beautiful daughter, Jemma, thank you for letting Dada be gone for so many days and nights. May you always dream big, my sweet girl.

To my mom, Lori, and my dad, Jim, thank you for giving me the strength and encouragement to take the road less traveled and to always pursue my dreams. To James, Jeremy, and Jonathon, I am honored I get to call you not just brothers but my friends. Thank you also to Steve, Gina, and the Critchlow family for your unwavering support.

To my advisor, the late David Shneer, you were not just a mentor but a friend, a role model, and an example of who I hope to become. Thank you for all you did for me, and I hope to continue to reflect your light to the world. To David Ciarlo, I appreciate the wisdom, insight, and guidance that you continue to provide. Without you, this work would not exist. And to Nick Underwood, my sincerest appreciation for all the time spent sharing your invaluable expertise.

Thank you to Simone Gigliotti for serving on my dissertation committee and your continued mentorship. Thank you also to Martha Hanna, Beverly Weber, and Eli Sacks for the feedback, revisions, and most of all, the encouragement while this was still a dissertation. Thank you sincerely to the Jewish Studies Program at the University of Colorado–Boulder (CU); I will always remember and cherish how you included me in your tight-knit community. Thank you also to Gregg Drinkwater and Adi Nester for your thoughtful feedback on my earliest forays into this research. I am deeply appreciative of Jane Thaler, Sarah Gavison, and Stephanie Yuhas for connecting me with the Harry Mazal Collection; being included in that experience changed my life and helped form the foundation for this project. To my other colleagues and classmates at cu, I thank you for your kindness and your collegiality.

Thank you to Edward Westermann and Anne Knowles for your astute observations and keen recommendations that have helped improve this manuscript in so many ways. I owe you both a debt of gratitude. My profound thanks also to Heather Stauffer, Bridget Barry, and everyone at the University of Nebraska Press. Thank you for believing in this project and for your assistance at every step of the publishing process. Additionally, I am enormously grateful to Brianna Blackburn at Scribe Inc. and Jennifer Boeree for the deft and insightful copyedits you suggested for this manuscript. I must also recognize Jessica Freeman at Freeman Indexing: thank you for your brilliant work on this book's index.

And to my original mentors, Bill Feis and Dixee Bartholomew-Feis, thank you so much for helping me find my voice and for subtly guiding me toward my future. Every student needs a teacher to ignite their spark, and you both did that for me.

I also extend my appreciation to the Jewish Historical Institute in Warsaw, the Karta Foundation (Warsaw), the Central Archives of Modern Records (Warsaw), and the State Archives in Siedlce. My research experience at each of these locations was exceptional, and the employees and staff were extraordinarily helpful.

Thank you to the American Academy of Jewish Research for the Summer Research Grant that helped get me to the aforementioned archives. I also thank the Singer Fund Fellowship, the Rabbi Daniel and Ida Goldberger Fellowship, and the Global Initiatives Scholarship provided by the Jewish Studies Program at cu. Thank you also to everyone at the Nevzlin Center at the Hebrew University of Jerusalem for selection and inclusion in the Conference for Young Scholars on Eastern European Jewry in 2017. It was so helpful presenting my work there and building a network of stellar colleagues.

Finally, to my colleagues and friends at Arizona State University (asu) and the National World War II Museum, I extend my sincere gratitude for the support, encouragement, and friendship over the last few years as I developed this manuscript. I am particularly grateful to asu's Center for Jewish Studies and Hava Tirosh-Samuelson, Lisa Kaplan, and Gloria Baker for the gracious subvention to help complete this book. Thank you!

INTRODUCTION

A leaden fog hung so low in the sky that it seemed
as if we would be able to reach out and touch
it. . . . The pine trees stood out from a distance as if
shrouded in black veils. The sun had become pale
and dim; it looked like a small, round human face
gazing down at us from above, like the twisted,
suddenly-aged face of someone newly bereaved.

—Rachel Auerbach, *The Death Camp Treblinka*

French theorist Henri Lefebvre once suggested that no space vanishes from
history without leaving a trace.[1] I believe he meant that human beings possess
the inherent ability to connect with spaces in ways that transcend what we
see. The universality of this trait appears in observations made by three well-
known post-Holocaust visitors to Treblinka. Surveying the pockmarked field
of sand, ash, and bone spread out before him, Soviet writer Vasily Grossman
struggled to pair these scattered physical remnants of the Treblinka death
camp with the immeasurable human suffering he knew had taken place there.
"This plot of land fenced off with barbed wire has consumed more human
lives than all the oceans and the seas in the world ever since the birth of
mankind," he wrote. "The earth ejects the crushed bones, the teeth, bits
of paper and clothing; it refuses to keep its awful secret. . . . The lupine
pods pop open, the tiny peas beat a faint tattoo as though a myriad of tiny
bells were ringing a funeral dirge deep down under the ground."[2] A year
later, Holocaust survivor and scholar Rachel Auerbach felt dissonance confronting the emptiness, struggling to fathom the magnitudes lost: "Believe
me, over a million people killed in the course of one year in one little place
is a million times more than a million human brains could grasp."[3] Thirty

years further on, while filming his renowned documentary *Shoah*, Claude Lanzmann discovered an utterly banal, otherwise forgettable landscape that obliterated his haunted preconceptions: "There was an incredible shock in Treblinka, with its endless consequences, triggered by the meeting of a name and a place, by the discovery of this accursed name on ordinary road signs and train stations as though, over there, nothing had happened."[4] Although each took something different from the space where the camp once stood, they all sought their own traces of Treblinka.

From the historian's perspective, the "traces" of Nazi camps seem well documented.[5] Among the vast network, six—Auschwitz, Majdanek, Chełmno, Bełżec, Sobibór, and Treblinka—stood apart from the rest. Demarcated as death camps, or hybrid concentration-death camps, the Germans and their auxiliaries murdered over three million Jews and other groups at these locations during the Holocaust. And yet, the latter three (Bełżec, Sobibór, and Treblinka) stood even further apart, envisioned as factory-style, "industrial" spaces of mass murder. Built after the Wannsee Conference of January 1942, during which Nazi leaders formalized mass murder as the "Final Solution" to their "Jewish Question," and named for the recently assassinated *Schutzstaffel* (ss) officer Reinhard Heydrich, the "Operation Reinhard" camps represented novel spaces within the Third Reich. With no Auschwitz-like selections at the railway platform and no large groups of slave laborers kept alive in service of the German war effort, the Reinhard camps' sole purpose was to murder the millions of Jews detained in the ghettos of occupied Poland.[6]

In a span of nineteen months, from April 1942, when construction on the camps started, to October 1943, when the program was shut down, more than 1.6 million people were systematically transported to and murdered at the three Reinhard camps.[7] More than half of this staggering death toll, a figure consistently estimated at 800,000 to 900,000 people, died at Treblinka alone, and though in operation for only one-third as long as Auschwitz (where 1.1 million were murdered), the pace of killing at Treblinka surpassed that of any other location during the Holocaust.[8] Alongside its lethality, Treblinka also represented something else to Nazi planners of the Holocaust—it was the model of a death-producing space where initially Jews, but then later others deemed "undesirable" by the Third Reich, could be "efficiently" slaughtered in isolated spaces sectioned off physically and ideologically from the rest of the world. In fact, Treblinka was so conceptually different that Reinhard personnel intentionally waited to build it until several months after Sobibór and Bełżec were operational in order to correct at Treblinka any "inefficiencies" discovered in the first two.[9]

Despite the Reinhard camps' horrific purpose, in 1943 the war irreversibly turned against Germany, and fearful that the advancing Red Army might uncover their murderous operations, the Germans razed Treblinka to the ground. Consequently, at the current site, visitors encounter an open field surrounded by a thick forest of evergreen trees. The trees, many of which the Germans planted as they retreated, now stand over eighty feet tall and serve as imposing visual barriers separating the field from the rural countryside that surrounds it. Laid out across the sandy soil are seventeen thousand stone markers of various shapes and sizes jutting haphazardly out of the ground. Erected in 1963 by sculptor Franciszek Duszenko and architect Adam Haupt, many are engraved with names of the towns and cities from where the victims came, and all serve as symbolic gravestones for the murdered.[10] In the middle of these formations rises a massive monument marking where the gas chambers once stood; etched on its stone exterior is a menorah, and nearby a plaque proclaims "Never Again" in seven languages.

Jarringly absent are the tangible structures—barracks, ovens, and electric fences—that one finds still physically preserved at places like Auschwitz, Majdanek, and Dachau. At Treblinka, the memorial instead relies on the introspective and conceptual, creating a narrative of remembrance that embraces the living who come to honor the dead. In this way, the Treblinka memorial is hardly a static site of collective memory, and while visitors are free to interpret the space within their own perceptions and personal contexts, negotiating something so ephemeral can be a dissonant experience that creates more questions than answers.[11]

While standing amid the memorial stones on my own recent visit, I found myself, much like Grossman, Auerbach, Lanzmann, and countless others, seeking traces of Treblinka. The warm, sunny weather felt at odds with how I thought Treblinka *should* feel.[12] It was only later, when dark storm clouds materialized on the horizon, ominous and heavy with rain, that Treblinka somehow felt more *appropriate*, more aligned with the dark and moody atmosphere of "night and fog" that we usually imagine of Holocaust spaces.[13] Wrestling with these discordant feelings, I made an uncomfortable observation—only the passage of time separated the present space from what it formerly was, and in fact, if I were standing here eighty years earlier, I would encounter radically different and horrifying surroundings.

Shuddering at the thought, I decided to exit the Treblinka memorial, but not by the designated path. Instead, I weaved through the trees and beyond the pillars denoting where perimeter fences once stood. Traversing a kilometer through the dense pines and thick undergrowth, I came to a clearing, exited the forest, and approached a small village named Wólka Okrąglik. In this town, just a short walk from the camp, I was surprised to find a business, a church, numerous houses, and indeed, people. For whatever reason, I half expected all the spaces around the former death camp to be bereft of life and devoid of everything, save ghosts. Needing to remind myself where I was, at that moment I turned and glanced over my shoulder toward the massive grove of trees hiding the Treblinka memorial from view. Perhaps it was my own imagination again, but I would have sworn the forest enclosing the site was now looming overhead like a dark green cloud, threatening to overtake the tranquil rural home in front of me like an onrushing wave. I quickly snapped a photo, assured that I had captured some fleeting remnant—indeed, some trace—of how it must have felt to witness Treblinka as it belched towering clouds of ash and oily smoke over the landscape.[14]

In reality, as you can see in figure 1, the photo captures none of that. Treblinka no longer exists; the images haunting my perception are byproducts my imagination has conjured up. My knowledge of what happened just on the other side of those trees has been distorted by my own discomfort at the random spatial juxtapositions that exist in our world—ones that put the sanctuaries of our intimate spaces of hearth and home directly adjacent to those where horrific crimes take place.

Accordingly, the pages that follow represent my attempt to come to terms with my own dissonant experience; but along the way, I seek clarity on what Treblinka really *was*, who witnessed or smelled or heard what was nearby, and how we come to terms with the no-longer-existent spaces surrounding us as we go about our daily lives in (perhaps ignorant) proximity to them. I aim to bridge the gap between past and present by reconceptualizing what is no longer there and by reimagining spaces colored not in black and white but in the same vivid, multisensorial reality that accompanies all human history. From this exploration emerges a deeply entwined narrative of life

FIG. 1. Looking northwest from the town of Wólka Okrąglik. Treblinka
sits within the forest behind this house. Author's collection.

and death, of fantasy and reality, of nature and humans, of interactions and
witnessing, and of knowing and not knowing.

Beyond all else, Treblinka was, to borrow the term from spatial theorist
Doreen Massey, a space of "contemporaneous plurality" in which "distinct trajectories" of experience, ideology, and perception from many different people—
Germans, Jews, *and* Poles—coalesced around the focal point that was the
camp.[15] This fundamental observation makes clear that there was not a
single space of Treblinka and therefore no one group whose experiences
accounted for its spatial reality. Instead, like all other human spaces, Treblinka existed as the simultaneous product of interactions between all human
beings who encountered it and in conjunction with the nonhuman, natural
world inside of which all human activity takes place. Thus, to chart these
disparate but connected lived experiences, I map the spaces of Treblinka in
a way that weaves together testimonies, oral histories, and recollections of
Germans, Jews, and the local Polish population. While historians have generally treated these witnesses as if they existed in different spheres—studies

examine Germans' motivations as perpetrators, Jewish people's experiences as victims, or Polish citizens' behaviors as "neighbors"—such categorization dividing witnesses into clean, disparate groups is antithetical to how human beings, present and past, actually live their lives.[16] Although the power dynamics dictating different behaviors remain important, interweaving these perspectives creates a more holistic representation of the spaces of Treblinka.[17]

This book's reconceptualization also redefines how we understand Nazi death camps as structures of genocide by highlighting the tenuous relationship between what perpetrators of genocide think they are creating and what they ultimately create. Moreover, I chose Treblinka specifically because this disparity between the imagined and the real was so great there. No matter how many variables the Nazis believed they had accounted for in designing, building, and operating their model death camp, they could not change how other people perceived the spaces of Treblinka or how many ways the camp ejected sights, sounds, smells, people, bodies, and trains into the surrounding world. This observation proves that there were *many* more witnesses to the death camps than we have previously acknowledged. In fact, it redefines the very concept of witnessing altogether by recognizing the spatial experiences of thousands of people whose daily lives were influenced by their happenstance proximity to Treblinka. In charting these "zones of witnessing," as I call them, radiating out from the camp, I show that Nazi ideological conceptions of what Treblinka *should be* were repeatedly undermined by both the scale of mass murder carried out there and the lived experiences of these newly considered witnesses nearby. Instead of the hoped-for isolation of a camp hidden from the prying eyes of humanity, Treblinka was witnessed far and wide. And instead of the clean, sanitized site of industrial killing that made the elimination of "undesirables" almost mechanistically easy (as the Nazis hoped), Treblinka was barbaric, brutal, and horrifying to almost inconceivable levels.

While contemporary and postwar recollections of the death camp describe in meticulous and gruesome detail the awful reality of Treblinka and its adjacent spaces, few have stopped to ask why survivors and witnesses consistently devote space to mentioning such frightful details. But there are reasons. To quote Samuel Willenberg and Kalman Taigman, the last two known Treblinka survivors, in a 2010 interview, "The world cannot forget Treblinka," and "Soon there will be no one left to tell."[18] Such warnings are more prescient and consequential than they might appear at first glance. In 2016, in fact, the latter was realized when Willenberg passed away as the last known Treblinka survivor. The former warning, though, was overlooked before the ink on the same article was even dry. Just paragraphs before the survivors are quoted, the article's author describes Treblinka as the "most chillingly efficient killing machine"—the same imagery of efficient, antiseptic, and factory-like killing that has proven pervasive in many postwar representations of the Holocaust. A 1946 German-language pamphlet entitled *Das Menschenschlachthaus Treblinka*, one of the first publications on Treblinka in Germany after the war, fetishizes the factory-like, clean imagery of the death camp.[19] More recently, a 2013 Smithsonian documentary on the archeological research of Caroline Sturdy Colls employed as its title *Treblinka: Hitler's Killing Machine.*[20]

Yet those who witnessed the camp consistently remind us that Treblinka was not some disembodied industrial apparatus.[21] Whether popular culture has kept the cleaner industrial myths alive, or whether simply sanitizing mass murder appeals to our own societal squeamishness, such devices persist at the expense of these spaces' horrific, human-created reality. Instead, to borrow the astute words of Holocaust scholar Georges Didi-Huberman, "Let us not shelter ourselves by saying that we cannot, that we could not by any means, imagine it to the very end. . . . In order to know, we must *imagine* for ourselves."[22] In taking a closer look, then, and peeling back the myths, we see genocide for what it really is—humans killing other humans, often in ways so horrendous that the accompanying smells, sights, and sounds shocked anyone who witnessed them. And because anything done by humans can be repeated, we must be careful not to fall into the (perhaps unconscious) trap of representing Nazi spaces of atrocity using the same types of technocratic imagery and language that they employed to distance themselves from the mass murder they were committing.

Space and Place

To understand Treblinka's spatial reality is to think more deeply about how we, as humans, conceptualize space. More than an abstract theoretical construct, Lefebvre wrote that "it is possible, and indeed normal, to decipher or decode spaces."[23] My use and definition of space in this book adheres closely to something geographer James Tyner has written: "Space . . . has no materiality and exists conceptually as a result of human relations and interactions."[24] That is, space is constructed from the conceptions, fantasies, ideological assumptions, and memories a person projects onto a physical location or place. Because of the universality of this trait, we continually project our abstract perceptions onto *all* the places we encounter, whether they are historically important, personally meaningful, or both. In this way, according to Lefebvre, space is not produced in the sense that a kilogram of sugar or a yard of cloth is produced; instead, this reciprocal relationship, where we both produce and are produced by space, gives structure to our everyday lives and frames how we create knowledge of our world.[25]

Place, though connected to space, is a more tangible concept. While theorist Yi-Fu Tuan argues that "undifferentiated space becomes place as we get to know it better and endow it with value," he is also clear to point out that "place is a pause in movement." Thus, while space can be said to exist in flux across both time and personal experience, place represents a more fixed representation of the here and now. In Tuan's own words, "if we think of space as that which allows movement . . . each pause in movement makes it possible for location to be transformed into place."[26] The temporal difference between space and place, therefore, is crucial: I study here only the *historical* space of Treblinka. Therefore, I maintain, as Massey does, that because place exists in the present, all past perspectives of experience belong in the category of space, especially as it pertains to the vanished Reinhard death camps.[27]

One problem with many historical spaces, like Treblinka, is that few physical remains, if any, exist today. Often the site has changed so greatly in appearance that its former state is unrecognizable. Kate Brown has studied these so-called nonplaces in her examination of the *kresy* region of the Eastern European borderlands. Brown argues that within "the redemptive power of memory spirits of the past" remain, "written on the landscape and into the cadence of oral culture."[28] In reimagining no-longer-existent spaces, therefore, as Simon Schama has also suggested, *memories* assume "the form of the landscape itself. A metaphor becomes a reality; an absence a presence."[29] In other words, the nonplaces of today's world remain historically relevant because their conceptual existence lives on in the memories of those witnesses most intimately associated with these spaces. In reconceptualizing Treblinka, that means that the perspectives of Jewish, German, and Polish witnesses *all* play significant roles in detailing its historical space.[30] Not only do these witnesses reveal the transnational nature of Treblinka's spaces, but given the various power dynamics at play, each witness group provides slightly different but inherently related—often overlapping and corroborating—conceptions of what occurred. Blurring the categorical boundaries often used to separate these groups, therefore, privileges the fact that each person witnessing the camp possessed a body capable of experiencing sensory phenomena and using those experiences to interpret their spatial realities.[31]

Indeed, one commonality of Treblinka's transnational witnesses is that almost all placed an emphasis on *sensory* memory. Lefebvre accounts for this by arguing, "It is by means of the body that space is perceived, lived—and produced."[32] More specifically, as geographer Paul Rodaway writes, "Through their structure and the way we use them, the senses mediate" a person's everyday spatial experiences. Therefore, our senses are "the ground base on which a wider geographical understanding can be constructed."[33] Simone Gigliotti's nuanced and insightful book *The Train Journey*, which explores the concept of "sensory witnessing" in relation to deprivations inflicted on Jewish bodies in transit to death camps, has critically shaped my understanding of the seminal role our senses play in witnessing and memory.[34] And while I devote a full chapter to Treblinka's existence as a sensory space, the use of sensory memory is a theme that runs throughout the book due to its primacy in how we perceive the world and create memories connected to our lived experiences.

Mapping Treblinka's Spaces

The starting point for this project is, in many ways, Lanzmann's *Shoah*. To borrow the words of scholar Shoshana Felman, *Shoah* is an important historical document because it shows "profound and surprising insight into the complexity of the relation between history and witnessing. It is a film about witnessing: the witnessing of a catastrophe. The limit-experiences, their overwhelming impact, constantly put to the test the witness and witnessing, and at the same time unsettle the very limits of our sense of reality."[35] Yet it is exactly this *perception* of reality that is so important in reconceptualizing Treblinka. Hence much in the same vein as Lanzmann, I rely heavily on oral testimonies of witnesses, specifically those held in the USC Shoah Foundation's Visual History Archive and the United States Holocaust Memorial Museum's oral history collection. These variegated perceptions of reality can be corroborated by, and placed alongside, archival sources to create a more complete spatial reconstruction. Beyond these sources, I also draw from postwar investigative reports conducted near Treblinka and postwar trials held in Nuremberg, Frankfurt, and Düsseldorf to rebuild the contemporaneous plurality of those who witnessed the camp.[36] The richest archive for this project has proven to be the Żydowski Instytut Historyczny (Jewish Historical Institute, abbreviated as żih), in Warsaw. In addition to the Emmanuel Ringelblum Archive (originally called Oyneg Shabes), which żih also holds, I cite over fifty individual testimonies from żih alone.[37] Other archives I utilize, especially to find local Polish witnesses, include the Regional Polish Archives in Siedlce, Poland; the Polish Central Archives of Modern Records in Warsaw; and the KARTA Foundation Archives in Warsaw. One other archive of particular importance is the Polish Institute of National Remembrance, which includes an array of first-person testimonies from immediately after the war (and is now available online).[38]

In plotting these testimonies onto various maps, like the one in map 2 (chapter 6), I have identified six distinct spaces that existed in and around Treblinka that constituted its historical reality: an ideological space, a behavioral space, a space of life and death, an interactional space, a sensory space, and an extended space. Each space is unique, and while all overlap in some manner, each offers a different way to understand Treblinka. One significant feature of this work is that as each subsequent space is revealed, the first two spaces—the ideological and behavioral spaces, both largely dictated by Nazi ideology—are consistently eroded. A function of the passage of time as the other spaces developed, this phenomenon also reflects the inherent fallacies of Nazi beliefs about what Treblinka should become. In this way, the book's organization reflects how quickly and widely Treblinka was witnessed after it became operational on July 22, 1942—offering a direct and instantaneous challenge to Nazi conceptions of an isolated, hidden, and technocratically "perfect" death "factory."

Chapter 1 examines the ideological space behind Treblinka's existence. As builders of the camp, Nazi thinkers, informed by their warped ideologies, instilled meaning into what was, for them, an otherwise abstract setting. Located, as all Reinhard camps were, in the forested "wilderness" of Poland, the site that became Treblinka was filled with preconceptions. For one, the land on which the Nazis erected the camp was within the so-called

Lebensraum (living space) in which they planned to build their "thousand-year Reich." And yet, perhaps paradoxically, it was within this same landscape that Treblinka came to serve as the apotheosis of a death-producing space in service of a phantasmagoric worldview of a *Judenfrei* (free from Jews) future. Every part of Treblinka's physical organization and layout was geared toward these ideological purposes, and because they believed they had created a new space adherent to an alternate morality, Nazi planners operated within Treblinka as if the camp was a microcosm of this moral universe itself—which gave them a space to commit mass murder outside the bounds of, or at least isolated from, the rest of human existence.

Chapter 2 explores how Treblinka's spatial layout contributed to German and Ukrainian behaviors within it. Nazi ideology, and the perceptions that grew around it, promoted the concept of the factory-like, clean killing process represented by the "human slaughterhouse" of Treblinka. This technocratic, industrial imagery also positioned German and Ukrainian guards as "masters" within the camp's cordoned-off spaces, and many adjusted their behavior accordingly. A mix of Nazi fanatics, euthanasia program employees, and ordinary men, Treblinka personnel displayed brutality, reveled in newfound authority, and acted as though free from consequences while they performed the "dirty work" required by the Nazi mission. Yet the terrible reality of Treblinka soon overtook these "privileged elite of hell," and finding themselves far from the "unfeeling automatons" Nazi ideology expected them to be, Germans and Ukrainians employed secrecy to hide their crimes and create psychological distance from the depraved violence they inflicted. At some point during the transformation of Treblinka from a "clean" and "industrial" death factory into its actual physical form, the horrific process of murdering thousands of innocent people every day morphed into a stark counterpoint to Nazi ideological premises.

The other humans within Treblinka were there against their will—the hundreds of thousands of Jews, Roma, Sinti, and other minority groups targeted in the Holocaust.[39] Chapter 3 explores their experiences of Treblinka as a space of life and death. For the vast majority, Treblinka existed as the space in which their lives were callously ended, and while their last moments are inherently unknowable, the spatial reconceptualization employed here allows us to learn more about that tragic experience. While often brief, the experiences of these hundreds of thousands of people included a combination of deception, hope, suffering, and ultimately death in gas chambers or an execution pit. For the small groups of mainly male Jewish workers selected to live for short periods of time to ensure the camp operated, however, life became almost inseparable from death. Adapting to this world of unavoidable death and destruction, these "living Jews" of Treblinka created a space where survival meant finding ways to confront and adapt, physically and psychologically, to the existential horrors facing them.

Those few who somehow managed to escape Treblinka found new challenges in encountering the spaces beyond its fences. Chapter 4 follows survivors who escaped the camp as they entered interactional spaces laden with life-and-death implications. As these survivors confronted both the natural and human spaces outside Treblinka, they made new adaptations to account for hope and freedom and for trial and tribulation. A space fraught with the hardships of survival, adaptations to the natural world—which often included a fundamental reassessment of one's relationship to nature—became expedient for both short-term and long-term survival. Moreover, the frequent interactions with other humans inhabiting these surrounding spaces created uncertainty, confusion, and potentially salvation as survivors faced the full range of human responses to their plight. Even the Poles inhabiting these spaces existed in a liminal world—one in which Nazi rule reduced them to colonial subjects and fundamentally altered the relationship many had with what had previously been their intimate spaces of home.

Alongside escaping people, Treblinka also released into the surrounding world a constant stream of sights, smells, and sounds of mass murder, a set of phenomena I call "sensory contamination." Chapter 5 reveals how despite Nazi beliefs in Treblinka's isolation, the sheer scale of mass death carried out there could never be contained within its small physical boundaries. As the sensory contamination flooded the landscape surrounding Treblinka, locals living nearby soon became "sensory witnesses" to the camp by experiencing these new sights, smells, and sounds. In charting this "zone of sensory witnessing," which spread around Treblinka for a sizable radius, I redefine *who* was a witness to the camp, and I show how sensory witnessing can affect individual behavior and aid in knowledge creation.

One did not have to live close to Treblinka, though, to witness something related to it. In chapter 6, I argue that extending out for many kilometers in all directions from the camp, like spokes on a wheel, were "spatial extensions" of the camp in the form of the railway corridors snaking to Treblinka from their points of origin. The cattle cars used in transporting Jews to Treblinka were microcosms of the camp they served, essentially becoming overcrowded boxes of suffering and death on wheels. Along these railway corridors, local people lived and worked in rural houses, farms, small villages, and larger railroad hub towns. These local populations frequently witnessed and even interacted with the trains, the Jewish survivors who escaped from them, and the bodies, remnants, and other objects left in their wakes. Such trackside interactions allowed thousands of people to witness a specific aspect of the Holocaust by creating intersecting contemporaneous spaces between Jews bound for Treblinka's gas chambers and those implicated by the arbitrary placement of nearby railway corridors.

Collectively, these were the spaces of Treblinka, and the ability of humans, trains, sights, smells, and sounds to travel far beyond the camp's confines meant that thousands witnessed the camp, or something related to it, during its existence. Along with this witnessing came knowledge about what Treblinka really was, and as this knowledge spread far and wide, Nazi conceptions of what the camp *should* be—the isolated, clean, and industrial death factory—were utterly destroyed. The contrary observations made throughout the following pages represent the contemporaneous plurality of Treblinka and hence the camp's clearest spatial legacies.

Redefining the Periphery

Within the past decade or so, Holocaust historians have focused on the numerous mass shooting sites scattered throughout Eastern Europe. The spatial nature of this "Holocaust by Bullets," as so thoroughly documented by Father Patrick Desbois and his Yahad-in Unum team, adds a new dimension to sites of atrocity by revealing the intimate, localized nature of this phase of the genocide.[40] After all, there were over 2,500 individual murder sites, and every town had a ravine, gravel pit, or quarry that the *Einsatzgruppen* (Special Squads) filled with the bodies of their victims.[41] This shift in research sometimes bypasses Nazi death camps because of the widespread assumption that research on them has been exhausted. However, in a 2010 synthesis of Holocaust historiography, Dan Stone suggested that while substantial research exists on the larger camp system (especially Auschwitz) scholarship on individual death camps—namely, those of Operation Reinhard—remains "vanishingly small."[42]

At Treblinka specifically, the benchmark study is still widely considered Yitzhak Arad's 1987 book *Belzec, Sobibor, Treblinka*. Only recently have scholars started to ask new and updated questions. Recent archeological work at Treblinka by Caroline Sturdy Colls has confirmed camp layouts, uncovered physical remnants of gas chambers, and helped create a computer model of how the camp once looked.[43] Others have begun to widen the lens to study the "neighbors" living beyond Treblinka's boundaries.[44] For example, in *Golden Harvest* (2012), Jan Gross explores what he calls "events at the periphery of the Holocaust," looking explicitly at the motivation behind local Polish grave-digging at Treblinka after the war.[45]

In *Spaces of Treblinka*, therefore, by seeking to put the voices of Polish witnesses in conversation with those of Jews and Germans, I attempt the most comprehensive analysis of Treblinka to date—one that connects recent research on space, archeology, neighbors, and the human body to Arad's foundational historical account. Making these connections across disciplines was directly inspired by both Lanzmann's work thirty years ago and that of the Yahad-in Unum team today. Just as both look to the spaces surrounding sites of atrocity to explore the experiences of everyday people living nearby, I too seek to expand the definition of who counts as a *witness* to Treblinka and, by extension, the Holocaust. This approach not only acknowledges the transnational character of interactions in and around spaces of atrocity, but it also reimagines these spaces previously labeled as the "periphery" of the Holocaust. Surely, all witnesses, both those next to Treblinka and those farther away, formed inescapable memories of how it looked, felt, smelled, and sounded living near a death camp. Lanzmann recognized this fact as early as the 1970s, writing in his memoir, "I talked to people . . . [who] seemed pleased to have found a stranger curious about a past they remembered with extraordinary exactness, yet one that they spoke of as if it were legend . . . a past both incredibly remote and yet very close, a past-present forever etched in their minds."[46] It is in these recollections that the traces of Treblinka lived on long after the camp itself ceased to exist, carried forth as remnants scattered across the Polish landscape and far beyond.

Spaces of Treblinka

An Ideological Space

In our mind's eye we are accustomed to think
of the Holocaust as having no landscape—or at
best one emptied of features and color, shrouded
in night and fog, blanketed by perpetual winter,
collapsed into shades of dun and gray; the gray of
smoke, of ash, of pulverized bones, of quicklime.
It is shocking, then, to realize that Treblinka, too,
belongs to a brilliantly vivid countryside; the
riverland of the Bug and the Vistula; rolling, gentle
land, lined by avenues of poplar and aspen.

—Simon Schama, *Landscape and Memory*

On June 22, 1941, Nazi Germany attacked the Soviet Union in the largest military invasion in human history. Following on the heels of Hitler's three-million-man-strong *Wehrmacht* (German Army) were four special squadrons, called *Einsatzgruppen*. Tasked with shooting Jews, communists, and other subversive elements, the Einsatzgruppen ultimately murdered close to two million people—three-fourths of whom were Jewish—in this "Holocaust by Bullets."[1] By early 1942 the Nazis began shifting the center of mass murder from these thousands of scattered mass shooting sites to just three death camps: Bełżec, Sobibór, and Treblinka. In the process of concentrating their victims, Nazi conceptions of mass murder, which had been relatively disconnected spatially and conceptually during the mass shootings, also became more concentrated. Specifically, it was at Treblinka where the Nazis most directly manifested their murderous ideology by aiming to erect a "factory" of death within the very spaces marking the frontier of the "thousand-year Reich."

As the builders of Treblinka, it was the Nazis' arrangement, utilization, and treatment of the camp's spaces that installed ideological meaning and purpose to an otherwise abstract setting. Treblinka was the apotheosis of the surreal and utopian Nazi vision of a death-producing space in service of their *Judenfrei*, or "Jew-free," worldview. Nazi thinkers imagined that in a Judenfrei landscape, "undesirable" elements could be industriously slaughtered within distinct spaces cordoned off and separated from the normal world, often by no more than dense trees and camouflaged fences. According to historian Hans Mommsen, the overzealous "ambitions of Heinrich Himmler and his ss to achieve the millennium in the Führer's own lifetime" drove the creation of such spaces before the war itself had even ended.[2] Nazi officer Erich von dem Bach-Zelewski gave a more forthright explanation at the postwar Nuremberg trials, explaining that the evolution toward racially cleansing all newly conquered eastern territories was simply "the logical consequence of our ideology."[3] Treblinka, as the physical manifestation of Nazi exterminationist ideology, held particular meanings for those who ordered its construction and operation. As historian Michael Ley writes, "In the eyes of Hitler and his true-believing supporters, the murder of the European Jews was, in terms of salvation-theology, the necessary prerequisite for the 'thousand-year Reich.'"[4]

In Nazi logic, spaces of mass murder like the Reinhard camps did not expose the moral shortcomings of the Third Reich. Rather, supported by its own (repugnant) rationality that recommended killing "inferior" groups to improve the Aryan gene pool, Nazi morality claimed to exist in a realm *beyond* Western ideals.[5] Michel Foucault astutely identifies the broader mechanism at work here: "If genocide is indeed the dream of modern powers, this is not because of a recent return of the ancient right to kill; it is because power is situated and exercised at the level of life, the species, the race, and the large-scale phenomena of population."[6] Indeed, Nazi ideologues presented the need to kill Jews in terms of life; however, life was only guaranteed to the Aryan race, and eradicating non-Aryans was justified by phrases like "biological survival." It was within this narrow, inverted conception of right and wrong that camp architects, designers, administrators, and guards alike were *supposed* to operate within Treblinka, as if the camp's space was somehow detached and isolated from the rest of the world and could create an alternate moral universe inside of which mass murder became normalized.

Because Treblinka spatially embodied these radical ideological fantasies, foundational principles of those ideologies are identifiable in every aspect of the camp's spaces as they once existed. Nazi ideals are seen most clearly in an examination of five areas of Treblinka: (1) the camp's location within Poland and the corresponding ideological components associated with the concept of *Blut und Boden* (Blood and Soil); (2) the actual internal physical layout and spatial divisions of the camp itself; (3) the deceptive components built into the camp's design and operation; (4) the horrific phantasmagoric "mission" behind the camp's operational functionality; and (5) the specific behaviors of camp personnel—diffusion of responsibility, moral adaptation, and secrecy—that created the camp's atmosphere of mass murder.[7] Each of these aspects coalesced to turn Treblinka, at least conceptually, into an industrial, repetitive killing "machine" that operated away from public view.[8] While the Nazis believed that someday they could reveal to the world and to the German people their horrific "accomplishments" at Treblinka, in the meantime they felt compelled to steadfastly conceal the camp by adding layers of isolation between their "progress" toward racial utopia and what the wider world would certainly recognize as cold-blooded mass murder.

While in lived reality even the model death camp at Treblinka turned out to be neither all that isolated nor cleanly industrial (as later chapters show), the Nazis believed both ideas were essential to what Treblinka *should* be, and they built the camp with their long-term goals in mind. Studies of Nazi architecture and the built environment have shown that the Nazis had embarked on rebuilding Germany even before the war started. In *Building Nazi Germany*, Josh Hagen and Robert Ostergren write, "The Nazis expressed and realized their most fundamental ideologies and objectives through the use of space, place, and architecture . . . [and] were fully confident in their ability to achieve desirable social, political, economic, and demographic outcomes through the calculated arrangement of specific places."[9] This aligns with something Adolf Hitler stated in a 1937 speech: "These buildings should not be conceived of for the year 1940, not even for the year 2000, but extend into the millennia of the future like the cathedrals of our past."[10] This orientation toward the future of Nazi Germany was just as applicable to German cities as it was to the "concomitant reorganization of the *Lebensraum*" in the East.[11] "From the mightiest work of technology to the plainest house," wrote Hitler's architectural advisor Gerdy Troost, "the German homeland grows into an ordered and structured whole and becomes the image of an ideologically united . . . nation."[12] When seen in this light, the death camps, built as they were while victory on the Eastern Front seemed guaranteed, give a glimpse into the dark future of what the Nazis had planned for their thousand-year Reich.

Before Treblinka

Prior to World War II, the landscape of what later became Treblinka was an otherwise ordinary tract of Polish countryside. Writer Vasily Grossman, who traveled through Poland with the Red Army in 1944, described the landscape he encountered: "The terrain to the east of Warsaw along the Western Bug is an expanse of alternating sands and swamps interspersed with evergreen and deciduous forests. The landscape is drear[y] and villages are rare. The narrow, sandy roads where wheels sink up to the axles and walking is difficult, are something for the traveler to avoid. In the midst of this desolate country stands the small out-of-the-way station of Treblinka."[13] Franciszek Ząbecki, Polish stationmaster of this "out-of-the-way" station, described the area in similar terms: "The surroundings of Treblinka were sad. Barren, sandy land. Fields were destroyed every year by the extensive floods from the Bug."[14] What Ząbecki adds to Grossman's description, as we would expect from a local person, are the intimate elements of emotion (sadness) and also of natural hazards (floods) that he feels best depict his known surroundings. Yet both he and Grossman paint the perception—through their use of words like *small, out-of-the-way, barren,* and *sandy*—of rurality, wilderness, even wasteland. Each descriptor of Treblinka's landscape conjures up a space relatively untamed, or at least one where natural features of wetlands, rivers, and forests take center stage and where an element of unpredictability, perhaps even a violent unpredictability (expressed by the flood threat), remains.

According to spatial theorist Henri Lefebvre, every space "has a history, one invariably grounded in nature, in natural conditions that are at once primordial and unique in the sense that they are always and everywhere endowed with specific characteristics."[15] As an inherently isolated space, a "wilderness" takes on symbolic idealizations for almost everyone who encounters it because "nature cloaks itself in nostalgias which supplant rationality."[16] For the Nazis, the isolation, wildness, and natural characteristics of Treblinka's landscape held important underlying assumptions that dictated how they ultimately transformed it. For one, Nazi ideology generally placed an emphasis on the rural, natural world because some believed that the city was an "unnatural fact in the life of the people" and its "denaturing" effects limited spiritual growth.[17] The *return* to nature, therefore, became a common refrain in Hitler's Germany, and alongside it sprouted theories connecting natural living spaces with what had become, in Nazi circles, the seemingly organic principles of racial purity.

The Nazi doctrine of Blut und Boden defined this link in a single terse phrase, and German ideologue Willy Hellpach captured the concept's essence in a 1944 publication:

> There is a fact of living space; in it climate and landscape appear to be closely linked, it belongs to both equally, it is a contributing factor to all climatic and primal conditions for all landscapes; it is the soil. . . . It likely composes essentially that which we call the "constitution," thereby modifying concepts of family and racial substance. It is the very place of life for beings, and a good part of their essential characteristics depends on it; not only due to the plants, which root in it and are bound to it in one given spot to get their nourishment, but also of animals and human beings, who grow away from it to a far-reaching extent by free mobility or by technical civilization. We must not fail to recognize that there are probably forces still unexplored, even yet unknown, by which the soil influences our organism.[18]

At the core of Nazi Blut und Boden ideology was the belief that the German *Volk* (people) represented a distinctive biological organism that required a specific ecological environment in order to survive and thrive.[19] A pseudo-scientific blurring of concepts of race, space, and science, Blut und Boden hinged on the idea that the individual German farmer possessed a creative relationship with the soil—one in which instead of exploiting the land, he created upon it a living space in "ever renewed service to," and in harmony with, the local environment. Prominent Nazis believed this Germanic race of farmers had innate capacities for rational organization and husbandry that allowed them to master any agricultural environment.[20] In the words of Nazi Party member and professor Erich Maschke, "It is for us an *unspoken, self-evident* fact that the creative service between the German farmer and the soil is only supported on freely available land, opened up by their own work."[21] Fellow professor Werner Knapp, who created a 1942 handbook on Nazi architectural design, noted that forming distinctly new German communities within the *Heimat* (homeland) was an "unequivocally clear" goal, claiming that since "Blut und Boden are the cornerstones of our new world, so thus are space and people the starting points."[22]

Connecting blood and soil, however, meant that Germany inherently needed new frontiers into which they could expand. In 1933, Alfred Rosenberg, head of implementing long-term Nazi planning and policy, wrote, "We want Lebensraum for a great cultural nation. We want to have space for the peasants in the East in order that the German nation be able to nourish itself."[23] To the east of Germany sat the very lands connecting these ideologies, because in Maschke's words, here was a "natürliche Dreieinigkeit von Rasse, Volk, und Raum," or "a natural trinity of race, people, and space."[24] Poland, in particular, united these conceptions of blood, soil, and identity to strands of German history. Specifically, Nazi historians believed Germany possessed a historic claim over Polish lands that dated back to before the Jagiellonian dynasty of the fifteenth century, and it was simply through centuries of Polish neglect that these spaces had "vegetated" to the point of "hopeless apathy."[25] Most found little need to go back centuries, though, finding a much easier target in the Versailles Treaty's resurrection of Poland in 1919, a country now counting among its population the largest proportion of the thirty million *Volksdeutsche* (ethnic Germans) that Nazi planners estimated lived—against their wishes—outside the redrawn German borders. Just months after Versailles, Hitler included in his "Program of the Nazi Party" specific points calling for self-determination for these stranded Volksdeutsche and stressing the need for new German colonies on the European continent to ensure the "maintenance of our people."[26]

After successfully reintegrating the Volksdeutsche-heavy territories of Austria and the Sudetenland in 1938 (and the less-Volksdeutsche-heavy remainder of Czechoslovakia in 1939), Germany seemed more poised than ever to reestablish its "historical" claims over Poland.[27] From this vantage point, it was a short step to suggest that for the "natural trinity" to be restored, and German history made right, the Germans must retake and revive Poland—saving it from its "unworthy" Polish overlords while simultaneously reuniting any remaining Volksdeutsche with their ancestral homelands. Resettling German farmers in former Polish territories, therefore, was intended not just in service of Blut und Boden ideology; according to a document later revealed at Nuremberg, resettlement was also meant "to form bulwarks of German culture and to encircle the Polish population, thus accelerating the process of Germanisation" throughout the region.[28] On the eve of World War II, Maschke wrote, "The recovery of the eastern German soil is and always will be the greatest and most consequential act of our past, by which our people determined their habitat . . . in which not the individual, but our entire nation—as a unified and closed body—was the hero."[29] By positioning the German nation as the hero, Nazi thinkers needed a villain for the upcoming battle of spatial and racial ambitions. In this case, the Poles and their "backward" agriculture stewardship embodied a rationale beyond imperialistic ambitions alone; as part of the pseudoscientific narrative of Blut und Boden, the sanitized language of cleansing the space of its current inhabitants seemed more palatable.

Thus, Nazi propaganda began to portray Poles in terms similar to those applied to indigenous populations of Europe's earlier colonial projects in Africa and Asia. In general, geographer Derek Gregory has concluded, colonizers view colonial spaces as a "blank page on which . . . [the] 'will-to-power' is to be written."[30] Indeed, just as other European colonizers had done in the late nineteenth and early twentieth centuries, Nazi racial planners imagined Poland as an uncivilized, remote wilderness where the German people could build their pure racial utopia upon virgin frontier lands.[31] The mechanism supporting such colonial language appears in a 1936 German report: "The question arises whether the illiterate masses of an agrarian population with the above indicated standard of life are capable of being organized at all in war time, or whether a degree of primitiveness is not attained which must make it extraordinarily hard for even an agrarian exporting country to be self-supporting when thrown entirely on its own resources."[32] Calling into question Polish standards of living and characterizing their land practices as primitive, Nazi planners fostered a narrative of contempt for the current inhabitants of their Lebensraum. As an internal Nazi memo entitled "Political Guidance as Regards Eastern Policy" positioned things, "In relations between Germans and Polish peoples, the first law is that above the Polish magnate stands the German peasant; above the Polish intellectual the German laborer; that there is no common measure between Germans and Poles, as that would deprive the German of his status as Master."[33] Taking the next step, *Gauleiter* (governor) of Danzig–West Prussia Albert Forster added in a 1939 speech, "It will be our highest and most honorable task to do whatsoever lies in our power so that in a few years everything that can in any way be reminiscent of Poland shall have disappeared."[34]

For Nazi planners, the rapid military victory over Poland that followed in 1939 seemed only to confirm their preconceptions, and upon occupying the country, they immediately ordered the clearing and restructuring of the land, a process of colonial erasure some scholars call "deterritorialization."[35] By the war's end, in the General Government of Poland alone, German occupiers had massively deterritorialized and reshaped the landscape. By exploiting forced labor, they built approximately 1,790 kilometers of roads and 220 hectares of dikes, drained 240,000 hectares, irrigated 5,600 hectares, broke up and tilled 9,200 hectares, regulated and cultivated 1,100 kilometers of riverbeds, dug 3,600 kilometers of new ditches, and constructed several new railways.[36] While transforming Poland's physical landscape, Nazi planners also embarked on a racial engineering project aligned with Blut und Boden. As they shuttled German farmers to these new frontiers, Nazi leaders segregated Poles as second-class citizens and passed laws carrying severe penalties for challenging the new status quo. Gauleiter of Posen (later renamed Wartheland) Arthur Greiser was frank, justifying the conquest as a foregone, even religiously ordained, reckoning: "German colonists have taken up the struggle . . . against the Polish peasant. . . . If God exists, it is he who has chosen Adolf Hitler to drive this vermin hence."[37] In the process, the more than three million Polish Jews, were, to quote historian Simon Schama, "reduced to the status of barnyard animals that could be stabled or slaughtered as the freshly reclaimed landscape required."[38] The interplay of racial fantasy with the reality of German territorial gain revealed the dichotomous nature of Nazi Lebensraum, something observed by author Francis Aldor, who wrote in 1940, "[What] the Germans mean by living space at the same time [became] the dying space of other peoples."[39]

As 1941 bled into 1942, a group of Nazi leaders led by Reinhard Heydrich and Adolf Eichmann met at a villa in Wannsee, a lake region at Berlin's outskirts, to discuss the implementation of what they called the "Final Solution" to the "Jewish Problem," a marked shift away from mass shootings to fixed death camps. In deciding where to locate these Reinhard camps, as they came to be known, Nazi planners chose the area of Poland that had not been incorporated into the Third Reich: the nebulous administrative zone called the General Government.[40] The logic of this choice reflected several spatial considerations, some conscious and some perhaps unconscious. Of the latter, the General Government represented a space where rules of modern civilization no longer applied. The enlightened conception that sovereign governments must guarantee and protect the rights of their citizens did not account for areas situated outside the defined boundaries of a state. By not being incorporated into the Reich, the General Government, therefore, offered no guarantees or protections to its subjects. Yet paradoxically, as administrators of the territory, the same government representatives, the Gauleiter, were still responsible for the fate of all those within their territories. As Hans Frank, overseer of the entire General Government, elaborated, "The Government-General, subject to the sovereignty of the Führer, forms part of space dependent on the authority of the Reich; yet from a legal point of view this territory is not part of the Reich. The peoples living in these areas live under the protection of the Reich, they are independent of German authority as regards their cultural life, and their needs will be administered to on condition that they show their loyalty to the Reich by the performance of tasks allotted them."[41] This created a particularly dangerous situation for Polish Jews of the General Government, who became stateless subjects completely at the mercy of Gauleiter unbeholden to any modern social and civil contracts. And since Jews had already been stripped of civil rights within Germany proper, Polish Jews in the General Government could never demonstrate the requisite loyalty to Germany that Frank mentions. They thus occupied the tenuous position of what Timothy Snyder has called a "zone of statelessness," which Nazi leaders used to justify the state-sponsored destruction of a group technically under state control but without the protections normally guaranteed to state subjects.[42] As Hannah Arendt once observed, "The destruction of a man's rights, the killing of the juridical person in him, is a prerequisite for dominating him entirely."[43]

The Gauleiter and Reinhard planners, however, were well aware of the contradiction they faced in building death camps intended to cleanse the area of unwanted and "indigenous" populations within the *same* spaces of the new Blut und Boden frontier. To avoid overlap between the two goals, the Nazis wanted the death camps, at least initially, to be entirely isolated from population centers. This concern stemmed from earlier lessons Nazi leaders learned during Kristallnacht and the T4 killings. Following Kristall- nacht, the German populace complained to Hitler's government not because of the pogrom-like violence against Jews but because they had witnessed it as a disruption of peace and order in their neighborhoods. During the subsequent T4 euthanasia program, Nazi leaders took this lesson to heart, reducing the number of murder locations to just six sites scattered through- out Germany.[44] Local German citizens soon smelled the smoke and heard the cries from these killing centers, however, and as the bishop of Limburg wrote in an August 1941 report (later forwarded to Reich Minister of the Interior Wilhelm Frick), "Several times a week buses arrive in Hadamar with a considerable number of such victims. School children of the vicin- ity know this vehicle and say, 'There comes the murder-box again.' After the arrival of these vehicles citizens of Hadamar watch the smoke rise out of the chimney and are tortured with the constant thought of the misery of the victims, especially when repulsive odors annoy them."[45] Following sub- sequent protests, including sermons by Bishop Clemens von Galen that condemned classifying *any* life as "unproductive"—a clear shot across the Nazi bow—Hitler "officially" shut down the program.[46] Many Nazi leaders, nevertheless, still believed that the indignation did not arise because of the killing itself but rather was aimed at the ongoing disruption and disorder; and as a result, few Nazi leaders shied away from pursuing future mass murder plans—as long as they occurred far away from German population centers.[47]

Other concerns informing the decision of where to locate the Reinhard camps arose from more practical considerations. The mass shooting phase of the Holocaust, which preceded Operation Reinhard, was defined by "cha- otic killings . . . carried out in broad daylight and [that] could not be kept secret."[48] Thus, Reinhard planners had two requirements for where to locate the death camps. First, the camps had "to be far from larger settlements and main roads in wooded and uninhabited areas." This aimed to ensure secrecy and isolation. Second, the camps needed to be within close proximity of a major railway link, which provided a way to transport victims from the ghettos in which they currently resided.[49] The General Government met both requirements, author Gitta Sereny observes, because its "railway system covered all of the country, with stations even in the smallest towns;

while large tracts of the Polish countryside, densely forested and very thinly populated, made isolation possible."[50]

In deciding where to locate Treblinka specifically, Nazi planners sought the perfectly isolated but accessible location northeast of Warsaw. They zeroed in on the small railway junction town of Małkinia-Górna, situated just west of the Bug River, which demarcated the border between the General Government and the newly Soviet portion of Poland.[51] In the two years since being incorporated into the General Government, this area had remained relatively obscure thanks to its distance from central Germany. However, as Operation Barbarossa—the massive German invasion of the Soviet Union—drew closer, the location gained importance for German military planners. Local Polish official Zdzisław Łukaszkiewicz witnessed the changes: "Before the war, two or three trains passed each day, after which the little station returned to its state of hopeless boredom. Little did the first years of occupation change in this respect. Only in 1941 before the eastern offensive, did the German station begin its role as one of the closest stops to the border. Since then, this region has attracted the attention of the occupation authorities as a place well-suited for special purposes."[52] Because Barbarossa would be launched from border areas like Małkinia, German troops soon flooded in to begin preparations. "The road from Warsaw was constantly utilized by the army, artillery of various caliber, and motorized weapons," Treblinka's stationmaster Ząbecki observed. "The war machine was on the Bug." The influx of German soldiers and war matériel temporarily altered the space from its rural, quiet wilderness to one dominated by loud, frenetic activity. "It was summertime, sunny, and yet the air in the area was slightly hazy," Ząbecki described. "Even the color of the greenery was a bit different, darker with dust and exhaust fumes from motor vehicles. One heard the clatter of concrete mixers and of trucks full of construction material being hastily unloaded amid shouts from the Germans carrying out the work."[53]

During the buildup, the German Army focused in on a small gravel quarry, which, though owned since July 1940 by a Polish man named Marian Łopuszyński, "was founded before the war—dating back even to tsarist times," according to local resident Edward Sypko.[54] Local Poles commonly referred to this quarry and the spaces adjacent to it as the "Milewo Estate," borrowing the name from a family whose farm sat adjacent to it.[55] The towns closest to the quarry were Kosów Lacki and Wólka Okrąglik. Founded in the fifteenth century, Kosów Lacki took its name from the Kosówski family, who established it. A small settlement, its main building is a parish church dedicated to the birth of the Virgin Mary. Wólka Okrąglik is also a small village, and its most revered landmark is also its church—a nineteenth-century neo-Gothic chapel with a large folk sculpture depicting St. Anthony.[56] In fact, if not for Nazi war planning, these two towns would likely have remained in relative obscurity to the modern day. But because the Wehrmacht utilized this gravel pit, an asphalt road was quickly built between Małkinia and Kosów Lacki to transfer raw materials extracted from the pit to a newly established concrete company.[57] In this way, the area became a modest but locally important hub for distributing the area's natural resources for use in the expanding German war effort.

After Barbarossa launched in June 1941, the concrete company experienced severe labor shortages as the front consumed German personnel. In response, Ernst Gramss, German administrator of the Siedlce district (which included the towns of Małkinia and Treblinka), decided to erect a labor camp near the gravel quarry so it could continue supplying the concrete company and thereby the Wehrmacht. Consequently, Łopuszyński had to surrender his remaining claim to the site. (In payment, though, the Germans allowed him to keep some wagons for private use, provided him a job in Warsaw, and gave him a small cut of profits generated by the pit and concrete company.) Next, Gramss conscripted local train worker Jerzy Gałach and his team of Polish railway workers from nearby villages to build the camp, which they completed in September 1941.[58]

The Germans named the camp "Treblinka" after a small village of the same name situated about four kilometers from the site. Inhabited in 1941 by Polish peasants, farmers, and forest workers, archaeological evidence shows that the lands around the village have supported settlements for thousands of years. In fact, in the area between Treblinka and Wólka Okrąglik (roughly where the camp stood), Bronze Age artifacts dating from 1200–400 BCE have been discovered. The town's name, and later the camp's, derives from an old Slavic term, *tereb* in Russian or *trzeb* in Polish, that is a root of the verb *trzebić*, meaning "to kill, clear, thin out, or exterminate." Although this provenance is eerie in hindsight, the name Treblinka likely had more pragmatic origins, as it is believed to reference an overgrown area around a local stream, which medieval settlers had *to clear* or *thin out* before building a village there. The earliest known use of the name "Treblinka" dates from a 1436 document that mentions the "Nobleman Albert of Treblinka," perhaps of the region's noble Prostyński and Suchodolski families. Alongside this nobility came peasants eager to work the noble lands, and eventually they founded other small villages, including Poniatowo (1 km), Prostyń (4 km), and Wólka Okrąglik (1 km).* Some of these early settlers had roots in Kievan Russia, but many others were Poles from the Mazovia region, and given the rural, agricultural landscape, most residents living near Treblinka in 1941 likely descended from these settlers.[59]

Alongside these Polish peasants lived many Jews. Anna Kazierodek, resident of Poniatowo (1 km), recalled, "Many Jewish families lived in Poniatowo and in many nearby places. Jabłkowski Srulek, a Jew, had a dairy in Poniatowo. Zelek Korytnicki lived opposite Srulek. He had a beautiful garden, and I came to him for matzah."[60] Indeed, the demographic makeup of the region around the camp was fairly typical of Poland in general, a country counting over three million Jews among its total prewar population of thirty million. As recorded in a 1920s census, Prostyń (4 km) had a population of 805 people, of whom 136 were Jewish, and nearby Złotki (4 km) had a population of 540 people, of whom 72 were Jewish. There were also Jewish communities of similar proportions in the larger towns of Stoczek (13 km) and Węgrów (25 km)—though as an inexplicable oddity, the town of Treblinka (4 km) counted zero Jews among its 276 residents.

Most Jews living in these towns did not own farms like the region's Polish peasants did. Instead, Jews ran shops, bakeries, and mills, while others worked as craftsmen—primarily as blacksmiths. Because of their limited agricultural opportunities, local Jews were generally poorer than their Polish neighbors, although they often had larger families.[61] And like the non-Jewish Poles in the region, most Jews had also lived in the same area for generations and would likely have been intimately familiar with the local landscape. It might have later seemed strangely reassuring, then, when upon arriving at the camp, they could glimpse familiar landmarks in the distance. Early prisoner Antoni Tomczuk had this experience: "In the field . . . near the Milewo site, I could just barely see from afar the church of Prostyń."[62] It is difficult

---

* Hereafter, all towns will include the approximate straight-line distance from the Treblinka death camp in kilometers (km).

to imagine how it must have felt to view this known spatial quantity—the steeple composing the meager skyline of one's hometown—while imprisoned within a newly constructed concentration camp.

Indeed, local German officials used the Treblinka labor camp (known later as Treblinka I) to imprison people they deemed *widerspenstige Elemente* (unruly elements). As new, brightly colored signs posted on walls throughout the Siedlce district began to warn, any local farmer who failed to meet grain quotas, or anyone who did not support the Wehrmacht's demands, could be sent to Treblinka I.[63] As time passed, violations warranting a trip to Treblinka expanded to include not providing punctual transport, violating price regulations, and illegally leaving one's place of work. Broader transgressions included disobeying on-the-spot German commands, and by the end of 1942, the range of offenses for which someone could be sent to Treblinka I became practically endless.[64] As Sypko described it, the prisoners of Treblinka I became a continually changing and "crazy" (his word) rotation of residents from the nearby towns of Hołowienki (20 km), Rogów (30 km), and Sokołów Podlaski (27 km) and other smaller villages.

The number of Poles living and working at the camp fluctuated daily, but the total number of prisoners gradually increased over time. According to Sypko, "Initially, when they brought me there, there were about 360 in the Polish barracks. . . . By the time I escaped there were about a thousand Poles."[65] Tomczuk recalled that imprisonment often included forced labor, and such "work in the gravel pit was murderous. . . . In the heat of the summer, [there was] no drinking water. The people working in the gravel pit were skeletons, little more than bones covered with leather."[66] Fellow Treblinka I prisoner Jan Zawadzki added, "The hunger was incredible. . . . Those with poorer health died of exhaustion and malnutrition. . . . These were terribly hard times, men were treated worse than animals."[67] The Germans undeniably treated Polish prisoners of Treblinka I cruelly, frequently forcing them to labor in the gravel pit fourteen hours per day. Consequently, Treblinka I became deadly in its own right, and ultimately between seven thousand and ten thousand people perished there from hunger, overwork, or disease or were shot for infractions.[68]

Outside of the suffering occurring at Treblinka I for certain Poles, though, other local witnesses generally agree that, in broader terms, a relative calm had returned to the region after Barbarossa. As Jerzy Królikowski, a Polish train worker living in nearby Prostyń, just four kilometers from Treblinka I, described it, "During this period . . . nothing hinted that this would become a place of such horrible experiences for hundreds of thousands of people. As usual in the spring, nature awoke to life, Bug willows and Treblinka orchards were covered in fresh greens, and among them were choirs of nightingales, well known in the evenings and mornings, when we returned from work or went to start it."[69]

Yet just as the level of German activity seemed to be waning, a coterie of several ss men came from Sokołów Podlaski (27 km) one day in late April or early May 1942. Their mission was to inspect thirteen hectares of forested land located between the villages of Poniatowo (1 km) and Wólka Okrąglik (1 km) directly adjacent to Treblinka I and its gravel quarry. While the few locals who noticed their presence were unaware of the reason for it, Ząbecki observed that "immediately after this visit, various construction materials began to arrive at the site, such as pipes, parts of sanitary installations, cement, boards, residential barracks, storage sheds, and a postal phone."[70] These were the inconspicuous beginnings of Treblinka II—the death camp.

Between when this material arrived and mid-June 1942, the Germans used prisoners of Treblinka I to build Treblinka II.[71] By this point, some local Jews had been imprisoned at Treblinka I alongside non-Jewish Poles. Szmuel Miedziński, sent there from Sokołów Podlaski (27 km) in December 1941, titled his postwar testimony "How I Built Treblinka." In it, he wrote, "Apart from 30 Jews from Sokołów there were also 150 Jews from Otwock, who built Treblinka. The leader of the Jews was Shimen, the blacksmith from Kosów [Lacki]. From the 150 Jews who were brought in, only 130 were left the next morning. Twenty died on the first night after their arrival. We built barracks for Treblinka II, where later gas chambers were. We built cellars in Treblinka I. Treblinka I had already been built before we arrived."[72] Other Polish laborers, including Jews from nearby towns of Węgrów (25 km) and Stoczek (13 km), were also brought in to dig ditches, build wooden huts, and erect structures that came to comprise the death camp. For two weeks in early June 1942, Lucjan Puchała, resident of Wólka Okrąglik (1 km), was put in charge of constructing the railway track leading from Treblinka's town station to where the camp was being constructed. He remembered, "It was not until the end of the construction that I learnt, from conversations of the Germans, that this branch line was to run to a camp for Jews."[73]

In addition to local labor, the Germans also sought and requisitioned locally available materials to construct the death camp. Nowhere was this more visible than in the destruction of an old factory's chimney in August or September of 1942. As pictures from Treblinka deputy commandant Kurt Franz's photo album show (see figures 2, 3, and 4), German camp personnel tore down this tall brick structure, probably in the town of Małkinia (7 km), to harvest the bricks for use in building several new gas chambers at Treblinka. While residents watched, this local structure, on the skyline for years, toppled to the ground, reduced to thousands of individual pieces that the Germans gathered up and took away.[74] The Germans also used other local materials in building Treblinka. "Near the camp was Kosów Lacki . . . and wood from the demolished Jewish houses there was brought into the camp," Sypko recalled. "It was cut into pieces so the Germans could sun-treat it for use in barrack construction."[75] In this sinister way, whether by design or happenstance, the very structures meant to destroy Jews contained not only physical remnants of their former lives but the same pieces comprising their most intimate spaces of home.

Nazi planners also took advantage of the area's "natural topography," which consisted of an overgrowth of young forests that seemed to make the camp "invisible from the outside," as a postwar report described it. The dense forests offered a simple visible barrier to local Poles and any other passersby on either the Kosów-Małkinia road or the Siedlce-Małkinia railroad line, both of which ran parallel, at a distance of roughly four hundred meters, to the camp's eastern edge.[76] Łukaszkiewicz described the advantages offered by the local terrain: "The area is convenient for the perpetrators. . . . The pine forest, growing on a hill that runs along the camp's borders, is an excellent barrier to prevent outside onlookers. From the east, the area is completely isolated. As far as the eye can see, there are no settlements. . . . In addition the area from the east and south is flat. From the camp's guard towers, it would be easy for a series of machine guns to scare or kill . . . any transitive passersby."[77] The one area somewhat vulnerable to the outside world was a section of meadows and farmlands near the camp's western boundary. Yet situated just three hundred meters beyond these open fields was another thick forest stretching to the north, essentially creating an enclosure that could be effectively monitored by guards from within the camp.[78] As seen in figure 5, the towns of Wólka Okrąglik and Poniatowo are situated in

FIGS. 2–4. Series of photos from Kurt Franz's album showing SS men destroying a chimney, likely located in the nearby town of Małkinia, as German nurses watch. The bricks were used to construct several new gas chambers in Treblinka in August and September 1942. Courtesy of USHMM, gift of Eugene Miller, acc. no. 1997.A.0240.

FIG. 5. Aerial view of Treblinka and surrounding landscape taken by German reconnaissance, November 1943. The camp sat within the triangular space left of center formed by the main Siedlce-Małkinia railway line (running top to bottom) and the railway siding cutting the top of the triangle (the special sidetrack connecting the camp). The town of Wólka Okrąglik is to the right of the Siedlce-Małkinia railway line, southeast of the camp. The town of Poniatowo is northwest of the camp and to the left of the Siedlce-Małkinia railway line. USHMM, courtesy of NARA, College Park MD.

close proximity to the camp (both approximately 1 km). Yet the areas to the east and northeast of Treblinka included open farmland, forests, and floodplains from the Bug River, which flows just beyond the photograph's northern boundaries.

The Germans utilized the existing natural landscape to situate a death camp that felt both isolated and easily accessible to them. Deliberately placed and relatively easily constructed, Treblinka also became an intentionally manipulated space—one that worked, often subtly, in conjunction with its local setting to become, in Nazi imaginations, the paragon of mass death—a space unlike any ever created. Survivor Oskar Strawczyński, who was familiar with the area before the war, reflected, "The terrain around Treblinka, which had previously been overgrown with pine forests now took on a completely different appearance."[79]

Treblinka's Spatial Layout

After strategically constructing Treblinka within a "wilderness," the Germans attempted to further isolate the camp by creating additional layers of separation, including the utilization of camouflage and the erection of other barriers to the outside world. This *double isolation*, as I call it, intended to turn Treblinka into a *zone of Nazi morality*. In this zone, German camp personnel functioned free from the moral and ethical constraints of the world, since they imagined the camp's space as truly separate from it. The imagined moral universe at Treblinka subscribed to its own internal logic and rejected Judeo-Christian morals, highlighting how morality, because it is man-made, is subject to spatial boundaries.[80] As geographer James Tyner has further explained, "The processes leading to moral inclusion or exclusion have a geographic component, one that is infused with power. . . . People whose ordinary reality contains sharp inhibitions against inflicting violence . . . may switch to an alternative reality—a different geographical imagination—that permits violence."[81] This is exactly what happened at Treblinka, where within the zone of Nazi morality, the laws of "civilized countries" that promote creeds like "Thou shalt not kill" were suspended in favor of the domineering Nazi principle, "Thou shalt kill" (if in service of engineering racial purity).[82] By removing obstacles to the contrary inside Treblinka's confines, the Germans felt free to pursue whatever ends their means demanded within this spatially segregated zone of alternative morality.[83]

Establishing Treblinka as a moral universe unto itself is most directly evident in the Germans' arrangement of the camp's spaces, each space's unique functionality, and the perceived mission to be carried out there. Treblinka comprised a rough quadrangle (ss guard Franz Suchomel referred to it as a "rhomboid") measuring six hundred by four hundred meters walled off by fences, which were then surrounded by chains of antitank obstacles that served the dual purpose of creating an imposing visual and physical barrier. It was not a large camp—in fact, it would have only taken twenty to twenty-five minutes to walk around the entire perimeter of Treblinka. Beyond the fences were ditches three meters wide and an open strip of land approximately fifty meters wide, all forming a defensible perimeter directly outside the fenced areas. Other security measures included the erection of eight-meter-tall watchtowers in each corner of the camp to provide the guards with multiple angles of vision and interlocking fields of fire. These towers were equipped with machine guns, lights, and reflectors and served as the camp's main perimeter defense system.[84]

The outer perimeter of Treblinka was enclosed by a barbed-wire fence roughly three to four meters tall, and it had pine and spruce branches intertwined within the barbed wire as a method of preventing outsiders from seeing into the camp. In addition to serving as a visual and physical barrier, the "porous shrubbery" had the additional purpose of enabling air to pass through freely, eliminating the risk that a strong gust of wind might knock the fence down. According to one witness, the Germans used fifty kilometers' worth of tightly interwoven barbed wire in the perimeter fence of Treblinka alone.[85] Though formidable, this main fence did not directly border the camp but sat across the ditches and cleared spaces directly adjacent to the interior perimeter fence.[86]

Lefebvre once wrote that the visual obstruction created by walls or fences represents a clear intention of "cutting off" one space from another.[87] Though this may seem fairly obvious, it had dire consequences in reinforcing how the Germans imagined the space within the fences. In addition to demarcating a zone of double isolation and Nazi morality, by camouflaging these fences, the Germans clearly desired to avoid the prying eyes of the world—at least anyone who managed to infiltrate the wilderness in the first place. Turning Treblinka into a private realm played a critical role in executing the program of mass murder the Nazis had planned for the camp. What happened inside the fences was fully intended to stay inside them, and for anyone who got close enough, the Germans wanted to control the visual narrative. "There was generally nothing [of the camp] you could see," Eugeniusz Goska, resident of Wólka Okrąglik (1 km), recalled, "because there was a fence, with wire mesh and braided branches. . . . It was entwined with pine branches."[88] As Sypko put it, "Unless you had a birds-eye view, when someone passed by, you could not see what was happening there." And maintaining the camp's barrier was so important to the Germans that they kept alive groups of Jews (who would have been killed otherwise) to maintain the fence's camouflage—making Treblinka's isolation literally a matter of life and death. Sypko recalled that from his vantage point in Treblinka I, he witnessed these groups working along the outer fences of nearby Treblinka II: "There were prisoners among the groves, they cut down the pine branches and wrapped the camp in them."[89] Known as the *Waldkommando* (Forest Brigade) and the *Tarnungskommando* (Camouflage Brigade) these teams worked to collect and replace the quickly rotting and dead pine branches in the fences with fresh ones, a task requiring almost constant attention.[90] Perhaps as an unintended consequence, the work done by these groups also changed Treblinka's outer appearance on a daily basis. Survivor Samuel Willenberg described, "There was a conspicuous difference between the repaired section and the rest of the fence: the new stretch had the living green color of the fresh branches we had inserted into it, in contrast to the dry branches elsewhere."[91] That Treblinka's physical appearance changed colors based on the pace of the Tarnungskommando's work became a spatial indicator of the ever-ongoing process of isolating the death camp.

Treblinka became operational on July 22, 1942, when the first trainload of Jews arrived from the Warsaw ghetto. Around the same time, the Tarnungskommando and Waldkommando, at the Germans' behest, began to perform other tasks aimed at isolation as new needs arose. These included planting trees within a radius of one kilometer around the camp to ensure that further approaches to Treblinka were hidden from outside observers. The groups also began planting young trees around the burgeoning "death field" of mass graves situated next to the camp to conceal its presence. Once this project was completed, the Germans sinisterly nicknamed the tree-lined area "the children's garden," a sadistic reference to both the young trees and the many children who lay dead in the graves there.[92]

These groups were also tasked with cutting down trees to build an additional wooden fence near the railroad track entrance and beyond the original barbed-wire one. According to survivor Abraham Krzepicki, the intent was "to better shield the camp from the eyes" of those arriving.[93] In this particular instance, Willenberg recalled, three meters of material were added to the tops of the fences because otherwise, from the tracks, "the Germans apparently knew that one could see the top of the pile of clothes and the crane which scattered the bodies."[94] Thus, as the mass murder process expanded, the Germans continually added new spatial measures to ensure Treblinka remained isolated unto itself.[95] As bodies began to pile up, Wiernik observed, "whenever an airplane was noticed flying overhead, the work was discontinued for the moment and the corpses were covered with foliage as camouflage against aerial observations."[96] In fact, the Germans' obsession with maintaining Treblinka's visual barriers included a ramshackle effort cobbled together after the outer fences were burnt in the prisoner revolt of August 2, 1943.[97] Wacław Bednarczyk, a Polish railway worker, noticed that "tablecloths, bedspreads and other similar things apparently taken from the victims' wares were spread on wire to obscure the view."[98]

While the fences ostensibly cordoned Treblinka off from the outside world, the Germans further subdivided the camp itself into three areas of nearly equal size that served to starkly reinforce the notion that distinct conceptual zones existed inside Treblinka. One was the German living area (*Wohnlager*), one was the reception area for incoming transports (*Auffanglager*)—which included a rail siding and unloading yard large enough to hold between two thousand and three thousand people—and the third was the *Totenlager*, or "extermination camp," which housed the gas chambers. The German living quarters were in the northern corner of the camp and therefore deliberately situated far away from the gas chambers, which sat in the southeast corner. In map 1, one can note that the commandant's living quarters (labeled "12a") were located at the northwest extent of the camp and thus the furthest possible linear distance from the Totenlager. This separation of internal spaces aimed to remove the Germans from having clear lines of sight of the gas chambers during their daily routines. In this way, physical and conceptual distance existed between the murderers and the murdered, a spatial manifestation of the ideological aspects of Operation Reinhard's stated goal of lessening the personal psychological burdens some Nazi leaders, including Heinrich Himmler, attributed to mass shootings by the Einsatzgruppen.[99]

The distinct functionality of each of Treblinka's internal zones further reveals the German conception of a subdivided world within the camp. In addition to being spatially remote from the killing area, the space housing the German quarters also included many "amenities of home," including gardens, barbers, tailors, shoemakers, carpenters, and a zoo (labeled "14" in map 1). There seemed to be a nonchalant atmosphere that accompanied this portion of the camp, according to survivor Yankel Wiernik, who noted that with cars parked haphazardly along the driveway, "to the casual observer, the camp presented a rather innocent appearance."[100] According to Rachel Auerbach, who conducted postwar interviews with witnesses and survivors, the zoo (see figures 6 and 7) included an enclosed space where "rabbits, foxes and squirrels were kept. There was also a pond in which ducks swam around, and there was even talk of bringing in a deer. . . . They also planted a garden in the sandy soil, with flowers—lots of flowers."[101] In addition to these well-maintained animal enclosures tucked safely within the living quarters, German personnel at the camp also took pains to transform the small strip of land between the fence and the barbed wire into a large vegetable garden.[102] Treblinka commandant Franz Stangl later reflected that these intentional spatial manipulations made the German living quarters of Treblinka "a special place" meant to provide relief from murdering people. To "escape" the horrors of the adjacent death space, Stangl visited animals, relaxed with a shave, and held "social gatherings" either in his own quarters or in the mess hall (often called the "canteen," identified as 6a in map 1)—activities ostensibly highlighting the "normal" life German camp personnel attempted to lead within their designated portion of Treblinka.[103]

The "normal" German living space could not have been more different from the Totenlager just a few dozen meters away. Of the thirteen hectares comprising Treblinka, the Totenlager accounted for only about two hectares and was tucked away in the southeastern corner surrounded by a tall earthen wall blocking the view and special screens hiding the entrances. As Yitzhak Arad wrote, the Totenlager was "completely isolated from the rest of the camp."[104] So instead of being doubly isolated like other areas, the Totenlager subsection of Treblinka was technically *triply isolated* from the outside world,

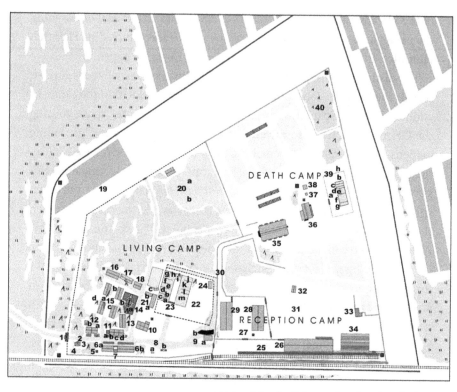

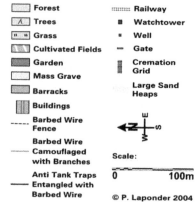

MAP 1. Map by P. Laponder showing the layout of Treblinka as it existed in 1943. Courtesy of Chris Webb, ARC, http://www.deathcamps.org.

Forest
Trees
Grass
Cultivated Fields
Garden
Mass Grave
Barracks
Buildings
Barbed Wire Fence
Barbed Wire Camouflaged with Branches
Anti Tank Traps
Entangled with Barbed Wire

Railway
Watchtower
Well
Gate
Cremation Grid
Large Sand Heaps

Scale:

0   100m

© P. Laponder 2004

Key

Living Camp

1 Main gate

2 Tyrolean guardhouse

3 Armored car (used for transporting to Lublin valuables taken from victims)

4 SS relaxation area

5 Officer's well

6 SS living quarters: a. Mess; b. Sleeping quarters

7 Arms storeroom and water tower

8 a. Petrol tank; b. Petrol pumps

9 a. Garage; b. Coal dump

10 New bakery foundations (later "farmhouse" housing Ukrainians guarding against locals plundering mass graves)

11 Service building for the ss: a. Air raid shelter; b. Sick bay; c. Dentist; d. Barber

12 a. Camp commandant's office and living quarters; b. Wine and spirits cellar

13 Polish and Ukrainian girls' staff sleeping quarters

14 a. Zoo with pigeon coop on top; b. Relaxation area for ss

15 Ukrainians' living quarters: a. Sleeping quarters; b. Night shift quarters; c. Doctor and barber; d. Roll call and exercise area

16 Ukrainian kitchen

17 Potato cellars

18 Gold Juden (where Jewish prisoners sorted valuables and gold stolen from victims)

19 Vegetable garden

20 a. Timber store and yard; b. Waste combustion area

21 Farmyard area: a. Stables; b. Pigsty; c. Chicken run

Roll-Call Square

22 Prisoner assembly area

23 "The Ghetto," Jewish prisoners' living and working quarters: a. Jewish kitchen; b. ss laundry; c. Jewish infirmary; d. Kapo barrack; e. Saddlery and shoemaker shop; f. Tailor shop; g. Jewish women's quarters; h. Carpenter shop; i. Blacksmith and locksmith; j. Tool storehouse; k. Jewish quarters 1; l. Washroom; m. Jewish quarters 2

24 Latrines

Reception Camp

Station Square

25 Victim disembarkation platform (accommodating 20 cattle cars)

26 Storage barracks for items stolen from victims (later disguised as a railway station called Obermajdan,

including a fake ticket window, locked doors, and signs such as "To first-class waiting room")

Deportation Square

27 Separation of victims: women to the left, men to the right

28 Barracks (initially male sleeping quarters, later a lumber store)

29 Undressing barracks for females (including "cash-desk" and barber area for cutting prisoners' hair)

30 "The Tube" (narrow camouflaged passage called the Himmelstrasse [Road to heaven] through which victims were chased to "the showers")

Sorting Area

31 Sorting yard

32 Latrine

33 Lazarett (field hospital), execution site disguised as a hospital

34 Double barracks (for victims' belongings already sorted)

Death Camp

35 New gas chambers (five steps with potted plants leading up to entrance and passage; 10 sealed gas chambers with trapdoors that opened onto platforms outside from which the corpses were removed)

36 Old gas chambers (originally three smaller gas chambers)

37 Water pump shelter

38 Guardhouse

39 Sonderkommando (special unit) camp (prisoners working in death camp section): a. Roll-call yard; b. Women's quarters; c. Doctor; d. Kapo; e. Ablution; f. Men's quarters; g. Kitchen; h. Laundry area

40 Concealed burial pit (revegetated with saplings and lupine)

FIG. 6. Photo from Kurt Franz's album showing the exterior of
Treblinka's zoo. Courtesy of Ghetto Fighters' House Museum.

and this triple isolation created an imaginary area of distinction dividing
the Totenlager into a space even further removed from "normal" human
existence. For Nazi planners, the Totenlager became a space marked not
by presence but by absence, where life no longer held meaning and all that
mattered was death. Inside this conceptually remote space, the substance of
human lives disappeared, and the individuality of death was substituted by
a repetitive process of common annihilation undertaken in a tiny closed-
off section of an already closed-off world. Treblinka's spatial arrangement
meant that while Stangl performed the banal tasks of tending his garden,
visiting the zoo, and relaxing, just a short distance away, the doors to the gas
chamber opened after a gassing, "but not a body [fell] out. Due to the steam
all the bodies [became] a homogenous mass stuck together with the per-
spiration of the victims. In their death agonies, arms, legs, trunks [were]
intertwined into a gigantic macabre entanglement. . . . The bodies [lay]
piled up like slaughtered cattle."[105] Juxtaposed here in stark contrast, these
two events—one tranquil, the other horrifying—could hardly seem more
remote, but at Treblinka, such events transpired in close proximity every day.

Perhaps the conceptual spatial division between the Totenlager and the rest
of the camp was so profound because it was also the demarcation between

FIG. 7. Photo from Kurt Franz's album of animals in Treblinka's zoo.
Courtesy of USHMM, gift of Eugene Miller, acc. no. 1997.A.0240.

life and death. The Jews who remained alive to work in other areas of Treblinka (discussed more in chapter 3) almost tangibly felt the differences
between these distinct spatial zones. Survivor Abraham Bomba recalled that
while the Totenlager was situated only sixty or seventy meters from their
barracks, communication with members of the Totenlager work crew was
impossible because, as he put it, "That was a different country . . . far away
like let's say from here to Australia."[106] What happened beyond the berm and
fences of the Totenlager was conceptually unimaginable and so foreign to
consider that, although nearby, the spatial chasm separating the two meant
it might as well have been on the other side of the planet. This imagined
gap was not only enormous, but it also seemed uncrossable. "From our side
it was invisible and inaccessible," survivor Jerzy Rajgrodzki stated. "The gas
chambers served as a border between camp I and camp II. . . . From Lager
[Camp] I, you could still drop into Lager II, but the reverse path was non-
existent."[107] Strawczyński added, "If anyone crossed the border into Camp 2
by accident . . . he had to remain there, there was no return."[108] Although,
in reality, this was not always the case, and both Willenberg and Wiernik

survived after not only witnessing but also working inside the Totenlager (sometimes internally called Lager or Camp II, not to be confused with the overall camp of Treblinka II). Thus, while the majority were, in fact, relegated to one side of the chasm or the other, survivor Aleksander Kudlik explained that there were a select few, including "laborers who did woodwork (especially a man called Wiernik)[, who] were able to move between both parts of the camp."[109] Perhaps more important than the reality of this dividing line, then, is that for Treblinka's Jewish prisoners, the specific spaces that they encountered contained deep meanings about how their immediate world functioned. Because of its isolation and inaccessibility, the Totenlager became the embodiment of a death space, one inside of which things happened that were beyond comprehension—a space Krzepicki described as "najstraszniejsze z najstraszniejszych" (the scariest of the scariest).[110] As survivor Chil Rajchman gave voice to this perception, "Lager No. 1 was a place for sorting clothes and belongings of the victims and cutting their hair, and so on. . . . Camp 2 . . . [meant] contact only with the dead. This was the devil's factory."[111]

While the separation between life and death was stark in these first two zones, the third section, the Auffanglager, was a transitional space, and as such, the Germans employed regular measures of deception there. Aside from maintaining the isolation they intended at Treblinka, the Germans believed deception was needed "to coerce the remaining 400,000 inhabitants of the Warsaw ghetto to depart, without excessive resistance, from their native towns in order to be 'resettled.'"[112] According to Wiernik, "The Germans carried out the deportations in such a way that the Jews themselves crowded into the trains without even knowing what was in store for them," and in the words of Krzepicki, "Everything is being done to lie to and fool people."[113] This seems to have been a feature of how the earliest deportations to Treblinka were carried out and may also explain why such large numbers of Jews were deported so quickly in the first month of Treblinka's operation (July–August 1942). Survivor Edi Weinstein described the general atmosphere of the ghetto before these initial deportations: "Many of us still believed that the Germans were merely behaving as they had at the start of the war. The conventional wisdom held that the 'unknown destination' was somewhere in the Russian hinterland. Nobody knew anything for sure, of course."[114]

Because of the lies being told in Warsaw, from which the largest number of Treblinka-bound victims originated, the Germans built complex facades at the camp to create a continuity of spatial deception aligned with the narrative that Treblinka was merely a way station en route to resettlement. Therefore, the most elaborate deception at Treblinka was, by far, the creation of a fake train station in the camp's unloading area. The arrival platform was nicknamed "Potemkin" and was "camouflaged as a quaint rural station. Timetables and advertisements were posted on the walls in a kind of gruesome joke."[115] The station included a seventy-centimeter diameter clock with painted-on numerals showing 3 o'clock, ticket windows, timetable charts, fake restaurants, signs for freight handling, and arrows indicating connections to destinations like Warsaw and Białystok. An artist even painted signs reading "First Class," "Second Class," "Third Class," "Waiting Room," and "Cashier." Another sign read "Station Obermajdan! Umsteigen nach Białystok und Wołkowysk! [Obermajdan Station! Change here for Białystok and Wołkowysk!]."[116] Willenberg recorded that the cashier's desks even had a notice on the front window that read "Kasse Geschlossen" (Register Closed), a detail to explain why there were no employees on the other side. (Yet at other times there actually were work Jews at the cash registers.)[117] The entire area around the station was also "beautifully decorated" with flower beds and decorative shrubs.[118] This mimicry of a real train station, down to the smallest details, created a facade everyone would have seen upon arriving at Treblinka.

For the same purposes of reassurance and deception, the Germans also disguised the execution pit as an infirmary, naming it *Lazarett* (hospital), and erecting a small building with a red cross, the international sign of relief, prominently displayed. The building measured sixty by eighteen by six feet, and the two men working there posed as doctors, wore white aprons with red crosses on their sleeves, and gave false reassurances to their victims before they shot them. Such deception also included thinly veiled irony in that these fake Red Cross workers were executing exactly those people they often helped most—the elderly, children, and the sick.[119] Indeed, the Germans often combined deception with irony, intending it not only to conceal but also to degrade and humiliate their victims.[120] For instance, they disguised the gas chambers to look like a Jewish temple and draped the entrance with a red ceremonial curtain containing a Hebrew inscription that read, "This is the gateway to God. Righteous men will pass through." They also installed the Star of David on top of the gas chamber's roof.[121] The Germans nicknamed this gas chamber building the *Judenstaat* (Jewish State) as a cynical way of referring to the death-producing site.[122]

Collectively, these measures of deception created odd, almost surreal scenes—after all, Jews being led to the gas chambers were told these were showers, and yet they looked like temples. From the German viewpoint, though, either worked to disguise their true purpose, and thus, creating elaborate fake spaces within Treblinka had both practical and abstract ramifications. The facades were intended to create more passive victims, making the work of mass murder smoother and thereby less psychologically burdensome for the Germans to carry out. On a deeper level, however, the Germans' inherent internalization of their own deceptive measures likely further reinforced their conception that Treblinka was, in fact, some alternate reality in which they could act according to their own warped morality. Thus, the juxtaposition between fake and real was potentially blurred for the killers as well as for their victims.[123]

The Imagined Treblinka

Treblinka was the apotheosis of Nazi ideology dictated in space, and the decisions regarding where to locate the camp and how to organize its spaces highlight exactly what the Nazis desired to create—a Judenfrei world within the Third Reich's living space. Positioned within this conception, Treblinka was meant to operate as an industrial, efficient death factory, which "manufactured" the deaths of the Jews at first but assuredly would be followed by other "undesirable" elements within Germany. "In all probability, the Germans will not want to limit themselves to the murder of Jews," a 1943 report buried in the Oyneg Shabes Archive stated. "Once set into motion, the death machine will not stop."[124] At Nuremberg, Bach-Zelewski confirmed that if not for the war's end, the methods of mass murder employed by his fellow ss members at spaces like Treblinka would have, in his opinion, resulted in the deaths of over thirty million people.[125] As the paradigmatic embodiment of a death-producing space, conceptually speaking, some Nazis indeed believed Treblinka was a system that, if properly concealed from the world, could run interminably. And thus, it seems that the Nazi vision of having industrial human slaughterhouses as a normal feature dotting the landscape of their thousand-year Reich is no casual speculation but a legitimate depiction of their disturbing "utopian" future.

These belief systems created a distancing of the killers from the processes of killing at Treblinka, which in turn created at least the perception of the industrial atmosphere they needed to carry out their "mission." Yet no space, however ideologically inspired and positioned, can function completely isolated from the larger world beyond. At Treblinka, the separation between the ideological space of the camp and the reality on the ground began to grow immediately. Treblinka became a place where clean, sanitized, factory-like destruction looked very much like the mass murder of innocent people; where hardened, murderous automatons were revealed to be human beings; and where all the isolation, secrecy, and deception in the world did little more than momentarily distract anyone who encountered these flimsy facades.

A Behavioral Space

All the witnesses remember one feature which ss
men in Treblinka all had in common: they loved
theoretical constructions, philosophizing. . . . They
boasted and explained the great significance for
the future of what was taking place in Treblinka.
They were all deeply and sincerely convinced of
the importance and rightness of their work.

—Vasily Grossman, *A Writer at War*

Human behavior is complicated. Multiple studies of Holocaust perpetrators
have pointed to different (sometimes conflicting) explanations for why people act the way they do. From "ordinary men" to "willing executioners" and
the gamut in between, we seek simplistic categories to help make sense of
something that is, in reality, infinitely complex. One study cannot account
for all the nuances explaining perpetrator behavior, and I do not attempt
to provide a comprehensive explanation here.[1] Instead, I aim to answer a
seemingly straightforward question: How did space and perceptions of it
affect perpetrator behavior at Treblinka?[2]

Spatial theorist Tim Cresswell has argued that the "socially constructed
meaning of place[s] directly affect judgments of the events in them," and to
understand a space is to understand the images and symbols associated
with it.[3] So if Treblinka was the nadir of the Holocaust, the most clear-cut
example we have of Nazi exterminationist ideology projected onto space,
then unpacking its images and symbols tells us more not only about the camp
that once existed but also about those who used it to pursue such horrific
ends. The previous chapter's examination of the physical and ideological
considerations of Treblinka's placement in Poland and the conscious (and

perhaps subconscious) construction and arrangement of Treblinka's spatial layout revealed Treblinka to have been a doubly isolated zone of Nazi morality tucked into Poland's "hidden wildernesses." This chapter digs deeper to ask how certain individuals transformed their behavior, demeanor, and purpose once placed within positions of authority at Treblinka. In so doing, two other components of ideology manifested in spatial practice come into focus—the "mission" many Germans believed must be carried out in this confined space and the secrecy that both pervaded the camp's built environment and influenced the behaviors of those in charge.

Treblinka personnel represented a mix of Nazi fanatics, career-minded officers, and an array of ordinary men—a combination of personality types that allowed for a deadly diffusion of responsibility that created the space for mass murder.[4] Historical and popular perceptions of these German and Ukrainian men have long perpetuated imagery of Treblinka as a mechanically perfected, industrial "human slaughterhouse" operated by ice-cold automatons. In fact, there are at least two sources in the Oyneg Shabes Archive, one from Abraham Krzepicki and one from Emmanuel Ringelblum, that refer to Treblinka as a "slaughterhouse."[5] Hence while the war was still ongoing, and the camp still operational, the perception of industrial killing was already proliferating widely, and this same technocratic description of killing cleanly still persists today in references to Treblinka.[6]

Here, we start the long process of unpacking and challenging this perception. On one hand, this imagery gives insight into why so many German camp personnel shifted their behavior so rapidly once inside Treblinka's spaces and why they also "shut off" their Treblinka-adapted personas after leaving the space. It was as if, upon crossing Treblinka's spatial threshold, they shed previous moral persuasions and inhibitions to assume their part in something they believed was far larger than themselves, something that the small confines of the death camp not only represented but provided them the spatial freedom to pursue. In fact, in one of the early Reinhard trials in Frankfurt, the court stated in its evaluation of a Treblinka guard that whether he believed his actions were justified or thought he would never be punished was "irrelevant. . . . It is not the personal view of the perpetrator that is decisive, but the generally recognized moral views."[7] Although inferring broader Nazi morality here, one could attach to the court's appraisal, without diminishing its validity, this phrase: *within spaces sanctioned for such purposes.* Put differently, the isolation, sectioning off, and erecting of facades at Treblinka enhanced the phantasmagoric belief that Treblinka was some spatial outlier where perpetrators felt uninhibited to behave according to Nazi moral principles and logic. In Donald Bloxham's estimation, such "places of exception conditioned behavior at least as much as did attitudes to specific victim groups."[8] Or, as Hannah Arendt put it, "It is not so much the barbed wire as the skillfully manufactured unreality of those whom it fences in that provokes such enormous cruelties and ultimately makes extermination look like a perfectly normal measure."[9]

On the other hand, the industrial imagery is also fundamentally flawed. Given the power dynamics at Treblinka, the German and Ukrainian guards were supposed to have relatively free rein inside the camp's spaces, and with such power, they were among the very few who moved throughout Treblinka's spaces without the specter of certain death hanging over their heads. For illustration, the same Frankfurt court judged that "a restriction on the freedom of movement of any of the 20–25 Germans in the larger Treblinka camp would have been completely incompatible with their tasks."[10] But despite this spatial freedom, many tasked with operating Treblinka withered under the weight of their heinous crimes. Simply put, ideology, perception, and fantasy accounted for much in creating Treblinka, but it could not account for the reality of murdering large numbers of human beings within a small, confined space. In a short time, even the "hardened" ss men, those supposedly incapable of human weakness, sought various salves to somehow better align the crimes they perpetrated daily with the ideological fantasies dictating what Treblinka, and they as its operators, was *supposed* to be.[11]

It is at the crossroads, then, between the ideological and moral spaces of transformation Treblinka represented and the awareness of the sheer brutality of murdering almost a million innocent people in the span of fifteen months that we see another noteworthy behavior related to Treblinka's space—the need to hide it. Extreme measures of secrecy defined the camp from beginning to end, influencing both its construction and how camp personnel operated within the space. These considerations reflected the ideological need for isolation from the world, and hence its Western morality and norms, and served as the prerequisite to creating the alternate moral universe required to conduct "clean, industrial" death on a mass scale.[12] However, the sheer *need* for practices of secrecy also reveals the utter inability of many Germans to break completely with the world outside Treblinka, and at least on some level, no amount of ideologically driven spatial transformation could distance them from their crimes. In the broader perspective, providing reality to the *idea* of something like Treblinka snatches it from the dark recesses of our nightmares and lays bare what it ultimately was—an inherently human creation that produced grisly and disturbing scenes of suffering. And teasing out this tiny shred of humanity from the perpetrators (whether identifying their guilt or simply calling them human) in no way justifies, condones, or otherwise relativizes Nazi ideology. Instead, it reveals a much more realistic view of the Holocaust by underscoring this fact: this was a crime committed by humans against their fellow humans, and only when we accept that do we start distancing ourselves from the same pervasive and imaginary tropes that the killers themselves used.

The Slaughterhouse Image

In 1946, Vienna's Stern Publishers released a pamphlet entitled *Das Menschenschlachthaus Treblinka* (The Human Slaughterhouse Treblinka).[13] On its cover is an image depicting a train pulling a line of cattle cars and steaming toward what looks like a modern factory, complete with sleek, streamlined buildings and smokestacks puffing out clouds of industrial smoke (see figure 8). Out of the smoke rise distorted faces with expressions of pain and fright, representing the final output of the death camp, which has transformed human beings into disembodied specters hanging above the landscape. The imagery is intended to present Treblinka as a clean, industrial death factory where the blood and carnage of murdering human beings through gas and bullets are removed from our view and instead presumed to be modern, efficient, quick, and despite the clear anguish evident on the faces drifting skyward, painless.[14] Likely a leftover from the Nazi period, using sanitized symbols to replace and conceal the killing process reinforces the conception that Treblinka was a nearly automated system that ran fluidly without needing to get human hands dirty. Equally as striking is how the camp complex itself sits atop a hill, providing *more* elevation from which to belch its smoke into its surroundings, and how its telegraph wires suggest a connection with the outside world.

These are images not of secrecy, deception, and hiding but rather of modernity, pride, progress, and awareness. Thus, taken holistically, Treblinka

FIG. 8. Cover of German pamphlet *Das Menschenschlachthaus Treblinka* (The Human Slaughterhouse Treblinka). The style invokes the perception of a technocratic, industrial, and clean killing center. Courtesy of Harry Mazal Collection, University of Colorado–Boulder.

appears as a model of refined killing, replete with modern amenities, unashamedly producing its product, which in this case was dead bodies instead of gadgets, as if it were a logical extension of the industrial era.[15] In fact, Vasily Grossman used just such language in his 1944 report, stating Treblinka was "run on the conveyor system, on the production line method copied from modern large-scale industry."[16] Hence it seems even from the earliest days after it had ceased to exist, the camp still had a particular reputation.

Yet this was not Treblinka's reality.[17] So where did this imagery come from? To answer, we go back to the construction and organization of the death camp's space and how ideology dictated what the Germans believed they could do inside of it. From the Nazi perspective, after being physically isolated from the outside world and spatially arranged to serve its purpose, Treblinka became a world unto itself—at least conceptually. Within the camp's confines was supposed to have existed a space beholden only to Nazi ideological premises, which brought together a twisted blend of pseudoscience, racialized antisemitism, and a technocratic faith in social engineering. "Everything that was done in the camps is known to us from the world of perverse, malignant fantasies," Arendt wrote. "The difficult thing to understand is that, like such fantasies, these gruesome crimes took place in a phantom world."[18] This atmosphere of pervasive lies and twisted connections between nationalism, duty, and murder, Rachel Auerbach points out, exploited the criminal tendencies of the Nazi murder program to unleash "a reservoir of annihilation energy essential to the service of the state and the war effort."[19] This energy found its clearest outlet within closed-off spaces like Treblinka, where hidden from the prying eyes of a world they worried would not understand, Reinhard camp inspector Kurt Gerstein found ss guards who believed that their tasks were "humane" and that the intentionality behind the death camp's design represented the "beauty of the task."[20] As historian Daniel Blatman has suggested, the "commandants and senior officers regarded themselves as warriors in the forefront of National Socialism's main battle, performing tasks that constituted a supreme historical mission."[21]

The camp's specific mission, according to a Nuremberg document, was the "complete destruction of the Jewish population in Poland, which necessitated the creation of a machinery by means of which the Polish Jews could be killed in large numbers."[22] Some Germans prided themselves on the specific language of machinery because it represented their technological mastery over a situation where mass shootings had become too burdensome for the shooters. "A German's skill was reflected . . . in his ability to master any situation," ss guard Kurt Franz once commented to survivor Yankel Wiernik.[23] Many looked no further than Treblinka's built-in mechanism by which "even the [Jewish] people employed within it—transiently—were only occupied with servicing this production of death, until their own time came."[24] This "ingenuity" reinforced its legitimacy for many, and when later asked if he could have stopped this "industrial machinery," Treblinka commandant Franz Stangl answered emphatically, "No, no, no, This was the system. . . . It worked. And because it worked, it was irreversible."[25]

This Nazi conception for how Treblinka, and potentially future Reinhard-style camps, might industrially operate carried a power of its own—even for non-Nazis. Treblinka survivors used similar language in describing the camp, like Richard Glazar, who reflected later: "This is something, you know, the world has never understood; how *perfect* the *machine* was. . . . Treblinka alone could have dealt with the 6,000,000 Jews and more besides. Given adequate rail transport, the German extermination camps in Poland could have killed all the Poles, Russians and other East Europeans the Nazis planned eventually to kill."[26] Besides conjuring up the dark killing potential he imagined of Treblinka, Glazar presciently suggests the camp might soon expand its reach to include anyone deemed "undesirable." In fact, Treblinka survivor Samuel Rajzman once conversed with an ss guard who indicated there were plans to increase Treblinka's gas chambers from ten to twenty-five. When Rajzman protested that most of Europe's Jews had already been killed, the guard replied, "After you there will be others, and there is still a big job to do."[27] As Kurt Franz repeatedly commented, "The gas chambers will continue to operate as long as so much as one Jew is left in the world."[28] Statements like these—invoking killing potential, coming from Nazis and non-Nazis alike, and combined with the unimaginable death toll Treblinka actually inflicted—have given immense imaginative power to the perceptions surrounding the Reinhard camps.

Attached to Treblinka's conceptual mission—that the system be perfected, machine-like, and operational until every Jewish person was destroyed—was the overriding, albeit paradoxical, belief that although the German people were not yet ready to understand the murders, the Reinhard program was critical for the long-term survival and viability of the thousand-year Reich (hence done in the name of these same German people).[29] Chief of the ss Heinrich Himmler endorsed this idea in his 1943 Posen speech, stating that the death camps were "a never written and never-to-be-written glorious page in our history. . . . We had the moral right, we had the duty to our people, to kill this people that wanted to kill us. . . . All in all, we can say that we have carried out this most difficult task out of love for our people. And we have suffered no harm to our inner being, our soul, our character."[30] Everything about this statement, from the disclaimer on discretion to the twisted logic of duty to the hypermasculine call to remain unharmed by the "difficult task," intends to reinforce ideological buzzwords for those running the camps.[31] Indeed, most Germans on the ground shared, at some level, Himmler's "Posen mentality," especially his refrain that mass killing was a national duty. Gerstein reported that ss doctor Wilhelm Pfannenstiel echoed these concepts, once telling a group of death camp personnel, "Your task is a great duty, a duty useful and necessary. . . . Looking at the bodies of these Jews, one understands the greatness of your work."[32] Another phrase that caught on was Himmler's call to become "inhuman to a superhuman degree" by overcoming tasks that might make "lesser" men squeamish.[33] Not idle words, the concept clearly had been circulating in Nazi circles for some time. In a November 1939 speech, for instance, Albert Forster, Gauleiter of Danzig–West Prussia stated, "We hope that in this struggle for the triumph of our German cause, we shall never become merciful, that we shall always show the *necessary harshness*."[34]

Yet despite his key role in creating Nazi ideological fantasies, Himmler did not personally exterminate Jews. Instead, he delegated these tasks to lower-level Nazis on the ground, to men like Christian Wirth and Odilo Globočnik. Far from being passive gears in the Nazi mechanism of death, Wirth and Globočnik were fervent Nazi ideologues, enthusiastic about their mission. In fact, it was Wirth, according to historian Yitzhak Arad, who "introduced the regime of terror and death" to Reinhard camps, and not just for Jewish victims but also for German and Ukrainian guards. Wirth began his Reinhard work as commandant of Bełżec before becoming inspector for Sobibór and Treblinka in mid-1942. Those who knew Wirth described him as "an exceedingly unpleasant and feared superior," whose harsh methods of operating the camps earned him the nickname "Wild Christian."[35] His two other nicknames, "Christian the Terrible" and "Christian the Savage," each invoked his inclination toward running around the camp with his whip and gun in hand, shouting, cursing, and swiping at anyone who crossed his path. Dieter Allers, a fellow ss officer involved in Operation Reinhard, later reflected on Wirth: "He was the arch-villain, how awful he was."[36]

Globočnik, who oversaw the management of Reinhard camps from his base in Lublin, shared Wirth's ideological fanaticism. According to some, Globočnik desired to become "the most proficient killer of Jews," and he often bragged about how many people he had killed.[37] His rabid enthusiasm is best shown in his own words: "Gentlemen, if there was ever, after us, a generation so cowardly, and so soft that they could not understand our work which is so good, so necessary, then gentlemen, all of National Socialism will have been in vain. We ought, on the contrary, to bury bronze tablets stating that it was we who had the courage to carry out this gigantic task."[38] Globočnik accepted that grisly tasks had to be carried out to achieve the Third Reich's "utopian" goals, but even he, holed up in his Lublin office, was at a remove from the camps themselves. "Globočnik cast himself as a dynamic and ruthless 'man of action' who believed one hundred percent in his mission, which matched what Himmler had in mind," historian Bertrand Perz has noted. "Still Globočnik had to rely to a large extent on personnel who executed the duties assigned to them." Therefore, even he, described often as "fanatic" and "obsessed with his mission," had to rely on, and dictate orders to, a group in charge of day-to-day operations.[39] In some sense, then, Globočnik thrived on a positive feedback loop that enhanced his own sense of purpose within a mechanism he oversaw from a sanitized distance.

While indoctrinated Nazis held key positions within Operation Reinhard, one must look at the day-to-day operators of Treblinka to see how far Nazi ideology permeated. The core personnel selected to work at the Reinhard death camps were 121 ss men who had previously worked in the T4 program.[40] Named after the location of the program's main office on Tiergartenstraße 4 in Berlin, Aktion T4 was a planned euthanasia program where Nazi "doctors" oversaw the murders of as many as two hundred thousand German citizens with mental or physical disabilities, the elderly, or those otherwise deemed a burden on Germany's economy. While some doctors determined from afar which cases merited euthanasia, others worked, alongside nurses and administrative staff, to run the six main murder facilities scattered throughout Germany. Begun in October 1939, but postdated by Hitler to September 1939 to coincide with the invasion of Poland, Aktion T4 officially ended in 1941.[41] Beyond that point, as a postwar trial noted, these "euthanasia employees" represented a latent "work force" who "had already been tested in a secretly carried out killing action of a grand style . . . [and] therefore were particularly suitable for use in the final solution."[42] Because gassing was used in some T4 centers (others used lethal injections), these T4 members also had the peculiar "technical and professional experience in killing people by gas" that the Reinhard camps required.[43]

The "repurposing process" for these T4 operators was fairly streamlined— upon arriving in Lublin, they were sworn in for their "special assignment," became subject to the Military Penal Code, received new uniforms and ranks, and were given weapons instruction at the Trawniki training camp near Lublin before being sent to a Reinhard camp.[44] Their destination, however, was conceptually (and spatially) different from other camps in the Nazi system; the Reinhard camps certainly differed in comparison with concentration camps like Dachau, Gross-Rosen, and Mauthausen but also from other camps in Poland like Auschwitz and Majdanek, which served different purposes. As hybrid concentration-death camps, these latter locations specifically maintained a large living prisoner population (sometimes tens of thousands) to perform forced labor for Germany, whereas Treblinka, Bełżec, and Sobibór intended fatal outcomes for everyone who entered. Even the initial choice of staff for Reinhard camps—using this "highly trained" subset of the SS (those with T4 experience)—set them apart from Majdanek and Auschwitz, both of which were originally staffed with economic and administrative SS divisions.[45]

In total, between thirty and fifty of these T4-trained men worked at Treblinka.[46] One in particular, Franz Stangl, whose T4 work included ascribing fake causes to the death certificates of those murdered, later became commandant of Treblinka. Stangl stringently believed his T4 work did not constitute mass murder, but instead, he saw it as a "cleansing" operation aimed to "protect the sensibilities of the [German] population."[47] He applied the same broad justification to his role at Treblinka, commenting in a postwar interview with Gitta Sereny, "I remember . . . that the definition of a crime must meet four requirements: there has to be a subject, an object, an action, and intent. If any of these four elements are missing, then we are not dealing with a punishable offence. . . . The only way I could live was by compartmentalizing my thinking. By doing this I *could* apply it to my own situation; if the 'subject' was the government, the 'object' the Jews, and the 'action' the gassings, then I could tell myself that for me the fourth element, 'intent' . . . was missing."[48] Aside from the unabashed attempt at self-vindication, Stangl reveals here the rationalization he used—likely shared by other T4 and Reinhard camp personnel—to account for his part in murdering hundreds of thousands of people. Because the system was designed so that little burden of intent fell on the individual, Stangl viewed his task as part of the greater collective mission for Germany—an undertaking in which each individual mattered less than the whole.

Indeed, the Nazi hierarchy and command structure, with Hitler firmly established at the top, thrived in a type of bureaucratic chaos where Hitler's lieutenants all competed to develop the best solution to every new problem. While some—like Heinrich Himmler, Hermann Göring, Joseph Goebbels, Albert Speer, and Reinhard Heydrich—operated from clearly entrenched positions of authority, Hitler sat so far above the fray that it became very easy to diffuse responsibility as one moved down the ranks.[49] A significant example of this mechanism comes from Otto Ohlendorf, commander of Einsatzgruppe D, who testified at Nuremberg that when Himmler gave him the orders to shoot Jews on the Eastern Front, Himmler specified "the leaders and men who were taking part in the liquidation bore no personal responsibility for the execution of this order. The responsibility was his, alone, and the Führer's." In another key statement, Ohlendorf added, "The SS, that is to say, Himmler, as Reichsführer SS, gave State offices no official authority to issue orders."[50] Hence entire organizational decisions were reduced to relying upon the whims and commands of one person, even though thousands operated under its auspices. Therefore, with a firm belief that mass murder represented some higher cause, and with ultimate responsibility lying in faraway Berlin, the person pulling the trigger found little fault in their own actions. Or, as Willi Mentz justified his behavior at Treblinka, "The Führer ordered it and he will have to answer for it."[51]

The same framework applied to many others operating the death camps. The Treblinka trials court stated unequivocally that Himmler bestowed upon Globočnik "extensive special powers" to make decisions as needed. Moreover, Globočnik was made subordinate to only Himmler himself, which

gave him extensive flexibility to interpret Himmler's wishes—and by extension, Hitler's—as he saw fit.[52] This trickled down to localized command
structures in occupied Poland, and a microcosm of this power dynamic
operated among Treblinka's ss personnel. Despite Stangl's later claim that
he was only a "little man" who "couldn't do anything about it," we know he
was promoted, alongside several other "deserving" Reinhard personnel, on
February 12, 1943, to ss-Hauptsturmführer (roughly equivalent to captain),
for being, in Globočnik's words, "the *best camp commander* who had the
greatest share in the whole operation."[53] Repeatedly true in other aspects
of the Nazi system, promotions and career advancement motivated many
camp personnel, and as a postwar court stated, "With particular reliability
and circumspection, [Stangl] sought his own advancement."[54]

But it was more than that—it was *how* Stangl acted in the space of Treblinka
that highlights his adaptation and adherence to what the space represented.
After all, being singled out by his superior as the best commandant was
probably not unsubstantiated, and as court transcripts expand on this point,
"The accused accepted the basic attitude of the National Socialist leadership about the unacceptable value of the Jewish race and he felt no inhibitions about willingly accepting and exercising the office of camp director
of an extermination camp.... He was successful in trying to ensure the extermination operation under his supervision . . . ran quickly and smoothly."[55]
Clearly, deference to authority and adaptive morality go hand in hand,
and though he viewed himself as a cog in the larger machine, in fervently
streamlining the murder operation at Treblinka, Stangl aligned his own
morality to fit within Nazi ideological goals once he entered the camp's
space. Stangl later gave voice to this transformation process, reflecting on
his first encounter with Treblinka's full pits of corpses: "It had nothing to
do with humanity—it couldn't have; it was a mass—a mass of rotting flesh.
Wirth said, 'What shall we do with this garbage?' I think unconsciously that
started me thinking of them as cargo. . . . I rarely saw them as individuals.
It was always a huge mass." However, this transformation functioned for
Stangl like a psychological "on/off" switch, because while piles of bodies
elicited no emotional response, when Sereny asked which was Treblinka's
"worst place," Stangl replied, "The undressing barracks. . . . I avoided it
from my innermost being; I couldn't confront them; I couldn't lie to them;
I avoided at any price talking to those who were about to die; I couldn't

stand it." Stangl compartmentalized the spaces of Treblinka and adapted his behavior accordingly, and as Sereny surmises, "It became clear that as soon as the people were in the undressing barracks—that is, as soon as they were naked—they were no longer human beings for him. What he was 'avoiding at all price' was *witnessing the transition*."[56] Treblinka's distinctly separated internal layout meant that such transitions occurred within specific spaces, eliminating his need to have to witness the process.

Something else Stangl told Sereny reveals just how sharp this dividing line was for him:

> [STANGL]: I *did* have contact with the work-Jews. . . . You know, quite friendly relations . . . that's what I enjoyed; *human relations*. Especially with people like Singer and Blau. . . . Blau was the one I talked to most. . . . He knew I'd help whenever I could. There was one day when he knocked at the door of my office. . . . His eighty-year-old father [had arrived] on that morning's transport. Was there anything I could do. I said, "Really, Blau, you must understand, it's impossible. A man of eighty . . ." He said quickly that yes, he understood, of course. But could he ask me for permission to take his father to the *Lazarett* rather than the gas chambers. And could he take his father first to the kitchen and give him a meal. I said, "You go and do what you think best, Blau." . . . In the afternoon, when I came back to my office, he was waiting for me. He had tears in his eyes. He stood to attention and said, "Herr Hauptsturmführer, I want to thank you. I gave my father a meal. And I've just taken him to the *Lazarett*—it's all over. Thank you very much." I said, "Well, Blau, there's no need to thank me, but of course if you *want* to thank me, you may."
>
> [SERENY]: What happened to Blau . . . ?
>
> [STANGL]: I don't know.

Sereny reflects on this exchange, "This story and the way it was told represented to me the starkest example of a corrupted personality I had ever encountered and came very near to making me stop these conversations."[57] In fact, this, what Sereny calls a "corrupted personality," underscores Stangl's complete adherence to the spatial reality Treblinka provided him—one in which he so wholeheartedly adopted his role that years later he still did not recognize the humanity of Blau or his father or even the heartbreaking scene he recounted, apparently emotionless, despite mere sentences before stating that he enjoyed "human relations" with these very people. One can sense the *same* compartmentalization taking place in Stangl's mind in Sereny's 1971 interview that probably occurred in Treblinka years earlier: "In *that* space I played *my* part." Any deeper contemplation was superfluous.

Another area we cannot overlook is Stangl's role as commandant. As such, Treblinka provided a spatial setting that Stangl could dominate and rule as an "unchallenged sovereign." Michel Foucault wrote about sovereignty in relation to the modern nation-state, but the logic uncannily applies to the world inside Treblinka: one of the sovereign's "basic attributes" is deciding life and death for his citizens, but the sovereign cannot "grant life in the same way he can inflict death"; therefore, "the right to life and death is always exercised in an unbalanced way: the balance is always tipped in the favor of death."[58] Geographer James Tyner has applied this concept to spaces of genocide, arguing that "mass violence results from the imposition of state-sanctioned normative geographical imaginations that justify and legitimate unequal access to life and death."[59] By many accounts, Stangl reveled in his role as sovereign and the power he possessed over everything within *his* spatial domain at Treblinka. Beyond his unwavering belief in the mission of killing people, there was his penchant for traversing the camp on horseback clad in a white jacket and jodhpurs. Although he later told Sereny this outfit was improvised because he was transferred east with no clothes, the image he cut speaks for itself (see figure 9).[60] Many survivors remembered seeing him in this ostentatious outfit, and survivor Samuel Rajzman described the accompanying attitude: "Stangl often stood on the earthen wall between the two camps.... He stood there like a Napoleon surveying his domain."[61]

When challenged after the war on his behavior at Treblinka, Stangl again invoked the camp's spatially divided interior to give his defense—claiming that he did not command the *whole* camp but was *only* responsible for registering valuables and maintaining the security of the warehouse. As for the killing operation (the sectioned-off Totenlager), Stangl pointed the finger at Kurt Franz, claiming it had been solely Franz's domain and responsibility. Though untrue, Stangl's response highlights many spatial adaptations all rolled together—that the internal space was mentally as well as physically

FIG. 9. Franz Stangl in his white outfit holding his whip, a clear projection of his authority within the spaces of Treblinka. Courtesy of USHMM, gift of Eugene Miller, acc. No. 1997.A.0240.

sectioned off, that deference to authority occurred within the camp, and given what we know about Kurt Franz, that Stangl's own adaptation to Treblinka's spaces had powerful ripple effects on those below him, who sought to replicate his actions, demeanor, and outlook. Trial records pinpoint this latter fact: "It was not the difference in rank alone, but the factual superiority and authority of the defendant as camp leader that gave subordinates reason to show greater zeal when he was around."[62] In other words, behavior aside, Stangl's mere presence as a superior was sufficient to inspire lower-ranking personnel at Treblinka not only to defer to his authority but to act in ways they thought he—and by unseen extension, Globočnik, Himmler, and ultimately, Hitler—would approve. The space of Treblinka, therefore, represented a microcosm of the entire Nazi bureaucratic system, and although he claimed he had merely "followed orders," Stangl himself had the same effect on those beneath him.

The transformation these lower-level personnel underwent is best exemplified by the utter disparity between their prewar lives and the roles they assumed at Treblinka. A cross section of these men shows that while most became accustomed to killing during their time in the T4 program, little in their personal histories flags them as somehow irregular or destined to commit genocide. They were not predetermined sadists, nor were they uneducated. In fact, some had advanced degrees from the best universities in Europe. Others came from agriculture, and here, perhaps, is the closest prewar connection some had to the genocide they committed—they had experience working in the slaughter of animals, which some believed made them "hardened men" unlikely "to break out in tears or develop nightmares because of their work."[63] But many others came from a variety of personal backgrounds and "normal" prewar occupations (not to mention the relatively banal lives most returned to after the war). Therefore, it was almost as if, for them too, a switch flipped on once they walked into Treblinka's space (and off again when they left).[64] As the Frankfurt court noted in 1951,

> Whether they let the gas into the extermination chambers themselves, or watched over the undressing of the victims, or drove them through the "Schlauch" [Tube] to the gas chambers or merely ensured that the guards were fed properly by monitoring the kitchen is all irrelevant....
> In such a case of organized mass crime, all such actions ... are the cause

of the predetermined result, the destruction of numerous people. . . . The success was only made possible by the interaction of *all* individual acts and would not have happened if they had not been carried out. Whether the participation of the individual was more or less extensive and his actions regarded as the predominant occurrence of success, or whether they only accelerated or promoted it, can be of decisive importance for the assessment of his criminal guilt, but for the question of causality . . . in carrying out such a well-prepared plan, [these issues] are immaterial.[65]

Thus, as a microcosm of the larger Nazi system, Treblinka's space promoted a diffusion of responsibility and encouraged individual excess, and if nothing else, these men's "banal" prewar lives only helped them further adapt. A Düsseldorf court later reflected on this point, suggesting that Willi Mentz's behavior was molded "by the defendant's long-standing membership in the Nazi party, where he was constantly told at party meetings that one had to obey as a subordinate, and finally, also by the defendant's professional activity as master milker, in which he always had to accept and follow instructions from landowners and estate managers."[66]

Another instructive example is deputy commandant Kurt Franz. Despite working as a waiter and cook before the war, Franz was known at Treblinka for his sadism and depravity and for unleashing his dog, Barry, to attack prisoners.[67] The court that tried Franz stated he "used the power at his disposal in a terrible and unrestrained manner, to help achieve the final goal set by the Führer of the complete annihilation of the Jewish people in his sphere of influence and to ensure the short span left of their lives was an agonizing hell. In doing so, he revealed such sadism and disregard for all Jewish life that the human imagination scarcely suffices to imagine. . . . A large part of the streams of blood and tears spilled in Treblinka are of his account." In trying further to explain his behavior, the court added, "He made a big show of everything that spread fear and terror and in which the accused *wanted to confirm himself*."[68] The spaces of Treblinka became "his sphere of influence," and he relished it, keeping a "well-groomed" appearance accenting his "pretty face" to the extent that Jewish prisoners nicknamed him *Lalka* (Doll in Polish).[69] In fact, years later, Franz titled a photo album from his Reinhard days "Schöne Zeiten," or "Beautiful Times," insinuating these years were fond memories.[70] The "Treblinka song," which several sources recount, was likely also Franz's creation, and the lyrics are telling: "Looking squarely ahead, brave and joyous, at the world, the squads march to work. All that matters to us now is Treblinka. It is our destiny. That's why *we've become one* with Treblinka in no time at all."[71]

The case of Josef Hirtreiter repeats this formula. A locksmith and bricklayer before the war, at Treblinka, Hirtreiter inflicted "unsurpassed brutality." In fact, a Frankfurt court stated, "Some of the crimes the defendant is accused of are so unimaginable and monstrous in their brutality that the jury had to overcome their disbelief that such bestial events were possible."[72] What explains this transformation from a mundane life of skilled labor before (and his return to it after) Treblinka? During T4, Hirtreiter had been a desk clerk at Hadamar, a forgotten member of the bureaucratic processes of euthanasia. His initial assignment at Treblinka—running the kitchen—was a role befitting his background. Yet he "soon 'advanced' to supervising the undressing of the arriving Jewish victims. . . . Next, he actively participated in the chasing of naked victims to the gas chambers, for the purpose of which he made use of a specially designed whip containing pieces of lead. Also, he 'accompanied' old people and little children to the so-called 'Lazarett.'"[73] Within the spaces of Treblinka, such opportunities to usurp and display authority were endless and encouraged, and Hirtreiter used the unique occasion to assert his dominance, perhaps for the first (maybe only) time in his life, over "lesser people" with impunity. "The defendant has clearly shown through his behavior in Treblinka," the court concluded, "that he had completely accepted the views that led to the establishment of the camp—that the Jews were inferior, and their killing and mistreatment was justified."[74]

A similar transformation can be seen in the example of Heinrich Matthes. A nurse before and after the war, Matthes worked in photography at the Berlin T4 office. While at Treblinka, however, Matthes was given control over the gas chambers, a duty he took "very seriously . . . overcoming all the difficulties that arose with great severity and brutality."[75] In his zeal, a Düsseldorf court summed up,

[Matthes] adopted the plan worked out by Hitler, Himmler, Globočnik, and Wirth to exterminate the victims brought to Treblinka. . . . Matthes was well aware of the important role he played as head of the

Totenlager. . . . While during his past as a nurse and educator he had to accept and follow instructions from his superiors, even on trivial things, he held an almost unimaginable position of power as leader of the upper camp, which gave him increased self-confidence. After all, he could give orders to hundreds of prisoners, beat them, and even kill them without being held accountable. For him, this was the best opportunity to vent his suppressed inferiority complexes in an extremely effective way.[76]

This prescient explanation pinpoints several key elements of the behavioral equation at Treblinka: the intoxicating power of authority, freedom from repercussions, the diffusion of responsibility, and above all, a specific spatial realm within which each was fostered.

Examples of behavioral transformation inside Treblinka's spaces go on and on. August Miete, a miller and farmer before the war, and a loan manager after, was known by Polish Jews as *Malchamowes* (the Angel of Death) at Treblinka.[77] Willi Mentz, a prewar and postwar dairy farmer, was called "Frankenstein" by Jewish prisoners for the robotic way he shot thousands of people at the Lazarett without emotion.[78] Gustav Münzberger, a cabinetmaker before and after the war, chased victims into gas chambers with lashes from his whip and ordered that children be violently thrown into gas chambers already "filled to the brim." The court's judgment: Münzberger's "special belief in authority" and his "subordination to orders and his gratitude to the Führer" made him "a cog in the cruel killing machinery" who "stubbornly" did his "prescribed work."[79]

Overall, it seems that once inside Treblinka, most German personnel collectively replaced vestiges of Western morality with the new ideological goals the space promoted to justify their murderous roles. What followed was a chain reaction that historian Eric Weitz describes as a "breakdown of preexisting norms of behavior and a reworking of the rules of social interaction including the promotion of political violence as the method of progress towards utopia."[80] Nazi officer Erich von dem Bach-Zelewski said as much in his postwar testimony, reflecting, "If for years, for decades, a doctrine is preached to the effect that the Slav race is an inferior race, that the Jews are not even human beings, then an explosion of this sort is inevitable."[81] While ideology alone does not commit genocide, when human beings who have internalized certain beliefs are given a spatial domain that is isolated and free from the constraints of the normal world outside—and told that they are performing the critical, if albeit dirty, work for generations to come—mass carnage ensues.

Yet there was another group who also occupied positions of power at Treblinka—the Ukrainian guards. Witnesses estimate that between 140 and 250 Ukrainians worked at Treblinka in ancillary roles, and their tasks included patrolling the perimeter of the camp, warning local Poles who approached too closely or failed to follow posted instructions nearby, manning the watchtowers in each corner of Treblinka, and supervising the victims as they passed through the camp. In practice, Ukrainians carried out most day-to-day operations, while Germans maintained more of a general oversight role.[82] Krzepicki explained the power dynamics at play: "For the Germans, [the Ukrainians] were lower-class people." In fact, the Germans even built a special detention center for Ukrainians who disobeyed German orders, and they shot any Ukrainian (there were several) caught trying to escape alongside Jews.[83] In their subjugated roles, the Ukrainians were seen, in the words of postwar investigator Zdzisław Łukaszkiewicz, as the "blind executors of orders from their masters in the ss."[84] One reason for this power dynamic was that most of the Ukrainian guards at Treblinka had previously been captured as prisoners of war. Most, therefore, readily accepted the German offer to work at Treblinka and cooperate with the ss simply to avoid the alternative, which for millions of other Soviet prisoners included incarceration, starvation, mistreatment, and death.[85] Some of these Ukrainians guarding Treblinka, therefore, probably relinquished control of the situation to spare their own lives—performing integral daily tasks but not adhering to the ideological prescriptions guiding the Germans.

This broad brush does not apply to all Ukrainians at Treblinka, however, and there were certainly others who "reserved a sizzling, boundless hatred for the Jews," according to survivor Samuel Willenberg.[86] These men—notorious examples include Nikolaj Marchenko and Ivan Demjanjuk—were rewarded for their zeal, and some received additional training at the Trawniki camp alongside the ss. Demjanjuk, in particular, was known as "Ivan the Terrible" because he often treated Jews cruelly and seemed to enjoy inflicting pain. His behavior included hitting those entering the gas chambers with a thick pipe and using a long cavalry sword to hack at people within his reach. With the latter, he slashed hands, killed young children, and sometimes cut off women's breasts.[87] While we might explain away this behavior as remnants of prewar Ukrainian antisemitism, Demjanjuk's own psychological state, or myriad other factors, it cannot be overlooked that as the person literally flipping the switch for the gas chambers, Demjanjuk worked within a small space where he possessed ultimate control over the lives of others, found reinforcement from the environment around him, and knew his actions were unassailable as long as the job got done. The court that tried him in 1981 even commented, "Ivan was always present at the gas chambers . . . and enjoyed *especially good terms* with the German officers at the camp."[88]

Taken holistically, it remains difficult to explain the ideology and motivation that drove Treblinka's perpetrators. Certainly, there are some parallels to Christopher Browning's analysis of Reserve Police Battalion 101, where he suggests that "ordinary men" not particularly indoctrinated in Nazi ideology but susceptible to the human influences of group dynamics "bonded" over committing mass murder.[89] But Treblinka offers a more complicated evaluation. Some, like Wirth and Globočnik, were radical Nazi ideologues, while others, like Stangl, fit a category Yehuda Bauer has adroitly called "run-of-the-mill" mass murderers who were "morally neutral" and "technically competent," although I would amend this description slightly to suggest they were not just neutral but morally flexible.[90] And yet the close look taken here suggests a third level—perhaps more or less in the vein of "ordinary" Germans, albeit ones with some technical knowledge from the T4 program—filled out the administrative ranks at Treblinka. This group ensured the "success" or the demise of the camp's mission, and their response, generally, was to follow their leader's (Stangl's) example to jettison outside moral restraints at the door, defer responsibility to some distant person (Globočnik, Himmler, even Hitler), and become what the space of Treblinka allowed—unquestioned sovereigns over life and death with no moral constraints of the outside world and every opportunity to assert the authority they might have previously lacked. Buttressing the entire system was the large workforce of Ukrainians, a group motivated to help by their own anti-Jewish animosity or desire to avoid being killed themselves. The result was a lethal combination of personality types that coalesced inside the unrestrained spatial reality that allowed for large-scale mass murder to operate within the confines of Treblinka.

Secrecy at Treblinka

The other pillar of German behavior at Treblinka was an adherence to strict measures of secrecy. Arendt once wrote, "Real power begins where secrecy begins," and for the Reinhard camps, secrecy provided the power to act upon the darkly phantasmagoric conceptions projected onto the killing "factories."[91] From the start, Nazi higher-ups went to great lengths to keep Operation Reinhard and Treblinka as secret as humanly possible. Grossman wrote,

> It was Himmler's intention to keep this camp a dead secret. Not a single human being was to leave it alive. And no outsider was permitted to approach the place. Anybody who chanced within a kilometer of the camp was shot at without warning. Luftwaffe craft were forbidden to fly over the area. The victims brought hither by trainloads over a special branch line were ignorant of the fate awaiting them up to the last moment. The guards escorting the trains were not allowed inside the camp grounds; instead ss men took over arriving trains at a distance of two hundred meters from the camp. . . . Thus, neither an engineer nor a fireman ever crossed the boundary line.[92]

Stefan Kucharek, a Polish engineer who drove trains to Treblinka, stated this boundary separating Treblinka from the outside world was rigidly enforced: "We came to the gate, the gate opened, we put it in, they unhooked the engine and that was it."[93] The Germans treated transgressions against Treblinka's spatial security very seriously. On one occasion, a woman transported to Treblinka tried to show proof of her identity, which claimed she was of "pure German stock." Her documents were valid and her two sons uncircumcised, but the Germans ruled that even these "Aryans" had to be killed to protect Treblinka's secret. Wiernik reflected simply, "Whoever crossed Treblinka's threshold was doomed to die."[94]

In practice, though, this was not always the case. On a separate occasion, a Polish driver wandered too close to the death camp and was detained for two weeks before being "miraculously" freed.[95] Hence the German maintenance of security and secrecy was often discretionary and likely dependent on two considerations: how much of Treblinka a witness had seen and their ability to spread this information if released. In this sense, the Germans running the camp monitored local public opinion, as Franciszek Ząbecki, the Polish stationmaster at Treblinka (4 km), remembered: "Stangl was interested not only in the extermination camp, but also in everything that was happening in the immediate and distant surroundings of the camp. In particular, he supervised the efficient rotation of wagons with 'resettlers' to the camp [but also] the behavior of the people in neighboring villages."[96] The Germans possessed a level of control over life and death in the east in ways unimaginable in other parts of Nazi-occupied Europe. Whereas when members of the German public learned of the T4 program and voiced opposition to it, the Nazis significantly scaled back the program publicly, in the "wildernesses" of Poland, they had near total spatial control and felt free to implement racial policy as they desired.[97] And yet the ever-desperate need for such tight secrecy at Treblinka clearly shows that the T4 protests had lasting effects. Why else go to such great lengths to isolate and hide the camp?

Part of the answer lies with the same Nazi government structure that allowed for the killers' diffusion of responsibility. By nature, the murder of millions of people in death camps required a larger, overarching bureaucratic apparatus encompassing many Germans and non-Germans alike. To keep Treblinka a secret from so many people and to prevent the outside world from finding out, Nazi leadership officially designated Treblinka a *Geheime Reichssache*, a "matter of Reich secrecy," and ordered that no written reports about the camp be created. As a further measure of security, they sacrificed their characteristic attention to detail and ordered that no "stat sheets," used by the Einsatzgruppen to record their mass shootings, be kept at Treblinka.[98] Other secrecy measures included requiring death camp personnel to sign a special declaration that prohibited writing, speaking, or otherwise disseminating information about Treblinka to anyone besides certain Reinhard personnel. This declaration also included a pledge to maintain the secret after the program's end and forbade photography in the camps.[99] According to one survivor, the Germans "attached particular importance" to ensuring that any photographs or documents that did turn up were burned.[100] In being aimed toward those with the most intimate knowledge of the death camps, these specific measures of secrecy theoretically ensured that while the paper trail was destroyed, the bureaucratic apparatus needed for Operation Reinhard could continue unhindered.

The Germans also took steps to limit the ability of those outside the Reinhard bureaucracy to learn about Treblinka. Ząbecki recalled that the Germans sent timetables and train schedules to local train stations to regulate operations, but these documents contained secret codes to disguise train movements while still allowing Polish personnel at train stations to operate the railways. "It was done with a code, which the Polish personnel did not know," recalled Siedlce (53 km) railway worker Józef Kuźmiński. "Ordinary freight transports had shipping lists and they were registered in the railway station records. Transports of Jews arrived without any shipping lists and it was forbidden to register them in the records."[101] Yet since Ząbecki worked with these documents daily, he ultimately deciphered the codes to track the trains passing by.[102] In fact, perhaps as a precaution against just what Ząbecki was doing, two German overseers, Rudolf Emmerich and Willi Klinzmann, soon arrived at the Treblinka town station (4 km) to supervise "the efficient management of wagons with prisoners," though on "essential work related to general train movements and office work," the Germans usually did not interfere.[103] This gave the Germans more direct oversight of the death trains while also reminding local workers of who was in charge. To prevent other information leaks, the Germans likely also encouraged it when misinformed local rumors began spreading, like one pervasive conjecture that speculated that Treblinka was either a Nazi missile factory or a work camp related to ongoing projects to regulate and deepen the Bug River.[104]

By October 1943, Germany had irretrievably lost the war, the Red Army was consistently rolling back German gains, and the death toll of the Reinhard camps reached into the millions; thus the Germans decided to terminate the program and tore the death camps down.[105] But even in Treblinka's final days, the Germans continued practices of secrecy and deception. Survivor Chil Rajchman commented on the persistent German *need* to cover up their crimes: "When [the Allies] discovered . . . the victims of Katyn . . . the mass murder of Polish officers . . . [the Germans] started to worry, 'Would the world discover the murderous deeds in Treblinka?'"[106]

A key step in trying to erase the evidence of the death camps was destroying the bodies of those murdered there. Himmler ordered ss colonel Paul Blobel to organize a commando of Jewish workers to open remaining mass graves and burn all evidence of the killings.[107] "The 'side product' of the death factory in Treblinka is the mass of human corpses," Łukaszkiewicz wrote, assuming the German perspective. "A troublesome product, they had to be hidden from human eyes. . . . At first, human strength was used for this purpose, but mass murder required methods for faster handling."[108] Death camp workers attended a special training program where they learned how "to organize the exhumation of the corpses from the graves, how to pile them on stacks, burn them, how to scatter the ashes, to crush the bones, to fill up the ditches, and how to plant trees and brush wood on the graves as camouflage."[109] The Germans even blew up Ząbecki's train station in an attempt to destroy documents that could become evidence—although Ząbecki was able to save (risking his life) many "timetables, messages, and various types of mailing lists for wagons sent from Treblinka."[110]

After the remaining bodies were incinerated, the Germans dismantled Treblinka and then leveled the field where the camp stood, planting vetch, lupins, and other saplings from the nearby woods to camouflage the ashes and sand covering the site.[111] A local Pole described the totality of this transformation, recalling how, after the Germans retreated, "nothing was left, the field was cleared."[112] As an unnamed survivor described Treblinka's new space, "Ash from human bodies is a fertilizer. In the lands of Treblinka, where millions of people were burnt, [the Germans] planted gardens, flowers, and trees. The grounds of Treblinka were quickly overgrown with beautiful flowers. But under the flowers—the blood of millions."[113] It was an odd juxtaposition between what had once existed and what remained both physically and conceptually. In razing Treblinka to the ground and destroying as much evidence as possible, the Germans sought to erase all traces of their crimes, and in the process, they attempted to restore the site to its previous existence as an unremarkable wilderness. In their minds, as local resident Stanisław Głąbiński recalled, they "were almost sure of the absolute secret that surrounded the camp. . . . It seemed to them that there was not a single witness to the genocide."[114]

And it is here at the intersection of secrecy, fantasy, and outright absurdity that we see the cracks in the whole Nazi scheme—tens of thousands of people witnessed Treblinka and no amount of covering up could hide the brutality of that mass murder. In fact, this same selective cognition is probably connected to the grandiose delusions that caused them to build a space like Treblinka in the first place. But before we track down Treblinka's witnesses, near and far, there is one thread of the Menschenschlachthaus image we can pull on to unravel it further. Simple logic dictates that if the Germans had, in fact, totally rejected Western morality and completely accepted the Nazi alternative in its place, secrecy would have been utterly unnecessary at Treblinka. As the *Das Menschenschlachthaus Treblinka* pamphlet illustrates, they might instead have *promoted* it from the hilltops. Yet this clearly was not true of how the camp operated—there was a desperate *need* to treat Treblinka with an almost paranoid secrecy from beginning to end. If nothing else, such secrecy betrays a fundamentally human element of guilt or caution on the part of the killers, and given their level of careful planning, organization, and attention to detail, it is clear they feared the camp would be recognized as the ghastly spatial abomination it was.[115]

Such feelings were perhaps exacerbated by the extreme human horrors attached to the death space they created. After all, at the end of the day, human beings do not become the automatic, unfeeling killers demanded by Treblinka's ideological space. In contrast, Wiernik ascribed an otherworldly countenance to the ss men he encountered at Treblinka, writing, "I never saw them show any compassion or regret. They never evinced any pity over the fate of innocent victims. They were automatons, who perform their given tasks as soon as some higher-up presses a button."[116] Krzepicki wrote similarly that for the typical Treblinka German, mass murder "doesn't burden his conscience and awareness"; he is simply "blunt and phlegmatic."[117] And although it seems like the same type of technocratic language used in the Menschenschlachthaus imagery bled over to color descriptions of the Germans operating the camp, other reports reveal that many of these same "automatic" killers recoiled at the gruesome reality of their "work" there. In fact, Rajzman recalled, "[Stangl] didn't want to get his hands dirty with blood. He never hit anybody. The whole camp operation was under his control and direction, but he kept his hands clean."[118] Wiernik also observed a certain deputy squad commander named Hermann: "The first time he came to Camp No. 2 and saw the heaps of corpses of the gas victims, he paled and looked at them with fear and pity. He left with me at once in order to get out of sight of the gruesome scene."[119] Treblinka survivor Heniek Sperling wrote the following regarding a different ss man, who "expressed disgust about the inhuman operations. The very first day after his arrival, he found everything so unbelievable. . . . 'Impossible, impossible,' he muttered incessantly, slowly shaking his head."[120] ss guard Franz Suchomel too, upon witnessing the undulating ground where thousands of buried bodies were violently decomposing, reflected, "It was a hell up there. . . . We puked and wept."[121]

Many Germans took frequent leaves from the camp, and while clearly a tactic later used to deflect guilt, these bouts of absentia also expose a constant need to escape from Treblinka's spatial horrors. As Hirtreiter later argued (albeit as a ploy in his defense), the "horrific events in the camp" had been the reason he requested a transfer elsewhere.[122] In fact, according to historian Sara Berger, 16 of the 121 Reinhard personnel requested and were granted transfer out of the death camps, preferring to serve in the Wehrmacht or *Waffen-ss* (military branch of the ss) over the comparative safety of the camps. While this number represents one in every eight members of the Reinhard personnel, many others took repeated "vacations" from the camps.[123] As Suchomel said in postwar testimony, "I would like to say that I took vacation four times from Treblinka."[124] Erwin Lambert, another transplant to Treblinka from the T4 program, recalled similarly how, soon after arriving, he was "sent back to Berlin for 4–6 weeks sick." He then spent between three and four weeks in other camps before returning to Treblinka.[125] Stangl also later brought up his own absences but with an odd exculpatory addendum attached. As the court trying him paraphrased his defense, "Any other hangings could have only taken place during his vacation or other absence from the camp, without his knowing about it. Such things would have been impossible during his presence in Treblinka because he could not have tolerated such excesses."[126] There is a peculiarity to this response—alongside highlighting the "I wasn't there" excuse, it also tries to justify or reinforce, twistedly, the idea that when he *was* there, the killing was "efficient" and "not excessive" and thus somehow excusable or different from killings that took place in his absence.

All the same, these examples highlight the inherent fallacies of the warped Nazi morality of death camps—human beings could never be as coldly technocratic as the processes they tried to create. Stereotypes to the contrary initially arose because of the perceived efficiency with which Treblinka seemed to operate. As survivor Aron Czechowicz once witnessed, an entire transport to Treblinka was completely "discharged" from the cattle cars in only eight minutes.[127] "The Germans came to possess such skill," another witness wrote, "that within 2.5 hours, the cars were unloaded and unpackaged, people stripped and thrown into gas chambers . . . things removed to the sorting yard, and the whole camp was ready to receive new victims, cleaned as if nothing had happened here before."[128] The reality, however, was more complex, offering a counterpoint to this narrative of efficiency. Only during its deadliest period did Treblinka actually develop into a place where, according to Auerbach, "those who went into the gas chambers arrived in time to watch the flames that would consume them that very day."[129] In fact, the mass murder at Treblinka was often slow and disorganized, so much so that Irmfried Eberl, the first commandant, was relieved of command in favor of Stangl, who promised to fix the disorder during Treblinka's first months of operation.[130] Thus, perhaps what witnesses were seeing, and subsequently painting into their descriptions of "automatons," was Germans trying futilely to assert their control over something rapidly becoming uncontrollable.

As rotting corpses began to stack up and horrific sights, smells, and sounds flooded Treblinka's spaces, the Menschenschlachthaus became an appalling space for all involved, and the Germans found themselves less distanced from genocide than ever before, the opposite of what the space was supposed to achieve.[131] Thus, many Germans often retreated into the shrinking spaces of the camp that they felt they could still "master." A stark example is Kurt Franz's decision in early 1943 to "beautify" Treblinka by remodeling the Ukrainian barracks and renaming roads within the camp after prominent camp guards in the hopes of creating "a place to be proud of."[132] Indeed, many Germans redirected their focus to their own spaces, their "reprieves" (or "special place," as Stangl called it) in which they could relax, visit animals in the zoo, have a shave, or even go jogging (see figure 10).

Riding horses were provided, and there were cinema screenings, football games, and "working Jews" who cleaned the German spaces, cooked on demand, and in one instance, painted family portraits for every guard.[133] Paradoxically, though, it quickly became a space where Stangl also found the need to cover his living quarters in perfume. "There was an intense smell in both rooms," an eyewitness reported. "The rooms were carpeted and it seems they were sprayed with this liquid. The smell was supposed to neutralize the smell of burning corpses pervading the interior of the room." The sensory horrors of mass death at Treblinka exploded Stangl's illusions that this was some special place of reprieve, so much so that he was forced to perfume his living area so he could stand being *there*, within his own "domain," as commandant, which had now become, as the same witness called it, "the perfumed hell of Treblinka."[134]

FIG. 10. An SS man jogging in the German portion of Treblinka. Note the antitank obstacles in the background, which betray Treblinka's purpose despite the apparent tranquility. Hannah Arendt called such examples of simulacra "skillfully manufactured unreality," a phrase that applies well to the delicate spatial realities the Germans tried to maintain at Reinhard camps. Courtesy of Ghetto Fighters' House Museum.

Instead of a "clean, industrial" factory of death, the Germans had actually created a hideous spatial abomination where the gruesome realities of death were neither hidden nor confined to an isolated world but instead magnified on an unimaginable scale. If we recall Himmler's Posen speech, such work at these camps, though difficult, was imagined to be for some greater glory of Germany and thus nothing to the "hardened" individual. But in reality, living within a space of such death and sensory horror for long periods of time affected many Germans. Suchomel recalled how Treblinka guard Erwin Kaina finally broke down working amid piles of corpses, exclaiming, "I'm finished. I just can't do it anymore." Soon thereafter he took his own life. When Fritz Küttner, a particularly brutal camp guard (and the person in charge of Treblinka I), learned of it, he called Kaina "a cowardly pig," which Berger suggests is a reference to what Küttner saw as "weakness" in Kaina's inability to deal with the grisly tasks of working at Treblinka. In fact, another death camp guard named Ernst Bauch, who worked at Sobibór, also died by suicide while on leave from the camp.[135]

Gerstein too was described as "a broken man" after touring the death camps, having once stated, "I feel like I'm being crushed by the most monstrous secret any man has ever known."[136] According to his biographer, even the fanatical Globočnik was nearing a nervous breakdown by the end of Operation Reinhard.[137] "It appears that the more one kills, the greater is the desire to remain alive oneself," Auerbach writes. "One's own small, mean existence becomes all the more important."[138] The Düsseldorf court concluded as much in its appraisal of Willi Mentz: "If he killed screaming and crying people first before the other victims, it was probably for practical reasons, because restless people who made the killing business difficult were eliminated first."[139] The longer these people disrupted the "system," the longer Mentz and others had time to consider their own mortality as reflected in the human responses of their victims.

Like other aspects of Treblinka's space, there was a trickle-down effect on the Ukrainians, and according to survivor Sol Liber, "even they *couldn't take* the slaughter" going on around them.[140] Other survivors noted how Treblinka's Ukrainians were "constantly drunk, and sold whatever they had stolen to secure drinking money."[141] In Edward Westermann's 2021 study on alcohol use by Reinhard personnel, he notes that camp auxiliaries "mirrored in many respects the drinking rituals, acts of mockery and humiliation, sadistic games, and homicidal behavior of their German superiors. . . . These auxiliaries were merely taking advantage of the expanded boundaries of accepted behavior created under the German occupation for ss and police forces in general."[142] One might add to the list of reasons for drinking *a way to soothe their nerves* over the crimes they committed. We know the Germans did this—daily social gatherings at the camp frequently included beer, wine, vodka, and even eggnog but often devolved into excess. Berger notes, "In addition to its function as a motor for social gatherings, alcohol consumption also had the character of compensating for and suppressing the atrocities witnessed daily, even if the men remained unaware of this."[143] In fact, Stangl was known to drink himself to sleep at night in his perfumed living quarters because of the horrors surrounding him.[144]

In addition to excessive alcohol use, Ukrainians frequently descended on local towns hoping to "organize orgies in nearby public houses."[145] Local Pole Jerzy Królikowski recalled how "Ukrainians . . . were heartily welcomed by *some* peasants. Daughters in such households, people were saying, provided company to these murderers and eagerly benefited from their largesse."[146] Prostitutes from nearby cities often flocked to the area hoping to be paid in gold and valuables from Treblinka for their services.[147] Indeed, as Oskar Strawczyński observed, "Local peasants and peddlers earned well. They demanded top dollar for everything and thanks to this, the local residents have greatly enriched themselves. But . . . money was no object in Treblinka."[148] After all, as Kucharek said, "the Ukrainians could get as much as they wanted back then" for dealing in stolen camp goods.[149] The "large quantities of everything" at Treblinka's warehouses made the Ukrainians rich in comparison to the local populations.[150] And subservient within the spaces of Treblinka itself, they used their access to this wealth to exhibit dominance over the Jews they were murdering and the local populations, both of whom they viewed as "lesser." Consequently, the Ukrainians' drunken and power-hungry behavior led to violence and predatory behavior, which included enforced sexual relationships and the rapes of several local women.[151] Such interactions also carried other consequences for local people. For illustration, one Ukrainian guard who felt slighted by a local woman reported this "transgression" to Treblinka's authorities "in order to provoke the arrest of the woman and the people surrounding her." Later, these same Ukrainians shot the woman's husband out of spite.[152]

Overall, as Ukrainians sought to escape the "Treblinka hell" they had helped create, they generally tried to exercise the authority they lacked within Treblinka over another group of people—the local Poles.[153] But as they did so, they also exposed Treblinka's secrets to the outside world, and the first rumors about the camp were probably spread by the same Ukrainian guards who entered surrounding villages. As Michał Kalembasiak, who lived four kilometers away, stated, "We knew exactly what they were doing because the Ukrainians sometimes came to tell us what was happening."[154] These Ukrainians, and sometimes Germans too, were "very well known in the town of Kosów [Lacki]," and "they used to come to have a good time, get drunk, and have their pictures taken."[155] Directly violating Nazi prohibitions, the behaviors of escapism displayed by these "privileged elite of hell" directly contradicted practices aimed at protecting Treblinka's isolation and secrecy.[156] As survivor Richard Glazar later reflected, "Secrecy? Good heavens, there was no secrecy about Treblinka; all the Poles between there and Warsaw must have known about it, and lived off the proceeds. All the peasants came to barter, the Warsaw whores did business with the Ukrainians—it was a circus for all of them."[157]

Treblinka's Human Reality

For sixteen months between July 1942 and October 1943, the German and Ukrainian guards at Treblinka left their preconceived notions of morality at its doorstep to play the role that the Menschenschlachthaus ideology demanded they play. They imagined the camp as a space in which they could reign over the lives and deaths of others without fear of repercussion for whatever depraved displays of authority and barbarity they exhibited. The results were devastating—Treblinka became a space where hundreds of thousands of innocent people were ruthlessly murdered.

But in reality, the only clean, industrial slaughterhouse the Nazis ever created at Treblinka was in their phantasmagoric ideology—a flimsy conceptual facade draped over a brutal and horrific killing spree. And even though they tried to erase the space itself when they had finished their orgy of violence, they could never wipe off the stain of what they had seen, heard, smelled, and done. These were human beings who had murdered other human beings, and that is not a switch one turns off as easily as the personas they seemed to adopt inside the spaces of Treblinka.

Rarely in history are we presented with irrefutable evidence of the motivating factors we claim drives specific behavior, but one would be hard-pressed to find something more coincidental than the following. At the finale of Gitta Sereny's weeks-long interview with Stangl in 1971, the most in-depth he ever gave, "he gripped the table with both hands as if he was holding onto it. 'But I was there,' he said then, in a curiously dry and tired tone of resignation. 'So yes,' he said finally, very quietly, 'in reality. I share the guilt. . . . Because my guilt . . .' He had pronounced the words 'my guilt': but more than the words, the finality of it was in the sagging of his body, and on his face. . . . 'My guilt is that I am still here. . . . I should have died. That was my guilt.'" Nineteen hours later, Stangl was dead. No one had visited him beyond a guard delivering food to his cell, and the postmortem revealed not suicide, as some expected, but heart failure. "His heart was weak and he would no doubt have died quite soon anyway," Sereny reflects. "But I think he died when he did because he had finally, however briefly, faced himself and told the truth; it was a monumental effort to reach that fleeting moment when he became the man he should have been."[158]

Treblinka was not an industrial, clean death factory—it was a veritable hell on earth; and that this hell was created not by monsters with evil eyes and devil horns but by our fellow human beings is, I often think, the far scarier truth.

3

A Space of Life and Death

They no longer shouted because the thread of
their lives had been broken. They no longer had
any needs or desires. Mothers held their children
tightly in their arms. There were no more friends
nor enemies. There was no jealousy. All were
equal. There was no longer any beauty or ugliness,
for all looked yellow from the gas. There were no
longer any rich or poor, for all were equal before
God's throne.

—Yankel Wiernik, *A Year in Treblinka*

Contrary to what is sometimes claimed, we can understand the Holocaust. Those who have suggested it is "uniquely unique" miss a fundamental reality. "The genocide of Jews," Yehuda Bauer points out, "was engineered and executed by humans for human reasons, and anything done by humans can be repeated."[1] We most clearly see this reality when examining what Treblinka actually *was*, regardless of Nazi conceptions of what it was *supposed* to be. Nazi ideology positioned Treblinka as a space where death was to be performed cleanly and in an orderly manner, but as the previous chapter began to reveal, Treblinka actually existed as a space defined by a constant confrontation with the grisly world of mass death.

In "normal" life, we often separate death from spaces meant for other purposes. As a result, according to Henri Lefebvre, "death is relegated to the infinite realm so as to disenthrall (or purify) the finiteness in which social practice occurs, in which the law that that practice has established holds sway."[2] Although modern societies create spaces for death, like cemeteries, these almost always carry sacred connotations, and while usually confined, they are carefully apportioned and maintained with a level of respect. In this process of moving death above or below our other social spaces, we create distance between life and death, where the former takes our focus and the latter is abstracted and spatially compartmentalized as much as possible. But at Treblinka, death was not relegated to the abstract, and the laws "holding sway" derived from the twisted morality invented by the same Germans who not only created the space but, in doubly isolating it from the outside world, seemed to possess unchecked power over it.

Yet what was the lived experience of those brought to Treblinka against their will and directly targeted by Nazi ideology?

The vast majority of the nearly one million Jews sent to Treblinka were murdered, and most died within an hour of arriving there. Their experiences of the camp's physical spaces (generally, the unloading area and the Toten-lager) were limited and brief, consisting of a near-constant confrontation with the many measures of deception designed and implemented by the Germans. While some may have tried to find hope in these elements, others saw through the facades to realize the fate awaiting them. As they moved rapidly through the interior spaces of the camp, the Jews murdered there likely experienced a mix of confusion, uncertainty, and understanding amid an often surreal spatial environment that juxtaposed veneers of reassurance with the ever-increasing certainty of death. While the individuality of these final experiences can never be definitively known, this chapter's exploration of the spaces that victims encountered not only reveals more about their final moments but, in so doing, also further erases the Nazi conception of Treblinka as a sanitized or industrial death factory.[3]

While Treblinka overwhelmingly existed as a space of death, fleeting spaces of life also endured there, sometimes only in the tiniest nooks and crannies. A very small number of Jews (mainly younger, "healthy" males) were kept alive at Treblinka to operate different parts of the camp and, though not as apparently obvious, to ensure the Germans remained free from the most gruesome work of mass murder. Some of these Jews died within a few days, some lived until they were "liquidated" at regular intervals to be replaced by new arrivals, and a few found ways to survive even longer. But regardless of their fate, for these "living Jews of Treblinka," life became so intertwined with death that the two became inseparable. Forced to work amid Treblinka's death spaces—including inside the gas chambers, within the burial pits, and

FIG. 11. Treblinka survivor Abraham Krzepicki. Courtesy of
E. Ringelblum Jewish Historical Institute, Warsaw.

alongside burning piles of corpses—these living Jews gained an intimate familiarity with death on a scale few could ever conceive. "It is impossible to imagine what we saw there," Treblinka survivor Abraham Krzepicki recalled. "It was more horrible than the scariest fairy tales from childhood: about wicked witches, bandits, seven-headed monsters that kidnapped and strangled people in caves where the bones of previous victims already lay scattered. . . . [Treblinka was] a monster factory that produces dead bodies."[4]

Survivor testimonies included throughout this chapter show in graphic detail how such experiences often blurred distinctions between life and death and how survival itself consisted of a difficult and almost surreal process in which the living Jews of Treblinka found methods to adapt to the spaces of death in which they were immersed. Though it varied for each person, this adaptation included, at some level, each of the following: a flashbulb confrontation with death; the variations of grief, shock, and numbness that accompanied immersion in the death space; physical and psychological torments; and finally, the tiniest flickers of hope, and indeed life, to which they desperately clung. Statistically, this experience—finding a space for life within such all-consuming death—was rare. Out of the more than eight hundred thousand Jews sent to Treblinka, only seventy are known to have survived.[5] Overcoming such odds left most Treblinka survivors with the feeling of never being truly able to escape the camp's reality, and the spaces they encountered and the things they witnessed were so profound that these experiences fundamentally reshaped the narrative arcs of their lives, representing a finite rupture between what came before and after. Krzepicki realized as much immediately after escaping the death camp, writing in a document that was later hidden in a milk can, buried under the Warsaw ghetto, and many years later unearthed from the rubble to which that city was ultimately reduced, "The killers killed not only our present and our future, but also our past. We, accidental survivors, temporarily buried, are all fugitives from Treblinka."[6]

Death at Treblinka

The Nazis intended for Treblinka to be hidden in the rural wilderness of Poland. But for some of the Jews sent there, the location of the camp and its surroundings would have been well known. As we saw in chapter 1, Jews lived in towns near the death camp, and their experiences of being deported (often via truck or on foot) through landscapes they intimately recognized were at odds with what the vast majority of Jews sent to Treblinka would have endured.[7] The largest number of Jews sent to Treblinka originated from the region's larger towns of Sokołów Podlaski (27 km), Siedlce (53 km), Warsaw (80 km), and Białystok (90 km), though some were brought from the farther towns of Radom (145 km), Wołkowysk (170 km, which is today Vawkavysk, Belarus), Kielce (220 km), and even distant Częstochowa (285 km).[8] According to Gedali Rydlewicz, who witnessed deportations to Treblinka from the relatively distant town of Biała Podlaski (98 km), "The inhabitants . . . didn't know that they were being taken to death. If they had, they may not have allowed themselves to be taken away so easily."[9] Indeed, many had little knowledge of their destination beforehand. "There was an inscription 'to Treblinka' on the freight cars where the Jews were loaded," described Blanka Goldhurst, from the distant town of Piotrków (210 km). "At that time, we still had no idea what that word signified, and that's why lots of people didn't even try to avoid the 'deportation.'"[10] Once the journey began, spatial indicators like signposts, landmarks, or passing villages provided few meaningful clues. As Linda Penn recalled of being sent to Treblinka from Grodno (165 km) in February 1943, "We traveled . . . overnight and the train stopped and as soon as the train stopped, we didn't know where we [were] going, we didn't [have] the slightest idea of what was going to happen. The train stopped and it stayed stopped. We saw a sign 'Treblinka,' but it didn't mean anything because we didn't know anything about it."[11]

Especially unfamiliar with the Treblinka region were Jews from outside of Poland. Czesław Sikorski, a Polish railway worker in Sokołów Podlaski (27 km), described how Jews from the Netherlands, Belgium, Yugoslavia, and other places seemed unconcerned about their long journey. He recalled, "When the train stood at the station, those on board could leave, enter the stores and buy something to eat and go back and forth between the wagons. And they had tickets."[12] Another Polish railway worker, Józef Kuźmiński, from Siedlce (53 km), witnessed two lavishly outfitted trains from Greece: "These trains consisted of Pullman carriages, with each passenger holding a ticket and bringing along a lot of luggage; there were luggage wagons in the train. . . . The tickets were issued to 6500 people. . . . I specifically checked the number. . . . People from foreign transports were able to leave their train freely at stations, and they were confident they were going to a labor camp."[13]

To further cloud conceptions of what awaited at the end of the train journey, Nazi planners passed around propaganda promoting the idea that Treblinka was a labor camp, rest area, or transit station en route to the broad end goal of "resettlement." Survivor Yankel Wiernik remembered that this concept was foremost on the minds of many Jews on Treblinka-bound transports: "The poor wretches kept poking their heads out of the train windows when they passed a station, asking casually how much further it was to Treblinka. Tired as they were, they eagerly looked forward to reaching an asylum where they could rest up from the hardships of the journey."[14] Since some perceived Treblinka as a restful, potentially relaxing destination, they imagined it as a nice place, and Wólka Okrąglik (1 km) resident Eugenia Samuel recalled that someone in a car waiting to enter the camp once inquired, "Where is this *beautiful* Treblinka colony?"[15]

The single largest origin point for Treblinka-bound Jews was the Warsaw ghetto, which by 1942 imprisoned over four hundred thousand people. From here, Bernard Goldstein recalled, "everything was done to bolster the fantasy that the Jews were being taken out of the overcrowded ghetto, away from hunger and epidemics, to work under happier conditions."[16] The Germans placed signs at the *Umschlagplatz* (the loading platform from which Treblinka-bound trains departed) that read, "Do not worry about your fate . . . you are all going eastward for work."[17] In fact, even when information first reached Warsaw that Treblinka was not a resettlement site but a death camp, many struggled to believe it. Jack Price, who witnessed the deportations in Warsaw, reflected on the confused atmosphere there: "A couple living eyewitnesses escaped from Treblinka. . . . They told the leaders . . . what they saw exactly with their own eyes. . . . The leaders . . . put up placards [warning] not to volunteer for resettlement, that going means death. A lot of them didn't want to believe it. . . . They didn't want to believe that such a thing is possible. They were still believing that such a thing cannot be true."[18] It seems that initially, at least, the idea of being resettled and forced to work for Germany was more believable than reports suggesting everyone would be killed. As Treblinka survivor Samuel Rajzman explained, it was simply easier for most to assume that the rumors coming from these early escapees were "crazy" and that "it was impossible that [the Germans] would burn men and women and small children!"[19]

One of the most logical examples Warsaw Jews could use as rationalization was that Germans allowed everyone boarding a Treblinka-bound train to bring along fifteen kilograms of luggage. The train guards also provided loaves of bread and jars of marmalade for the journey. For the hungry people of the ghetto, the food itself was a godsend, and many reasonably asked that if they *were* headed for death, why were they being fed and allowed to take belongings?[20]

The narrative of resettlement also benefited from the shocking speed of the first waves of deportation. According to the *Informacja Bieżąca* (Current Information), a pamphlet distributed during the war by the Armia Krajowa (the Polish Home Army, or AK), in the four weeks between the first deportation on July 22, 1942, and August 17, 1942, an estimated 200,000 people, or roughly 50 percent of the entire ghetto's population, were deported to Treblinka. In fact, in just the first two weeks alone, 113,000 people had been transported.[21] Consequently, by the time the first escapees from Treblinka even returned to Warsaw to give their warnings, whether or not their stories were believed was increasingly becoming an irrelevant matter.

Even though Warsaw was the largest starting point, the initial hopefulness regarding what deportation might mean seems to have persisted (at least for some unquantifiable number of people) at all places of origin. Treblinka survivor Aron Czechowicz discovered evidence supporting this point; while sorting through the same fifteen-kilogram luggage bundles people brought with them to the camp, he said, "I found notes and diaries. They wrote: 'I am going to Treblinka colony.'"[22] Perhaps this hope of a chance at resettlement or the persistent doubt in the death camp rumor led many to justify the odd scenes they initially encountered upon entering Treblinka. When Krzepicki arrived inside a cattle car, for instance, someone crammed in near him commented on the gigantic mountain of clothes piled several stories high just beyond the train platform. Instead of expressing fear, the person calmly theorized, "People will be employed sorting these rags. . . . Here it is sorted and sent to Germany for processing." Krzepicki believed this to be a logical explanation based on an earlier odd sight: "Near Treblinka, we saw Jews being led to work by a Ukrainian. This good news was also shared with everyone, to let them know that they are taking Jews to work here."[23] Survivor Zdzisław Goldstein observed a similar rationalization after his transport rattled to a stop at Treblinka: "Through an open gate we saw a whole lot of barracks—a dozen or so, inconspicuous buildings in the foreground." When it quickly became apparent that these twelve buildings could not "absorb" the large number of people arriving, someone else simply surmised that "underground buildings had to exist."[24] After all, up to this point, underground buildings still seemed less far-fetched to many than the existence of a death camp.

Others relied on simple rationality to comfort them amid the odd scenes they confronted. Tanhum Grinberg, giving voice to the collective mentality inside the cattle car, commented, "It was unfathomable to us that such young, healthy people who could be useful were only going to be murdered." He went on to provide another rationalization used by many—that the natural forested landscape surrounding Treblinka, with its seeming tranquility, was simply *not* how a death camp would look. "Through the window we saw the forest," Grinberg wrote, "but we did not understand that they were taking us to death."[25] Saul Kuperhand commented similarly, "In another time we might have been tourists enjoying the lovely scenery."[26] Even non-Jews arriving at Treblinka shared this experience. Wiernik witnessed a transport of Roma who "thought they had entered an enchanted place" as they disembarked at Treblinka.[27] It is human nature to form conceptions of places we have never seen, and these imaginings often impact our narratives regarding what we expect to find. For so many, then, Treblinka, with its overgrown forests, might not have been what they expected, but it certainly did not fit narratives suggesting mass murder.

In terms of the physical spaces of the camp, the Germans designed the arrival platform to reinforce the resettlement lie for anyone who still wanted to believe it. For instance, they hung a sign giving these directions: "Be calm about your fate. You are all going east to work. You will work and your wives will run the household. But before you go, you must take a bath, and your clothes must be deloused. You should deposit your valuables and moneys at the cash register, where you will receive the appropriate receipts, and after bathing and delousing, you will get everything back."[28] Passive measures like signage were used in conjunction with active measures such as the behavior of Treblinka personnel to reinforce the deception. As survivor William Schneiderman recalled, a group of Ukrainians welcomed his transport, using the nonthreatening term *Pensjonat Treblinka* (Hotel Treblinka) in reference to their location.[29] Some guards went further, giving what Dawid Nowodworski—whose writings were later found in the Oyneg

Shabes Archive—called "sympathetic speeches" at the unloading ramp, which included such statements as "You will not be returning home, [you are going] to work, near Kiev." In response, Nowodworski noted, "people were happy."[30] This often-surreal spatial juxtaposition came to define the initial experiences many Jews had of Treblinka, and as Rachel Auerbach later reflected, "Even on the grounds of the death camp, a few hundred meters away from the machinery of the corpse factory, there were some who refused to face the facts."[31] While helping offload trains, Rajzman witnessed just such an example: "An elderly woman came up to Kurt Franz, took out a document, and said that she was the sister of Sigmund Freud. . . . Franz read this document through very seriously and said that there must be a mistake here; he led her up to the train schedule and said that in 2 hours a train would leave again for Vienna. She should leave all her documents and valuables and then go to the bathhouse; after the bath she would have her documents and a ticket to Vienna. Of course, the women went to the bathhouse and never returned."[32] In this case, likely representative of others, German behavior reinforced the deception of resettlement, but constructed facades like fake train schedules (discussed in chapter 1) also upheld the narrative.

To what extent Jews accepted this fake reality depended largely on individuals and their beliefs about what fate awaited. To be sure, this was a complex equation in which many factors weighed heavily.[33] Some who arrived at Treblinka quickly questioned the deception, and for them, the facades would have rapidly crumbled after entering the camp. To this end, according to postwar investigator of Nazi crimes Zdzisław Łukaszkiewicz, "Contrary to other camps, at Treblinka, no amount of planning could be taken to convince victims that the camp was only a place of work, and not of execution."[34] An anonymous Treblinka witness wrote in a report that circulated widely through both the Warsaw and Białystok ghettos that it was possible from Treblinka's arrival platform to see the raised towers mounted with machine guns that pointed toward the wagons.[35] Auerbach gave voice to the logical follow-up: "The new arrivals . . . noticed some strange things. They had been told they would be 'resettled' somewhere far away in the 'East,' where they would be put to work. . . . They could see the whole structure of barbed wire fences, camouflaged with green branches, the heavy machine guns on the roofs of the barracks and in the watchtowers, ready to release a stream of bullets at a moment's notice. . . . Was this how a resettlement place was supposed to look?"[36] For some, these details clearly hinted at something more sinister, while others needed more evidence before the facades completely crumbled away. Krzepicki, for instance, recalled that after exiting the cattle car, a large section of his group became separated: "After a few minutes, we heard excruciating screams. However, we could not see anything, because a forest of trees blocked our view."[37] Here, the placement of trees as a visual barrier removed the line of sight Krzepicki and others needed to confirm their suspicions. After all, hearing screams may have been disturbing, but the group could not visually witness the cause.

It also merits noting that many arriving Jews probably had little time to make such lengthy considerations, focused as they were on more pressing concerns within the often chaotic unloading of the cattle cars. Part of why the Germans tried to move new arrivals from the train to Treblinka's gas chambers as quickly as possible, in fact, was to prevent any mounting speculation. Rajzman testified at Nuremberg that the time from unloading the train to arrival at the gas chambers was supposed to take just fifteen minutes, "including the undressing."[38] The speed of the process meant that arriving Jews could not always be sure of exactly what was happening around them. Survivor Oskar Strawczyński gave voice to this reality: "Everything happened so fast and in such a panic, there was complete confusion."[39] Amid the chaos, more immediate concerns took precedence over being able to observe subtle spatial clues that might undermine Treblinka's disguises. As Abraham Bomba remembered of the whirlwind disembarkation, he was so quickly separated from his family that they "had no chance to even say goodbye to each other."[40] Within the tumult, intense individual dramas played out spontaneously, distracting people from all else. When asked about the camp's fake train station, survivor Zygmunt Strawczyński (Oskar Strawczyński's brother) recalled, "There was a rough outlay but it couldn't very well hide this—and to tell you the truth, the first moment I didn't even notice it. . . . There was such a commotion that you just looked to keep your own close by, to get into this yard where they divided us anyway. But at this moment I didn't see anything. . . . I cannot imagine that anybody could have noticed anything—only a very perceptive person could have noticed all that."[41] Most likely, then, many who were murdered at Treblinka simply had very little time in which to form any specific understanding of the spaces they encountered after stepping off the train. In Auerbach's words, "The new arrivals did not have a moment's chance to come to their senses."[42]

Yet the perceptions they were able to form are telling. Zygmunt Strawczyński's first observation was not the train station, fake as it was, but instead what seemed most out of place: "When you saw those mountains of clothes, you saw that this is it . . . that [death] is not the lot of ten percent or fifty percent, but that this is the lot of one hundred percent. For all of us."[43] Interestingly enough, people on Krzepicki's transport hoped these same piles of clothes would mean work. For those who came to the opposite interpretation and saw the piles as alarming, one specific detail disturbed them most—their sheer size. Czechowicz estimated that despite the height of the fences themselves (3–4 m tall), the "piles of shoes and piles of clothes . . . [were] 3–4 meters above the fence." Bomba made a similar estimate, putting these piles at six or seven stories high.[44] The logical question that followed, according to Krzepicki, was, "So many clothes, what happened to the people?"[45]

Highlighted by competing interpretations of the same sights, the level of *confusion* elicited by Treblinka's spaces continued beyond the train platform. The massive size of the unloading yard, which had room to accommodate between two thousand and three thousand people, offered subtle deception. As the largest open space that Jews experienced inside Treblinka, it was supposed to offer some measure of reassurance. A report found in the Oyneg Shabes Archive stated, "The battered and nervous masses of people spilled out [of the trains], breathing in a sigh of relief in the open square."[46] After the cramped quarters of the train journey, many welcomed the simple spatial freedom of being able to stretch out their bodies.

The Germans recognized the power of controlling how this arrival space looked. When Leon Finkelsztein arrived at Treblinka, the open square had not yet been cleaned from the previous transport. "I saw a great number of dressed corpses in this courtyard," he stated, "and I realized that we had been brought here for extermination."[47] This immediate connection between seeing death and knowing that death awaited was what the deceptive spatial measures tried to prevent. Therefore, as a further precaution, Bomba reflected that steps were taken to ensure the newly arrived Jews "shouldn't be suspicious that they're going to be killed."[48] This included not only clearing the unloading spaces between arriving trains to prevent a recurrence of what Finkelsztein experienced but also ensuring that disembarking Jews went straight to the undressing barracks before having time to look around.

Survivor Chaim Grabel described what happened next: "When a transport arrived, they sent people for a bath. Everyone had to buy a ticket worth 20 złotys, undress in the cloakroom and hang his or her clothes on a hanger. Everyone took a towel with him or her."[49] Once in the undressing barracks, the Jews removed their clothes and placed them on hooks, reassured by the *Sonderkommando* (special unit, a reference to the Totenlager's Jewish workers) that this would guarantee their orderly return. There was also someone who took away the folded clothes under the guise of temporarily storing them; though these clothes actually went directly to the massive piles in the sorting area.[50] At this point, "Each victim was told to keep one złoty, which was to be used to pay for a bath," survivor Henryk Poswolski recalled. "These 'fees' were collected by a Ukrainian sitting in a wooden box whose window faced the pathway leading to the gas chambers."[51] According to Krzepicki, even at this moment, there was still a mix of responses from the Jews moving through Treblinka. His description is powerful: "Instinctively, like animals in the slaughterhouse, they sensed what awaited them. But, in the crowd of women, there were also naïve ones, who really believed that they were being led to the baths, and they took along with them a towel and a piece of soap."[52] The option to believe that everyone was undressing for a bath before being advanced to the next stage in the resettlement process was readily available and encouraged by spatial deception for anyone still clinging to this narrative. And yet at the same time, with each step toward the gas chambers, it became clearer to many that this may be, in fact, the road to death.

The Germans referred to the path leading from the undressing area to the gas chambers as the *Himmelstrasse* (Road to Heaven), though its other nicknames included *Himmelweg* (The Way to Heaven) and *Schlauch* (Tube) because of its narrow, twisting design. The path was eighty to ninety meters long, approximately four to five meters wide, and included a ninety-degree bend to hide the gas chambers from view to those in the tunnel until the very last moment. It was also enclosed by fences taller than a person's height that were so thickly camouflaged that it was impossible to see through them to the left or right.[53] At the entrance to this pathway hung a sign with the words "To the showers," which, as survivor Samuel

Willenberg noted, "was put there to reassure the already naked victims walking to their deaths."[54] Oskar Strawczyński observed what happened along the pathway: "When I was working on the rooftops of Treblinka, I had many chances to witness the last walk of my naked, unhappy people. Mothers carrying infants and leading older children, young girls—already shaved—covering their breasts with their hands, all running as quickly as possible through the rows of Germans and Ukrainians who sneer at them."[55] Littering the grounds of the pathway were gold coins, jewels, diamonds, and banknotes that previous groups had torn up or discarded as a final protest before entering the gas chambers. These piles of valuables were so thick that the Sonderkommando often had to use rakes to collect them all, because if they were not cleared immediately, these spatial remnants of those who went before would have alarmed the next group of Jews coming down the pathway.[56]

The Germans and Ukrainians guarding the pathway often became more violent at this juncture. As Rajzman described, "The Germans hit very hard; many people were killed from the beatings alone. Everybody was pushing to get to the gas chamber sooner because the Ukrainians and the Germans were beating so hard that everybody was stampeding forward. The whole place was covered with blood. People didn't know that it would be the end there; the idea was to get out of the place where they were beating you. And in doing that, they went straight into the gas chambers."[57] These beatings frequently focused on victims' sexual organs, heads, bellies, and other areas most sensitive to pain. In response to the violence, groups of Jews ran faster down the pathway to escape the "smacks of canes on the naked skin, from indignities, from the cold in the wintertime. And so, they [ran] and leap[ed] over one another."[58] If the gas chambers were full, Wiernik recalled, people had to wait in a backlog within the pathway, exposed to the elements and sensorial evidence of the horrors they increasingly knew awaited them. Here, on at least one occasion, "the soles of their feet froze and stuck to the icy ground."[59] The Jews in the pathway could probably also hear the screams of those in the gas chambers while they waited. To quote documents from Franz Stangl's postwar trial, "In certain knowledge of their impending fate and in the barely conceivable fear of death, they often still had to listen to the screams and cries of the people already in the gas chambers."[60] Combined with the increasingly brutal treatment they received, at some point along the pathway, in the words of Łukaszkiewicz, "it was only certain that the small, naked, helpless children" were the only people left unaware of what awaited.[61]

At the pathway's end stood a narrow gateway opening onto a small enclosure with a relatively plain single-story brick building on a concrete foundation. Disguised to mimic a "public bathing establishment," this building contained an internal central aisle with three to four gas chambers on either side.[62] Attentive to even the smallest details serving the constant narrative of deception, the Germans planted "the most beautiful and variegated" flowers at the gas chamber's entrance. This odd spatial juxtaposition, according to Krzepicki, made it look to the unassuming person like a "cozy, clean bathing house in the middle of a green forest."[63]

Drawing from her interviews with several survivors, Auerbach compiled a nuanced description of Treblinka's gas chambers:

A gray-white building with all the accoutrements of a regular public bath on the inside: "cabins," plus a few chimneys protruding from the roof. You entered the cabins from a corridor through doors just big enough to admit one person at a time. The door had been made so narrow on purpose, so that people who were already inside would not attempt to break down the door and escape. The cabins were lined with white tiles halfway up the walls. The floor sloped down to wide, hermetically sealed chutes facing the entrance gate. Real shower heads were set in the ceilings of the rooms, but they were not connected to any water pipe.[64]

Meticulous spatial details also included fresh coats of paint on the walls, floors covered with red-yellow terra-cotta tiles, and finely finished nickel-plated showerheads. The slight slant in the floor was to allow bodily fluids to drain, since many victims of gas inhalation hemorrhaged when they died. But because the gas chambers mimicked showers, this slanted channel leading to a drain may not have been an alarming detail in itself. This would not have been true of the "special thick-sheet doors sealed with rubber at the entrances, which betrayed the true purpose of the 'showers' for anyone who noticed these details."[65]

The surface area of each of the original gas chambers was approximately thirty to forty square meters. Czechowicz described that "each chamber had a gate like a barn and a ramp before them. . . . There could have been about 300 people in each, but they pressed in more."[66] The German and

Ukrainian camp personnel consistently loaded them with upwards of six hundred people, and after the new gas chambers were built in October 1942, each with a capacity of eight hundred, the guards often crammed in more than one thousand people.[67] As a Sonderkommando survivor who witnessed such horrors told Auerbach, "People were jammed together so closely that they pushed each other into a standing position. Some witnesses report that the people inside the gas chambers had to raise their arms and pull in their stomachs so that more could be fitted in. And then, when they stood pressed together, little children were slipped in above their heads like so many bundles."[68] According to one report, the gas chamber floor was slippery, and people who fell "could not get back up anymore, because new crowds of victims were driven in on top of them."[69]

Once it was crammed full of human beings, a German or Ukrainian finally shut the gas chamber doors and turned off the lights. Jews working near the gas chambers heard "terrible screams . . . of human pain, terror and despair," right after which "there was an outbreak of collective hysteria in the gas chamber."[70] Two Ukrainians seated inside a booth next to the gas chambers then switched on a diesel engine, and carbon monoxide began to flow through pipes connected to the gas chambers. Colorless and odorless, carbon monoxide is highly diffusible and has roughly the same density as air. A standard combustion engine like that used at Treblinka produces gas containing between 7 and 12 percent carbon monoxide—a concentration of only 5 percent is fatal within fifteen minutes. Not poisonous by itself, carbon monoxide triggers a chain reaction in bodily cells by combining with the iron of certain enzymes that block cellular oxidation processes. Carbon monoxide poisoning results in asphyxiation, which produces anatomical and functional failures of tissues and cells. This is accompanied by cardiac and respiratory reactions including respiratory alkalosis, whereby the body's desire for respiration causes hyperventilation as the blood PH rises above ordinary levels—ultimately leading to uncontrollable convulsions and seizures. Eventually, the lack of oxygen in the blood creates full, irreversible acidosis as the chemical structure of the blood changes. At this point, the victim experiences anoxia, or the absence of oxygen, which ultimately culminates in death.[71]

According to a postwar study on the biological effects of carbon monoxide poisoning, the difference between the fastest and slowest absorbers of carbon monoxide is as high as 25 percent.[72] This means, in the words of Wiernik, who worked in close proximity to this process at Treblinka, "the speed with which death overcame the hapless victims depended on the quantity of combustion gas admitted into the chamber," and thus some died earlier than others within the gas chambers, meaning those who lived longer had to experience the deaths of those around them before they too succumbed.[73] Czechowicz, who worked loading and unloading the gas chambers, described the entire process from what was probably the most complete viewpoint aside from someone physically inside the gas chambers: "As the gas gushed out, silent screams followed moans after 6–7 minutes, and after 15 minutes the door wedges were unlocked, the door opened, sliding as if on a wagon, and the corpses fell out. . . . Women and children together. I saw the dead children, holding their mothers by the neck, when they fell out, they detached. The corpses were damp, as if sweaty, and with wet hair. A little foam formed on the lips, some blood from the nose."[74] Given their limited vantage point, Jews working nearby speculated wildly as to what went on inside the gas chambers between when the doors closed and when they reopened. Survivor Nachman Diament testified after the war, "People were mass murdered in this way: 500 people stood on an iron plate, water began to spurt, people stood in the water up to their ankles, through which later an electric current passed and people died."[75] Given the speed of death and then opening the doors to find bodies soaked in various fluids, Diament's explanation (though inaccurate) seemed like a logical way to account for what happened once the doors to the gas chambers closed.

The vast majority of those murdered at Treblinka died violently within the gas chambers, but other groups—anyone old, young, or frail—were killed at the *Lazarett* (hospital). As Czechowicz witnessed, "Everyone who could not go, we had to lead them by hand, help undress, and [tell them] it was because they were going to the doctor for examination to see if they were healthy."[76] The Lazarett had its own features of secrecy and deception. It was "fenced with barbed wire, opaque, intertwined with pine branches" so that it could be hidden from the rest of the camp, and like the gas chambers, it was decorated with gardens of flowers. Inside the Lazarett hut was a small waiting room with a velvet embroidered bench upholstered with red plush.[77] As was also true in the gas chambers, though, these small details of the Lazarett were fleeting, and before being shot, every victim would have seen, laid out before their eyes, a massive pit approximately eight meters wide and ten meters deep with a raging fire at the bottom consuming the bodies of those previously murdered. Additionally, as they waited, many had to first witness the murders of others.[78] At the final moments, according to survivor Julian Leszczyński, a German wearing a white coat with a red cross on his shoulder—an attempt to deceive to the very end—approached and seated the victim "on the edge of the pit of burning fire, and then . . . shot them in the back of the head and the person, sometimes only wounded, fell into the bottom straight into the flames."[79]

Horrific, brutal, and bloody, death was the ultimate outcome for nearly every single person—more than eight hundred thousand individuals—who crossed into Treblinka's space. The painful and difficult reconstruction of their final moments displays the tragedies that played out within the camp, but the task of retelling is not in vain. It shows that mass murder at Treblinka was far from the clean, sanitized process Nazi planners imagined, eroding the myth that these lives were swallowed by a black, nameless void about which we can know nothing.

Yet some lived.

Life and Death at Treblinka

The Germans "employed" a set number of Jews as "work commissions" to keep all areas of the camp functioning and to serve as a buffer between the Germans and the areas where mass death occurred. For these Jews, life at Treblinka was tied to keeping the camp running, although their outlook was equally as dire as those murdered right away. "The masses of inmates in Treblinka died in one way—death being the chief product of the camp, but the death of the Jewish operators at the murder factory was of quite a different sort," Auerbach writes. "Their final agony lasted longer and was interspersed with intervals of hope. Transformed into a delirium of conflicting emotions, it was perhaps even more difficult, in the last analysis, than death in the gas chambers."[80]

The number of Jewish prisoners alive and working at Treblinka at any one time ranged from seven hundred to one thousand.[81] Those chosen were usually young, "fit" males, and preference was given to people who worked in specific professions, especially carpenters, engineers, goldsmiths, cooks, tailors, shoemakers, barbers, and physicians. The Germans divided and color-coded all groups of "work Jews" at Treblinka to show which spaces they "belonged" to inside the camp. The group of professionals was known as the *Hofjuden* (court Jews) and they wore pants with yellow stripes, which symbolized long-term workers. They generally worked within specially designated workshops that kept them out of the elements, and they had slightly better living conditions—and higher overall chances of survival—than almost all other groups.[82]

The Germans selected unskilled workers as needed, and their roles varied, though they often became chauffeurs, custodians, and clothing sorters. They also worked along the corridor of death, "undressing the people who did not want to disrobe on their own and clearing the courtyard."[83] This group was given red stripes, which indicated the temporary nature of their work at Treblinka. The "Reds," as they were called, comprised the largest group of all work Jews, and while many worked sorting the massive influx of goods, a set of around three hundred within this group were employed operating the Totenlager and the gas chambers. These Jews, called the Sonderkommando, handled bodies, dealt with corpses after gassing, cleaned out the gas chambers, and oversaw the burning of bodies. A subgroup within the Sonderkommando was the *Goldjuden* (gold Jews), whose nickname derived from their jobs handling gold and valuables, often in the form of gold teeth, which they had to take directly out of the mouths of those murdered in the gas chambers. Because they were intimately familiar with the most secret spaces of Treblinka's killing process, the Germans routinely murdered every person in the red group every two to three months and replaced them with new arrivals (many other groups were also "rotated" in a similar manner).[84]

Indeed, one constant for work Jews, regardless of category, was an extremely short life expectancy. Some were murdered while working, and many others died from exhaustion. "Generally speaking," Poswolski recalled, "the treatment of laborers can be characterized as cruel, with individual laborers and even large groups of laborers being constantly killed."[85] A 1943 report noted that "as a result of the debilitating and inhumane treatment by the Germans," few survived longer than two weeks.[86] Rajzman estimated that while the number of workers at any given time stayed relatively constant, "During my stay, several dozen thousand people worked in that group (with their numbers being constantly replenished by newcomers from new transports), of which at least 25,000 were killed or died from exhaustion."[87] Adjusting to such attrition often meant finding relief wherever and however it presented itself. Wiernik described how, "in the meantime, 'life' ran its 'normal' course. . . . [The Germans] organized compulsory theatrical performances, concerts, dancing, etc. The 'artists' were recruited from among the inmates, who were relieved from work for several hours to participate in rehearsals."[88] Though the performances were bizarre and degrading, Wiernik's use of the phrase "relieved from work" suggests they also offered those chosen to perform a break from the constant exposure to death, a reprieve from their forced labor, and potentially a shot at finding a role that might mean longer survival.

Another group, which was in charge of offloading the wagons and clearing out corpses from the train journey, wore blue bands on their left arms and were thus known as the *Blaue Kommando* (Blue Group).[89] According to Rajzman, the Blue Group included between thirty and fifty members, and they had to complete their work in the unloading spaces "at such a pace that another transport could be brought within 40 minutes after the arrival of the first one, and the victims were not supposed to be aware where they were being transported."[90] This meant rapidly and thoroughly cleaning the arrival area to erase any remnants of previous transports.

Aside from these main groups, the Germans occasionally selected other Jews to provide "personal services" to the Germans.[91] These Jews had more spatial freedom within Treblinka than the color-coded groups, whose distinctive stripes indicated the spaces they needed to stay within. As Rajzman remembered, one teenage boy who washed and pressed ss uniforms "walked all over the camp, free. He was just about the only prisoner who could do that."[92] The other groups with some mobility not just within Treblinka but also outside of it were the Tarnungskommando (Camouflage Brigade) and Waldkommando (Forest Brigade). Composed of about fifteen people each, these groups were responsible for the daily replacement of leaves and branches camouflaging the barbed-wire fences. In their roles, they became intimate with the natural world directly adjacent to the death camp. "We climbed nearby trees, sometimes in pairs," Willenberg described. "We threw the cut branches to the ground; once enough had been accumulated, we jumped from the trees and tied the branches into bundles with some belts."[93] Such unique tasks gave these individuals some level of spatial freedom because they were able to escape the camp's death spaces for extended periods. Krzepicki described how that felt: "The door closes behind us. In the forest, we felt a little freer. We weren't watched as closely by those dog-catchers. But once you cross back over the camp's fence, it felt as though the whole world was caving in. We find ourselves once again in the *Mordbetrieb Treblinka* [Murder Operation Treblinka]."[94]

A loose class structure also emerged among those living in Treblinka, and according to Oskar Strawczyński, it had three layers: the aristocracy, which included the Kapos (barrack leaders), doctors, and warehousemen; the middle class, consisting of tradesmen from the workshops and some of the better "speculators" profiting from outside trade; and the lower class, consisting of the regular camp workers. In this world, life was measured by resources and the ability one had to acquire more. Getting a job sorting clothes and packages from the arriving trains meant one could siphon extra noodles, beans, and flour for nutrition alongside other goods that provided both sustenance and means with which to barter.[95] After all, as Wiernik observed, "Treblinka was filled with all one's heart might desire and there were large quantities of everything."[96] Indeed, almost every item imaginable flowed through the sorting area, creating another spatial oddity where among the thick forests of rural Poland sat storehouses laden with enough expensive goods to rival any town square of Europe. On this level, what the outside world considered valuable retained the label in Treblinka, especially for use in bribing Ukrainian and German guards. After all, as Zdzisław Goldstein noted, the Jews at Treblinka lived "among the abundance of diamonds, vodka," and other things the guards specifically desired.[97] However, the Jews often attached much higher value to more ordinary items—food, cigarettes, shoes, and eating utensils—that, inside of Treblinka, made a bigger difference between life and death than did precious metals.

Among those seen less often within the living spaces of Treblinka were women. Krzepicki observed, "Women had a much heavier fate than men. If some of the young men managed to stay alive for a while, and in isolated cases get out of this death factory, it seems that no woman survived a single day here."[98] Although the trend he indicates regarding the predominance of male survivors is valid, women did exist within Treblinka for different durations. Oskar Strawczyński noted the presence of a group of "working girls" consisting of "about 30 women . . . most of whom were employed in the German, Ukrainian, and Jewish laundry areas. . . . A few others knitted, embroidered, or performed similar work" (see map 1 in chapter 1). This group also included women who worked in the kitchen areas preparing meals for the work Jews.[99] While there may have been Jewish women among this group, other research has shown it likely consisted of between twenty and thirty Polish and Ukrainian women who also served as maids and servants for the Germans. These women also had special barracks within the German living spaces, and their spatial experience of the death camp and their interaction with male Jewish prisoners would have been limited.[100]

Possibly the only other Jewish women kept alive in the camp for longer periods, as Jerzy Rajgrodzki witnessed, were a dozen women whose barracks "were on the eastern side [of the camp,] and dance parties were sometimes arranged there."[101] Rajgrodzki's mention of dance parties, at odds with the fate of other women in Treblinka, insinuates that these women were sexually abused by the Germans and Ukrainians. Given that little is known about them, we might also assume that they were murdered and "rotated" with some frequency (as happened to other groups of Jews). Moreover, sexual violence certainly occurred in other areas of Treblinka, notably when Ukrainians sometimes raped or attempted to rape Jewish women before sending them to the gas chambers.[102] As Wiernik recalled, the Ukrainians "frequently selected the best-looking Jewish maidens from the transports of nude women passing their quarters, dragged them into their barracks, raped them brutally and then delivered them to the death-chambers."[103] The German guards almost certainly committed similar acts of sexual violence, and Otto Horn admitted to frequenting the laundry area in order to talk to the girls there: "They had their own barracks and were locked in there at night. Later on, I sometimes let them out on a Sunday to go for a walk in the woods behind the camp."[104] Horn's description here adds dark undertones to the gendered nature of Treblinka's spatial layout because it shows how the very few spaces in which women could exist were tightly controlled by the same individuals responsible for their lives. Therefore, "in a regime that glorified a hypermasculine ideal," as Edward Westermann writes, German guards saw women and girls "as disposable if not dehumanized objects" and thus chose to commit sexual violence under any pretext. At Treblinka, and certainly at other camps, sexual violence often took on a spatial manifestation as guards exploited the power imbalance that came with offering women temporary reprieve from the gas chambers or allowing them time not locked inside their barracks.[105]

While most other women arriving at Treblinka went straight to death (as was true for most everyone regardless of gender), there is at least one remarkable exception. Linda Penn (born Kremer) recalled a singular experience inside of Treblinka's death space where, just before having her head shaved (and presumably being sent to the gas chambers), a man saved her life by sending her to another barrack. Here, Penn recalled, "there were a group of women standing that were also picked, and before we knew it, very quickly . . . they counted a hundred at the door, a hundred women, and [anyone] over a hundred went back to the crematorium." Some workers then brought food and told them, "Today is your happiest day. You are the first people ever to come out from Treblinka alive." Penn never learned why this group of women was saved, but the next day they were all sent by train from Treblinka to Majdanek, from where Penn survived the war.[106]

Though unique in that she was one of the few women to survive Treblinka, Penn's experience highlights the role sheer luck often played in determining who lived and died within the camp's confines. As Rajzman remembered, he only survived an immediate death in the gas chambers because a man named "Galewski," one of the Blue Group, happened to recognize Rajzman as he disembarked the train. Rajzman later reflected, "[Galewski's] thirteen-year-old daughter went to school with my daughter. I didn't know him personally, but his daughter used to come to my house to do homework with my daughter. . . . When he saw me standing there naked, he remembered where I lived—near him. . . . So he told me not to push to the front of the line going into the gas chamber; he told me to hang back, and he brought me a shirt and a pair of pants."[107] From his transport of approximately seven thousand people, only Rajzman and one other man were selected to work (and to live)—making his fortuitous meeting with Galewski even more remarkable. Bomba had a similar experience: he was one of only five, out of three simultaneously arriving transports holding perhaps eighteen thousand people, selected to live and work at Treblinka, and only then because, like Rajzman, someone in the Blue Group (in this case a relative) noticed Bomba. Bomba added that the number of Jews selected to live from any arriving transport depended solely on current camp "needs," which meant that, as a postwar trial document stated, from each new train, "usually there were only a few, and in many cases none at all, who were spared immediate death."[108]

Beyond luck, others who survived the initial chaos at Treblinka relied only on intuition and adaptation. One account of an unnamed survivor found in the Oyneg Shabes Archive explained that when one of his group began to undress, "he put on some clothes and pretended to be one of the Kapos, urging others to hurry. One of the Kapos wanted to make him undress again, but another defended him."[109] This split-second decision had life-or-death consequences, and it seems to have saved this man's life. In a similar instance, Finkelsztein also risked everything on an immediate spatial adaptation to his surroundings: "When the men were separated, I was able to join a group of laborers, who had red marks on their trousers. I learned from them that they were used to work in the camp and so I fixed the red mark on my trousers, and this was how I survived."[110] Few found cover in the chaos as effectively as Isadore Helfing. In what can only be described as a sudden and total immersion into the death spaces of Treblinka, upon disembarking the train, Helfing said, "I jumped right in and started dragging those bodies just like I was one of them."[111] In this way, he pretended to blend in with the other workers removing the corpses of those who perished on the train journey, and he survived thanks to this cerebral, instantaneous adaptation to the specific space in which he suddenly found himself.

To be more exact, this space was one defined, as almost every Treblinka survivor reiterates, by an up-close, daily interaction with death. For some, like Helfing, this interaction occurred almost immediately, while it took others longer to confront the spaces of death surrounding them. Survivor Mosze Klajman recalled that it was only after he started to work sorting clothes at Treblinka that everything became clearer. "I asked my friend where all these naked people were," Klajman said, "and he answered me, 'Right beside us. On the other side of the cabins you see thick, black smoke. That is all of them.'"[112] Zygmunt Strawczyński described the moment this realization clicked, the flashbulb moment of understanding when after being separated from his wife and children at the rail platform, he was sent to "this big field where these big mountains of clothing were, while naked men were running with their bundles on their shoulders, and they had to throw them down and run back." As he reflected, "These were the ones that were sent right away to the oven. I couldn't comprehend, but of course, I knew that this is it, this is death."[113] For Chil Rajchman, awareness came in a terribly personal manner: "On the second day, while separating clothes, I recognized my sister's dress."[114] For others, the realization only came when confronting Treblinka's horrors up close: "We sorted the packages. . . . In one of the packages I found a strangled half-year-old child. I was terrified, [and] I threw the child in among the garbage that was burning in the Lazarett."[115]

Confronting death and handling bodies represented a novel experience for some, invoking spontaneous emotions of terror, fear, or sadness, but others may have already become somewhat acclimated from previous experiences. For instance, many coming from Warsaw had witnessed death amid the deprivation, starvation, and disease in the ghetto. A group of resistance fighters from the Warsaw ghetto observed, "From the Summer of 1941 to the Summer of 1942 . . . the restrictions put on the ghetto were tightened more and more, with the visible result of the increasing number of corpses lying on the ghetto streets."[116] The biggest difference was that in Treblinka, the confrontation with death was constant; as survivor Shalom Kohn noted, "Every day we looked death in the face and witnessed the German atrocities."[117] Therefore, whereas the ghettoes were fluid spaces in the evolution of genocide, intended foremost to isolate and concentrate (not necessarily to kill), death at Treblinka was the fixed spatial reality from which there was no outlet.[118]

However, even within Treblinka, the exposure to death varied in different areas of the camp. While everyone encountered it, no one became more familiar with Treblinka's grisly reality than the Sonderkommando in the Totenlager. Several times each day, these men opened the gas chamber doors to find this scene: "The corpses were found standing erect like so many dolls, their dead eyes wide-open. They were usually tangled in a mass, their arms and legs wrapped so tightly around each other that it took a great effort to drag out the first batch. . . . The bodies were naked; some of them were white, others were blue and bloated. They were always wet, covered with their final sweat, befouled with the filth of their final defecation, with rivulets of blood running from their mouths and noses."[119] More terrible still, the Sonderkommando next had to take the corpses out, as Willenberg remembered: "They're still warm. They're all crushed into one great mass of meat, and we've got to pull them apart."[120] This group then had to take the bodies to the burial pits nearby. Initially, they used a wagon, but it soon became faster to tie a belt from the corpse's hands or legs and run to the open rows of pits behind the gas chambers while dragging the body along.[121]

Far beyond anything experienced on the streets of the ghetto, this constant interaction with death on a mass scale had no precedent.

In times between transports arriving, the Sonderkommando was tasked with digging up previously buried bodies and burning them. Krzepicki described the sensory horrors of witnessing what he estimated were ten thousand recently exhumed bodies lying in a pile: "There was a terrible stench all around. The corpses were swollen, their bellies horribly bloated. They were covered with brown and black spots, and worms swarmed all over the corpses. . . . We, the new arrivals, were overwhelmed by terror. We looked at each other, each asking: Is what we are seeing actually real? We could not believe our eyes."[122] Once the bodies were exhumed, survivor Edward Sypko recalled, "the Germans used . . . an excavator with a grappler. It took out these corpses and put them on the rail grates. When it took too much, it sometimes dropped body parts; I saw them fall off."[123] After that, two Sonderkommando had to pick up the disinterred corpses by their limbs and arrange them on the grate.[124] And those who somehow survived these awful experiences were forever left with the dark, unwanted knowledge imprinted by being forced to interact with Treblinka's death spaces in order to live.[125]

Many in the Sonderkommando died from exhaustion or were killed by the work itself, but the psychological effects of what they witnessed also undoubtedly added to their high mortality rate. Hejnoch Brener, who was selected to work as a barber, recalled, "On the very first day of my work in this group, we were sent to so-called camp no. 2 . . . in which one of the chambers intended for exterminating people had been turned into a barber's shop. . . . After the trial of shaving off the women's hair in the chamber, each subsequent shaving of hair took place in a hut located on the left side of the undressing courtyard."[126] Describing the ordeal as a *trial*, Brener was unnerved by the spatial awareness, not lost on him, that he had been inside the very same gas chambers where so many others had been murdered. Indeed, simply being immersed in such spaces of mass murder caused great stress. Rajzman remembered seeing another Jewish worker who, upon arrival, "was a middle-aged, handsome man with black hair. By the time of the uprising, he was completely white. Every day he became whiter and whiter."[127]

For others, it was not only seeing dead bodies and being in the same spaces where murders occurred but witnessing the killing process itself that took a toll. "I almost went insane on the day when I first saw men, women and children being led into the house of death," Wiernik recalled. "I pulled my hair and shed bitter tears of despair."[128] Czechowicz wrote similarly, "At the beginning, when I fell into this hell, I do not know what happened to me. I was left rather insane."[129] That both men invoke insanity to describe their mental states reveals that life inside Treblinka was consumed by a constant, visceral anguish and anxiety.

Undoubtedly adding to this psychological distress was the ever-present threat to their own lives. Sypko recalled, "Everyone trembled because every hour was an unknown; they could have killed us randomly."[130] In fact, just as luck often determined who was selected to live right away, it also went far to determine who survived at Treblinka in the long term. For illustration, Krzepicki remembered one morning when his group of Jewish workers was scheduled to be murdered, but "an extraordinary miracle happened. . . . It was said that something broke in the gas chamber. In the morning, no one came for us." Although eighty from this group were eventually shot, Krzepicki and others were saved, given new jobs, and spared from the gas chambers, seemingly out of nowhere.[131] Indeed, the longer one stayed alive in Treblinka, the clearer it became just how thin the line was between life and death. As Brener the barber explained, "The barbers were not allowed to talk to the victims. If a supervising German noticed such a conversation, the barber had to undress and was sent to a gas chamber. I remember a woman recognizing her brother [as] one of the barbers and greeting him. The barber was immediately ordered to strip naked and was killed."[132]

The mental suffering did not relent at night either, when, in Krzepicki's words, "broken in body and soul, dying of thirst, we returned to our barracks."[133] Survivor Richard Glazar described, "At night we were put into barracks. It just had a sand floor. Nothing else. Each of us simply dropped where he stood."[134] As they tried to rest in the cramped spaces allotted to them, the workers, who were finally physically separated from the spaces of death that had occupied their waking hours, in Willenberg's words, "were afflicted with terrifying nightmares which were actually re-enactments of the things [they] had witnessed during the day."[135] Survivor Mieczysław Chodźko recalled poignantly, "Like a nightmare, the specter was recalled during the night . . . and with a shudder one was awakened to think about this hell, about this 'work,' about the constant beating, and murdering of people who could no longer work, swollen with hunger."[136] These constant nightmares meant many never had an escape from the death surrounding them, and the consequences were terrible. Every morning the survivors found two or three people in each barrack who had taken their own lives during the night. Krzepicki described the air of fatalism that took hold: "You can imagine our mood when we were alone in the barracks. Final night or the last hour? None of us knew that, but it was clear the end was near."[137]

The barracks, primitive spatial creations in themselves, offered no reprieve from an already unremitting world, and they instead served only to exacerbate the despair of Jews still alive. Sypko, upon first seeing these structures, exclaimed, "Dear God! These barracks looked so gloomy and black."[138] Inside the barracks was a "different world," as Willenberg recalled: "Here we were, in this hut in Treblinka . . . piles of rags on the floor; pajamas and towels strewn about; razors and mirrors, forks and spoons jammed between the boards and planks; cups of various colours and shapes resting on the boards. Signs of human habitation. It was incomprehensible."[139] There was no consistency and little comfort in the spaces in which the Jews spent their nights. Each person had a bunk space only about forty centimeters wide, and as Chodźko recalled, "It was mostly dark in the barracks. . . . During the night, it was forbidden to leave the barracks for upwards of 15 hours during the winter. . . . In the morning, when the doors and shutters could be opened . . . the prisoners could see large puddles from the overflowing 'tub' and buckets [provided as toilets]."[140] Suffering in the barracks seemed to come from all sides at all times. "When it rained, we were soaked. . . . The barrack was not heated," Sypko described. "There was no water . . . and in the summer it was terrible; bed bugs bit us so much that the straw in the bunk was covered in red."[141]

Aside from the physical discomfort the barracks created, they had more subtle and macabre elements of psychological torment. Willenberg noted that the electric lights in his barrack were powered by the same motor that "provided the burning gas for the gas chambers, where tens of thousands of humans were poisoned day by day." These lights left a pale glow in the hut, he added, not just because of their weak light but also because of his realization that this same electricity was directly used for mass murder.[142] In this unnerving atmosphere, prisoners had few options, and as one survivor observed, "In the barracks . . . some cried, others prayed."[143] Above all else, no one had any amount of rest, relaxation, or rejuvenation from the daily horrors they witnessed in abundance. Instead, most remained bombarded by the death all around them. Krzepicki gave voice to this disconcerted feeling: "Of my earlier companions, no one remained alive. They were already sleeping on the other side of the [barrack] walls, on the other side of the fence, in a great fraternal grave."[144] For living Jews at Treblinka, it was as if the constant physical and mental proximity to spaces of death and dying began to dominate all facets of daily existence.

Piotr Kisiel, a local Pole who knew many Treblinka survivors, recalled how torments piled up one on top of the other until eventually something had to give: "Summer 1943 was extremely hot in this area. For a long time, there was not a drop of rain nor any wind. Prisoners working among burning corpses could not shake off the physical and moral hardship. . . . Many prisoners looked for death and sought to violate the rules of discipline established by the Germans. Prisoner Jan Kobus told me, 'To die from an ss bullet is a luxury.' Other prisoners said among themselves in the barracks that to be condemned to live in Treblinka was simply worse than being condemned to death."[145] For those who survived, adaptation to life in Treblinka underwent several stages, marked first by shock, then despair, and lastly, a near resignation to fate.[146] This last stage was not necessarily a "death wish" but instead an acceptance of the utter predominance death had over life inside the spaces of the camp. Rajzman recalled the precise moment when he realized that he had reached this last phase. One day, a German directed twenty-five or thirty people, including him, along the path leading to the gas chambers. As he later described, "I was sure that this [was] it—this [was] the end. I was somewhat confused—I had nothing to lose anyhow, so I said, 'Scharführer, it's a pity that our torn clothes and torn shoes should be burned with us. Why don't you ask us to get undressed so you'd have more shoes?' I said it with evident sarcasm. I didn't care much at that point."[147] It turned out that Rajzman and the others were being put on assignment near the gas chambers, and this was not, in fact, their turn to die, but the nonchalant attitude Rajzman displayed in the face of death highlights his acceptance of its inevitability within Treblinka. Krzepicki reflected, "It is unbelievable how people learned to live not by the day, nor the hour, but literally by the minute, and how they cleverly repressed the thoughts of impending death."[148] Glazar put it succinctly: "It was normal that for everyone behind whom the gate of Treblinka closed, there was death, had to be death, for no one was supposed to be left to bear witness."[149]

Part of this final stage of adaptation was accepting that someone else likely decided one's fate at Treblinka, and to survive, one had to adjust to this ephemeral, precarious world. Krzepicki remembered an example of just how quickly a camp guard could pass judgment on life and death inside the camp's spaces. One day Krzepicki was speaking with a German near the death pits when the German noticed a young Jewish man working with corpses at the bottom of the grave. The German decided that the young man was working too slowly and commanded, "Don't move, turn around!" The German then shouldered his rifle, and "before the boy could understand what was happening, he already lay dead along with the other corpses. The effort of transferring his body was saved. He was immediately covered by another layer of corpses."[150] Krzepicki, trying to understand his reality, reflected further on this moment: "Here, just a moment ago, the man standing next to me, harnessed together with me, carrying corpses to the pits, now lies naked with glassy eyes, in the same pit. In a moment, you won't be able to see him anymore in this grave, because the next dead bodies will be placed on top of him."[151] The cold truth was that within a matter of moments, any living Jew at Treblinka could be anonymously swallowed up by its death spaces.

Rajchman summed up the benumbed fog that overtook many as they accepted this reality: "We became . . . incoherent. Our vision was overcast. We did not know what was happening to us."[152] Helfing provided a similar description: "I became like a void person. Just didn't bother me because I know I'm going to be dead, now or in five minutes or ten minutes, and I became just like a person who has been doing this for years."[153] Eliahu Rosenberg recalled, "Until the day of the revolt, I saw nothing but the sky and the sand, sky, and sand, and corpses on the ground."[154] The only thing to focus on became the repetition, and Krzepicki had the same simple credo: "*Ziemia, niebo i trupy* (earth, sky, and corpses)."[155] Any other mental processes within Treblinka were superfluous.

This familiarity with and acceptance of death extended to those outside of the Sonderkommando as well. After all, despite the ostensive restrictions to the contrary, many outside the Totenlager constantly interacted with death. Zygmunt Strawczyński, who spent much of his time repairing barracks, recalled that "from the roofs you saw everything—you saw the whole process of extermination from the roofs of the barracks."[156] Similarly, Willenberg, who worked in the sorting room, recalled accidentally stumbling upon the pit next to the Lazarett while passing to another part of the camp: "At its bottom were heaps of corpses which had not yet been consumed by a fire burning under them. I stopped in my tracks, paralyzed with terror. The sizzling, half-burnt cadavers emitted grinding and crackling sounds. The flames, once having enveloped them, either dissipated into little jets of smoke or reignited into a blaze which forced firewood and corpses into a devil's embrace."[157] When he returned to the sorting room, Willenberg told the foreman what he had seen, and the man "reassured" him, "Not to worry: in the end all of us [will] end up there."[158] It seems not only were intimate experiences with death shared outside the Totenlager, but so too was the acceptance of the fate awaiting every Jew inside Treblinka's confines.

But alongside this acceptance came not resignation but perseverance and perhaps even hope—attributes that, when combined, not only led these Jews of Treblinka to stage a major revolt against their oppressors on August 2, 1943, but ultimately ensured some of them would survive the camp and the war as well.

Adapting for Hope

Those who adapted to the spatial demands of Treblinka in order to survive raise comparisons to the idea posited by Primo Levi at Auschwitz of "the drowned and the saved."[159] Levi suggests that Auschwitz survivors often had to adapt to the morality dictated by the new space in which they found themselves. At Treblinka, Zygmunt Strawczyński recalled similarly that while some Jews risked their lives to help others within the camp, there were others who, "when they grabbed something, it was only for them. They didn't care; they could go over somebody's dead body to get it."[160] Krzepicki described once being ordered to remove thirty-five corpses from a water well. But as he was doing so, a group of workers approached with a bucket to fill with water. Krzepicki explained, "In the hope of getting a drink [despite knowing that bodies contaminated the well], I tried to join them, but the German guarding us slammed me in the face with his rubber truncheon and told me to go back to work."[161] The acclimatization to death meant that the dead bodies in the well troubled the living less than the survival instincts that gripped them. "You went through a fire, and either you melted or you hardened," Zygmunt Strawczyński later reflected on adapting to life in Treblinka. "Some people were corrupted; the ghetto and the camp corrupted them, and they are corrupt for all their lives. . . . I know people here who went through all that, and I've seen that they were corrupted for life, in the sense of inhumanity."[162]

Yet adapting to Treblinka's death spaces did not mean the living (and those who ultimately survived) completely shut down their feelings. Survivor testimonies reveal that many experienced moments of vivid emotion despite their adapted survival instincts. Take Krzepicki, the same man who so nonchalantly drank water contaminated by dead bodies: "Dozens of times a day, I fought from collapsing at the sight of human suffering and fear. My heart burned with pain and rage when I saw the terror, fear, and confusion in the thousands of powerless souls rushing into the clutches of the devil."[163] Thus, despite the survival mechanisms to which he resorted, he was still affected daily on a deeper emotional level by what he experienced.

Others found ways, however small, of employing hope. Willenberg reflected, "Overhead I saw a lovely autumn morning, illuminated with warm sun, and at my feet, a mounting heap of corpses."[164] Although highlighting the juxtaposition between the beauty of nature above and the space of death below, one sees here the subtle reminder that the world and the seasons continued to move forward outside Treblinka, allowing for a momentary reprieve from the spaces of death—a glimmer of hope. Indeed, another way some sought optimism was through picturing the spaces outside Treblinka's fences as "free" from the death spaces they inhabited. "We imagined that there was an open and unguarded field beyond the barbed-wire fence surrounding the barracks," Krzepicki recalled. "We didn't know then that behind this first fence there stood another one."[165] The realization of what was beyond—which, in fact, was more barriers in this case—was much less important than the idealization of the free spaces outside Treblinka that they *hoped* were there. In fact, immediately after escaping, Willenberg stopped to reflect: "From afar, past the fences, a glowing world displayed itself to us in its wonderful colours as the sun crept into the blue, innocent sky. The first light of day revealed the full horror of our humiliation and misery in the depths of the abyss named Treblinka."[166] The world outside the confines of Treblinka was infinitely better than the one within it—to a survivor, spaces deserving of the descriptors *glowing, wonderful*, and *innocent*.

It is unsurprising, then, that those living within Treblinka made frequent escape attempts, and even though this also often meant death, the potential benefits of reaching the free spaces beyond Treblinka far outweighed the consequences. Perhaps, too, escape meant something intangible, something to account for the hundreds of thousands who would never get the chance. Perhaps it was, in Krzepicki's words, a chance "to run away, to experience revenge, to look at something else with the same eyes that had seen so much pain."[167]

4

An Interactional Space

It was different in the forest, Gavriel. The forest
meditates; it listens to voices instead of stifling
them. The forest has ears, a heart, and a soul.
In the forest, simplicity is possible; simplicity
belongs there. And unity, too . . . those righteous,
just men who took refuge in the forest and learned
the language of the trees, birds, and clouds. . . .
They paid with blood and tears for their right to
solitude and peace, but at least the blood and tears
were their own.

—Elie Wiesel, *The Gates of the Forest*

Most of those who escaped from Treblinka did so during the prisoner revolt
on August 2, 1943, when, encouraged by news of the Warsaw Ghetto Uprising
and concerned about the slackening pace of murder at Treblinka, a group
of around seven hundred "work Jews" destroyed a portion of the camp,
killed several Ukrainians, and fought their way into the woods.[1] Yet many
survivor testimonies suggest that Jews continuously escaped, or attempted to,
throughout the camp's fifteen-month existence. In fact, in the early months of
Treblinka, before greater security measures were taken, as many as thirty to
forty Jews may have tried to escape *per day*. One popular method was to hide
in the massive piles of clothing in the camp's sorting area. An unnamed survivor, whose recollection was found in the Oyneg Shabes Archive, described
how it happened: "Many workers escaped . . . while sorting clothes near the
piles of sand thrown out by the [excavator]. They hid in these clothes until
the night. At night, they climbed on the piles of sand from the graves that
were as high as the fence and jumped to the other side."[2] In similar inventive

ways, a steady flow of Jews escaped Treblinka, but the spaces they now entered—both natural and human—posed new challenges that required further adaptations for survival.

The first interaction most Jews had after escaping was with the natural world of forests and fields around the camp. Sociologist Suzanne Weiner Weber calls these natural areas "liminal spaces," which she describes as places "where traditional beliefs, norms, and values are reversed, muddled and subsequently transformed."[3] Alongside psychological adaptations to surviving in nature, escapees also encountered very real physical challenges associated with these environments. Religious scholar Didier Pollefeyt notes that many survivor testimonies speak about the "indifference of nature regarding their suffering or to the radical rupture between the beauty of nature and the trauma of genocidal evil."[4] Finding cover among the forests, bushes, and crop fields usually provided short-term safety from recapture, but surviving long term often meant utilizing the natural environment to produce shelter, food, and supplies as well as developing the skills needed to live *within* nature.

Alongside natural spaces, Treblinka escapees also encountered other human beings within the spaces around the camp. Some were refugees like themselves, and some were partisans operating in the forests; but the vast majority were the Poles who called the farms, villages, and towns around Treblinka home. Because most escaping Jews were unfamiliar with the area and unsure of where to go next, interactions with these local Poles almost always occurred at random. And since the attitudes of the local Polish population often determined much about the fate of individual escapees, these initial encounters were laden with life-and-death implications—usually for both parties.

Researchers have generally categorized Polish behavioral responses to Jews during the Holocaust into three categories, which Anna Bikont defines succinctly: "Some people killed, others saved . . . and still others didn't do anything."[5] Nearly one hundred Poles living near Treblinka alone are remembered at Yad Vashem as the "Righteous Among the Nations" for aid they gave to Jews.[6] On the opposite end of the spectrum, though, many other Poles, whether through coercion by the Germans or of their own accord, helped round up and kill escaped Jews. And yet in all probability, nearly all other local residents, perhaps unwilling to become involved or simply perceiving the circumstances as beyond their control, became relatively passive witnesses to what was occurring—only brought into the fold as random interactions dictated. Consequently, how someone responded when a Jewish escapee from Treblinka knocked on their door in the middle of the night truly varied on a case-by-case basis, creating a human space around the camp that was defined by uncertainty. Escapees could be shot at by a Pole in one house while the person next door might provide them food and shelter.

Historians continue to be frustrated by the difficulty in making blanket statements explaining *why* there was such variance in Polish-Jewish interactions during the Holocaust. Most continue to blame prewar antisemitism or imagined wealth disparities between Polish Jews and non-Jews.[7] Yet far more nuanced explanations take into consideration the complicated situations introduced by the changed atmosphere of wartime occupation. As historian Jan Grabowski notes, many Poles were "seduced by modest prizes and inducements offered by the Germans," while others acted "out of fear."[8] Writing from the Warsaw ghetto, Emmanuel Ringelblum reminds us that the Germans also employed threats and made sure "posters threatening capital punishment for this 'crime' [of helping Jews] appeared before every 'liquidation action.'"[9] In this charged atmosphere, in the words of historian Jan Gross, some Poles simply "took advantage of the norms imposed by the Germans" for their own benefit.[10]

Nonetheless, when it comes to explaining Polish behavior, it is obvious that each individual case merits its own evaluation and judgment. As Warsaw Ghetto Uprising planner Yitzhak Zuckerman astutely put it, "You can't generalize about the Poles."[11] Thus, aside from documenting the widely varying Polish responses to escaping Jews, I am most interested here in exploring how the concept of space also played into the equation. In doing so, I acknowledge that during the war, Poland was actively being colonized by the Germans.[12] Subsequently, Poles lost jurisdiction over many spaces, even their most intimate ones—their homes—a spatial domain that geographer Yi-Fu Tuan argues is universally recognized as offering basic security from the outside world.[13] As spatial theorist Tim Cresswell explains further, home is "an intimate place . . . where a person can withdraw from . . . the world outside and have some degree of control over what happens within a limited space."[14] Consequently, as the Germans imposed unlimited jurisdiction over Polish spaces, they stole this control, this simple sovereignty to govern one's everyday life, from Poles. In the process, the human landscapes around Treblinka became liminal spaces not only for Jews escaping into them but, as we also must recognize, for the Poles who lived there.[15] It was this complex world that escaping Jews entered and tried to navigate as they sought to escape the horrors of the death camp behind them.

Forests and Fields

Among the first things mentioned by almost every Treblinka survivor when describing their escape from the death camp are the natural spaces they encountered.[16] Distinctly different spaces from what they had just left behind, the natural world surrounding Treblinka seemed to promise freedom and hope. These particular feelings usually started well in advance of the escape attempt. On his first morning imprisoned inside Treblinka, Jerzy Rajgrodzki tried to focus on the larger natural world he saw beyond the camp: "A beautiful September morning with clear, cloudless skies. The birds are heard. It was a true Polish golden autumn. Among the forests, the air was marvelous. I felt I should say goodbye to this beautiful world of nature, however, because soon it would be the end."[17] Though we can sense his foreboding, Rajgrodzki finds some solace in the simple pleasures of nature above and beyond the horrors surrounding him. Fellow survivor Abraham Krzepicki got a longer taste of freedom when, as part of the *Waldkommando* (Forest Brigade), he was able to leave the camp for short work stints: "I am beyond all the wires and fences now, on the sandy forest road. I allow myself to look at the clear sky above and at the green trees rustling around me. Will this be the path to freedom?"[18] Survivor Samuel Willenberg, also in the Waldkommando, had a similar experience: "The next day we went out to work in the forest as usual. . . . Then a little squirrel caught [the guard's] eye, and he ordered us to chase and capture it. . . . The little animal, already within my grasp, looked at me with fear-filled glistening eyes. I could not trap it. It symbolized freedom."[19]

At Treblinka, the nearest natural spaces consisted of large expanses of forest. As local Polish witness Władysław Rażmowski described the setting, "The Jewish camp . . . was fenced with barbed wire surrounded by a young pine grove, beyond which stretched forested woodlands leading to the Orzołek forests. The Polish camp lay on the open sandy space—it was also fenced in with barbed wire. Beyond it, the Maliszew forests stretched north."[20] The immense forests were visible from within the camp, and Jews imprisoned there envisioned freedom and mobility in the tall trees and dense undergrowth that they were denied in Treblinka. Thus, prisoners formed plans that if they ever escaped, they would head straight for these forests first in hopes of finding shelter and perhaps creating a partisan unit there.[21]

Planning for their emergence into the world beyond Treblinka probably paled in comparison to those first few steps of freedom during the escape. "Night fell and we could not get our fill of the intoxicating joy of freedom," Tanhum Grinberg wrote. "All the time we had dreamed about the moment we would find it, the first meter of ground outside the damned camp, and now we were 15 kilometers away."[22] Aron Czechowicz was so overjoyed that he risked the peril of a quick celebratory embrace of another escapee just after exiting Treblinka. Having hidden in a pile of clothes all night, when their brief escape window came, Czechowicz and another man jumped the fence, then as they helped each other up, they stopped and "kissed and wept" before finally running off into the forests for cover.[23] Crossing over the spatial boundary demarcating life and death and hope and despair, regardless of what came next, merited celebration.

This elation often had to wait, however, since many who escaped were pursued by guards (especially during the revolt), creating a chaotic environment where finding temporary cover became an immediate priority. "We ran across swamps, meadows and ditches, bullets coming after us fast and furious," Yankel Wiernik described. "Every second counted. All that mattered was to reach the woods, because once there, the Germans would be loathe to go in after us. . . . After penetrating a little deeper into the thicket, I sat down among the bushes. . . . I was alone, resting."[24] Those escaping had to make decisions on the fly because immediate survival trumped all other concerns; consequently, the length of this initial survival phase varied widely. As survivor Oskar Strawczyński experienced, "Once outside the camp, people broke into smaller groups and ran in all different directions. A group of twelve of us ran eastward. We ran for a long time. We ran through a village, over a railway line, through fields and swamps. Finally, exhausted and out of breath, we found a ditch thickly overgrown on both sides. We slipped into it and lay there until evening."[25] For many, true *escape* from Treblinka was not complete until they had finally found a forested space impenetrable enough to relax in and rest for a moment. And though the natural world around the camp certainly provided many areas like this, what constituted a truly safe or secure space was open to individual interpretation.

Indeed, the more distance people put between themselves and the death camp, the more it became clear that alongside freedom, the spaces of the natural world also presented challenges and threats to long-term survival. A group of inmates who tunneled under Treblinka's fence in December 1942 learned this lesson painfully, since "as the first snow had just fallen, the tracks of the escapees could be traced. . . . At least three of the escaped were returned to the camp alive and hanged . . . on a gallows by the neck."[26] Specific climatological phenomena, therefore, meant more in the natural spaces around Treblinka than it might have inside the camp, and in this case, simple snowfall had transformed the natural landscape into a space of treachery and death instead of one of hope and survival.

Another issue some found upon reaching the spaces beyond the camp was what to do or where to go next. "From the distance, we [saw] black, this was woods," Isadore Helfing recalled. "We were running straight into the woods. And we hided [sic] out overnight. . . . The next day, we didn't know where to go."[27] For some, the answer was simple—they would go home. Chaim Kwiatek, who lived in Stoczek (13 km), was rounded up by trucks and sent to Treblinka, but he escaped from the truck roughly three kilometers before the camp and, being in familiar territory, simply returned to his house.[28] Similarly, William Schneiderman threaded his way through familiar forests upon escaping Treblinka to return to his home twenty-five kilometers away.[29] Others had more difficulty, as survivor Richard Glazar wrote: "We want to get back home, somewhere off to the southwest. First past Warsaw and over the Vistula. We can both remember at least that much of our geography lessons. But we're complete failures when it comes to navigating by the stars. . . . Up to this point we have actually been heading toward the Russian front. And this is probably our great good fortune, since the Germans will hardly have thought of sending a search party off in this direction. What a marvelous blunder."[30] For most, home was not close by, and escaping Treblinka meant encountering unfamiliar terrain. Combined with the disorientation of the escape itself, many faced the very real possibility of getting lost in the natural landscapes beyond the camp. Abraham Bomba, originally from distant Częstochowa (285 km), had just such a dizzying experience. Making his escape from Tre-blinka around ten o'clock at night, he, along with a small group of others, sought to navigate a way to freedom through the thick forests. Yet by five o'clock the next morning, they found themselves right back at Treblinka. For the first seven hours of their escape, they had simply circled the camp.[31] Something similar happened to Abraham Kolski: "We [didn't] know at night where to walk. There's . . . such a big forest. And we started to walk by the moon, with the moon. We walked the whole night. . . . In the morning we saw we were in the same place. . . . I mean we want[ed] to go away from Treblinka. Again we [were] in Treblinka. . . . [We had traveled] three kilometers . . . but we [were] still in Treblinka."[32] A tense and disorientating experience to begin with, escape became infinitely more perilous the longer one stayed in proximity to the camp.

Certainly, the dangers mounted as time passed. Krzepicki described the anxiety he felt, where "at the slightest rustle of a bird, or a squirrel jumping on branches, our breaths accelerated from fear."[33] The biggest worries included being recaptured or encountering someone or something hostile in the woods. Saul Kuperhand recalled this uneasy feeling: "We headed for the safety of the dense Kurczewsky forest, but we did not feel very secure there. Something smelled fishy; there was danger in the air . . . perhaps . . . we were being followed."[34] This constant fear altered their behavior. "At night we walked single file, carefully and in great fear that someone might hear us," Krzepicki remembered. "Everything was quiet. There is an uneasy calm in the fields, as if the homeless, frightened souls haunted by death had never wandered by."[35] Such constant, almost paranoid worry of recapture stayed with escapees throughout their time in the forests but also often scarred them for years after. "The wound of Treblinka was still far from healed in his mind," Rachel Auerbach writes of one survivor she met later after the war. "His manner was still that of a hunted animal, and probably would never be any different."[36]

Once the adrenaline of the initial escape wore off, the daunting task of facing the natural environment for long-term survival became more apparent. As an unnamed survivor wrote in a document found in the Oyneg Shabes Archive, "For a moment I delighted in the feeling of freedom. The nightmare of the past days disappeared, but it was to return soon with another nightmare, that of the future."[37] In this moment, survivors recognized the need to develop some type of adaptation to the natural world. Several had an advantage, having gained experience and knowledge during their imprisonment at Treblinka. Mosze Klajman explained that he was not worried as he hid in the forests after escaping the camp. Having previously been in the Waldkommando, he wrote, "I knew the forest well because I had worked in this forest for some time. So in silence, I avoided all the patrols. . . . I got to the buckwheat field, which was growing white, and I moved farther away from the camp."[38] Here, Klajman took advantage of his spatial knowledge of the nearby world, first to hide, then to avoid capture, and finally, to move steadily in a direction he knew led away from the camp. In another instance, Chil Rajchman observed how a member of his group—a former military officer he calls Masaryk—"[was] able to orientate himself at night by the stars." As Rajchman explained, "With him leading the way, we move[d] on."[39] Escaping alongside someone possessing this unique skill set undoubtedly set his group up for success. (One cannot help but compare this scenario to Glazar's a few paragraphs earlier, where he mentions his *inability* to navigate by the stars.)

Nonetheless, however well prepared one might have been, adapting to the natural world never came easy. Krzepicki and those escaping with him soon faced obstacles: "We then enter a new forest, and bury ourselves in a thicket and go to sleep. . . . There was nothing to lie on and nothing to cover ourselves with, and we can't sleep because of the cold."[40] Even the primitive amenities of Treblinka's barracks had offered some protection from the elements, but being on the run meant exposure quickly became a major issue. As Grinberg described, "We lay low in that place for two whole days, without any food or water. We ate only wild berries from plants growing above us, and they made us sick. . . . We reached a stream which divided the woods into two parts. We flung ourselves to the ground, drank our fill of the icy water and ate some bread. Then we crossed the stream silently and entered the virgin forests. A torrential rain was pouring down. We quickly broke off some branches and built ourselves a little hut." Though many escapees found the natural environment indifferent to their plight, they had to adapt to it or they would die. For those who succeeded in this adaptation, overcoming nature's hardships actually reinforced the initial feeling of freedom (and joy) many felt. As Grinberg added after building a hut and surviving the soaking downpour, "From that moment on, we saw ourselves as free men, denizens of the wild Sterdyń woods."[41] One can sense his transformation here from the exposed, cold, and wet fugitive to the belonging denizen who sought not only to inhabit but to master these natural spaces.

Weiner Weber uses the term "landscape agency" to define the ability of nature to remake one's conceptions about survival. Within this adaptation process, a pattern emerges where only through repeated encounters does a person finally come to learn that they must adapt *to* nature, not the other way around. The first experience with landscape agency is usually a study in contrast, especially when juxtaposing the space of Treblinka with that of the natural world beyond. This initial interaction happened immediately as Jews escaping into the forests darted behind trees and beneath shrubs to hide themselves and avoid immediate recapture. Almost every escapee had to utilize the existing "material landscape" of the forested spaces around them—meaning the location, density, and types of plant and animal life available—to make it through the first day or two.[42] For many, this meant trying to blend in with whatever landscape in which they found themselves, however unnatural an adaptation this required. Survivor Samuel Rajzman, for instance, was forced to spend the first two days of his escape lying motionless in a potato field while he tried to blend into the awkward terrain, avoid recapture, and figure out his next moves. Later on, he periodically found himself hiding variously within piles of hay or amid cornfields for the same purposes.[43]

If one survived the initial escape, one then had to contend again with landscape agency, but now for long-term survival. Sometimes on their own and sometimes banding together with other groups of survivors, these "forest fugitives," as Weiner Weber calls them, lived in the forests for months, and sometimes years, after escaping.[44] Long-term adaptations meant not imposing one's own will on nature but recognizing that the natural world asserted its own set of rules (and indeed its own agency). For forest fugitives, these adaptations included learning from animals what could be eaten, watching insects to determine the drinkability of water, creating mental maps to aid in navigating unfamiliar forest terrain, figuring out both how to create fire and which materials burned less smoky (oak worked best), and discovering makeshift forest remedies for wounds and lice infestations. Some even learned through trial and error to fashion moccasins out of tree bark steamed over a fire.[45] For Willenberg, adaptation included using the hard-to-reach location of a river sandbar not only for hiding but for the advantages offered by its water: "I lay on the island several hours longer, until my hunger and thirst would let me rest no longer. I drank from the river, bathed, and slowly began

FIG. 12. Treblinka survivor Samuel Willenberg outside Warsaw after escaping the camp. USHMM, courtesy of Shmuel and Ada Willenberg.

to move on."[46] For Richard Glazar, it was studying local livestock for spatial clues: "Grazing cows, like guideposts, let us know which direction we should be taking. From the other side we are protected by long rows of bushes that are supposedly here to keep the wind from scalping the low-growing vegetation off these flat fields."[47] Such adaptations to nature were universal for forest fugitives throughout Poland, and these survivors developed ingenious solutions to a wide range of problems. Take, for instance, the story of a man named Joseph, who escaped from the Przemyśl ghetto but was wounded in the process. Other survivors living in the woods taught him to "take stale bread, rye bread, and . . . mix it with some spider webs. We kneaded it and we put it on the wound." After this forest triage, Joseph stated, "[The wound] slowly started healing, and slowly we adjusted to life."[48]

The body's natural abilities, those sometimes taken for granted in the modern world, become critical while on the run through the fields and forests. As Treblinka survivor Edi Weinstein reflected, "The moonlight picked out the low scrub that covered the marshes, occasional clumps of trees, and now and then a glimmering pond." Using his night and peripheral visions, Weinstein added, "We kept our eyes straight ahead, afraid to blunder into the railroad guards." Navigating unfamiliar and wild terrain was complicated by the need to avoid recapture, and Weinstein also noted that one always spoke in whispers and communicated frequently by hand gestures and other nonverbals.[49] So critical was maintaining stealth, as Chil Rajchman explained: "We take turns every few hours to make sure that no-one snores loudly if he falls asleep, since every rustle resounds in the forest."[50] One also avoided dangerous situations, even if it meant taking the long way around. "Shortly before the bridge over the Liwiec River we climbed down from the embankment, in case there were guards on the bridge," Weinstein recalled. "We trod through hundreds of yards of swamp water, channels, and rivulets, detoured around the bridge at a safe distance, and returned to the embankment."[51]

Indeed, traveling anywhere in the natural world meant doing so mainly at night. This tactic aimed not only to avoid people, but nighttime conditions offered additional benefits for those attuned to the natural world. Rajchman remembered, "I went back to the field and laid there until midnight. Because at night, in the evening, you hear every movement."[52] Both a climatological adaptation—nighttime often includes a lessening of wind and decreased temperatures, both of which allow for better acoustic conditions—and something simply learned by traveling at night, these subtle changes often made the difference between life and death.[53] For Mojżesz Mydło, this meant forcing himself to stay up all night after his exhausting escape while he "wandered through forests and fields" to find safety near a familiar village before dawn broke, a task critical to his survival.[54] Rajgrodzki recalled similarly, "We stopped somewhere in the woods because it was getting light. We laid in one place all day, hidden among the bushes."[55] When daylight came, one hunkered down wherever, even if it meant being uncomfortable and remaining motionless among thorns and thickets for hours. As an unnamed survivor wrote in a document found in the Oyneg Shabes Archive, "We wandered by night and slept by day in roadside ditches under the sky."[56] This was not a hard and fast rule, however, and others adapted as the situation dictated. Take Glazar, for instance, who wrote: "We're going to have to risk traveling by daylight, at least for a while, so that we can avoid settlements. It's OKAY. We have the feeling that this has become less dangerous than moving at night."[57] Whether unsuccessful in adapting to nighttime conditions or for some other urgent reason dictated by unique situational factors, what worked best for one person may not have worked for another.

Adjusting to the agency imposed by the natural environment also meant adapting to a new pace of life. "We lived quite a few days in that hideout [in the forest]," Krzepicki recalled. "Life there was very boring and tiresome. There was nothing to wash with, we became terribly dirty and run down. Some of us, having nothing to do, sat in the sun and searched our bodies for lice."[58] Surviving in a forested world meant accepting the long, slow process whereby physical comforts like cleanliness became less important. Menachem Treist described the appearance of another group of forest fugitives: "They are all overgrown with hair, their skin peeled because they had nothing to wash with. They were dressed in rags and their bare feet were swollen."[59] Yet they were alive.

Acclimating to the natural world went beyond the purely physical, and forest fugitives found mental adaptations just as important. Historians Waitman Beorn and Anne Kelly Knowles suggest, "In order to escape this threat to their mental well-being, individuals seek to change either their beliefs or their actions to bring their mental and physical states into congruence."[60] Those who survived long term in the forest had to alter their perceptions not only of survival itself but of what life in the forest *meant*. Holocaust survivor Alex Levin recalled his own experience in the forests around Lublin: "We sought protection in those woods. They were our refuge and our hearth. Every tree became a fortress. Every shrub was a fort. The forest became our best friend. I am sorry that I am not a poet or songwriter who could find the words I can't to praise the forest as my savior and my faithful benefactor. The forest saved us."[61] Not as trees and shrubs alone but as refuge, hearth, and fortress, the natural world served survivors best when they made their peace with it.

Since most escapees had been urban dwellers before being sent to Treblinka, though, adapting usually included a fundamental reassessment of one's previous relationship with nature. In turn, this changing mindset often created, according to historian Tim Cole, "a greater blurring of the boundary between [one's] embodied self and the natural world he hid in."[62] For Glazar, this meant embracing his new existence as a forest fugitive:

> By now we look exactly like the ragged speculators of the region—both of us barefoot, one of us with dry muddy boots slung over his shoulder, our pants torn practically to shreds. It is impossible to tell what color our crumpled shirts and jackets once were. With a new sense of self-assurance, we simply walk along the sidewalks past houses big and small, continuing on our way. From road signs we read the names of places we have never heard of before—Rembertów, Solejówek. We head in the direction in which civilization is rapidly thinning out and heave a sigh of relief once we find ourselves moving freely through open land.[63]

Glazar and his companion had to pass through a small settlement, during which they were potentially exposed. Yet their appearance was so disheveled from living in the woods, they walked through with confidence, and as they reemerged into the forests and fields, Glazar gave a "sigh of relief" to be back in a place he admits is still unfamiliar (he doesn't recognize the towns on the sign) but no longer threatening.

Elie Wiesel beautifully captures a similar moment of this transformation (one many Treblinka escapees likely could relate to) in his novel *The Gates of the Forest*: "Without knowing how or why, he felt in harmony with the visible and invisible forces of nature which run through every inch of the human body. . . . And it seemed . . . quite natural that the same segment of eternity should contain the outcry of the tortured prisoner and the song of the forest. Both belonged to the same ancient and secret design and bore witness either for, either against but their testimony was clear: perfect harmony between me and this design, between me and this witness."[64] The juxtaposition between the fear of hiding from potential murderers and these moments of "perfect harmony" with nature created striking memories for many who found shelter within the forested landscapes of the Holocaust. In myriad ways, therefore, as Cole explains, this psychological adaptation often meant embracing the forest as a comforting place of "peaceful coexistence between humans and animals, and humans and the natural world . . . [that] provided a paradise compared to the corrupt and dangerous human world outside the forest."[65] Pollefeyt similarly suggests that nature could provide its own comfort and hope because it "offered a structure to keep oneself in life (time schedule, day and night, the rhythm of the seasons, etc.)."[66] If nothing else, simply the layout of the forest landscape itself could provide some reassurance. A group of Jewish fugitives hiding within the Białowieża forest of eastern Poland made this point: "With its jungle-like growths, islands of swampy terrain, and irregular, poorly built country roads, this forest promised safety to many of the persecuted."[67] Here, the interpretation of the forest's natural setting assured those surviving within it of their perceived security from recapture and provided them a refuge, physically and mentally. Willenberg, while living in the forests after Treblinka, took similar solace in the natural world that was his haven: "I walked into the field, uprooted a few shoots of straw, burrowed into the great heap, wriggled in and closed the opening with straw. When night fell, I emerged and enjoyed the silence of an enchanting August night. . . . The mingled scents of cut rye and wild foliage filled the air. Innumerable twinkling stars lit up the sky."[68] Nothing here suggests he is a fugitive of Treblinka struggling to survive and adapt; instead, he has a moment of clarity and calm as he connects with the elemental forces around him in the natural world.

Human Interactions

The Jews who escaped Treblinka soon discovered that alongside the natural spaces of forests and fields, the landscapes beyond were also full of other humans. In fact, the two spaces were rarely mutually exclusive. As Rajgrodzki recalled of his escape from the camp, "There was only a woman, an old woman, and a little boy. They did not have anything; they only gave us carrots. . . . Along the way we met an audience of Jews who were going in the opposite direction. . . . We could not have been more than a kilometer from the camp. We waited for evening with longing. . . . When it was already darkening, we got to a village, we chose a hut . . . and asked the occupant to make several potatoes for us."[69] Clearly, the world around Treblinka was not simply a natural space but one where people lived, worked, hid, and generally existed. As Rajgrodzki also shows, one group that fleeing Jews often encountered was other Jews who had escaped. In fact, while Krzepicki was making his own escape through the woods and villages around Treblinka, he came across a group of ten people, several of whom were refugees from the camp.[70] Jews who had escaped from other places also took to these same forests. A report from 1944 noted, "The Jewish detachments which forced their way through the walls of the Warsaw ghetto, were also to be found in the woods and hills where they organized and strengthened their forces by recruiting young Jews from the Polish ghettos and labor camps and death camps." These Jewish partisan groups not only hid in the forests but also attacked German garrisons and sabotaged railways, ammunition dumps, and other installations. Between April and August 1943, for illustration, a crucial railway line supplying the German war front was cut eleven times, and the same groups blew up a convey near Husiatyn (in present-day Ukraine) that killed many Germans.[71] While some Treblinka escapees stumbled upon these Jewish partisan groups by chance, others had the explicit goal beforehand of linking up with them or forming their own.[72]

The very real possibility also existed of encountering other partisan groups—including those not as welcoming toward Jews. Celina Kalembaziak noted that many "gangs or partisans . . . prowled in the nearby forests."[73] Some forest landscapes were thus a free-for-all containing a medley ranging from roaming bands of opportunists and criminals, to individuals hiding from the Nazis, to paramilitary groups of Polish nationals resuming the battle against the Germans. Notable among the latter was the Wilków Military Organization (WMO) in Węgrów (25 km), which operated in the area around Małkinia (7 km) and Treblinka (4 km) from 1940 to 1942. The field commander of the WMO, Władysław Rażmowski, stated that he worked to "train a platoon for night and sabotage operations and to conduct exercises aimed at controlling the Małkinia railway junction and the Treblinka camp."[74] The WMO was affiliated with a larger, better-known paramilitary group called the Polish Home Army (commonly called the AK), which had a number of units operating throughout Poland. Yet the AK was not always sympathetic to the plight of Jews, and in fact, they killed Jews on occasion.[75] Nonetheless, several Treblinka escapees assumed the risk and joined the group anyway, often using fake identities. Edward Sypko took this route after escaping from Treblinka: "I made contact with an organization. They made new documents for me in a different name. My new name was Henry Molski. . . . I immediately went to the partisan unit and was put into the sabotage and subversion section."[76]

Another group of people found in the woods near Treblinka were German and Ukrainian guards. As Rażmowski experienced while performing reconnaissance for the AK, a person "could not go any farther in the forest because there were so many patrols of SS and Ukrainians who were guarding the camp."[77] Treblinka survivor Szymon Goldberg recalled that the zone of danger around Treblinka varied and that several Ukrainians chased his group for what he estimated to be four to five kilometers after he escaped the camp.[78] Since they often tortured or killed anyone they caught, these guards posed a constant threat to anyone trying to survive long term in the forests. As Rajchman, escaping with a man named Masaryk, described, "When [Masaryk] saw the Germans near the field, he cut his veins. He did not want . . . the Germans to take him alive. . . . I bandaged his arm. I grabbed his arm and stopped the bleeding. . . . We don't know if he survived."[79] The fear of these patrols often decreased precipitously the farther one moved away from Treblinka, but no matter the distance gained, the threat of being denounced by the local population never abated.

Far and away the largest number of people occupying the spaces outside Treblinka were local Poles who lived there. Different from the other, more transitory groups roaming the forests, these Poles were intimately familiar with the landscapes around Treblinka—spaces consisting for them of family, home, and often livelihood. Some of the first Polish-Jewish encounters around Treblinka occurred before the escapes even took place. Many Jewish survivors (and Polish witnesses) recalled a trade system that occurred between local Poles and the Jews of the Waldkommando that was able to take place because Ukrainian guards looked away, were bribed, or sometimes even joined in the process. Krzepicki recalled the first time he encountered this situation, when, as part of the Waldkommando, he overheard the Ukrainian guards whispering to "a peasant couple bustling among the trees, alongside another peasant."[80] Schneiderman noted similarly, "We used to go up with the Germans in the woods to chop, to bring in the young trees . . . so farmers used to bring up some food there."[81] Grinberg said that after several excursions, they had developed a rather elaborate system of trade with local Poles, in which "the peasants would bring packages, set them down some distance away and hold two fingers up to their eyes. This meant they wanted 20 dollars."[82]

In fact, trade and interactions between these groups became so commonplace that Jews sometimes took advantage of the familiar situation to try to escape. An anonymous survivor whose writings were found in the Oyneg Shabes Archive noted that one day, he and four other Jews went into the forest to gather sticks and branches (ostensibly as members of the Tarnungskommando, or Camouflage Brigade). When they reached what he estimated to be between one and one-and-a-half kilometers from the camp, their Ukrainian guard stopped to buy vodka from a local Pole who frequently traded with the Tarnungskommando, and while the Ukrainian was distracted negotiating the trade, the five Jews fled.[83]

The black market established between the local Poles and the Jews (and Ukrainians) from Treblinka continued for the duration of the camp's existence. Through this trade, those inside the camp acquired bread, cigarettes, alcohol, salami, canned goods, and even some of the weapons later used in the 1943 revolt.[84] The weapon trade was especially delicate. Stanisława Stefańczuka, a native of Kosów Lacki (7 km) who worked with the local AK unit and frequently traded with Tarnungskommando members, recalled how it happened while volunteering for a Polish work contingent one day: "After reaching the camp, we met an ss-man who told us to transport the gravel from a nearby pit. Driving up to the gravel pit gate, we encountered a dozen or so Polish Jews. . . . I managed to communicate in whispers with one of them regarding the next transport of firearms." On the specified date when Stefańczuka returned, he recounted, "I informed [the Jewish prisoner] that there was a weapon under the cart. . . . After some time, about 20 minutes, I received an empty cart from the gravel pit and found there was no longer a weapon hidden there because the Jew had taken it. In total, in this manner, I transferred 11 short firearms and four defensive grenades to the camp."[85]

Polish-Jewish interactions occurring *after* the Jews had escaped Treblinka, however, often looked much different than these mutually beneficial encounters at the camp's fringes. Specifically, these escape encounters were almost always random and depended on several variables, including which direction Jews traveled after escaping, the proximity of various houses along any given escape path, and even where Polish people were located—inside the home, out in the field working, traveling between villages—as escapees passed by. The strategy Jews chose as they escaped also determined much regarding these happenstance encounters. As Rajgrodzki recalled, his group's strategy was to travel only during the night, while "during the day, [they] approached the cottages that stood next to the forest [for food]."[86] Here, they chose to interact only with houses located on the edges of forests, bypassing many others. Chaim Grabel pursued a similar strategy, "We hid in the forest during daytime, and we traveled at night. . . . I spent nights in the forests, I asked for directions in solitary cottages and I also asked for food."[87] For some, the idea of approaching stand-alone residences near the forest edge seemed safer than entering villages potentially full of people. Others, though, pursued different tactics, changing the complex calculus that determined who they encountered, where, and when. Dawid Nowodworski, for instance, reasoned that increasing, rather than decreasing, his interactions with local Poles meant a higher likelihood of receiving aid. Near the village of Kosów Lacki (7 km), Nowodworski "knocked on the door of *each* hut" he came across—though, having no luck, he ultimately stole eggs from a farm and then hid in an abandoned barn.[88]

Strategies aside, most Polish-Jewish interactions took place adjacent to or within proximity of a Polish home. And here sits a stark juxtaposition between the relative safety and comfort we associate with spaces of home and the struggle, fear, and uncertainty a fugitive from a death camp experienced. Willenberg illustrates this dichotomy when retelling the story of his own escape from Treblinka. Emerging from the thick forests surrounding the camp, he was struck by the relatively tranquil, perhaps "normal" village scene he encountered: "I heard cows lowing in their barns, the sound of water being pumped from a well, a group of children wandering about the village streets. Weak light illuminated house windows." Remarkable when seen through the eyes of a Treblinka survivor, this serene, even quotidian scene offered the comforting simulacrum of a normal village, replete with inviting glows and country sounds, where life carried on only a few kilometers from the camp. Though he might have been tempted, Willenberg could not linger. Injured and in need of assistance, he took the risk of randomly selecting one of these houses, with its illuminated windows, and knocked on the door.[89] The chain of events that happened next, dictated by nothing more than proximity and chance, meant life or death.

Barbara Goska, a local Pole who lived in both Treblinka (4 km) and Wólka Okrąglik (1 km) during the war, recalled what it was like (though on a different occasion) to be on the other side of that door. One evening, she was startled by a sound: "A Jew knocked on the window of our house asking for clothing and food. We gave him what he asked for and urged him to run toward Rytele [5 km]. However, we later discovered that he had turned back to the camp out of fear."[90] Willenberg too received the help he needed when he chanced knocking on a stranger's door in the dead of night. But it becomes clear that these interactions were every bit as random for Poles living "safely" inside their homes as they were for Jews raising their knuckles to the doors.

Yet if you were a Pole living in the general vicinity of Treblinka, it seems the chances of an escapee suddenly showing up at your door were relatively high compared to areas farther afield. In fact, as Eugenia Samuel from Wólka Okrąglik (1 km) remembered, from her home, "you could see [the Jews] fleeing through the woods, across the fields from one side to the other."[91] Henryk Slebzak, also of Wólka Okrąglik, recalled similarly that since his house bordered a wide, open field through which escapees had to cross, he had the following view during the August 2 revolt: "From the forest, they ran away here, you know, they dropped into the village. . . . From the village they ran away into a meadow there. . . . I was watching all these Jews . . . one group of seven or eight, the other of ten. . . . They walked in groups [and] they went as if they were escaping." When asked by the interviewer if he stood by his window watching this scene, Slebzak replied, "Yes, that's how I know how many there were."[92] The imagery of a man standing in the comfort of his own living room watching people escape from a nearby death camp is striking for its spatial contrast—safety and security separated from despair and anguish by a pane of glass and a few meters of real estate.

It was not only the major revolt of August 2 that spurred these encounters, though, and Anna Kazierodek from Poniatowo (1 km) stated, "I was witness to *several* such escapes" (from inside her home).[93] In fact, Czesław

Borowy, who lived in Treblinka (4 km), recalled that some nights, he had to sleep on the floor inside his house to avoid stray bullets coming through the walls accidentally. With its flimsy wooden walls and its location along a main road elevated on a slight hill, his home became a backdrop to the "very dangerous" drama of escaping Jews and the guards firing away at them.[94] Considered spatially, his home's happenstance proximity to the route escaping Jews took altered Borowy's most basic behaviors inside the (no-longer-promised) safety of his own domestic space for the duration of the camp's existence.

Given the frequency of these encounters, passive witnessing from inside one's home often gave way to direct interaction. Stanisława Rytel, who lived in Rytele Wszołki (7 km), recalled, "During the time of the camp at Treblinka, Jews were at my place three or four times. They escaped from the camp and asked for food. We brought them food under a pine tree."[95] Treblinka (4 km) resident Halina Borowa (born Socha)—daughter of Karol Socha, who was later named "Righteous Among the Nations"—recalled the moment she discovered the person who had been living, unbeknownst to her, within the spaces of her home: "I was a child at the time, and my parents didn't talk about the Jew hiding in our barn. By chance, I discovered this man. . . . As I entered the barn, I noticed a human head leaning out. He initially thought I was my dad. Maybe he was hungry and anxiously awaited his return. I found myself in the role of uninvited guest, but later also in the role of his savior. I had to hold my tongue, I had to be a prudent and thoughtful child, since I was entrusted with adult duties."[96] In this case, what undoubtedly started as a random encounter between an escaping Jewish person and a local Pole turned into a long-term interaction through the shelter provided.

Indeed, opening one's home to strangers represented among the most intimate of interactions between Jewish survivors from Treblinka and local Poles, and examples abound. Many Poles later spoke of a person near Treblinka named Kolasiński who often "risked his own life" by hiding Jews in his cellar, many of whom "probably survived to this day" because of him.[97] So it was also for the Karczmarczyk family, who lived near the small village of Brzózka (9 km), an area the Germans used as a makeshift collection point for Jews they were transferring from nearby areas to Treblinka. Here, these groups "camped in the vast woods . . . next to the Karczmarczyk household. . . . Jews from all corners began to be gathered in the meadows of birch. . . . Almost everyone went to a 'better life' in Kosów and then to Treblinka. . . . Only a few remained in the house of the Karczmarczyk family." With the increasing awareness that the "better life" ahead actually meant death, the Karczmarczyk family began to hide Jews in their home. When the obvious hiding spaces filled up, the family altered their house—constructing a room with no floor where up to eight more people could hide. Yet opening their home to Jews meant German guards also frequently infiltrated their space, and the guards often "searched the whole house thoroughly. They looked in every little corner."[98] In a way, therefore, by the random nature of the holding area that sprung up near their house, the Karczmarczyk home became closely intertwined with the lives (and sometimes deaths at the hands of the guards) of all those who passed through that space. And certainly, death did frequently follow into these Polish spaces. Hejnoch Brener and the five others he escaped with ended up at the farmstead of Stanisław Pogorzelski, who lived near the village of Orzeszówka (18 km). When they asked Pogorzelski for help, he took them to his home, prepared hiding places, and hid the Jews for over a year. During this time, however, one of the escapees, Heniek Klein, fell ill with tuberculosis, died, and was buried near the Pogorzelski house.[99] His grave and body are now located near the homestead of a Polish family he only met at random, and only because he escaped a death camp that happened to be located nearby—his remains now a permanent spatial marker of the intersecting lives of the human landscapes of Treblinka.

The spaces where local Poles worked—often in or near their homes, where they were usually grazing cattle or tending fields—also became sites of interactions with Jewish survivors. Eugeniusz Goska from Wólka Okrąglik (1 km) described the randomness of these encounters: "Once, when I was walking amongst the cows grazing here . . . there was an escaped Jew."[100] Slebzak had a similar encounter in the town of Treblinka (4 km): "When we fed our cows, [the escapees] came out of the forest. . . . I used to graze this land here . . . near the camp, I grazed cows. One [escapee] came to me. . . . I gave him something to eat, and I told him the Germans are right here nearby, so I told him to go to the forest, there was a rake there, and I told him to go get that rake, go to the forest, but I don't know if he survived."[101] Stanisława Bruszewska (born Gałązka) from Boreczek (4 km) had a more perilous encounter:

I was grazing cattle in a meadow. I looped the end of the chain in my hand, and I fell asleep. When I woke up, I saw two naked Jews near me. They were about eleven or twelve years old. I was scared. I had heard that Jews ran away. . . . They told me they wanted to eat. I told them, "Wait here, I'll run home, which is close by, and I'll bring you bread." When I came back to them with bread they were gone. Two Germans were there instead. If they had come this way earlier, they would have killed me along with those Jews.[102]

Although this interaction occurred within a space familiar to her, Bruszewska was lucky to escape with her life, considering the consequences these experiences could carry.

Random, frequent, and often intimate, these Polish-Jewish interactions also had another common facet: uncertainty as to *how* the encounter would go. Though existing on a behavioral continuum—ranging from helping, to showing indifference, to hurting and including a variety of gray in between—the responses Jews received when interacting with Poles were unpredictable (probably for both sides in most cases) and imminently consequential. Rajchman's experience after escaping Treblinka illustrates the precarious nature of these encounters:

I looked like a living skeleton. We all did. When I wandered from village to village . . . I met a man. He [came] close and I greeted him in Polish. . . . The man paused and asked me, "Are you a Jew?" I said, "Yes." Then he said, "Are you one of the people who burned Treblinka?" I said, "Yes." This Christian man, who was walking in the opposite direction from where I came, turned back, and taking . . . my arm said, "I am taking you to my home." When his wife saw the way I looked, his wife looked at me. . . . She ordered me . . . to take off my soiled shirt and gave me a clean one. You know what she said to me? "This is my husband's only extra shirt." They gave it to me. They gave me a healthy meal.[103]

One can sense Rajchman's uncertainty in this interaction, and he reveals only at the end that this encounter was helpful and probably saved his life. Indeed, in the areas around Treblinka, several survivors encountered this altruistic behavior. Szmuel Miedziński, who managed to escape Treblinka and return to his hometown of Sokołów Podlaski (27 km), encountered a Polish neighbor named Bolesław Pietraszek who not only hid Miedziński and seventeen other Jews but also tried to provide for them. "Within the first months we lived . . . in a room upstairs, after that we were in a barn," Miedziński recalled. "One shelter we had was under a pigsty and another was in a barn. . . . Every week the owner baked pastries for us and gave us 25 kilos of bread and coffee two times a day. . . . We had enough food. All these Jews survived."[104]

Helping behaviors obviously gave Jews a better chance at short-term and long-term survival, and even the simplest gesture could prove meaningful. Sypko recalled that after escaping, he came to a village (perhaps on the opposite side of the Bug River, between 4 and 7 km from Treblinka): "At the edge of the forest, there was a house. I went quietly to the house and said to the woman in the yard 'Good evening, ma'am.'" The woman had heard of Treblinka, and she gave Sypko milk and bread before he moved on.[105] During his escape, Nowodworski recalled that near Sadowne (13 km), he met "good peasants" who "pitied and sympathized" with him and with the plight of the Jews, asking, "Why are you being killed?" The peasants then gave Nowodworski milk and potatoes and explained that there was a group of Jews hiding out near the village of Stoczek (13 km) and that he should go there next. (He followed this advice and was "welcomed" by the group.)[106] Many who survived remembered these simple gestures long after the war. Auerbach recalls how a Treblinka survivor she was traveling with asked for a brief detour so that he could "visit 'his' peasant and . . . give him a new shirt, with thanks, to replace the shirt the man had given him when he was a fugitive, wounded and bleeding, after the uprising, with the manhunt pursuing him from all sides."[107]

Aside from what seems to have been altruism, others may have helped Jews for different motives. Kolski explained the reasoning of the Pole who helped him: "After the war he want[ed] to show he helped guys from Treblinka. . . . He brought us out bread and butter and butter and milk. . . . He [let] us shave and [brought us] water to wash. . . . He bought the tickets . . . [to] the train [that] goes every day in the morning at seven, eight o'clock to Warsaw."[108] The clear question here is, *Why* did he care about his postwar image? We have only Kolski's words to speculate from (for instance, Kolski leaves unclear whether the man said this or only implied it), but regardless, determining clear motives for behaviors was (and still is) a very murky process. As Helfing recalled of his own encounter, "The next day, we didn't know where to go. . . . I saw a little farm, a farmer, all by himself. I was with another guy. And we got into his place, and we told him the story and he kept us, hiding . . . but later he used us to help him work."[109] Helfing's statement that they were later *used* for work highlights the shades of gray in determining motivation. Did this man help altruistically, and the work was simply unrelated? Did he employ the Jews as a clever way to avoid arousing undue suspicion from passersby? Was the work offered in exchange for continued support, a detail Helfing leaves out? Impossible to determine definitively here, it does insinuate that for some Poles, the risk of helping had to be worth the benefit. In fact, Krzepicki stated as much when remembering an interaction with a Pole: "If not for the fear of the Germans, he would take me in for free, but it's not worth it, the risk is too great."[110] The price required to offset the danger was high—after leaving Treblinka, Sonia Lieber encountered a Pole who gave her food, but only in exchange for a quantity of gold.[111] Similar stories within Holocaust testimonies abound.

There was always the chance, though, that their knock on the door or the request for help would be met with hostility or worse. Szymon Goldberg escaped Treblinka with a large group of Jews, but few made it beyond about ten kilometers from the camp, because, he recalled, as they passed through "all the villages around [the camp]," most of them were caught by locals and led back to the Germans. Goldberg added that even if they evaded recapture, they still faced mortal danger, and once, about seven kilometers from Treblinka, a Polish person shot at him and unleashed his dog to chase the group down.[112] Maria Krych, who lived with a partisan group near Treblinka, recounted the following story an escapee told: "Eight of us escaped. We sat in the forest behind Siedlce for two days without food. At night we went to the colony. We tried to give a peasant a gold ring for bread. On the third day, he came with some individuals who had grenades, and they pulled us out of hiding, robbed us, and threw the grenades at us. I don't know what happened to my companions. Naked I escaped back to the forest."[113]

Despite clearer examples, many interactions between Jews and Poles cannot be quantified in simple binary terms of helpful or hurtful. Take Rajchman's encounter: "The first night I was sleeping in a field. It was raining all night. I rambled toward a farmhouse and started talking to the peasants. At that moment we heard shots and shouting. The peasant crossed himself and started to shake. 'Please,' he urged, 'run away! If they will find you with me, I will be killed.'"[114] Panicked by the nearby gunfire, the peasant wanted the interaction to end, hastening Rajchman on his way. His fear arose because, as Henryka Sinakowska of Kosów Lacki (7 km) remembered, "it was announced you could be shot for hiding or helping [Jews]. The death penalty!"[115] In such an atmosphere, many interactions were characterized, like Rajchman's, by hurried dismissals. Samuel Rajzman also met a Pole who told him, "'You must be from Treblinka.' . . . He said, 'I'll tell you—you better get going. There's such a search going on all over this neighborhood; it's unbelievable. They're looking for those who escaped from Treblinka.'"[116] From a spatial standpoint, this trend seemed more common in the areas nearest the camp, and it seemed to lessen somewhat the farther one traveled. "The peasants around Treblinka refused to give me shelter even for a night. Everyone willingly gave me food and even money. But they didn't even give thought to the overnight stay because Ukrainians working in Treblinka often visited them," survivor Samuel Puterman observed. "As I got closer to Warsaw, they gave me accommodation for a night, but there was no question of stopping permanently."[117]

Escaping Jews soon learned they should be ready for any reaction when they knocked on doors or otherwise encountered local populations. Rajgrodzki and his fellow escapees developed a cautious but calculated method to approaching houses: "Usually my companion stood at a distance with his rifle, but in such a way that he was still visible, and I approached alone to ask for bread." In one encounter, he recalled, they paid a peasant for the requested supplies, and in response, the man let them stay at his house for a time, even offering vodka. Cautiously accepting the kindness, Rajgrodzki could not let his guard down: "For a moment, the thought passed our minds that maybe he would bring the police, but the peasant was decent and had a drink with us before we moved farther on."[118]

Given the danger, many found it easiest simply to avoid other people altogether. Krzepicki employed this approach when, upon reaching the village of Stoczek (13 km), he and the others hiding with him decided to pause and wait for the peasants to leave their fields: "We went out to the meadow where the haystacks were located and buried ourselves in hay and slept."[119] For many, this avoidance was less a strategy than a realization that only a limited number of places existed where they could find shelter and not risk being recaptured and sent back to Treblinka. As Czechowicz recalled of his escape, "We walked all night until we got to Kosów [7 km]. . . . When I was in Kosów, I watched 600 people who were driven on foot to Treblinka from there." Recognizing this was clearly not a good place to hide, Czechowicz continued onward until he reached Warsaw. And while he managed to survive in the city and evade recapture, another man with him was recaptured, sent back to Treblinka, and murdered in the gas chambers in January 1943.[120] This illustrates another stark spatial aspect of the escape: the specter of being returned to Treblinka followed survivors everywhere.

For many, this meant taking even further evasive steps once freed from the confines of the camp, like disguising themselves or finding ways to mask their Jewish identities. Upon approaching a cottage on the edge of a village to ask for bread, Klajman recalled,

> I didn't look especially Jewish. An elderly woman was busy in the home, and the rest of the family was out working in the field. Only this elderly Christian woman, alone, was sitting on the doorstep. She gave me a piece of bread and a glass of milk. I sat down and ate. The old lady asked me where I'm from. I told her that I am from Warsaw and that I am looking for a job. She told me that the military police were out looking for just such people who wander around. She said, 'If they find you, they'll send you to a concentration camp.' . . . If the old woman knew I was a Jew, she wouldn't just let me sit, she'd chase me away. But she didn't know I was Jewish.[121]

While Klajman relied on his "not especially Jewish" appearance (as he put it) to aid his survival, others had to manufacture stories to explain their presence in the woods. Rajgrodzki remembered, "We of course said we were from the Polish Army, which operated in secret. [People] didn't recognize us as Jews. I was fairly well dressed, and I didn't appear suspicious."[122] In this way Rajgrodzki passed himself off as a partisan and consequently probably received more assistance.[123] In fact, if one's identity was disguised well enough, one might attempt to come out of the woods and embed oneself in "normal" non-Jewish life. Mojżesz Mydło took this path: "All night [after escaping Treblinka] I wandered through the forests and the fields until I arrived at the village of Paproć. I turned to the village administration, Volksdeutsche [ethnic German] Jan Knajp, asking him to accept me as a shepherd. Knajp agreed. For a long time, he didn't know that I was Jewish at all. When I became convinced that he was a good man, because he gave food to a Jewish manufacturer from Wołomin hidden in a barn, I finally confided in him that I was Jewish."[124] Though risky, hiding in plain sight worked well for Mydło, and it is plausible he might have kept it up indefinitely had he not felt comfortable disclosing his real identity.

Mydło's example highlights something else—the sheer extent of the interactional space around Treblinka. Measured in a straight line, Paproć sits approximately twenty-five kilometers away from the camp. While it took several days and nights to travel this distance on foot, others found quicker options. After initially walking fifteen kilometers, Chaim Grabel recounted, "We then took a cart and two horses from some peasant and we continued on by cart," thereby more rapidly increasing the distance from Treblinka.[125] Charted spatially, these disparate escape vectors extended out in almost any direction from the camp. For instance, while Paproć sits almost due north of Treblinka, Rajzman, after three days on the run through the forests, found himself near the village of Węgrów, twenty-five kilometers *south* of Treblinka.[126] This random but consistent spread of escaping Jews into all the spaces around Treblinka created a situation where, in Auerbach's words, "all the Poles of that area, the Siedlce region and particularly the Sokołów districts, had seen a lot and knew plenty."[127]

Yet the reach of these interactions cannot be measured simply by geographical distances. Perhaps one of the most striking features of the entire interactional space around Treblinka was the transnational character of it. The Central Commission Report states that after the war, "a collection of coins, Polish, Soviet, German, Austrian, Czech, Greek, Belgian, French and even American" were dug up during leveling operations at Treblinka. Willenberg recalled even seeing a coin from China amid many others from "all over the world."[128] Another local witness stated that other documents found lying about in Treblinka included identification papers from a Jew from Göttingen (Germany), several Soviet passports, and even a diploma issued by Cambridge University (England).[129] Though discovered in Treblinka, these material objects represent the internationality of not only those sent to the camp but likely those who escaped as well. Who knows how far out into the surrounding world this panoply of foreign currency, documents, and other items journeyed alongside those seeking safety from Treblinka (or if some of it still remains forgotten in attics, hidden in storage sheds, or buried underground in the nearby fields and forests).

The Polish World around Treblinka

The many Polish-Jewish interactions in the areas around Treblinka and the variety of behavioral responses exhibited have often raised questions about the mindset and motivations of local Poles. Were their behaviors the result of prewar antisemitism? The quest for financial gain? Using the chaos of war as a cover for settling personal scores? The inherent altruism and virtue some seem to be born with? Undoubtedly, we can only sufficiently answer these questions on a case-by-case basis, taking into consideration the confluence of circumstances factoring into each specific encounter. One factor that should be considered, however, in explaining complex behavioral motivations and responses is the unique spatial aspects of occupied Poland.

Existing as an independent nation since the 1919 Versailles Treaty resurrected it as a buffer zone between Germany and the Soviet Union, Poland and its citizens had known relative freedom in dictating their own affairs over the twenty years preceding the outbreak of World War II. After the 1939 German invasion of Poland, however, Poles were largely reduced to subalterns as their formerly sovereign territory was absorbed into the Reich in some places and colonized in others. Nazi ideologue Alfred Rosenberg once wrote, "In the East, Germany is carrying on a three-fold war: a war for the destruction of Bolshevism, a war for the destruction of the greater Russian Empire and finally a war for the acquisition of colonial territory for colonizing purposes and economic exploitation." As a result, Polish cities and rural family homesteads were replaced by spaces defined by uncertainty, fear, and hostility, and Poles were subject to new foreign-born laws that included the compulsory confiscation of their property *if* it was "required for the public welfare." Far from an idle phrase, by May 1943 alone, the Germans had already seized (and presumably ransacked) 693,252 large estates and farms in the combined eastern territories, 9,508 of which they ended up confiscating entirely.[130]

Without mincing words, Hans Frank, head of the General Government, decreed that "Poland shall be treated as a colony," and since Nazi racial hierarchies positioned Poles only slightly above Jews, Frank added, "The

Poles shall be the slaves of the Greater German World Empire." In fact, at Nuremberg, prosecutors found a "secret thesis" from the Academy of German Law dating from January 1940 that encouraged an intentional reduction in the overall Polish population through "deportation of Jews, intellectuals, and leaders of the Polish economy, and by measures to discourage and stifle Polish propagation. . . . The fertility of the Polish people was to be reduced by keeping hundreds of thousands of Polish workers in Germany for forced labor, and by employing one million Poles in Germany as wandering agricultural workers. The annexed territories were to be Germanized by the settlement of German population in strips, designed to encircle those areas containing Polish majorities." The document goes on: "The strictest care is to be taken that secret circulars, memoranda and official correspondence which contain instructions detrimental to the Poles are kept steadily under lock and key."[131] Although not directly marked for destruction like the Jews, Poles were targeted by subjugation and elimination from public life as determined by Nazi policies (which changed on a whim) like *Generalplan Ost* (General Plan East), which suggested potentially deporting or starving millions of Slavic people in the newly annexed German territories.[132] In the meantime, the AK's *Biuletyn Informacyjny* (*Information Bulletin*) from December 16, 1943, reported, "The deliberate instilling of terror and panic through spreading news that is unfounded, exaggerated, and sometimes absurd, is a German work . . . of mental terror that is supposed to break down Polish society."[133]

Moreover, amid this atmosphere, Poles were also in constant danger of ending up in Treblinka themselves. The local Nazi administration passed laws threatening Poles with arrest and imprisonment for offenses including failing to meet grain quotas, disobeying German orders, and giving aid to Jews (later punishable by death). "It was a bitter reality," local railway worker Franciszek Ząbecki observed. "Exceeding the provisions of Nazi law was necessary and unavoidable. It was a struggle for a proverbial piece of bread." In a world where daily survival meant breaking German laws, giving aid to Jews became just one further way to incur risk—especially since Germans often followed through on their threats to punish anyone they caught.[134]

Beneath the contempt Germans held for Poles as colonized subjects and in concert with perceiving Polish land and property as free for the taking, Poles lost even the sovereignty over their private spaces of home. Lucjan Puchała of Wólka Okrąglik (1 km) recalled, "One day, my house had been

searched and they had found packages and letters to people in the camp."
For this, he was sentenced to six months at Treblinka I (the work camp).[135]
Suspicious of Puchała's behavior, the Germans simply came into his home to
find the incriminating evidence they sought, but in reality the Germans could
enter Polish spaces without pretext and could search for and take anything
they wanted. Given the threat of this type of intrusion, Ząbecki explained,
"I had to be more cautious, especially since the Germans had a lot of free
time. . . . They wandered around, visited farmers, extorted dairy products
and eggs. . . . They were interested in life in the surrounding villages. Such
penetration of the area gave us a lot to think about."[136]

In one instance, Treblinka commandant Franz Stangl ordered a thorough
investigation of the nearby town of Treblinka (4 km) to find an escaped
Ukrainian guard.[137] Such investigations probably took a similar form to
something Celina Kalembaziak witnessed in September 1942. While looking out the window of her house, she saw eighty Germans armed "with
machine guns, speeding toward the village of Złotki [4 km]." She continued,
"I ran out of the house and followed the Germans toward the village. I saw
how the Germans immediately surrounded the village . . . preventing any
escape from the peasants." In this "roundup action," perhaps looking for
contraband or escaped Jews, the Germans proceeded to search every house
in the area. Kalembaziak noted that other peasants, blocked from escaping
until the search ended, "in panic, began to flee or hide in the barns, in
haystacks, or in the recesses of their homes."[138] Spatially, when threatened
near the safety of one's home, one's instinct is to retreat back inside of it;
yet here, even these "recesses" inside a familiar space were no longer safely
available. The story of Stanisław Przyborowksi reveals how deeply this
truth ran in occupied Poland. A steam engine driver from Wólka Okrąglik
(1 km) working in Małkinia (7 km), Przyborowski refused a German order
to drive trains to Treblinka transporting cattle cars loaded with Jews.
Instead, he went into hiding. One day, after emerging for a meal at his
brother's house in Wólka Okrąglik, Przyborowski was arrested and sent
to Treblinka I, where he later perished.[139] The reach of the occupying Germans seemed pervasive, omnipresent, and unnerving, and even Ukrainian
auxiliaries could show up for an unannounced search. "The Ukrainians
invaded peoples' homes and demanded gold," Wiernik recalled. "They . . .
applied terroristic methods."[140]

Local residents could also end up in Treblinka without having broken any specific law. One day Eugenia Samuel of Wólka Okrąglik (1 km) was walking home from the town of Treblinka (4 km). She later stated, "I was stopped by the ss-men along with some Ukrainians who took me for a Jewish woman who had escaped . . . and they took me to the camp . . . [and] beat me." Samuel was finally able to convince them she was not Jewish, but her uncle, a Pole named Józef Podleś, was not so lucky. According to Samuel, Podleś was murdered in Treblinka after also being caught and admitting to helping Jews.[141] The terror continued even after one's release from Treblinka. Jan Suł-kowski, interviewed after the war by the Commission for the Investigation of German Crimes in Poland, said that upon being released from Treblinka I, "the commandant forbade us to tell anybody about what we had seen in the camp, and threatened that if we did, we and our families would die."[142] Those who had experienced the camp firsthand held no illusions as to the veracity of these threats.[143]

Adding to the atmosphere of uncertainty and fear were two other ele-ments: the random nature of German spatial intrusions and how far the "jurisdiction of Treblinka," as I will call it, reached into the lives of those nearby. For instance, when Stangl heard that weapons were being traded in the nearby village of Grądy (2.5 km), he sent ss men and Ukrainians there who arrested between twenty-two and twenty-eight people, including women and children. These Grądy residents were sent to Treblinka with their hands raised and were never heard from again.[144] In this instance, Stangl's authority over the camp extended into the nearby world, and ss men from Treblinka literally came to get people in their homes and took them back to the camp.

Spontaneous reprisal actions to avenge Germans who were killed (whether by Poles, partisans, or accidents it mattered little), might have represented the most indiscriminate expression of German spatial con-trol. "I remember they brought eighty-two peasants arrested from the nearby village of Rogów [30 km]," Sypko once observed. "A German was killed somewhere nearby. . . . Women, the elderly and the children were released, but the young men, in their prime, were packed into a car and brought [to Treblinka]. After five weeks, seventeen of them were dead."[145] Moreover, the threat of Treblinka loomed for many kilometers beyond the camp and surrounding towns, and even Poles from more distant places could end up there. Zygmunt Chłopek remembered that in June 1943 in Rogów, Germans under the direction of Siedlce district leader Ernst Gramss rounded up several townspeople, probably as a reprisal, and sent them to Treblinka.[146]

Ząbecki later summed up the overall feeling among local Poles resulting from the constant intrusion upon their daily lives and spaces: "As long as the smoke rose above the forest, the Germans were not to be trusted."[147] Jerzy Królikowski, who worked on area railways and built bridges, noted that a type of siege mentality developed, and "a very sober Polish collective formed on the construction site, constituting a kind of family together; solidarity connected with a sense of hatred for the occupiers and a willingness to defend against them."[148] Yet resistance in light of promised punishments and spatial intrusions meant risking everything, and the high price put on choosing prewar *right* over *wrong* reflected the new, upside-down morality Germans tried to instill in their colonized people and places. In this way, Polish landscapes around Treblinka often became liminal spaces for Poles as they navigated a strange new reality in which they lacked not only sovereignty but, increasingly, moral direction.

Therefore, when someone like Stanisława Bruszewska, living in Boreczek (4 km), states that "war weakens people's moral sensitivity," she is probably not solely offering an apologetic justification for the actions taken by some Poles.[149] She may, in fact, be invoking the very real "gray zone," to borrow again from Primo Levi's astute concept, whereby situational reality (including the changing spatial environment) often dictates human behavior, something that is already malleable—and fickle—to begin with.[150] Often, though, the only way most learned how they would respond to this new morality dictated by the ethics of German colonization was to be thrust into a situation where they had to act.

This contemporaneous spatial plurality of experience meant that outcomes of these interactions almost always varied, which resulted in a space where escaping Jews not only dealt with unfamiliar natural spaces outside Treblinka but also never knew what response they would face when knocking on the door of a local inhabitant. If this chapter has shown anything, then, perhaps it is that *most* Poles probably did not know how they would respond either. As Ząbecki once ruminated aloud about the spaces he and other Poles around Treblinka occupied during the war, "How can someone live here? How can someone look at these macabre scenes . . . that tear at the nerves and threaten a mental breakdown?"[151] This question takes on even more prescient, if not more horrifying, substance when we understand that alongside escaping human beings and German guards threatening punishment, Treblinka also expelled into Polish landscapes the full range of smells, sights, and sounds of mass murder.

A Sensory Space

The weather was extremely hot, and each grave,
when opened, gave off a nauseating stench. Once
the Germans threw some burning object into an
opened grave to see what would happen. Clouds of
black smoke began to pour out at once and the fire
that started glimmered all day long.

—Yankel Wiernik, *A Year in Treblinka*

Though Nazi planners tried to isolate and hide Operation Reinhard, the death camps were not, and could never be, isolated from the world in which they existed. On one hand, there was a veritable flow of humans escaping Treblinka who interacted with people around the camp. On the other, there existed a much wider opportunity for those outside Treblinka to witness the death camp "next door"—the sheer *scale* of human destruction being carried out there. During the camp's "busiest" times, roughly from August to December 1942, "the gas chambers were in operation until 1 am and finished off more than 20,000 corpses within 24 hours."[1] This level of mass killing was not contained within Treblinka's small physical boundaries, and the reality was that the smells, sights, and sounds of mass murder—a set of sensory phenomena I call "sensory contamination"—spread so widely throughout the nearby countryside that, as one witness remembered, "it often '*filled* the air for many kilometers.'"[2]

Scholars familiar with the Reinhard camps in general, and Treblinka specifically, have acknowledged the existence of this sensory contamination. Doris Bergen, the author of *War and Genocide*, writes that because of the smell, "no one in the area could be unaware of the massive killing operations at Treblinka."[3] Still, few have made deeper inquiries into what these sights, smells, and sounds *meant* for people experiencing them.[4] In this chapter, therefore, I address three specific questions: How *far* did this sensory contamination reach, and *who* was encompassed within the radius of this zone? How did these witnesses *interpret* the sights, smells, and sounds they experienced? How did these interpretations *impact* and potentially *alter* their subsequent day-to-day lives?

In answering these questions, I privilege sensory experience because, as human geographer Paul Rodaway writes, "through their structure and the way we use them, the senses mediate" a person's everyday spatial experiences, and therefore the senses are "the ground base on which a wider geographical understanding can be constructed."[5] In focusing on the corporeal, I also borrow from Simone Gigliotti, who, in her 2009 book *The Train Journey*, analyzes the sensory deprivation inflicted on Jews locked inside overcrowded cattle cars. Gigliotti writes, "The model of sensory witnessing that I identify with train journeys is also applicable to other intense spatial experiences of forced closeness," but I expand on and apply her model to the nonenclosed spaces surrounding Treblinka to show the universal nature of humans interpreting their surroundings sensorily.[6] Thus, while the physical place of Treblinka was fixed, the reach of its sensory contamination into the surrounding world outside its fences acted as a spatial extension of the camp itself. I call this extension a "zone of sensory witnessing," because if one was close enough to smell, see, or hear the camp, even from several kilometers away, that person should be called a witness to Treblinka. In addition to expanding the number of Treblinka witnesses potentially into the thousands, examining how these people interpreted what they experienced—as well as how this then affected and often changed their daily lives—shows how even distant sensory witnesses were impacted by their spatial proximity to the camp. Notably, many describe in gruesome detail how the sensory elements of Treblinka infiltrated their spaces, "obliging" them—as it does us today—to confront the "oppressive imaginable," as Georges Didi-Huberman describes the process of imagining the most horrific elements of the Holocaust "in spite of our own world, full, almost choked, with imaginary commodities."[7]

Although we generally rely on all our senses to gather knowledge, I organize the analysis of sensory witnessing that follows into three distinct categories of sensory stimuli—smell, sight, and sound. This breakdown allows for a focused examination that accounts for the nuances unique to each sensory modality while also highlighting the overlap between them. Moreover, witness statements at a variety of distances from the camp pinpoint these three senses as the ones extending farthest from Treblinka. Thus, despite limitations for those with impairments, the probability of someone in this zone experiencing at least one of the three was extremely high—a fact that, by itself, increases how many people witnessed such sensory contamination.[8]

Another reason to delineate sensory inputs is because they also operate differently at various distances. Spatial theorist J. Douglas Porteous suggests that the senses of smell and sound only operate at geographically "close quarters," and even at a "middle distance" only a "picture world" remains as smell and sound disappear. Nevertheless, even the number of visual witnesses to Treblinka had limits, because as the horizon curves, visual contact is eventually lost. (Though if plumes of smoke or glows from fires extended above the horizon, that could extend visual witnessing.) So while no clear boundaries exist to differentiate close quarters and middle distance, we can confidently call anyone who smelled, saw, or heard something related to Treblinka an "intimate" sensory witness to the camp. After all, only a limited number of people, spatially speaking, could have had any of these experiences.[9] While it is impossible to know for sure the exact dimensions of the zone of sensory witnessing, I approximate it here by referencing how far away (in kilometers) each person outside the camp was when they had their sensory experience. Based on the extent of this evidence, I estimate that the zone of sensory witnessing extended in a roughly circular radius encompassing the space within twenty kilometers around the death camp, with occasional, though rare, exceptions exceeding this area.[10]

Smell

For evolutionary reasons, humans have developed a particularly strong olfactory system, and as a result, smells aid rather robustly in long-term memory creation. As Porteous explains, smells arouse us "strongly and rapidly because olfactory signals plug directly into the brain's limbic system . . . crossing far fewer synapses than do signals emanating from other senses."[11] For sensory witnesses, smells are immediately noticed, offering signals that newly formed spatial stimuli exist nearby. Paradoxically, while "smell memories" can be very accurate, even more so than visual ones, according to some researchers, smell is also easily habituated, which means that after some duration, new smells must enter a particular environment to be noticed.[12] Each of these unique properties of smell existed in the zone of sensory witnessing around Treblinka.

The first new smell to emanate from the camp was the stench of rotting bodies of murdered Jews, which for the first several months were buried in vast pits dug into the earth. As Polish train engineer Lucjan Puchała recalled, these "pits full of corpses covered only with earth opened up as a result of decomposition of the corpses, and there was a horrible stench."[13] As Kazimierz Dudek, a Pole from Wólka Okrąglik (1 km) imprisoned at Treblinka I, described in ghastly detail, "Initially, their bodies were buried 10–15 deep and filled with lime and sand. After some time, these bodies erupted. . . . The gas from the decaying bodies threw a geyser of earth into the air, mixed with slime. It stank up the whole area."[14] Those in closest physical proximity to the pits were Jewish Sonderkommando (special unit)—a group tasked by the Germans with burying bodies. One of their number, Abraham Krzepicki, observed, "The monstrous stench of the decaying bodies was literally . . . nauseating."[15] To evade this sickening stench, fellow Sonderkommando Aron Czechowicz constantly sprayed himself with a bottle of perfume he discovered at the camp's sorting area.[16] Yet as the number of transports to Treblinka increased, especially within the first few months of operation, bodies could not be buried fast enough, compounding the sensory nightmare. As Treblinka survivor and Sonderkommando Yankel Wiernik noted, "The corpses had been lying around for quite some time and decomposition was already setting in, making the air foul with the stench of putrefaction."[17] Survivor Samuel Willenberg remembered that the odor arising from these bodies scattered everywhere was "unavoidable": "The pungent, nauseating stench of decomposing corpses wafted across the camp, penetrated our nostrils, filled our lungs and hung on our lips."[18]

Sensory witnesses have frequently described such smells of Treblinka using the descriptors *fill*, *hang*, and *penetrate*—terms that suggest the smells' power to transform and dominate one's spatial experience even at a distance from the camp. According to a report about Treblinka presented at the Nuremberg trials, "The smell of corpses escaped to poison the surrounding air."[19] As it spread beyond the camp's confines, the smell retained the similar, invasive qualities reported by the Sonderkommando. Jerzy Królikowski recalled from his home in the town of Treblinka (4 km), "It was difficult to get away from when it squeezed into homes through the porous wooden walls, windows, and doors of the country houses in which we lived."[20] Here, sensory contamination from the camp infiltrated local Polish residents' most personal spaces—inside their homes—by *squeezing* through barriers previously believed to separate one from the outside world. In the process, sensory elements created by the killing at Treblinka were deposited inside the intimate spaces, houses, and daily lives of people otherwise physically located at a distance from the camp. Franciszek Ząbecki, the train station-master in the town of Treblinka (4 km), gave voice to this sensory invasion of space: "You must imagine what it was like living here: every day, as of the early morning, these hours of horror when the train arrived, and all the time—after the very first days—this odour, this dark foggy cloud that hung over us, that covered the sky in that hot and beautiful summer, even on the most brilliant days—not a rain-cloud promising relief from the heat, but an almost sulphuric darkness bringing with it this pestilential smell."[21] Ząbecki's description shows how smell can transform a normally pleasant summer day into one where instead of rain clouds, one imagines noxious fogs foretelling darkness. And his use of a synesthetic metaphor—the description of one sensory input using the language of another—is especially telling, because such devices show "knowledge of the factual properties beyond the referents and hence knowledge of the world in general."[22] In other words, Ząbecki's description demonstrates—through extrapolating based on a single sensory input—the process of knowledge creation in action, which is the essence of sensory witnessing.

Królikowski suggested that these new "clouds" of smell did more than invade the local atmosphere; they compelled him to discover the smell's origins, evidently to learn what had changed in his once-familiar landscape. "At first, I thought that somewhere beside the road in the fields lay the remains of some animal," he recalled. "However, after we went a few hundred paces from that place, we could still smell the cadaver scent that came from Treblinka."[23] Instead of remaining a passive witness, he was compelled by the new smell to seek out knowledge about his current spatial reality—a behavioral response that Rodaway suggests exemplifies "the senses both as a relationship to a world and the senses as in themselves a kind of structuring of space and defining of place."[24] Put differently, Królikowski's behavior represents one of the most fundamental spatial realizations a person can have: deriving awareness sensorily, an action triggered merely by a lone sensory input in this case.

The behavioral changes of local Poles went beyond simply trying to understand new spatial realities, though, and the new smells invading their homes usually upended daily life. As Królikowski described, "[The] sickening smell, which could make the faint-of-heart vomit [also] deprived every one of his desire to eat." He recalled that something similar was reported farther down the road in Małkinia (7 km), where a German guard stationed there complained that even from that distance, "it stinks so damned bad, one cannot eat." Królikowski explained that while the smell became "the direct cause of *physical* torment," it also caused specific *psychological* reactions, which sometimes manifested in people he met as "extreme nervousness . . . [that] bordered on a mental breakdown."[25] Indeed, it is not hard to imagine the anxiety, frustration, and dread such a terrible smell could bring in situations of prolonged saturation.

The ability of Treblinka's odors to impact towns several kilometers away highlights both the extent of Treblinka's smellscape and how certain environmental factors, such as the direction and strength of the wind, spread sensory contamination. Królikowski actually began his aforementioned testimony with the qualifier that "a terrible cadaver odor was brought to us by the southern wind blowing from Treblinka."[26] This suggests the smell was worse when the wind came from a specific angle. Stefan Kucharek, a Polish resident of the town of Małkinia (7 km), remembered similarly, "When we would sit at the table and there was a wind from the south, from Treblinka to Małkinia, then you weren't able to sit still. It stank so badly."[27] Yet human sensitivity to smell meant it could be noticed from even farther if conditions were right, and Józef Pogorzelski recalled that from Kostki (18 km), "after the first transports, there was a horrible smell of dead bodies."[28] According to Królikowski, "Even [in] Ostrów Mazowiecka (15 km north of Małkinia), people sensed the smell when the midday wind blew."[29] The ability for smell to travel twenty-three kilometers from the camp highlights the unpredictable nature of the spread of sensorial contamination into the world, making it clear that the zone of sensory witnessing around Treblinka was impermanent and fluid. And so while it is difficult to know for sure who in the region sensed the odors pouring forth from Treblinka, it is fair to suggest that there were many more Polish sensory witnesses than those whose stories are documented here.

We know that this witnessing was not limited to Poles, however, because the Germans at the camp also noticed the smell. Commandant Franz Stangl, who was transferred from Sobibór to Treblinka in September 1942, smelled the camp before he ever saw it, recalling in a postwar interview, "I drove there, with an ss driver. . . . We could smell it kilometres away. . . . When I entered the camp and got out of the car . . . the smell was indescribable; the hundreds, no, the thousands of bodies everywhere, decomposing, putrefying."[30] In fact, Stangl was brought to Treblinka to remedy the underlying disorganization that had caused the smell problem in the first place—when it reached its maximum "killing capacity" between the months of August and December 1942, the corpses equivalent to an entire small town accumulated daily in the small confines of the camp and its adjacent fields. In Stangl's "streamlining" of the murder process, therefore, he decided to "clean up" the camp by burning all the bodies—both of new arrivals and by unearthing the hundreds of thousands already buried. Stangl even called upon a combustion specialist from Bełżec named Floss to oversee the process.[31]

Yet this switch to burning bodies—intended to erase evidence and eliminate "problem" smells—actually created a dual-sensorial contamination of both the smell of burning bodies and the sights of smoke and flames from the fires, which *increased*, rather than decreased, the likelihood of the camp being witnessed by outsiders.

The first of these—the burning of bodies en masse—introduced a new odor into the spaces around Treblinka, that of charred flesh. In a graphic description, Edward Sypko, then a Treblinka I prisoner (0.5 km), depicted how it smelled to him: "When my wife used to cook *skwarki* (pork cracklings), and even older bacon, I would run away from home because I felt sick . . . because I was reminded of the camp and the stench of these burned bodies—it was the same."[32] According to Rachel Auerbach's postwar interviews with survivors, this burning smell initially "commingled" with that of rotting bodies, and as Krzepicki confirmed, these smells "issued forth together" from Treblinka.[33] Oskar Strawczyński stated that this combination of "the horrible smell of burning and rotting bodies and bones" made it "impossible to breathe outside."[34]

The distinctiveness and power of the burning smell, however, meant that it soon overpowered all other olfactory outputs, a fact evidenced by the first impressions of several Treblinka survivors who arrived at the camp after the burning started. The moment the doors to the cattle car opened, Edi Weinstein recounted, "We were struck by the sickening stench of burning bodies."[35] Survivor Fred Kort noted that upon his own arrival, a German greeted them by announcing, "What you smell is how Treblinka smells."[36] This signature odor of the camp existed as a constant reminder of the death all around, and for survivor Abraham Bomba, the smell was so potent, he and his fellow prisoners often could not eat—even though the scant food they received kept them alive.[37] According to Sypko, the smell was simply too invasive: "[It] was in my nose, in my ears, in my clothes, everywhere. I was soaked in it."[38] Strawczyński too recalled *feeling* the odor with his body: "The smell of roasted flesh was breathtaking."[39]

Part of the smell's potency came from its sheer volume. In order to keep up with the vast burning "needs" at Treblinka, the Germans used railway track sections as primitive grates that could hold around 2,500 corpses at a time—and they always kept this "eternal flame," as Willenberg called it, going.[40] Survivor Samuel Rajzman witnessed the gruesome process: "They made these fires with grates and they brought steam shovels. They pulled the dead out of the ditches and loaded them on the fire where they burned them twenty-four hours a day. The Germans put oil on the corpses and oil underneath, and the fire burned continuously."[41] This nonstop sensorial contamination meant that, as Czechowicz noted, "the smell of burning bodies floated throughout the night."[42] Because smells are notorious for lingering, even on rare days when no new transports arrived, Weinstein described how the odor of charred corpses still "*hung* in the air" as thousands of bodies burned around the clock.[43]

A similar sensory reality probably existed for anyone within close proximity of Treblinka. Polish railway worker Stanisław Adamczyk, who worked at a pointsman's hut (a structure situated at railway intersections) about two kilometers from the camp, recalled, "The furnaces in the camp must have been working without a break, since there was *always* a smell of burning in the air."[44] Kazimierz Gawkowski, who lived in the town of Treblinka (4 km), had the same experience even at this distance: "One could smell awful burning within a radius of several kilometers."[45]

Polish judge and postwar investigator Zdzisław Łukaszkiewicz wrote of the behavioral responses of locals in light of their new smellscape: "During the burning of corpses, the smell was so strong within a few kilometers that people did not dare to open doors and windows."[46] Bronisława Jakubik, a resident of the nearby town of Grądy (2.5 km), had this exact experience: "If it were not for the smell of burning bodies, which prevented the windows from ever being opened, sometimes it would be possible to think that nothing terrible was happening."[47] And as Czesław Borowy and Michał Kalembasiak, both residents of Treblinka (4 km), reflected, it was not just some houses; "*everyone* tried to shield themselves from it" by closing windows, even denying themselves relief on hot days "because there was a terrible smell of burning human bodies."[48]

Although recorded at different points in time and at different locations, the consistency of this evidence reveals how the sheer power of the smell altered normal life because it dictated how locals lived portions of their daily lives—even within their own homes. While at first glance, the behavioral response of shutting out an unpleasant smell may seem banal, both the frequency with which it was employed by local witnesses and how it overrode concerns of comfort (i.e., closing windows during hot days) underscore the new local spatial reality associated with adapting to living with a death camp next door. Yet these behavioral responses also stemmed from practical concerns. One in particular is a horror known all too well to Holocaust witnesses: once a smell got into a house, it often stuck around. A witness to the massacre of Jews at Radziłów once told author Anna Bikont, "The stench and fatty smoke—it was human fat—hung in the house for weeks."[49] Eugenia Samuel of Wólka Okrąglik (1 km) remembered of such instances near Treblinka, "It was a terrible stench, you could hardly bear it. . . . You had to clog your nose and everything."[50] And if the stench still managed to infiltrate one's home, one had little choice but to carry on *despite* the smell. Claude Lanzmann, who filmed the 1980s documentary *Shoah*, reflected on this fact in his 2012 memoir, *The Patagonian Hare*: "The peasants who lived near the camp struggled heroically not to smell. They ate and they made love in the unbearable stench of charred flesh." Lanzmann was particularly struck by the latter when he learned that Borowy and his wife, both of whom he interviewed, conceived their son during Treblinka's operational period.[51]

While the act of having sex amid the smell of burning bodies seems repulsive, it highlights two important realities of human experience. First, as Porteous claims, humans adapt to new smells fairly quickly, and even bad smells cease to be noticed after a time.[52] Think of someone who returns home after an extended absence only to recoil in disgust at the smellscape to which they had previously habituated. Second, people are quick to employ measures or devices to counteract or cover up unpleasant smells in their lives. Marian Piertzak, a resident of Sokołów Podlaski (27 km), frequently traveled to the areas near Treblinka during the war. On these trips, she noted, "When the Jews were burned, there was such a nasty smell, such a stench that people couldn't stay in their homes. I mean, it was four or five kilometers from Treblinka. So people brought torchwood and juniper leaves home because when the wind blew from Treblinka, it was impossible to stay at home—the stench from the burned bodies was so potent."[53] This example highlights two methods by which local sensory witnesses could avoid or adapt to the stench—simply leave home when it became too strong or burn fragrant plants and branches to mask it. In fact, one of the most blatant examples of this type of masking was already discussed in chapter 2, where Stangl splashed his walls and carpets with fragrance to mask the smell of burning bodies, turning his living quarters into the "perfumed hell of Treblinka."[54] Nonetheless, it seems a similar description could be applied to countless others living nearby amid the smells contaminating their landscape.

As with the smell of rotting bodies, the smell of burned flesh, specifically its potency and reach, was often subject to environmental factors. Borowy remembered how the odor was at its worst when dew points were high, because "dew carries the smell. . . . For example, when there's sun, a little wind, then during the day it's not that bad . . . while during the night, with the dew, it always came." This meant that on hot, dry days, locals might not necessarily have needed to close their windows because the smell was worse on humid days or at night. But as Borowy added, the wind played the biggest role in determining both the reach and direction of the smell: "In this climate, the wind blows in all directions, so there are winds from the north, the center, wherever . . . so fortunately sometimes there were periods when you couldn't smell it."[55] These environmental effects are corroborated by the fact that most witnesses beyond a radius of about five kilometers from Treblinka started their testimonies with a qualifier about the wind. For example, Kucharek, who lived seven kilometers from the camp, recalled, "*When the wind* was from the south, it stank in Małkinia [7 km], to high heaven. . . . When they were burning them, that is."[56] This was apparently a frequent occurrence, even at this distance, and according to one testimony, the smell "overtook the inhabitants of Małkinia *very often*."[57] Rural resident Piotr Ferenc stated, "I lived about ten kilometers away and *when the wind blew* over there, it was . . . such a burnt stench. . . . It stank so."[58] Władysław Rażmowski, who led a partisan unit in the town of Sadowne (13 km), stated, "*The wind brought* the smell of smoking bodies to my place of residence."[59] In fact, as Sypko reported, "My mother, who lived some twenty-five kilometers away, sensed Treblinka *when the wind was right*."[60] The fact that the smell returned *each* time the wind was right not only speaks to environmental impacts on smell but also hints at the magnitude of the odors escaping Treblinka. And the wind-determined directionality of smell also highlights its random spread into the world beyond the camp. The uncontrolled release of odors meant that even transient people within these spaces could witness them. Warsaw ghetto survivor Mary Berg heard reports about the smell: "People who have traveled in trains past Treblinka say that the stench there is so poisonous that they must stop up their nostrils."[61]

One remarkable aspect of the potency of the burned flesh smell in particular is that it lingered in the remains of Treblinka for many years after the camp was torn down. According to the Central Commission, which investigated the site in 1945, "Within a radius of several hundred yards from the camp site an unpleasant smell of burnt ash and decay is noticeable, growing stronger as one approaches." These sensory remnants came from the German practice of mixing the ashes of burnt bodies with sand and then later using this mixture as backfill to cover up the former site of Treblinka.[62] Even as late as 1947, Barbara Kadej, a local resident of Prostyń (4 km), still noticed "the fetid odor of the rotting bodies" surrounding the area where the camp had once stood.[63] The longevity of smell at Treblinka, therefore, poses a compelling challenge to Wiernik's cry that "ashes are silent," because in this case, in fact, they were not and instead served as sensory markers of what had previously occurred in the space of the death camp.[64]

Sight

As powerful and invasive as it became, the smell from Treblinka was only half of the emerging sensorial contamination created by burning bodies, and if it did not reach far into the surrounding environment, the glow of the fire or the curtain of smoke hanging high above the camp certainly did. As Rodaway reminds us, we think of sight as the "primary" sense, and because it can provide up to 80 percent of one's knowledge of the world, witnesses often privilege sight by ascribing emotive language to what they see.[65] Therefore, for Saul Kuperhand, imprisoned at Treblinka, it was not just smoke he saw: "The only sight of our loved ones was in the lazy smoke drifting heavenward above the furnaces."[66] That *lazy* smoke drifted *heavenward* reflects his almost spiritual connection to what he was seeing and the horrible reality he knew it represented.

This contrast between the black smoke of Treblinka's fires and the blue sky above was similarly vivid for many other witnesses. According to Willenberg, from within the camp, "We saw black smoke billowing from the area behind the towering bank between the sorting-yard and the death camp. The smoke rose hundreds of meters into the air."[67] On the "other side" of the barbed wire, Barbara Goska, a local Pole from Wólka Okrąglik (1 km), recalled seeing this "same" smoke: "During a bath in a nearby stream one day, I saw in the sky billowing thick black smoke."[68] Despite being on opposite sides of the proverbial fence, that both Willenberg and Goska use the term *billowing* suggests the power of the particularly heavy smoke of burned bodies to remain long suspended in the air, a fact that created lasting impressions in the minds of other witnesses. As Celina Kalembaziak, a local Pole from Prostyń (4 km), recalled, "Large smoke *floated* visibly" above the forested area of the death camp.[69]

The appearance of smoke floating or billowing often reflects much about the person witnessing it because their choice of these particular words suggests the plumes now hung or loomed over their lives like an ever-present specter of death. This is quite apparent in the example of Ester Gaist, a young Jewish woman who survived by hiding on the farm of local Pole Gustaw Diehl. Diehl lived close to Treblinka, and Gaist remembered approaching his farm for the first time: "The sky darkened with smoke. I am scared. I asked Mr. Gustaw where we are. [He said] that is . . . Treblinka, which is located about two kilometers from the farm, we are separated only by a small forest."[70] The sky, gloomy with smoke, cast the whole farm into a particularly ominous haze for Gaist, who undoubtedly saw it as a constant reminder of her own threatened existence.

The smoke plumes over Treblinka, lingering as they did, may not have been quite as strongly affected by environmental factors as smell was. While the strength and direction of the wind might have pointed the billowing clouds a certain way, the sheer height and volume of these plumes, given the sustained burning operations going on in Treblinka, meant they were probably a near-constant sight for some distance beyond the camp. In the nearby town of Treblinka (4 km), Gawkowski noted, "There were *always* clouds of smoke rising from the camp."[71] A report passed around the Białystok ghetto in 1943 extended the range of visibility: "Smoke from the burning piles [of bodies] is visible all around in a radius of 15 kilometers."[72] Yet the *Menschenschlachthaus Treblinka* report (published after the war) pushed the boundaries of this distance even farther, recording, "Dense, black, fat smoke columns rose up into the sky and hung as a heavy, motionless curtain in the air. Even thirty and forty kilometers away . . . [these sights] rose up from the camp above the tips of trees of the spruce forest."[73] While we might assume forty kilometers was somewhat overestimated, the central point stands true nonetheless: since the Germans were burning bodies all day and night, the visual effects could be viewed in the sky for many kilometers, and however far it actually reached, it created ever-larger numbers of sensory witnesses to Treblinka.[74]

For reference, two photos capture what the skies above Treblinka may have looked like on any given day. Figure 13 is a photo taken by Ząbecki of the smoke plume arising from Treblinka on the day of the revolt (August 2, 1943), where portions of the camp were set on fire by escaping Jews. It is shocking that the plume here, seemingly quite large, likely paled in comparison to what it must have looked like when thousands of bodies were being burnt daily at the camp. For a scalable comparison, figure 14 shows a smoke plume over the Majdanek concentration camp in October 1943, when the bodies of thousands of murdered Jews were burned there. Taken from nearby Lublin (about 1–2 km from Majdanek), the massive scale of the smoke plume is indisputable. While a rarer occurrence at Majdanek than Treblinka, the image clearly shows the volume of the smoke ejected into the atmosphere by large numbers of burning bodies.[75]

Another visible element of Treblinka was the fire responsible for creating this smoke. The prevailing descriptions come from those nearest the flames, the Jews imprisoned at Treblinka, and they consistently reflect foremost on the sheer *enormity* of the conflagration. To demonstrate the simple fact that the camp was surrounded by the burning grates, an unnamed member

FIG. 13. Photo taken by local railway man Franciszek Ząbecki. The smoke comes from Treblinka during the revolt on August 2, 1943. The camp's smoke plumes probably appeared larger during the daily burning of thousands of bodies throughout Treblinka's operational period. Courtesy of Yad Vashem Photo Archive, 2B08.

FIG. 14. Photo taken of the Majdanek concentration camp from the suburbs of Lublin, approximately 1.5 kilometers distant. This photo, taken during the burning of bodies, provides a comparative perspective of the scale of smoke released into the surrounding world. USHMM, courtesy of Panstwowe Muzeum na Majdanku.

of the Sonderkommando put it bluntly: "It was a hell of a fire."[76] As Wiernik described, it was a "huge inferno . . . which from a distance looked like a volcano breaking through the earth's crust to belch forth fire and lava."[77] Another survivor also invoked volcanic imagery, stating, "There was a long, sand-scattered embankment where an armed guard patrolled. On the other side smoke *poured* out as if from a volcano."[78] That flames and smoke *poured* out into the world illustrates the intensity of the fires at Treblinka, and the repeated comparison to a destructive force of nature—the volcano—portrays how overwhelming and uncontrollable such experiences must have felt to the Jews who witnessed them.

With flames came light and heat, and survivor Chil Rajchman remembered the blaze being "so immense that it was impossible to stay close to the place. . . . After a few hours, [from] even 50 meters [away], we wouldn't be able to stay there. And this burned night after night."[79] From other evidence, we know the flames themselves sometimes rose as high as twenty meters above the ground, and as a result, they were often visible above the trees. When Mosze Klajman approached the camp from a cattle car, he witnessed this very scene: "Fire burst through the thick forests and the train slowly entered 'Treblinka' through the tall green trees until the train stopped."[80] The visibility of the fires was most distinctive at night, according to survivor Richard Glazar: "One night, through the barbed window of the barrack; the flames rose high, high above the camp, flames in all colours: red, orange, blue, green, purple."[81] The emotive description here gets much of its power by highlighting the stark contrast between the dark night's sky and the bright, unnatural colors of light emanating from what Auerbach calls Treblinka's "funeral pyres."[82] Glazar added, "Suddenly, from the part of the camp called the death camp, flames shot up. Very high. In a flash, the whole countryside, the whole camp seemed ablaze."[83]

The obverse of black smoke set against blue sky, the bright light against the dark night sky indeed became another consistent feature of the local landscape while Treblinka operated. As Franciszek Byszewski, a prisoner of Treblinka I (0.5 km), noted, "Camp II was visible from our camp. You could still see . . . a low glow at night. Something was burning there, probably corpses. The fire was visible all the time. . . . We had to stay in the barracks at night, but the door was open, there were containers below the door at night, in which we took care of our needs. . . . When you came to the door, you could see the glow."[84] Adamczyk, working at his pointsman's hut about two kilometers away, recalled that from this distance, "you could see a glow in the sky at night."[85] A little farther away in the town of Treblinka (4 km), Borowy stated that the fires were not necessarily always visible, but "at night there was a glow over the camp."[86]

This glow of Treblinka was probably visible at much farther distances. After escaping during the prisoner revolt of August 1943, for instance, Rajzman encountered a peasant woman about eight kilometers from Treblinka: "[She] knew we came from Treblinka, because she had seen a terrific fire burning there."[87] Tanhum Grinberg, a Jewish prisoner who escaped in the same revolt, wrote that even from what he estimated to be fifteen kilometers away, he could still see that "the distant skies were red" over Treblinka.[88] Others, like Strawczyński, also remembered how the sky over Treblinka often "turned *red* from the flames."[89] And in fact, a postwar article based on Glazar's experience is entitled "Der Himmel war rot über Treblinka" (The heavens were red over Treblinka), placing specific emphasis on this color. In the article, Glazar states, "The whole heavens above Treblinka were red in those frosty nights [of winter 1942]."[90] Here again, we see synesthetic language, albeit subtly, in the juxtaposition of a cold winter night with the red glow of Treblinka's sky—a haunting allegory of a fire burning in the hearth, providing not glimpses of death but promises of warmth and comfort.

The specificity of the red glow hints at another environmental impact on sensory witnessing—cloud cover, which can scatter light originating from below back toward the ground. This "light pollution," often identified in studies of large cities, offers another way to understand the nocturnal visual landscape that existed around Treblinka.[91] Specifically, it helps us visualize how the sky above the camp changed on a nightly basis depending on the weather—an important fact of sensory witnessing but also a reminder that the extent of visual cues issuing from Treblinka varied widely. For comparison today, one might drive along a highway on a cloudy evening and see the lights of a major city reflected in the sky from many kilometers away, while the same trip on a clear night yields these visual clues only in closer proximity. The light emanating from Treblinka would have been affected similarly.

Light pollution from the camp had another source besides the fires, as a wartime report noted: "The whole area [of the camp] is illuminated at night by strong reflectors [search lights], to prevent escape of Jews not yet exterminated."[92] Krzepicki described this artificial illumination in more detail: "At the top levels of the watchtowers, there were machine guns, searchlights that sent out broad beacons every few minutes to every part of the camp, making the night as bright as midday. Only on nights when Warsaw was bombed did the searchlights remain dark."[93] This lighting also helped the gas chambers operate in the dark, and as records from Stangl's trial stated, on days when up to eighteen thousand people were killed at Treblinka, "the gas chambers were in operation for over 12 hours, including after dusk under the searchlights."[94] The very phenomena of artificial light and light pollution, especially during all hours of the night, would have been strangely out of place in this rural area of Poland, where industrial factories were exceedingly rare.

Aside from viewing bright lights, flames, or smoke, many people, especially those who lived close by, *visually* witnessed, and often intimately so, the mass murder process within the confines of Treblinka. Theoretically, according to Nazi principles of secrecy, no outsider should have been able to get close to the camp. However, in practice, this proved untenable for the simple fact that people lived nearby and conducted their daily lives in proximity to the camp. Originally, some of those living in the vicinity were displaced by the construction at Treblinka when, "during the first night [of building Treblinka II, the Germans] took all the Poles. The little farmers were kicked out, and the Treblinka camp was extended."[95] Nevertheless, the Germans allowed some farmers to move back into their homes after construction, and many continued working in their camp-adjacent fields to fulfill grain quotas. And even while some areas, such as the fields to the southeast, were banned for security reasons, farmers often passed through to and from work at other authorized locations.[96]

To be sure, many of those imprisoned inside of Treblinka saw, from their vantage point inside the camp, these Polish farmers through the fences. Glazar recalled once seeing a Polish boy standing in a Treblinka-adjacent field who "aped strangulation, rolled his wide-open eyes back, and stuck out his tongue" before running off.[97] Bomba was also well aware that "outside [of Treblinka] people lived; they could see from the outside that people were killed over [here]."[98] Krzepicki's recollection emphasizes the psychological discord such experiences caused him: "As we passed through the enclosed area . . . we would often see from a distance peasants working their fields. I looked at them, and I would feel a furious jealousy eating away at my heart. These were human beings, and I was a human being too. But they were free, and I was under guard all the time. The sky and trees were beautiful; this world was not big enough for me."[99] These were two worlds—one of life and one of death—that almost overlapped, close enough to be viewed from both sides but not quite traversable.

Just as they were noticed from inside the camp, these same "free" Poles on the outside certainly saw into Treblinka. As Mieczysława Filipowicz, a resident of nearby Grądy (2.5 km), recalled, "The lands [around the camp] still had to be cultivated, but you were not supposed to look in the direction of the camp or raise your head."[100] Yet Ząbecki noted that peasants working these nearby fields often had full view of the horrible scenes unfolding within Treblinka: "You see, there were fields all around [Treblinka] belonging to peasants who . . . continued to work their fields throughout the existence of the camp. So it wasn't as off-limits, or as guarded as all that—ever."[101] In fact, Borowy recalled that peasants continued to work in spaces abutting the very edges of Treblinka: "There are 3 or 4 [farmers] who have their fields right near the camp . . . 3, 4, 5 meters from the camp, you could work the land."[102] One of these farmers, interviewed in Lanzmann's *Shoah*, worked in a field situated one hundred yards from Treblinka, and his recollection shows what was visible from that location: "There's a small hill; he could see quite a bit. . . . They couldn't stop and watch. It was forbidden . . . but they could work a field a hundred yards from the camp . . . so occasionally he could steal a glance if the Ukrainians weren't looking. . . . He worked by the barbed wire . . . right up close, it wasn't forbidden to work there. . . . Where the camp is now was partly his field."[103] This farmer's workspace overlapped with the space of the camp, and during his daily existence, which included working his fields, he became an intimate witness to the murders occurring directly adjacent to his land.

This close proximity to Treblinka and the sights accompanying it greatly influenced the behavior of those living next to the camp. In Borowy's words, as a result of such terrible sights, "Of course [the farmers] worked, but they didn't have their usual work ethic; they were forced to work, but when they saw what was going on here, they said to themselves: OKAY, what if they come in the night and surround our houses and take us away, too? . . . Yes they were afraid."[104] After all, their visual confirmation of mass murder occurring "next door," often replete with knowledge of the shapes and forms the killings took, imparted a level of witnessing many probably never fathomed beforehand. Local witness Wacława Dyoniziak of Grądy (2.5 km), who tended cows with her family in a field near Treblinka, vividly remembered what she saw occurring inside the camp: "People were running around. . . . Ukrainians stood on the sides and behind them. This is the path in which the people were rushing. And these people could often barely walk because they did this all day. Unconscionable. There was neither water nor anything . . . and in the summer, the days were long."[105] Her description is noteworthy because Treblinka survivors have described in their testimonies how Ukrainian guards sometimes formed a "human wall" meant to funnel Jews toward the pathway leading to the camp's gas chambers. The specifics of Dyoniziak's recollection mean she possibly witnessed the final moments of Jews—an experience, from the Nazi perspective, that was never meant to be observed by an outsider. In fact, they only ever intended this terrible epicenter of Treblinka to be viewed by the Jews about to die, members of the Sonderkommando (who were murdered and replaced at frequent intervals), and a select few German and Ukrainian camp personnel authorized to work near the gas chambers.[106]

As surprising as it is for Dyoniziak's experience to have occurred at all, it is potentially more so in that it might not have been unique. Eugenia Samuel from Wólka Okrąglik (1 km) said she worked in her uncle's field near Treblinka. She described what she witnessed from that vantage point: "During the occupation, I saw everything. . . . I saw . . . the murders of the Jews they brought from all the transports. . . . It was in a grove, and it was such a space that you could see something from there: how they unloaded the Jews, how they undressed them. They did not segregate them, they only sorted everything out . . . and . . . there was a chamber like a little barrack, and they pushed the Jews in there. Women and children and old people undressed . . . and they did not come out anymore."[107] Stanisław Kucharek, also from Wólka Okrąglik, who had a field near the camp, stated similarly, "Working in the field I could observe, from time to time, what was happening in the camp. The area was initially not surrounded with a fence, so I could see huts being erected and pits being dug. Later, when the transports of Jews started to arrive, the fence was built and so the observation of the camp premises was more difficult."[108]

However, such barriers did not prevent locals from seeing into the camp. Henryk Slebzak, another Wólka Okrąglik (1 km) resident, claimed he once climbed a tree in the forest and, from this vantage point, saw within the camp a procession of people, "only they were naked" and being attacked by dogs.[109] Even without such extraordinary efforts, sometimes other local Poles, even those without Treblinka-adjacent land, caught views inside the camp. Wacław Bednarczyk, a local railway worker, explained, "While working on a hill located in such a way that one could see the area of the extermination camp, I once saw a transport . . . with people being driven out of the wagons. All people, fully dressed, were herded into a large hut. . . . I do not know if any extermination took place in that hut."[110] Most likely, Bednarczyk observed the undressing barracks of Treblinka, but his experience displays the lack of control German personnel had in isolating the camp from those outsiders who worked nearby. Władysław Chomka, a train engineer who sometimes drove the cattle cars to Treblinka, recollected similarly, "One day, while I was in a steam engine that was moving wagons full of Jews onto the camp ramp, I was able to observe people being thrown out of the wagons. Immediately after the wagons were emptied, the people were ordered to hand over their luggage, the men were separated from the women, and they were ordered to strip naked."[111] Polish train engineers were supposed to back the cars into Treblinka and disengage the engine before entering, but this rule did little to prevent furtive glimpses into the death camp.

Another way outsiders had visual contact, though perhaps less immediately apparent, was by viewing components of the camp that rose above the fences. As Gawkowski noted, "While traveling alongside the camp, in the direction of the gravel pit, I could also see four . . . diggers working, digging pits in the camp."[112] These tall digging machines stuck out, perhaps as the watchtowers also did, as man-made objects standing amid the natural canopy of trees above the camp. Probably also visible above the fences were the piles of clothes of murdered Jews, which according to several witnesses occasionally reached six or seven stories high—a height that would have rivaled some of the taller trees around the camp.[113] Treblinka I prisoner Stanisław Nasiłowski, while out on mandatory work detail, recalled just such a sight: "When I was going to Małkinia, [Treblinka II] passed on our left. . . . Above the fence I saw these great piles [of clothes]."[114] These inanimate objects towering above the camp's fences and occasionally above the treetops extended Treblinka's space vertically, just as the smoke and flames did, making ever more evidence visible to the outside world.

Horizontally, the Jewish work groups from Treblinka II—the *Waldkommando* (Forest Brigade) and the *Tarnungskommando* (Camouflage Brigade)—extended the zone of visual witnessing into the local landscape through their frequent excursions into areas beyond the camp. Dyoniziak illustrates this point in her postwar recollections: "In the morning, we went to this field and we used to feed these Jews. There was no more than fifty meters from the pasture to the camp. Jews cut branches in the forest and carried bundles on their backs, and they covered the camp's fences with them. And I saw . . . the Germans adjust their machine guns and shoot at the Jews and the Jews fell into these pits. At that time, they did not burn them yet, they buried them."[115] Here, Dyoniziak not only witnessed the Waldkommando working in spaces outside of the camp but also watched the outright murder of Jews

FIG. 15. A postwar photo of the forests near Treblinka. The indentation in the ground is perhaps from camp structures or possibly a mass grave. Courtesy of Yad Vashem Photo Archive, 2BO6.

that sometimes accompanied these work details. These individuals may not have died inside the camp, but they were victims of Treblinka all the same—a reminder that genocidal violence knows no spatial bounds.

This terrible reality of mass murder meant that although witnessing the killings taking place may have been rare, a more common experience might have included encountering grisly evidence left behind in unexpected places beyond the camp's confines. Local Pole Krystyna Pamrów explained that her husband had just such an experience. While searching for mushrooms one day, approximately five hundred meters from the Treblinka I penal camp (possibly near Treblinka II), "he saw a hole in the ground . . . and saw lots of human corpses. He remembered that the murdered victims were still fully clothed. The sight of such a crime filled him with great fear."[116] This quotidian activity—mushroom hunting—made Pamrów's husband an unwilling visual witness to the horrors associated with and emanating from Treblinka. According to Puchała, who was imprisoned at Treblinka I for several months in 1943, "In the woods located near the camp, there were constant executions, and, as far as I know, there are 32 graves there."[117] Each of these sites could have potentially been discovered by someone else working or living nearby or even a person just passing through the area.

How far from Treblinka these hidden graves extend is unclear, but evidence suggests they may spread out for several kilometers. For illustration, sometimes Jewish prisoners from Treblinka II found their way into Treblinka I work details that traveled deep into the Polish countryside. Małkinia (7 km) resident Stefan Kucharek estimated that as many as six hundred Polish and Jewish prisoners worked in Małkinia daily, and he claimed to have once seen Jews from Treblinka working at the Małkinia engine house cleaning the recently emptied trains from Treblinka.[118] All the violence occurring within the camp (as previously seen) followed these groups also, something Noemi Wajnkrano-Szac witnessed in Małkinia: "The workers from Treblinka . . . unloaded coal. We sat on the grass, I strained my eyes, and saw the Jews working in dirty old rags. . . . Their Lithuanian [guards] . . . beat [the Jews] endlessly, I closed my eyes."[119] Fred Kort, who survived Treblinka I, said these work details from Treblinka occasionally traveled as far as Ostrów Mazowiecka (23 km), with mistreatment, murder, and death through overwork and exposure constant accompaniments.[120] Thus, the Treblinka body trail followed wherever people from inside the camp went, and in this way, the violence of genocide—and the chances for outsiders to witness it visually—extended well beyond the camp's confines.

Sound

Historian Kate Brown suggests that "sound is more frightening than sight" because of the imaginative powers sound alone can unleash.[121] Sound is also an acutely geographical sense because humans need to locate sounds within spaces to determine intensity, direction, and threat level, each of which helps one form knowledge about auditory origins.[122] This reality is proven in the example of Stanisław Borowy, who worked at the town of Treblinka's railway station (4 km). Despite the distance and despite his inability to see into the camp, he noted, "I was able to *observe* some facts. I know that after unloading the wagons, men were separated from women and children. After some time, there was a scream that lasted about 20 minutes and then it was silent."[123] His synesthetic choice of the word *observe* for something he only heard shows his attempt at discerning Treblinka's true purpose as a purely auditory witness.

Halina Szymańczyk, a Polish resident of Poniatowo (1 km), wrote a poem about Treblinka recalling her wartime experiences. The first lines read,

> Between two villages, half a kilometer from the road
> was Hitler's extermination camp called Treblinka.
> We heard the voices of tortured people.
> Voices full of pain and despair, shrill cries for help
> drowned out by loud music and awful barking of dogs.[124]

That Szymańczyk gives primacy to the auditory, mentioning a cacophony of sounds within the first few lines of her poem, shows the impact the specific soundscape of Treblinka had on her memories of that experience.

Czesław Borowy recalled his own auditory experience traveling near the camp: "There you could hear something that sounded like bird calls, like music, and sometimes you could hear people speaking Jewish. . . . Then there were strange noises from time to time, and you'd hear Jews shouting."[125] Shouting and screaming were among the most common auditory experiences near Treblinka, and as Wólka Okrąglik (1 km) resident Stanisław Kucharek remembered, "One could constantly hear terrifying screams . . . coming from behind the fence."[126] These sounds likely originated as men, women, and children screamed out in agony and pain as they were driven along with blows and shouts toward the gas chambers. Survivor Oskar Strawczyński recalled of this experience, "People pass through and there is silence for a few minutes. Immediately thereafter, however, a distant, choked cry coming from many throats is heard; 'Ah, Ah, Ah.' It didn't last long, becoming weaker until it completely fell silent."[127]

Since, according to naturalist and author Diane Ackerman, our senses "crave novelty," human screaming in a forested, rural environment would have been a startling new aspect of the area's "normal," probably quieter, daily soundscape.[128] Marian Łopuszyński, who owned the Treblinka gravel pit, reflected later, "On my way to the gravel pit I had to walk alongside the extermination camp. The journey made a terrifying impression on me, since there was constant moaning and hysterical screams from women. The impression was so strong that I am still shocked today."[129] The visceral response to screaming was common. As Bomba described it, "Your hair . . . stood up just listening to the screaming of the people before they were gassed."[130]

Auditory witnesses to Treblinka sometimes provided startlingly similar recollections of what they heard there—often despite the passage of many years. Consider Isadore Helfing and Abraham Kolski. In a 1992 interview, Helfing recalled, "People, the minute they got into Treblinka, they saw what was going on . . . and they were screaming, that's all, everybody was screaming, screaming, crying. The screaming, you know, and that was going on all day."[131] In his own interview slightly earlier, Kolski gave the following description: "When the people came . . . the screaming was so high. . . . Everybody was screaming. Any screaming. Scream. Raus. Raus. Raus. [Out. Out. Out.] Screaming. . . . The screaming was until they get dead [*sic*] . . . the whole time everybody was screaming. Raus. Schnell machen. [Out. Go faster.] Anything. Screaming."[132] Fifty years later, both men recalled the same profound soundscape, and it is striking that they both repeat the word *screaming* multiple times, a reflection of how overpowering and constant this sound was at Treblinka. It is also noteworthy that Kolski includes the German words that accompanied the experience. Aside from highlighting the transnational character of Treblinka's soundscape, it evokes synesthesia by painting in our mind's eye a scene of action to which we add the presumed context, as if in a movie, where Germans are shouting at Jews, perhaps as they also hit them with truncheons, to get out of the cattle cars and run to the undressing barracks.

While the screams were constant when transports arrived, they were also random in their escape into the outside world at other times. Environmental factors account for part of this fact. As Adamczyk (working in his pointsman's hut 2 km from the camp) recalled, "When the wind was blowing from the camp, you could hear screams so piercing that you could not stand it."[133] Yet the random bursting forth of these sounds also resulted from the terrible fact that individuals screamed at different times during their confrontation with death. Vasily Grossman's report on Treblinka highlights this randomness: "Inhabitants of the village of Wulka [*sic*], the settlement nearest to Treblinka, say that sometimes the shrieks of the women being murdered were so terrible that the whole village would run for miles into the forest to get away from the piercing cries that rent the air. Presently the screaming would subside only to break out again as terrible and soul-searing as before. . . . This was repeated three or four times a day."[134] Such dramatic experiences were likely only had by sensory witnesses inhabiting the spaces closest to Treblinka, but they show the power of sound to command an immediate behavioral response from the surrounding world. After all, it is distinctly noticeable when, as a 1943 report on Treblinka stated, "women's cries and lamentations, along with the curses and imprecations from Germans, *break the silence* of the forest."[135]

In fact, Krzepicki was taken aback by the startling nature of this juxtaposition between the quiet forest and the loud sounds emanating from Treblinka. As part of the Waldkommando outside the camp, he recalled, "[We] workers in the woods could hear the cries of the women and children, like the squeaking of chickens or of pigs in a slaughterhouse. At times we thought we could hear deeper voices, the voices of men bellowing like oxen in a slaughterhouse."[136] Though Krzepicki could not know exactly where he was in relation to Treblinka, he estimated this experience happened within a kilometer of the camp, roughly the same distance as the town of Wólka Okrąglik.

While screams would have frequently radiated outward from the camp, the types of sounds emerging from Treblinka varied substantially. "The concrete road I was driving on was at most 200 meters in a straight line from the camp," Ząbecki recalled. "I heard the desperate screams and crying. I heard the prayers of the penitential Psalms, loud prayers in Yiddish and Polish, calls to God and the Most Holy Mother for help . . . and above all, there was a violent rattle of machine guns."[137] Goska, from Wólka Okrąglik (1 km), also remembered the gunfire in particular: "One day, somehow some Jews managed to escape. . . . The Germans opened fire and shots rang out. We fled home in a panic."[138] Guards frequently shot at Jewish prisoners while they tried to escape, but gunfire also burst forth from the camp's execution area (the Lazarett). Krzepicki stated that during larger executions, bursts of "heavy gunfire" could last upwards of half an hour, saturating the neighboring world with the sound.[139]

While many witnesses remembered the screams, the gunfire, and the horrible sounds of death, it also merits noting that in such a sound-laden world, silence could also be piercing. Survivor Sol Liber recalled the first time he experienced this juxtaposition: "You didn't hear a sound anymore. Thirty-one hundred people, it took about two hours to get rid of them in the gas chamber."[140] The sudden silence formed an indelible memory because it replaced what had been such a cacophony. Jakubik, from Grądy (2.5 km), remembered, "From where I lived, you could not see much, but unfortunately, I could hear the moans, shouts and cries of the prisoners. . . . These sounds were usually most prevalent in the morning, because that's when the transports arrived at the camp. During the day, there was usually silence."[141] Thus, the timing of different sounds allowed local sensory witnesses to learn more about what went on in the camp, and any unfamiliar sounds injected into this increasingly familiar soundscape alerted those nearby that something new might be occurring.

One such sound, which initially seemed out of place in the middle of the Polish countryside, was music. The Treblinka orchestra was composed of Jewish musicians whose only right to live was to play their instruments as people entered the gas chambers.[142] The group was originally led by well-known composer Artur Gold. According to Oskar Strawczyński, "A Czech Jew wrote lyrics and Gold composed the music. He composed some beautiful pieces. . . . The band also included a soloist, a Warsaw artist, several amateurs and . . . a cabaret dancer. . . . A tailor crafted white costumes with navy blue collars and lapel. Gold appeared in a white coat with navy blue trimmings, patent leather shoes, and smoothly pressed trousers with stripes, all in a white shirt and bow tie. . . . There were even varnished music stands with the inscription 'Gold Orchestra.'"[143] Polish farmer Jerzy Skarżyński, of the town of Treblinka (4 km), recounted that when new transports of Jews arrived at the camp, this orchestra played, which he believed was an attempt to "drown out" screams and shouts.[144] Other contemporary witnesses also believed the sounds they heard accompanying mass murder represented German attempts at camouflage. For instance, a wartime report noted how German and Ukrainian personnel at the Sobibór death camp "raised flocks of geese on farms in the camp, and whenever a massacre took place, they would excite the geese and cause them to call. In this fashion, the Germans were able to drown out the moans and cries of their victims."[145] It stands to reason that covering up the sounds of mass murder was one explanation; however, the orchestra played for other purposes too. Survivor Tanhum Grinberg remembered, "We ate supper to the sound of music," and there were "various pieces for three violins and two clarinets."[146] Later, when the number of transports slowed down, the orchestra came to serve another role—to provide musical entertainment for the ss men during lulls.[147] Music of all types is a well-documented characteristic of the "ritual of mass murder" during the Holocaust, and many theories have been raised as to why the perpetrators employed it, including normalizing the killing process, creating a festive atmosphere, and reinforcing hypermasculine concepts of comradery, sacrifice, and group bonding.[148] Regardless—and also certainly a component of why it was employed—this experience was cruel and degrading for the prisoners. As Rajzman described, "After all this . . . hell, we had to stand here and sing, and listen to such music for half an hour!"[149] Yet the duration and frequency of these "concerts" made them another common feature of Treblinka's soundscape.

One other sound that soon defined Treblinka's space came from the machines used in exhuming bodies to be burnt. Auerbach's report identified one particular machine, a modified bulldozer named the *Kopachke* (a diminutive of the Polish *kopacz*, meaning "digger"), which was "forever" digging ditches around the camp, and "its hammering was the characteristic sound of the death camp and could be heard for miles around." The machines often ran from four o'clock in the morning until nightfall, unearthing bodies and loading them onto the grates, meaning their drone was a constant sound streaming out of Treblinka.[150] In this way, another byproduct of intended evidence erasure—the digging up and burning of bodies—likely attracted locals interested in learning why heavy machinery was operating in the forests near their homes.

Among the most abnormal sounds recalled by witnesses were those noticed for their beauty. From her home in Wólka Okrąglik (1 km), Goska recalled hearing a song coming from Treblinka: "In the morning, as the sun rose, from the camp . . . one could hear a loud song 'Kiedy ranne wstają zorze' [When Morning Light Is Breaking]. It was as pronounced as someone singing in my own house."[151] While this example highlights a sound's ability to infiltrate the home spaces of local Poles, it also shows that this sound was notable because it did not fit with the "normal" sounds coming out of Treblinka. The music from Gold's orchestra might have caused similar reactions in anyone nearby who heard it. As Czechowicz reflected, "I remember someone saying, 'Hear the trumpet, maybe it's the trumpet of our salvation.'"[152] That this triumphant sound disguised the reality of Treblinka, though, was part of the purpose for its very existence. This was probably also true for the hymn Goska witnessed. After all, the singing of Polish songs by Treblinka

FIG. 16. The Kopachke, or digging machine, operating at Treblinka.
The sound of heavy equipment operating day and night was at
odds with the otherwise rural landscape of the Polish countryside.
Courtesy of USHMM, gift of Eugene Miller, acc. no. 1997.A.0240.

prisoners during daily roll call was a tactic the Germans employed because, according to Willenberg, "perhaps they wanted the villagers in the vicinity to hear the heart-gladdening little thing; perhaps, too, it was another way of camouflaging the atrocities of Treblinka."[153] This planned deception likely failed, as the dissonant sounds of mass murder vastly outstripped the more benign ones. Nonetheless, the chaotic soundscape created at Treblinka lived on for anyone close enough to have actually witnessed the death camp's auditory outputs. Sounds of joy mingled with sounds of agony, pain, and sorrow, all while heavy machinery droned on and guns fired into the night.

Creating Knowledge

By considering the modes of sensory witnessing that took place in the radius around Treblinka, it becomes all too apparent that not only were there many traces of this genocide and large numbers of witnesses to it, but in fact, one did not have to even be within the camp's barbed-wire fences to experience the horrors created at Nazi death camps. The sights, smells, and sounds pouring out of Treblinka on a daily basis far exceeded the camp's confines, and this sensory contamination spread into the nearby world, effectively extending the zone of sensory witnessing for many kilometers in all directions beyond the camp. Although often affected by environmental factors and day-to-day variations in the level of killing, Treblinka's sensory contamination of the world around it appears to have been relatively constant for the duration of the camp's existence.

While this chapter has detailed the actual experiences of many individual sensory witnesses to Treblinka, the fact remains that many more unspoken individuals lived their daily lives in this zone of sensory witnessing who have never given their testimony. Yet because of what others have described here, we now know at least part of what their experiences must have been like. Furthermore, the spread of information and the creation of knowledge about Treblinka was certainly enhanced by the reach of such sensory contamination into the nearby environment, wherein witnesses combined these sensory elements with other pieces of knowledge (including their own deductive reasoning) to learn about the reality of the camp. "People [nearby] might not have known exactly how the killings happened," local judge Zdzisław Łukaszkiewicz reflected, "but the fact that thousands and thousands of people arriving in transports did not return, in conjunction with the windblown stench of burning bodies spread out for many kilometers, spoke for itself."[154] Sensory witnessing helped connect the dots for many, and as a result, the Nazi belief that Treblinka would become an isolated, secret death camp was completely undermined almost from day one of the camp's operation.

6

An Extended Space

> Almost always, at the beginning of the memory
> sequence, stands the train, which marked the depar-
> ture toward the unknown, not only for chronolog-
> ical reasons but also for the gratuitous cruelty with
> which those (otherwise innocuous) convoys of
> ordinary freight cars were employed for an extraor-
> dinary purpose.
>
> —Primo Levi, *The Drowned and the Saved*

Slicing through backyards and forests, farmsteads and villages, the train tracks of Poland branched out like arteries from major city centers to all parts of the country. By 1942, even residents in remote villages had grown accustomed to trains as portents of the slow, steady encroach of modernity. "I used to like working as a railway man," Franciszek Ząbecki, train stationmaster for the village of Treblinka (4 km) reflected after the war. "The passing trains of peacetime carried the fruits of the labor of human hands. The trains passed with dignity and pride; in the sound of the long whistles of the steam engine, there was a cry for a clear journey, because people waited for the loaded trains. The lingering whistles and the characteristic clatter of wheels were something happy and cheerful. I always listened to their melodious tones, and sometimes I even stopped, for they were pleasant to my ear." Few could have imagined how these steel rails winding through the landscape would soon utterly transform the spaces around them as they conveyed hundreds of thousands of people toward their deaths. "Here, in Treblinka, I now encounter a train with sixty wagons rushing past like the phantom of death," Ząbecki continued. "And the whistle of the train leaving with empty wagons frightens me terribly. It was a harbinger of unavoidable destruction."[1]

One of humanity's most enduring inventions, trains, and the tracks they travel upon, were used by Nazi planners for sinister purposes—transporting millions of Jews to the death camps. In fact, totalitarian dictators and the perpetrators of genocide and mass violence have generally preferred, at least in the first half of the twentieth century, to use trains—perhaps because the fixed tracks provide them the feelings of control they crave—to transport victims to exile, forced labor, or extermination.[2] Those who had grown accustomed to the nuanced and perhaps pleasurable experience of sensing trains as they passed nearby now became involuntary witnesses to mass murder, exposed to the full range of the life-and-death dramas playing out in their backyards. The numbers alone are staggering: from July 1942 to October 1943, 390 different trains, composed of 7,800 individual cattle cars, carried more than three-quarters of a million people to Treblinka.[3] Moreover, the cattle cars themselves became overcrowded boxes on wheels where heat, cold, deprivation, starvation, and bodily suffering overwhelmed those trapped inside in what one survivor called "Dantésque scenes."[4] And all this took place continually along the same few stretches of track.

In her book *The Train Journey*, historian Simone Gigliotti suggests that the "intense bodily assault" of the train experience caused in victims "changes to perception, distancing from the natural world, and sensorial disconnection from landscapes because of mechanized transit." In this way, the vehicle used in transporting Jews to their deaths became a space of targeted genocidal violence—"a hidden Holocaust" of spatial and somatic traumas inflicted within.[5]

Yet what happens when we widen this scope to also consider the spaces through which these trains passed?

We find that death trains came to function as mobile microcosms of the death camps toward which they traveled—extending the sights, smells, and sounds of the deprivations inflicted on Jews within these cars into the landscapes surrounding the railroad tracks cutting across Poland. All along these "railway corridors," as I call them, lived and worked countless people scattered in their rural houses, farms, villages, and larger railroad hub towns. Given the thousands of *potential* witnesses within these corridors, the sheer number of humans passing by in confined boxes, and the ability for sensory elements of sight, smell, and sound to radiate far beyond their origin, it is conceivable that witnesses to these train journeys lived not only along the railway corridors but also at farther distances beyond the tracks.

Along with sensory witnessing, Treblinka-bound trains also created moments of interaction between people along the railway corridors and the Jews temporarily passing through. These interactions resulted from intersecting spatial trajectories between those outside and those inside the trains, and they occurred mainly in two ways. First, sometimes the local population directly interacted with the trains themselves, through either their jobs as railway workers, their physical proximity to the railway lines and main stations (in homes and work sites), or the increasing backlog of trains waiting to enter Treblinka. The second potential interaction was more indirect. Once the trains passed by, they left in their wakes Jews who had successfully jumped out, the bodies of those killed in the attempt, and often other objects thrown out by people trapped inside. Ultimately, therefore, even if someone did not witness a train itself, the remnants left behind turned these railway corridors into trails of death and devastation snaking inexorably toward Treblinka.

There were three main railway corridors, one from each of the main Treblinka-bound origin points—Warsaw (southwest and the most heavily used), Białystok (northeast), and Siedlce (south). Combined, these three corridors accounted for hundreds of kilometers of track over which the death trains traversed, essentially extending the space of the Treblinka camp in one- to two-kilometer-wide tentacular swathes like spokes on a wheel.[6]

As indicated in map 2, each corridor met at the junction town of Małkinia-Górna, a roughly equidistant point for all three lines. Because of Małkinia's centralized location, the Germans used it as the hub for death-camp-bound trains. (The camp was situated 7 km slightly southeast of Małkinia.) Situated four kilometers south of Małkinia was the *town* of Treblinka—from there, the Germans built a special side track leading to the camp, and thus, the town of Treblinka became the final stop for all death-camp-bound trains.[7]

For each recorded interaction along these paths, however, there were likely innumerable additional witnesses to these trains or their remnants whose experiences have never been recorded, revealing the unbounded nature of these spaces. But whether these experiences were spoken or unspoken, charting how these witnesses interacted with the mobile extensions of the death camps traveling in their midst inherently shows the process by

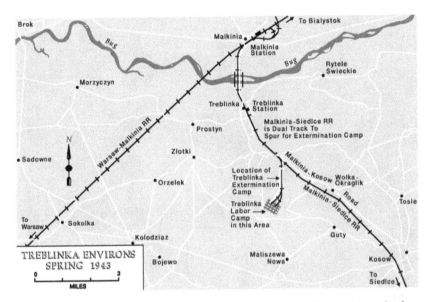

MAP 2. Map showing railway corridors that connected at Małkinia-Górna, leading to and from the three major starting points for Treblinka-bound trains: Warsaw, Białystok, and Siedlce. Several local towns are also identified. Courtesy of USHMM.

which they became connected to the larger spatial narrative of Treblinka. Ultimately, while most were not witnesses to Treblinka itself, these people experienced something *related* to the death camp—something that was, in fact, *only* passing through their world *because* the camp existed nearby and because of their own happenstance proximity to the very railway corridors the Germans decided to use in transporting Jews to be murdered.[8]

Death Camp Microcosms

Intending to dehumanize Jews, Nazi planners deliberately utilized degrading and destructive methods of transport from the ghettos to the death camps. They discarded considerations for spatial comfort and basic human needs, and instead, as Treblinka survivor Saul Kuperhand recalled, people "were piled into boxcars like cattle on the way to the slaughter."[9] A 1943 report explained, "The very method of transport was deliberately calculated to cause the largest possible number of casualties among the condemned Jews."[10] Gigliotti calls this directed assault on the body "the political immobilization

FIG. 17. Aerial view of the Małkinia-Górna railway junction taken by
a German reconnaissance plane, 1944. The line running to the bottom
of the photo is the Małkinia-Siedlce line heading south toward the Bug
River and Treblinka. USHMM, courtesy of NARA, College Park MD.

of personal mobility," and it was used to treat Jews not as people but as
freight or cargo; in fact, German reports often referred to Jews as "pieces" or
"items."[11] Consequently, with the exception of a few international transports to
Treblinka from Czechoslovakia, Belgium, and Holland—which, according
to Polish witness Czesław Borowy, arrived with orderly rows of people "in a
Pullman train . . . smartly dressed in white shirts . . . [with] flowers in their
cars . . . [and] playing cards"—the vast majority of Treblinka-bound transports occurred in thousands of overcrowded, tiny cattle cars that became
mobile boxes of death.[12]

Rated to hold between 40 and 50 people—or eight horses—the Germans often loaded each cattle car with anywhere between 120 and 200 Jews. They packed people so tightly that each person had a total area of less than two square feet, and therefore, not everyone could sit down or even stand without touching other people.[13] In this targeted assault on individual human space, survivor Sol Liber described, "you couldn't turn, just like sardines."[14] In the crowded cars, Ząbecki added, "everyone was deprived of air access and the possibility of taking care of natural needs. . . . It created unbearable conditions, even for healthy, young, and strong people."[15] As Cypora Jabłoń-Zonszajn, who witnessed a train in the Siedlce (53 km) ghetto, observed, "People became wild, they fought for access to the window. The air was unbearable—people jumped over one another. . . . A small window could not satisfy all these people."[16]

Climatological phenomena, especially warm weather, amplified this suffering. A document from Franz Stangl's trial states, "The victims squeezed into the cars had to suffer great bodily torments . . . when unbearable heat arose in the cars from the intense sun."[17] Abraham Krzepicki, sent to Treblinka in August 1942, described what he witnessed inside: "It was only about 7 a.m., but the sun was already scorching, and the heat steadily intensified. All the men had taken off their shirts and were lying half-naked, in only their pants or underpants. Some of the women, too, had thrown off their dresses and were lying in their underwear. People lay on the floor moaning, tossing around deliriously, twisting their heads, and trying to catch some air in their lungs. . . . Some had completely resigned, no longer able to move."[18] These "hot ovens," as Ząbecki called them, created appalling, inhumane conditions. "Under conditions worse than any ever imposed upon calves shipped to the slaughterhouses," Rachel Auerbach reconstructs from interviewing survivors, "the Jews licked the salt from each other's skins to slake their thirst. Terror dried up the milk in the breasts of nursing mothers who begged in vain for something with which to moisten their own parched lips or those of their babies."[19]

Though the largest deportations took place during the warm summer months of 1942, trains continued to Treblinka through the following winter. One local bystander said that he believed winter was tougher on those in trains because the brutal Polish winters could reach twenty degrees below zero. Though, as he added darkly, "they were so packed in the cars, maybe they weren't cold." ss Treblinka guard Franz Suchomel reflected how brutal the conditions were in the winter of 1942–43: "It was cold as hell. Between fifteen and minus four. I know: at first it was cold as hell for us too."[20]

Cramped spaces, lack of air, and exposure to weather conditions contributed to a high death rate on Treblinka-bound trains. Survivor Szymon Goldberg observed that the "elderly, infirm, and children" usually perished first in the wagons, but everyone faced the same torment.[21] Even those who managed to reach Treblinka alive, Krzepicki observed, "were as weak as flies."[22] Within such a universally degrading experience, those struggling to survive made horrific adaptations, as Chaim Grabel witnessed in regard to overcrowding: "When somebody fainted or died he or she was put on the floor and people stood on that person."[23] Therefore, when the trains finally arrived at Treblinka, as Edi Weinstein, who worked unloading them, discovered, "in every car there were corpses, lying in every conceivable posture."[24] One survivor suggested that on average forty to fifty people, roughly one-third of *each* car, died en route to Treblinka. Suchomel put the number higher, stating that in August 1942 (perhaps because of high temperatures), "about 2/3 of the transported inmates were already dead on arrival at Treblinka."[25] If a train was especially slow, with summer heat pounding down on it for days, the results were even deadlier, and Józef Gutman recalled that during his first days in Treblinka, some trains arrived in which everyone was dead and bodies were "already decomposing." One train, he estimated, had spent upwards of two weeks in transit.[26]

The high mortality rate meant that these cattle cars essentially became rolling coffins carrying numbers of dead bodies throughout the Polish landscape. In this gruesome reality, most cars, mobile and stationary, emitted odors into the outside world. Hubert Pfoch, a German soldier passing through the area to the Eastern Front, noted, "When we reach Treblinka station the train is next to us. . . . There is such an awful smell of decomposing corpses in the station, some of us vomit."[27] In response, the Germans covered the floors of the cars with quicklime and chlorine to mask the smell of death; however, other stenches soon coalesced within the enclosed atmosphere, overwhelming not only the quicklime but also those trapped inside. For instance, the performance of necessary bodily acts of excretion and urination, Gigliotti writes, "contributed to the psychological ruin of deportees when combined with the heat of the bodies and the overflowing outlets for the disposal of human waste." This now-public action that both men and women had to perform in front of each other "represented the closest of parallels to what they perceived as immodest, deeply traumatizing, and on par with animal or animal-like behavior."[28] The coinciding sensory emissions overwhelmed all who experienced them as people relieved themselves in all four corners of the car, since there was no toilet on board. The conditions created such an overpowering smell that Krzepicki said, "I found a crack in the floorboard where I stuck my nose to catch some air."[29] Even those outside the cars, like local Polish witness Józef Wierzbicki, observed, "The carriages were cesspools."[30]

In addition to the smellscapes they created, the trains were also extremely loud. In fact, Ząbecki wrote of how, on July 22, 1942, he heard the very first train *before* he saw it, "not because of the noise of the train, but because of the cries of the people, and the shooting."[31] Nachemiasz Szulklaper, a Polish railway dispatcher in Małkinia (7 km) heard a similar cacophony approaching: "I suddenly heard a terrible noise, human moaning and whining. . . . Ukrainians sat on the roofs in booths . . . firing salvos from automatic weapons and pistols."[32] For those living next to railway corridors who were accustomed to hearing the mechanical noises of regular train travel, the sounds of screams and shooting indicated something new was now taking place.

The human voices emerging from death trains most frequently resulted from the bodily torments suffered by those inside. As Polish train worker Jerzy Królikowski recalled, "I remember . . . one of the scorching days of July or early August 1942 . . . I heard voices screaming for water from a passing train as it went by."[33] Another survivor stated that at *each* stop on the way to Treblinka, "everyone shouted. . . . Several thousand people chanted 'wasser, wasser' [water, water]."[34] The cries from thousands of people pervaded the landscape for some distance. In fact, as Stanisława Bruszewska, who lived in Boreczek, about one kilometer from the town of Treblinka (4 km), said, "It's these 'waters,' that here in Boreczek could be heard when a big transport passed by."[35]

Other human sounds mingled with these pleas for a drink. From the train station at Treblinka, Ząbecki heard "wailing, screaming, crying, calling for water, for a doctor. There were also protests like: 'How can people be treated inhumanely? When will they finally let us out of the carriages?'"[36] As Jabłoń-Zonszajn witnessed from Siedlce (53 km), "The shouts merged into a great cry of despair of murdered, innocent, and helpless people."[37] In fact, the rising discord became so incessant that the Ukrainians guarding the trains sometimes fired into the cars to silence the people inside. This often led to horrible moments within the wagons, where, as survivor Mosze Klajman remembered, "mothers suppressed the screams of young children so they would not cry."[38] An untold number of children likely suffocated in this way, casualties of sensory-induced violence.

The gunfire itself composed another component of the railway corridors' soundscapes. Czesław Sikorski, a Polish train worker at Sokołów Podlaski (27 km) described, "As the train ran farther on, shooting was heard *all* the time."[39] According to Weinstein, most gunfire "came from soldiers stationed on the roof of the train, who shot at anyone who attempted to escape by leaping from the tiny windows."[40] These soldiers, whom Suchomel called "hellhounds"—sometimes Germans but often Ukrainians or Latvians—were positioned either on the roofs of cars or on special platforms called *brennkarts*.[41] From the brennkarts, Marian Pietrzak, resident of Sokołów Podlaski (27 km), reflected, "They stood with their rifles, with their machine guns, and when the Jews jumped out, they started shooting—they killed many Jews."[42]

Gunfire became a constant accompaniment to trains passing through the railway corridors, and nothing provoked it like Jews attempting to escape. As survivor Samuel Weiler remembered, "Some of the boxcars were pried open and the doomed prisoners began jumping from the running train. . . . All were mowed down by the train guards save three."[43] Adolf Lewin escaped in a much larger group, which "provoked a *salvo* of bullets from which 60 persons fell."[44] The volume of gunfire responsible for such casualties had to be enormous, and during these escape attempts, guards opened fire with abandon. To be sure, local Pole Marian Łopuszyński recalled an instance where, "since many people from the transport tried to escape, the personnel opened fire that was so heavy that after a while they ran out of ammunition."[45] Interspersed within the barrage of gunfire and deafening noise would have been random lone gunshots fired at various points and for various reasons. As Liber once witnessed, "[A] person stuck his head out the window and was shot through the throat."[46] It is not hard to also imagine the crack of a single shot as a warning or random act by trigger-happy guards.

Taken together, the smells, screams, and gunfire created a multisensorial contamination of the spaces through which these trains traveled. And while these were sometimes fleeting moments as trains raced past, survivors more often describe the slow pace of Treblinka-bound trains, suggesting a more saturated space of sensory witnessing as trains lingered within the railway corridors. Grabel, deported from Bełżyce, 160 kilometers from Treblinka, reported that his train took four days to reach the camp—an average speed of just 40 kilometers per *day*. Yaakov Rabinowitz recalled similarly, "The engine moves forward only grudgingly and stops at various stations for many hours."[47] These frequent stops, perhaps to let other trains pass, to change drivers, or for no reason at all, were common. "They ran us around and around and around all over," survivor Fred Kort remembered.[48] Not even the departure point seemed to factor into this equation, since even from Warsaw, only 80 kilometers from Treblinka (a trip taking two to three hours in peacetime), one train journey took over two days and "often stood in fields for several hours," according to a survivor.[49] In fact, even the "quickest" Warsaw-Treblinka trains, such as one recorded by Dawid Nowodworski, still took twelve hours to cover the route.[50]

Since trains took conspicuously longer than usual, they subsequently inundated the adjacent spaces with sensory outputs of smells and sounds for longer durations, and the longer they stayed in the railway corridors, the more opportunities locals had to become witnesses. Roughly four hundred thousand people, or half of Treblinka's victims, came from the Warsaw ghetto, and as a result, the location of its *Umschlagplatz* (loading platform), from which Treblinka-bound trains departed became the first point, chronologically speaking, of potential contact. The spatial layout of the Umschlagplatz was described by an eyewitness as "huge, oval in shape, partially surrounded by houses, and partially by fences . . . [and it] could accommodate up to eight thousand people," which made it particularly conducive to widespread witnessing.[51] Moreover, branching out from the Umschlagplatz in several directions ran streets through which flowed, during the initial roundups of July 1942, a near continuous procession of Jews carrying bundles of food, clothes, and other possessions amid rows of ss men and Jewish policemen armed with rifles and clubs to maintain order. Tangentially connected to the loading platform and hence the railway corridors themselves, these routes to the Umschlagplatz had their own level of violence. As local witness Antoni Szymanowski once witnessed, an elderly man in the procession stumbled and stepped out of line to rest against a wall when "a German hit him on

FIG. 18. Jews moving to the train station near Siedlce, Poland, for deportation to Treblinka. The photo was likely taken by a member of the local Polish Home Army unit between August 21 and 24, 1942, and its composition, with obstructions framing the shot, suggests it was captured quickly and discreetly. Courtesy of Yad Vashem Photo Archive, 1597/277.

the back of the head. He fell over. The German pulled out a revolver, fired at him, and turned away without looking back."[52] In this way, according to Zdzisław Łukaszkiewicz's report, even "the road . . . to the station was covered with people killed along the way."[53] The photos in figures 18 and 19 show how visible such roundup actions were, and the clandestine nature of both photos suggests that many witnesses caught glimpses of the deportations and the loading of death trains as they carried out their daily lives.

Once people arrived at the Umschlagplatz to board the trains, new horrors played out in full view. As a witness described the scene,

[The Jews] did not hide their despair: the men spoke with raised voices, and the women, whose children had been taken away, screamed and spasmed. But after a while, they too were overwhelmed by the atmosphere of apathy and numbness prevailing at the Umschlagplatz. . . . The whistle of the locomotive came from a distance and the rumble

FIG. 19. Photo of Warsaw ghetto deportation of Jews in April 1943, secretly taken through a window above the street by Leszek Grzywaczewski, Polish underground member. USHMM, courtesy of Howard Kaplan.

of railcars on the tracks came closer. . . . I turned around and shuffled forward in the middle of the deserted street, crying loudly, while from the direction of the train siding I heard the faint cries of people locked inside the wagons, like the muffled screams of birds in cages, filled with a mortal fear.[54]

Krzepicki observed similarly, "The girls were screaming, weeping, stretching out their hands begging 'I'm young, I want to work!'"[55] Such scenes often elicited emotional responses from those living nearby, as Szymanowski recalled: "After filling the wagon, they wired it with barbed wire. Worse than cattle. It was raining and the view of this misery was . . . unbearable." With their frequently slow schedule, some trains did not leave right away, and in this prolonged wait, Szymanowski once maneuvered his way onto the Umschlagplatz to receive a note from someone inside. It read, "I am already two days without food, lying on the floor in terrible conditions. We're leaving now—I don't know to where, probably to death, but I don't care."[56] On another occasion, a witness watched a train sit at the Umschlagplatz for a week, during which time "executioners approached and shot into the barred windows, killing or wounding many people."[57] The longer a train waited, the clearer the fate of the people onboard became—one the German guards no longer disguised. For those watching from the relative "safety" of the Polish side of Warsaw, larger trends became observable. "Trains returned after a dozen or so hours empty, cleaned with lime and new transports were prepared," Jan Przedborski recorded. "That's how entire weeks went."[58] Arising from this simple spatial proximity to the Umschlagplatz alone (or other deportation points), witnesses built knowledge about the genocide as they peered out of their windows to witness a scene like that which appears in figure 20. Here, the loading of Treblinka-bound trains in Warsaw's Umschlagplatz is clearly visible from a nearby building.

The photo's very existence, and what it so clearly shows, invokes the realization that countless people could have had eyes on the trains at any given moment—people like Józefa Miros, a Polish girl living in the Warsaw suburb of Falenica. "I was sitting at home because my building was right next to the station and we were watching through the window," she later recounted. "The curtains were drawn, but a child always sees a lot. . . . When the people were entering the wagons and when they couldn't enter by themselves, these Germans hit them with the butts of their guns. So this is how they loaded the first wagon, took it away and brought about the second one. Three wagons were standing then."[59] Such conspicuous moments of witnessing likely occurred at many different points along the railway corridors of Poland (and undoubtedly, other parts of occupied Europe).

Upon setting out from the Umschlagplatz (or a different origination point), these trains and their occupants entered a world full of potential witnesses. In response, the Germans tried to hide their operations up and down the railway corridors. The Reich Main Security Office, the Reich Ministry of Transport, the German *Reichsbahn* (Imperial Railway), and the Eastern Railway (organized by the General Government) worked to coordinate timetables of death-camp-bound trains.[60] They also tightly guarded information regarding individual train movements, implementing a strategy where "on single-track lines, an interval of at least fifteen minutes [was] allowed in passing stations between the time a train moving in the opposite direction moved through and the special train carrying Jews arrived."[61] On August 27, 1942, the Germans issued the even more restrictive General Directorate

FIG. 20. A witness's photo of the Umschlagplatz and Treblinka-bound trains, likely taken covertly, as though glancing over someone's shoulder. This photo reveals the visibility of the deportation process to witnesses, even those beyond the ghetto walls. Courtesy of E. Ringelblum Jewish Historical Institute, Warsaw.

of the Eastern Railway, which barred passenger trains from stopping at the Treblinka town station (4 km). Ząbecki, who received the directorate, said that this measure ostensibly aimed "to limit the ability of outsiders to notice anything related to mass genocide."[62] Nevertheless, even these secret timetables became predictable to those in the know (Polish railway workers and people living along the tracks). As Henryk Gawkowski, a train engineer from Treblinka town station (4 km), remembered vividly, "There was a schedule of trains, but often there were unscheduled or unexpected trains that operated outside their normal hours. These were the 'ghost' trains because they didn't exist."[63]

Clandestine directorates and schedules failed to prevent local Poles from witnessing trains, and few had closer interactions than Polish railway workers. Królikowski, who worked repairing tracks near Treblinka, recalled his first inescapable encounter with a death train:

By the bridge on the Małkinia-Siedlce line, next to which we worked, passed a strange train. It consisted of covered "goods wagons," whose windows were barred with coiled wire. The haggard, pale faces of people could be seen through the dense barbs. Soon thereafter, on the same day passed three more such trains. . . . The worst for us was to observe a transport at close range. It was not always possible to avoid. Sometimes transports surprised us as they crossed the bridge, which was 350 meters long, making it not always possible to get off and out of the way. At that time, you had to stop on the bridge and watch the wagons rolling next to you.[64]

Having this unobstructed vantage point, railway workers witnessed the death trains up close. In fact, their own lives were sometimes caught in the ongoing life-and-death struggle the trains brought with them. Ząbecki described one incident, perhaps involving Królikowski's group: "Workers of the bridge construction on the Bug [River], under repair at that time, fell to the ground to protect themselves from bullets [shot at people escaping]."[65]

As constantly staffed, fixed locations, train stations became major witnessing sites, and some of the first station workers to observe death trains were those like Piotr Ferenc, who worked in the switch tower two hundred meters from the Małkinia (7 km) station main platform. From this vantage point, between August and December 1942 alone, he watched as an average of three death trains, each composed of about sixty cars, passed by daily.[66] From Małkinia, the trains moved on to the town of Treblinka (4 km), where Ząbecki, who oversaw the station there, distinctly remembered the first train he saw: "Wagon doors were bolted, windows barred with barbed wire. A dozen or so SS-men with automatic weapons at the ready were lying on the railcars on both sides of the train and even on the roofs." Ząbecki also saw chalked figures on each car, which he soon determined denoted the number of people inside, and he used his unique situation to "note down the figures that very first day, and . . . never stopped for over a year." Becoming a critical witness to passing Treblinka-bound trains, Ząbecki recorded—rather accurately—that each passing cattle car carried between 120 and 200 people, giving each train a capacity of between 7,000 and 10,000 people.[67] These numbers were also noticed in Wólka Okrąglik (1 km) on the Siedlce-Małkinia line, as railway worker Henryk Slebzak saw on each car, written in clay or chalk, "120 in here, 80 there."[68] Even in Małkinia, Ferenc kept count, noting with some accuracy, "We counted by the cars that about a million [people] had passed through Małkinia."[69] Something else the railway workers observed was the frequency of passing death trains, which during Treblinka's first weeks of operation included three or four trains daily—though this number fluctuated as time progressed.[70]

While they watched, train workers tracked other patterns as well. Henry Kruger, a railway worker at the Małkinia (7 km) station, recalled, "After we start[ed] working the railroads we used to see twice a day trains going, packed with Jews. Two or three hours later they were coming back empty. We even saw Jews from Western Europe—France, Holland, Belgium, Norway, Denmark coming in [Pullmans], dressed in furs and diamonds, eating beautiful French bread with whatever . . . in the cars protected by Ukrainians."[71] Ząbecki (and maybe others) also figured out the code the Germans used to organize and disguise the trains—those from the General Government were marked *PKr*, returning trains were marked *Lp Kr*, transports from outside the General Government (like from Białystok, for example) were marked *PJ*, and transports from abroad were marked *Da*.[72] In noting the frequency, occupancy, and distinctive *type* of passing train, Ząbecki began to piece together details about their final destination, all without ever entering the camp itself. As he later put it, "While working at the station in Treblinka [town], I became *aware* of the most important events regarding the camp."[73] After all, despite how they appeared while passing by—whether in comfortable trains with curious faces pressed against picture windows or crammed into loud, stinking cattle cars—the silence of the return journey spoke volumes.

Simply put, one could glean enough information just from observing Treblinka's railway corridors to fill in the larger picture of what happened at the end of the line. Through the knowledge they formed, many railway workers began to spread information to other railway workers, creating some of the first channels relaying details about Treblinka to the wider world. As survivor Zygmunt Strawczyński commented, the "railway people" spread the first news of "exactly how it is in Treblinka. That they bring the people there, [and] they empty the wagons."[74]

Many of these Polish railway workers also probably first took the next step—going from passive witnesses to establishing contact with the trains and the people inside. Because the railway siding at the death camp could hold twenty cars at a time, the Germans divided each transport of sixty cars into thirds. In exceptional cases, the "unloading" of a train at Treblinka took fifteen minutes, after which the empty car was shunted back to the Treblinka town station to be exchanged for a waiting full section. Witnesses are quick to point out, however, that it was *rarely* this fast, and therefore, it was common for multiple twenty-car segments to be waiting at the Treblinka town station (4 km) for long durations, even overnight—especially if two or three trains arrived at once, which frequently happened during Treblinka's first few months of operation.[75] In fact, the backlog at the town of Treblinka was sometimes so heavy that train sections were made to wait even further down the line at Małkinia (7 km).[76]

Amid these backlogs, Ząbecki observed, "Railway men, especially at night, with flashlights in hand, had access to the train. This circumstance was often used to enable Jews to escape. . . . There were no German overseers or dangerous people near us, so we opened the doors of the wagons and the Jews fled. We gave them directions and places where they would be relatively safe."[77] Polish train engineer Stefan Kucharek recalled that once, while working near a waiting train, he saw a Jewish woman indicate she was hungry: "So I got off the engine and I checked the cranks here and there . . . and she was in the first car, right behind the engine. I simply threw this sandwich at her and she grabbed it."[78] Krzepicki remembered a similar instance where Polish railway workers gave bread and water to people in his cattle car despite German threats against this behavior.[79] As Antoni Tomczuk reflected, in this manner, "the Polish railway men who worked on the railroad also showed great help to the prisoners."[80]

Such interactions most often took place at larger stations but were certainly also possible anywhere along the railway corridors where trains stopped for any duration (which they frequently did). For instance, Sikorski, the train station worker in distant Sokołów Podlaski (27 km), witnessed the following interaction: "Because it was summer, it was hot. These Jews [on the train] were undressed, the windows were barred with barbed wire, and they could only look out the window. . . . They asked for water. At first the Germans allowed water to be given to the Jews, and they carried buckets and gave this water to the wagons. . . . Later the stationmasters got into trouble for this. . . . [The Jews] were sweaty and screaming all the time. Sometimes, they threw money from the wagons through the windows."[81] As this scene reveals, interactive spaces along railway corridors sometimes were subject to German oversight. Thus, anytime an outsider approached a cattle car, they assumed a risk to interact with those inside. In fact, Edward Sypko remembered that once the Germans arrested a railway worker caught smuggling bread and interned him at Treblinka I. From that point forward, Sypko added, "the railway men were afraid because the smallest piece of bread threatened them with camp imprisonment. . . . They could not help anymore."[82]

Backlogs at village stations also allowed *non*railway workers to witness and interact with trains. Ząbecki recounted, "There were cases that, due to lack of space, the Treblinka station could not accept trains with 'resettlers,' so these trains were stopped for several hours at the Wólka Okrąglik station, which made it possible for several thousand wounded German soldiers passing from the Eastern Front in sanitary trains to the hospital in Sokołów Podlaski, to observe . . . what was going on. . . . The tragedy taking place at the station could not be hidden from the soldiers . . . and upon exiting the sanitary cars in Sokołów Podlaski, they curiously asked Polish railway men what these transports and the people in them meant."[83] Pfoch, the German soldier passing through to the Eastern Front, witnessed the following: "The guards—Ukrainian volunteer ss, some of them drunk—cram 180 people into each car. . . . When all of them are finally loaded there are cries from all cars—'Water,' they plead, 'my gold ring for water.' . . . When some of them manage to climb out through the ventilating holes, they are shot the moment they reach the ground—a massacre that made us sick to our souls, a blood-bath as I had never dreamed of."[84]

Transitory witnesses aside, the spatial layouts of small Polish towns meant that many local Poles (nonrailway workers) lived near train tracks and stations. Slebzak noted how the residents of Wólka Okrąglik (1 km), although technically prohibited from doing so, went out to view the trains. "There was a ravine there; the railway was low and there were high embankments on one side and high embankments on the other," he recounted. "So the transport was standing such that you couldn't see much of it from the village, only the steam locomotive that was standing there, while the wagons were all standing back in these embankments. We *always* went to that embankment and sat there and watched."[85] Similar scenes transpired all along the railway corridors. From Sokołów Podlaski (27 km), Pietrzak recalled, "I personally saw such transports, not the ones from Sokołów but other transports as they passed through Sokołów, and I was watching these transports pass. And back then, you know, you watched secretly, you watched from afar. Because you were not allowed—when the Jewish transport was at the station, passenger trains would not stop. . . . When the Jewish transport would leave from the station in Sokołów, then the regular passenger train would arrive."[86] In all likelihood, there were always Polish eyes on these death trains. As Henryk Radzisze-wski documented, the Polish Home Army (the AK), for which he was the regional commander in areas near the towns of Węgrów (25 km) and Ostrów Mazowiecka (23 km), kept "very strict" records of passing death trains, including the destination, the number of transported people, the cargo, and the time of day they went by. He added that the "observation service had to run 24 hours a day without a break" to keep an accurate count. Although he estimated three million people were sent to Treblinka—a figure three times too high—it is fair to conclude that rare was the train headed to Treblinka or elsewhere that passed by his post unobserved.[87] In fact, it was a local Polish villager from the town of Treblinka (4 km), Kazimierz Skarżyński, not a railway worker, who told Soviet reporter Vasily Grossman after the war that as many as six trains (he counted either any passing train or each twenty-car Treblinka-bound segment as its own) passed by his village daily.[88]

One notable spatial quality of the railway corridors is that outside of major stations, they were relatively open to any curious witness. Kruger, who lived in Wołomin (62 km) along the Warsaw-Małkinia line, had the following experience one summer night in 1942: "Beneath the railroad tracks was a big pipe with water going through. We went in underneath the train. We pay the Pole not to raise the signal green, only stay red. And the train was stopped. . . . And then we heard talk in Jewish and praying, and crying, and the kids were hungry, and things like that. We came back to the ghetto. We say, 'Those were Jewish trains going some place.'"[89] Though Kruger himself was in a unique position—a Jewish person living in a work ghetto not liquidated until October 1942 (and thus able to witness the first wave of Warsaw ghetto trains)—his story shows the unbounded nature of the railway corridors, a reality for other Poles living in Wołomin and elsewhere along the tracks. The Germans could not isolate and confine these spaces as they felt they could at the Reinhard camps, and who knows how many other witnesses had experiences like Kruger's. For illustration, survivor Richard Glazar remembered, "The train had stopped. On one side was the wood, and on the other were fields. We saw cows watched over by a young man, a farmhand. . . . Not in words, but in signs, we asked: 'What's going on here?' And he made that gesture (draws finger across throat)."[90] Laden with the implications of this farmhand's knowledge of Treblinka or the trains (or both), this example makes quite clear the random spatial intersection of lived experiences created by railway corridors.

At stops near villages or towns, proximity equated to more frequent interactions. Dawid Nowodworski, whose testimony was found in the Oyneg Shabes Archive, described the following scene at the Treblinka town station (4 km): "A lot of Poles came to the wagons. . . . I spoke to the [train] driver, a Pole, and to the question of whether groups often go to work from here, he replied: they only arrive, from here no one leaves."[91] The suffering occurring inside these waiting trains would have been on full display. As Samuel Willenberg experienced from inside a cattle car, "On the track opposite stood a train just like ours, its passengers crushing one another as they tried to peer through the tiny, barbed-wire grilles." He added that among these waiting trains and such dire scenes walked many local Poles who frequently interacted with those trapped inside.[92] Ferenc, one of these Poles outside the trains, recalled from Małkinia (7 km), "We could [see into the trains] because the windows were wired but not shut. . . . And [the Jews] were sticking their faces and heads out and they were screaming: 'Give us water, give us water!'"[93] Responding to these requests, some Poles, according to Weinstein, "carried buckets of water over to the cars and filled the bottles that passengers pushed at them. But they charged dearly for each bottle." Survivor Yankel Wiernik reflected that water went for one hundred złotys a bottle, while bread sold for five hundred złotys per kilogram.[94] A similar atmosphere met stopped trains all along the railway corridors. As an anonymous author, who escaped Treblinka in September 1942 and returned to Warsaw, wrote in an Oyneg Shabes Archive document, "The peasants knew about the regular transports and were already waiting for the train," and on overnight stops at different rail sidings, purchases of water and food took place constantly.[95]

Others simply *lived* next to the train stations or adjacent to the tracks themselves. Barbara Goska, whose house in Wólka Okrąglik (1 km) was near the station, remembered, "A train transport destined for Treblinka stopped near our house."[96] Czesław Borowy, whose house was located next to the Treblinka town train station (4 km), revealed that he often "saw everything. . . . The train cars were overflowing. . . . They would cry out for water."[97] For these witnesses, the happenstance of proximity meant that their homes became part of the landscape of the death trains and the suffering occurring within these spaces. "What was happening in Treblinka, just at the railway station, is impossible to explain or describe," Ząbecki later wrote. "Nobody can conceive or re-create these horrors, this hell on earth."[98] Królikowski further added, "For many prisoners, the Treblinka station was the last station on their path of life."[99] As this fact became more apparent to those inside the waiting cars, tension and anxiety increased. "One train went in, then . . . came back empty," survivor Abraham Bomba described. "The second train went in, it came back, took about an hour or so, also empty, and then the train I was in started to roll into Treblinka extermination camp."[100] In this frenetic environment, trapped Jews frequently tried to escape, and local Poles living nearby were caught amid these life-and-death struggles. Królikowski, whose home sat four hundred to five hundred meters away from the Treblinka town station, reflected, "The gunshots at the station at escaping prisoners often *came our way.* Sometimes we could see through our windows people running completely naked fleeing through the fields. They usually fell under the shots of the guards and only a few escaped."[101] This extraordinary experience puts escape attempts (often from moving trains) in stark juxtaposition with spaces of homes, where people watched from the "safety" of their living room the life-and-death dramas occurring just outside their windows.[102] Claude Lanzmann later wrote of one such witness, "This gentleman has lived here a long time; he can't forget it."[103]

Yet these surreal moments may not have been that uncommon along the railway corridors of Poland. Wólka Okrąglik (1 km) resident Halina Sikorska reflected, "Our family lived . . . in a railway booth in Wólka Okrąglik. . . . From the windows of this place, Jewish transports were visible. There was not yet a railway station . . . but there was . . . a siding. In front of me, while the train was stopped in transit, the Germans killed a tall and slender 17-year-old boy escaping through the train's window. He was wearing a red sweater with green stripes."[104] Distinctions between watching and being immersed in the tragedy occasionally vanished entirely. "There were convoys where quite a few people would force open doors or escape out the windows," Czesław Borowy witnessed, "so, if they were caught, they would be killed right here [in front of his house]."[105] Situations like these affected the day-to-day lives of those living nearby, as Ząbecki observed: "Residents of station buildings and nearby farms were under constant threat, and during shootings, they were forced to hide or not leave their apartments."[106] As an involuntary backdrop for escape attempts, these residents' homes came under siege from the hail of bullets that followed. "A transport was already moving and [someone] jumped out. . . . It was snowing and he fled," Slebzak recounted. "They fired at him with machine guns, but this one escaped into some buildings and survived. And then, I do not know where he went."[107] Hence anyone who escaped from the confines of the cattle car amid the gunfire immediately sought refuge in any nearby structure—abandoned buildings, sheds, or even homes with people inside, as Kucharek discovered one evening when two women who escaped from a waiting train in Małkinia (7 km) showed up at his railway-adjacent home (Kucharek sheltered them for three days).[108] It was here, then, that the experiences of interacting with the vehicles transporting Jews to Treblinka merged with encounters with Jews fleeing from them.

Survivors, Bodies, and Remnants

One constant of the death train journeys to Treblinka was that people inside attempted to escape at nearly every point along the railway corridors. "When the train started and was moving, they were jumping out," said Sikorski, the Polish train worker at Sokołów Podlaski (27 km). *Everyone jumped wherever they could. They pulled out the attached wires and jumped through the windows. Many of them did not escape, but there were always a few who tried.*"[109] From the perspective of the person escaping, the decision to jump meant liberating themselves from the suffering of the cattle car and avoiding the fate they increasingly came to understand awaited at Treblinka. Of the latter, Liber recalled that by the first stop outside of Warsaw, everyone inside the car already "knew we were going to Treblinka . . . because we knew the roads. . . . If you went west, you went to Treblinka. We recognized the station. . . . Everyone started panicking."[110] Kuperhand reflected similarly that there was a certain junction where if the train turned left, it was headed toward Małkinia (7 km) and, thereafter, Treblinka. Once his train made this left turn, he later wrote, "Many of us broke down and lamented the certain death that we now knew awaited us."[111] Other times, people waited longer before deciding to jump, and according to Ferenc, who witnessed such events, it was often at Małkinia (7 km), "when the train started going toward Treblinka [that] the Jews were jumping out because they . . . knew—Małkinia was the last station."[112]

The palpable fear of Treblinka, especially prevalent in later deportations, injected elements of desperation and panic into an atmosphere already fraught with the debilitating conditions inside the cattle cars. As Nochem Babikier described,

> After a while, the observers near the window shouted in despair: "We are dead, we are going to Małkinia, and so to death at Treblinka." A panic broke out in the wagon, people were wringing their hands. Young people decided to violently break down the door and jump off the train. A piece of iron was torn from the door and a few people did jump. . . . A significant number of jumpers were killed on the spot [by bullets]. . . . In the car, a 30-year-old owner of a cosmetics store . . . was cutting his throat. Nobody gave him help. . . . A doctor took an injection. . . . Another doctor gave his 13-year-old son poison . . . "Child, I do not want to die, but I prefer death by our own hands than by the German's hands."[113]

Babikier adds that their train, in fact, kept moving right past Treblinka, ultimately ending up in Lublin, inexplicably. And yet, the dread of Treblinka was so great it provoked frantic choices—taking one's own life or jumping from a moving train. The latter, especially, was often an instantaneous and unplanned decision. "They took us to the trains to go to Treblinka," Jack Price recalled of his own experience. "Then I got over to that little window and I pulled out the barbed wire with my clothes because I couldn't pull it with my hands and I slipped out. I dived down and they were shooting after me and the train kept going and I went back to Warsaw."[114] While the spontaneity of Price's jump was common, his survival makes the experience unique, because escape attempts, as Zdzisław Goldstein estimated, often ended in "one hundred percent failure" because of "jumping during the day, exceptional speed of the train, [and a] very strong escort."[115]

Despite the odds, however, people still tried to escape, many accepting that if they died in the attempt, they did so "preferring it to death in Treblinka," survivor Elias Magid observed.[116] "My jumping out did not mean I would rescue myself, but simply, make my death easier, because I was very afraid of death in Treblinka," then twelve-year-old Luba Frank reflected. "When the train moved with the highest speed, I crawled through a small window and jumped out. I don't really remember more."[117] Jacob Freier spoke of preferred jumping strategies: "We were told that if you wanted to jump from the train, as soon as you see the telegraph post, jump, because if you wait, hesitate a second, you will jump into the [next] post, and a lot were killed in that way."[118] In the category of obstacles one might not have considered, people did perish in this manner; as Frank recalled, one man on her train "jumped but he hit his head on an electric post."[119]

In these dire escape scenarios, miraculously surviving the jump ushered in a whole new range of perils. "Much is talked about jumping from the cars, only very little is known about the mortal danger and the thousands of perils in it," a man named Finkelsztajn, who escaped from a Treblinka-bound death train, wrote. "Hundreds have succeeded in it, but many hundreds have suffered grave injuries, broken limbs and crushed skulls, and for these there was no hospital, no medical help, only an all-liberating death. No less perilous was the fate of those who succeeded." These new challenges to survival arose the moment the tumble ended. Though momentarily knocked out on impact, Finkelsztajn remembered upon awakening from his own escape, "There was a gang of local peasants, aged 20 to 40, armed with sticks and iron rods, who were catching escapees and beating them to death. . . . Still, some two-hundred and fifty beaten and injured people gathered alive. . . . Peasants searched the little wood nearby. . . . Later they telephoned the railway police in Łuków [80 km], who came immediately. Peasants and policemen encircled the escapees and drove them back to Łuków."[120] The presence of people walking along the railway corridors seems to have been normal, and local witness Noach Lasman wrote, "It was dangerous to walk close to railway tracks because it was known that the Germans had a special formation called *Bahnschutz*, whose armed members patrolled the railway lines day and night."[121] Ząbecki recalled that the Bahnschutz had outposts in the villages of Bielany (35 km), Sokołów Podlaski (27 km), and Kosów Lacki (7 km), essentially giving them "coverage" all along the main tracks leading to Treblinka. Bahnschutz formations were particularly troublesome for jumpers injured in the process, since the groups were "sent specially to the railway tracks to catch the fleeing Jews . . . catching the wounded, robbing them, and then finishing them off there."[122] And since so many who jumped injured their legs, ankles, and feet, they often could not escape this fate.[123]

If a person survived the jump and evaded the Bahnschutz, they entered a new spatial reality—one that offered many different things: hope, survival, uncertainty, and inevitably, more challenges. The first of these, hope, came well before the jump, and many expressed the emotion in terms connected to the rural landscapes through which their Treblinka-bound trains passed. "By the light of dawn we beheld green fields, rivers and lakes, a forest on the horizon," Willenberg described from inside a cattle car. "Gleaming sunbeams lent the forest a reddish hue which, to this day, I see only as so grey-blue. It was a lovely autumn morning."[124] Not simply a visual space of tranquility, the world outside the cattle car was one from whence "a cooler wind wafts into our sealed boxcar and the pastoral scent of fields and farms reaches us," Yaakov Rabinowitz wrote. "Outside the ghetto, nature still smiles on Poland; the fields and forests, birds and flowers, still thrive in the large—and free—world."[125]

Though speaking of hope, Rabinowitz's words also reveal anxiety in the juxtaposition of the *free* and *large* world outside with the horrors occurring inside the *sealed* cars. Others also reference this spatial contradiction, including an unknown survivor who wrote in their Oyneg Shabes Archive record, "The dawn sun had already risen and a beautiful rural day greened against the clear azure sky. The train has been in the field for several hours. An empty green meadow stretched out next to the train, a very even road ran by, and in the background stood a rural, brick cottage surrounded by a garden. Two young ladies stood in the garden, idyllic. In the meantime, in the wagon, my mother could barely gasp for air, with dried-up lips, and was moaning softly."[126] Highlighting the agony inside the cattle car offers a vivid contrast to the nearby world where local people, often visible from within the cars, seemingly carried out their normal lives as if the boxes of death on wheels were not hurtling by their homes and fields. Thaddeus Stabholz gave voice to this contrast: "The sun is shining; the sky is blue; the world is beautiful. We pass lovely resorts near the outskirts of the city. Lilacs are blooming; children play merrily in the fields, but we are riding toward death, toward a terrible death."[127]

Another survivor captured the moment she encountered the landscape beyond the cattle car after a successful jump:

She stood up and looked around. The railway embankment was located at a distance of several dozen meters. It was a little overgrown at the edges but with a clean ditch of water in the middle. . . . There was a path on the right side of the pond where you could not see any dwelling, but you would end up at some type of residence. . . . The area was almost flat, slightly undulating, the view was open to a great distance. There were cows grazing, and somewhere far away a dog barked, but people could not be seen. *Nothing indicated the war was going on and that traveling along the nearby railway line were wagons tightly packed with corpses and dying peoples.*[128]

Indeed, the starkest contrast for those trapped inside cattle cars was the visibility of rural residences dotting the countryside along the railway corridors. Looking out from a cattle car, Weinstein described, "I approached the door and peered out carefully. . . . Farther away, on the horizon, I could make out a green forest, here and there, the silhouette of an isolated house."[129] These rural trackside houses not only served as reminders of how life went on outside the cars, but they also usually became the precise locations of the interactions between those who escaped the trains and local populations. As Sadowne (13 km) resident Władysław Rażmowski recalled, his neighbor, a man named Zduńczyk, frequently encountered surviving Jews because they "came to Zduńczyk's house, lying next to the railway track, asking for a piece of bread and directions to the Bug, which promised their greatest chances of survival."[130]

Since people jumped wherever they could, most of the subsequent Jewish-Polish interactions occurred at random. As Frank remembered, "All I can remember is jumping, and hearing shots, and I made summersaults, I was so light, and the shots going between my legs, and the next thing . . . I must have fallen unconscious on the railway lines. And minutes later, I think it could have been only minutes when a woman, an elderly Polish woman came over to me and spoke to me in Polish and she said, 'Wake up, child, wake up. You just jumped and the Germans are cleaning up whoever is alive, they are finishing them off. Run!" That this encounter happened almost immediately after Frank jumped from the train underscores how many local people occupied the railway corridor spaces. In fact, soon after encountering this first woman, Frank came across three more men digging potatoes; they gave her directions.[131] As Frank's experience further illustrates, the interaction was random for Poles as well; people could be walking near their homes and suddenly come across Jews who had just escaped from a passing train. Eugeniusz Goska, who lived and worked near the train tracks, had this very experience: "Once as I walked and the cows were grazing . . . this one Jew who had escaped . . . he asked me to take him to Siedlce. I didn't have a horse or anything, so I directed him to go farther away from the camp. . . . I wanted him to run, because here was too close [to Treblinka], so he should not go that way over there."[132]

For survivors, the presence of local people along the railway corridors served as a reminder that they were now in a disorienting landscape of unease, hostility, and unfamiliarity. As Frank wrote, "From that day on I was wandering alone in an unfamiliar neighborhood. Days and nights went by, and I was barefoot and naked."[133] Even if someone knew the area intimately before the war (unlikely for most Treblinka-bound victims, who were far more familiar with the city landscapes of Warsaw than the rural areas stretching northward), there was often no way to tell exactly where along the line they had jumped. In these foreign and uncertain landscapes, therefore, in the words of author Nella Rost, "the atmosphere of the surroundings through which the death transports went had a fundamental importance" to survival.[134] Jacob Freier recalled the diverse responses he encountered after escaping a Treblinka-bound train:

> It was winter, it was still cold, and we jumped out and when we were walking through the woods, six of us; we were free, supposedly free. We were not in a concentration camp, we were not in any jail or anything, and we walked, and then we saw in a small village . . . a poster that for hiding a Jew it is [the] death penalty. For delivering a Jew, that's appealing to the Polish population. . . . You get . . . 10 kilograms of sugar and [their] clothes, which meant a lot . . . because everything was in short supply . . . and now we didn't know what to do. We came to one farmer, and he says, "For heaven's sake, just go away, I don't want to have anything to do with you because I don't want to die." And we understood. He is honest. . . . We used to sneak into the barn, and we used to sleep, and that was three nights like this. We came to one farmer and [he] says, "Oh yeah, come on in here, I'll give you soup."

And then, meanwhile, he said something to his daughter, and she ran out [into] the backyard, and we go, "She's going to notify the police, and we better run."[135]

Jews who did escape occupied precarious positions within the spaces they now found themselves—ones in which, as Freier noticed, they were no longer imprisoned but still not out of danger.

Local Polish reactions upon encountering these Jewish survivors ranged widely (as was also true for escapees from Treblinka itself; see chapter 4). Some were hostile, like a person Frank encountered on her escape: "There was . . . a shepherd looking after cows, and when he saw us four walking, he recognized that we were Jews, and he picked up a stick, and he was . . . threatening to hit us or kill us."[136] Others assisted. Stanisław Falkowski, who lived in Nowe Piekuty (50 km) on the Białystok-Małkinia railway line, hid a Jewish survivor in a church and obtained "Aryan documents" for him—probably saving his life. Similarly, Józef Perkowski, who lived along the same route, hid a fourteen-year-old Jewish boy named Józef Kurtzebie, who escaped from a Treblinka-bound train. German ordinances against helping Jews did not distinguish between those escaping camps and those escaping trains, however, and so these interactions too were fraught with life-and-death consequences. For instance, Julianna and Stanisław Postek, who lived in rural Stoczek (13 km), hid several Jews who fled from deportation trains to Treblinka, but when the Germans raided the farm in September 1943, they found these Jews hidden throughout the residence and later executed the Postek family.[137]

Given the uncertainties facing them, the logical question for many who survived escaping the train became where to go next. As one diarist from the Warsaw ghetto recorded, "One of our carpenters, Haim Srebnik, came back, having been . . . as far as the Treblinka station."[138] Essentially traveling the entire eighty kilometers back to Warsaw, Srebnik made a journey wherein he probably followed closely the same railway corridors through which he just passed. However, returning to the ghetto, especially the larger ones like Warsaw and Białystok, was fraught with danger, and because transports to Treblinka continued from both places until August 1943, the threat of recapture (and deportation again) remained high. In fact, Stanisław Zeminski once witnessed a woman who escaped from a death train near his residence in the town of Łuków (80 km): "She went to the village, nobody gave her food, nobody let her in. Resigned, hungry, and cold, she decided to return to the Łuków ghetto." As subsequent trains passed through Łuków to Treblinka, they stopped to collect Łuków ghetto Jews that they "pulled out of various hiding places." The woman Zeminski described may have met this very fate.[139]

An alternative for many survivors was to join up with or form their own partisan communities in the rural areas around the tracks. When the Soviets liberated the Treblinka area in 1944, they found a group of Jewish refugees in the forests of Szydłowiec "made up mainly of Jews who had managed to jump off a train that was on its way from Szydłowiec [175 km] to Treblinka at the end of 1942." Instead of returning home, this group survived in the nearby woods for over two years—despite losing sixteen members in the intervening period.[140] For many, the inherent risks of partisan life outweighed the chance of being forced on another train journey. As Frank observed, "We heard the . . . trains going to Treblinka that were passing that spot where we were" hiding out in the train-track-adjacent forests.[141] These were the haunting auditory reminders of both the fate they had escaped and the one still stalking them.

The presence of train survivors up and down the railway corridors created many opportunities for interactions with local Poles, but these local populations likely more often encountered the bodies of those who did not survive. Raźmowski, who lived in rural Sadowne (13 km) near the Warsaw-Małkinia railway line, observed, "The railway track was constantly strewn with the corpses of murdered Jews who jumped out of the wagons to save their lives. . . . Almost all of them were killed by the bullets from ss guards in the first and last wagon."[142] One could not travel far along the tracks without finding these remains, it seems, and as Szulklaper, the Polish railway worker, commented on the frequency of these horrors, "After transports passed, I saw . . . on both sides of the tracks the bodies of people lying who were trying to save themselves by jumping out of the windows of the wagon."[143] Bodies ended up alongside the track for other reasons as well. As Adolf Lewin noted, "We threw the bodies out through the window" of those who died en route.[144] Moreover, these train remnants included not just bodies; as Weinstein, who was forced to clean the train tracks as part of a Jewish detachment from Treblinka, recalled, "In addition to the bodies [around the tracks] there were severed legs, arms, hands, and other body parts lying between the railroad tracks."[145] Presumably, these remains came from those who jumped but did not clear the tracks.

These frightful scenes were widespread and commonplace. In the words of Wacław Sawicki, "*Piles* of corpses remained on the line."[146] While working along the railway, Królikowski recounted, "We tried to avoid the sight of dead or wounded people [along the tracks], because sometimes the escape attempts took place just after crossing the bridge, where our construction site and a number of barracks were located below the embankment."[147] This seemed to be true all along the railway corridors. (Figure 21 shows bodies of Jews who attempted to escape along the tracks in Siedlce—53 km—in 1942.) A Polish man named Marzec told Rachel Auerbach in a postwar interview, "Many corpses lay strewn along the railroad tracks at *every* stop."[148] In this way, witnesses with no connection to Treblinka and perhaps even those who lived nowhere near the tracks themselves happened upon these remains. Józef Sobolewski, an engineer based out of Białystok (90 km), recalled one experience on a non-death-camp-bound train from Białystok to Warsaw: "I encountered about 15 dead Jews lying at the Łochów-Tłuszcz section [26–46 km] near the adjacent track of the double-track line. As I realized, a Jewish transport had gone through there."[149]

The most concentrated number of bodies were found at larger stations. Treblinka station worker Stanisław Borowy testified to this fact: "While the train was traveling through the Treblinka station, the victims tried to escape from the wagons, while the transport guards . . . killed many people. At the station in Treblinka, there were very often a lot of corpses."[150] There were times, Polish train worker Kazimierz Gawkowski recalled, when "so many people were killed in this way at the Treblinka railway station that later four flat wagons were filled with the corpses."[151] Even Pfoch, the German soldier passing through Treblinka to the Eastern Front, observed the bodies strewn about: "When at last our train leaves the station . . . at least fifty dead women, men and children, some of them totally naked, lie along the track. . . . Eventually our train followed the other train and we continued to see corpses on both sides of the track—children and others."[152] In distant Sokołów Podlaski, some twenty-seven kilometers from Treblinka, local railway worker Wacław Wołosz remembered similarly, "After the trains had passed, there were a lot of corpses lying around at the station and along the

FIG. 21. Two Jews shot during the deportation process, lying
near the railway tracks in Siedlce, Poland, August 23, 1942. Photo
taken by German soldier Hubert Pfoch as he passed through the
area. Courtesy of Yad Vashem Photo Archive, 2586/1.

tracks."[153] This horrific spatial reality was even noted some 175 kilometers away in Szydłowiec, where the September 1942 deportation of five thousand Jews to Treblinka left "700–800 bodies . . . scattered in the fields."[154]

After the trains passed, the Germans generally forced local Poles to bury the bodies left behind. Czesław Borowy, who lived in the town of Treblinka (4 km), recalled, "Mostly it was local authorities who directed the digging of graves, and the burial of bodies, because they spread disease. . . . You can't leave bodies to decompose out in the open . . . eventually animals will come scavenge."[155] Something similar occurred in nearby Wólka Okrąglik (1 km), where, as local residents Eugenia Samuel and Michał Kalembasiak both remembered, the "local farmers" not only had to bury the corpses but also had to build the mass graves and utilize their own carts to collect and transport bodies.[156] This left a spatial legacy whereby Jews from all over Poland and parts of Europe ended up buried in towns, villages, and other locations scattered randomly along Polish train tracks. Sobolewski reflected on this when he witnessed the murder of several escaping Jews while once passing through Małkinia (7 km): "I drove away, but other engine drivers told me later that the Germans ordered a hole be dug near the engine shed and the bodies of the murdered Jews were buried there."[157] It is unclear if anyone has ever searched for a mass grave near the Małkinia engine shed, but the larger trend, in Wołosz's concise words, is clear—between Siedlce and Treblinka, "the entire railway is a grave."[158]

Besides bodies, Treblinka-bound trains left other things along the tracks. Królikowski observed that "through the windows of the wagons, paper money from all countries of the world fell on the tracks." While working on railway bridges, he also saw people throw jewelry and gold coins out of cattle cars into the Bug River below.[159] Ząbecki described this as an act of defiance: "Through the windows of the wagons, the Jews threw torn money, clothing, cards with addresses, asking us to warn families not to believe in resettlement, because resettlement . . . is death."[160] Other items littered the railway corridors, as Kruger remembered: "When we were working on the railroad tracks, 100 of us, everyday under guard, we saw trains going back empty. . . . We used to find pictures, letters, notes, and we saw it was [sic] Jewish."[161]

The leaving behind of material objects represents a cogent attempt by those trapped inside to reach the outside world, and in many cases they did. For illustration, a Warsaw construction worker taking a shortcut across the train tracks on his way home from work one day found a hammer resting next to the rails. He discovered it had a false handle with a note tucked inside, which read, "We implore the finder to deliver the attached notes at once to the addresses given. We were caught yesterday in the streets of Warsaw and are being transported to some unknown place. Thirty zlotys are enclosed for expenses. Please hurry. We dropped the hammer out of a hole we made in the car."[162] This remarkable interaction between a random person some eighty kilometers from Treblinka and a remnant from a death-camp-bound train, deposited into the world as a desperate plea by people doomed to die in gas chambers, reveals in unmistakable clarity how disparate spatial trajectories among human beings intersect and overlap in ways we often take for granted.[163] It also shows how someone's life outside of the train (and long after it passed by) could be impacted by those who had traveled over the same space earlier. These impacts varied widely, though, and Treblinka station worker Stanisław Borowy remembered that once the Germans arrested and shot a Polish railway bridge technician in Małkinia (7 km) because he had found several notes dropped from transports, and they were worried about the information he had gained from them.[164]

Other material objects flowed along these railway corridors as well, albeit in the opposite direction. The same trains that brought Jews to Treblinka also took away the property stolen in the camp and redistributed it throughout Germany. This was no small quantity; according to Odilo Globočnik's February 27, 1943, report, the Germans had stolen and transported over one hundred million Reichsmarks worth of goods by that date alone, including 1,800 kilograms of gold (some of which was dental gold from murdered Jews) and 10,000 kilograms of silver, collectively worth over five million Reichsmarks. Of the estimated one thousand cattle car loads shipped out of Treblinka, 25 carried hair packed in bales; 248 carried men's suits; 100 carried shoes; 40 were filled with medicines; 260 contained bedding and quilts; 400 carried random items such as pens, eyeglasses, dishes, and 14,000 carats of diamonds; and several hundred others contained miscellaneous items.[165] "You cannot imagine the huge fortunes that traveled in the opposite direction, through Warsaw to Berlin," one Warsaw ghetto diarist wrote.[166]

In addition to using the same cattle cars, the Germans also used the same tracks to ship these objects, presenting local residents with another chance to interact with these trains. And they certainly did. As Ząbecki observed from the Treblinka town station (4 km), "As for the transports with the belongings of the victims sent from the camp to the Reich, I suppose . . . that about a thousand wagons with clothes, shoes, and other materials passed by the station."[167] Another Polish railway worker named Pogorzelski also recognized what was happening: "Very often, trains passed through the train stations with 40–50 cars loaded with clothes and destined for Germany."[168] Flowing all along and beyond these railway corridors—and potentially far into the heart of Germany itself—were the material objects Treblinka-bound Jews had once carried, forming unquantifiable spatial connections between those murdered in gas chambers and the countless Germans who benefited from receiving their plundered goods.[169]

Yet evidence that local Poles all along the railway corridors knew about these trains of goods is found from an unexpected source—those Jews who escaped Treblinka by hiding in the cars leaving the camp. Strawczyński, who worked sorting clothes at Treblinka, stated, "There were many . . . who escaped in the wagons when we loaded the clothing. This was almost a daily occurrence. You got in—if nobody saw you, you just jumped in there behind and covered yourself up, and that's all."[170] Weinstein, who escaped in this way, recalled that while hiding, several bundles were removed or stolen from the train as it sat stopped overnight in the Treblinka town station: "From this [I] inferred that the inhabitants of Treblinka [town] and the vicinity had opened the door to exploit the new economic opportunities created by the Germans' monstrous schemes." He added that this was not a one-time occurrence, and locals pilfered bundles at several stops (each time unaware of Weinstein). From his unique vantage point, Weinstein speculated, "From the standpoint of the locals, the contents of our train were assuredly German property during the occupation. . . . Everyone made off with whatever could be moved and saw nothing wrong with that." In fact, these break-ins became so frequent that the Germans began stationing guards on the cars full of stolen goods as they traveled to Germany.[171]

The Transformation of Banal Space

Resulting cumulatively from the sensory contamination from the trains, interactions with the cars themselves, encounters with survivors who escaped or their remains, and perhaps even from the constant flow of stolen goods in the other direction, people living up and down the railway corridors to and from Treblinka became witnesses to the Holocaust. In ways sometimes indirect and tangential and at others direct and interactive, these railway corridor witnesses became linked to the horrors occurring at the end of the line. And although the tracks were fixed, the interactions were usually random in how, when, and where they occurred.

Therefore, and perhaps above all else, studying the railway corridors of Treblinka provides a tangible lesson in how otherwise banal spatial arrangements—homes and human beings positioned near train tracks or train stations—take on different contexts and create intersecting trajectories of contemporaneous spatial experience during periods of chaos, war, and genocide. Our modern systems of transit and infrastructure, places that we so often take for granted in our daily lives, can also become sites of irrevocable, horrific memory when used in the perpetration of mass crime. In fact, we need go no further than the survivors of such experiences to reveal the profound legacies these inseparable connections create. As interviewer Stefania Beylin recorded while traveling after the war with survivor Gedali Rydlewicz on a Warsaw-bound train, "When the train . . . went by the siding between Małkinia and Treblinka, Rydlewicz grew silent and stared into space with a painful expression: 'That's where my wife and daughter died; they took them *this way* to their death. It was their last journey.'"[172]

CONCLUSION

Human reason will never make peace with the
reality of Treblinka.

—Alexander Donat, *The Death Camp Treblinka*

Designed as the model of clean, technocratic killing carried out in complete
secrecy and industrial isolation, the Treblinka death camp was, in reality, a
brutal place of mass murder witnessed far and wide. Alongside the sights,
smells, sounds, humans, and train cars spreading from the camp into the
world beyond its confines traveled whispers, rumors, descriptions, and ultimately, awareness of the camp and its horrors. Knowledge formation is not
always a linear process, but evidence at Treblinka shows it is a steady one.
Within just days of the camp's beginnings, nearby Poles could determine
quite a bit through deductive reasoning. "We began to guess that we were
dealing with mass murder," Polish train worker Jerzy Królikowski reflected.
"Local peasants asked about how large the area of the camp was and whether
or not there were many barracks in it, since some claimed it wasn't very big
and only a dozen or so barracks existed there. It was obvious, therefore, that
the people who were brought in were murdered, but it seemed unbelievable
to us that so many people could be murdered every day."[1] At first, belief
often coincides with disbelief as witnesses try to understand events in real
time. In many respects, this phenomenon still plays out in our modern
society's obsession with "breaking" news. Accordingly, the existence of a
1944 report claiming Treblinka covered an area of five thousand hectares
(eight square miles)—in reality, the camp covered only forty hectares—is
somewhat unsurprising.[2] Vasily Grossman, gazing upon the remnants of
this small space later in 1944, captures the logic behind such speculations:
"What became of all these people of whom there were enough to populate

a small state or a large European capital? If their lives had been spared for only ten days, the human streams flowing here from all corners of Europe, from Poland and Byelorussia would have overflowed all barriers."[3]

Yet many people living near Treblinka did, in fact, have quite accurate information of what happened there. The first concrete details probably came from the Ukrainian and German camp guards, who descended upon local towns to trade, find alcohol, exert their power, or search for Jews who had escaped the death camp.[4] The knowledge they often shared, relatively openly, with local Poles explained the sensory contamination that was already pouring out of Treblinka and filling Polish spaces.[5] Moreover, the escaping Jews these guards sought created their own indeterminate, but far-reaching knowledge vectors through which information was transmitted to the outside world. As one Warsaw ghetto diarist explained, "Jews who escaped from those Dantean boxcars, from Treblinka, and other extermination camps . . . in the end, returned to the ghetto. That's how information . . . filtered back."[6] Antoni Szymanowski, also writing from the Warsaw ghetto, added, "[Treblinka] is covered with a thick wall of silence, but fractional messages are leaking back."[7]

The leak soon became a torrent. Coinciding with stories told by survivors who had seen the camp firsthand came bulletins from the Polish Home Army (the AK), which reported even "the smallest detail" emerging from the area.[8] Just five days after Treblinka-bound deportations began in Warsaw, the July 27, 1942, edition of the AK's *Informacja Bieżąca* (Current Information) reported, "It is obvious that the transports are headed for death, perhaps to Bełżec." This information evolved rapidly and can be tracked in subsequent editions. The August 13, 1942, bulletin stated, "As we have discovered, in the camp near Treblinka, death takes place in a gas chamber. Specialists dredge a deep ditch throughout the day into which the bodies of the murdered are thrown." Four days later, in the August 17 edition, even more intimate details appear: "Jews were forced to undress, supposedly to go to a bath, put into a gas chamber and executed." By September 15, 1942, the bulletin even goes so far as to detail that Treblinka's gas chambers were "hermetically sealed."[9]

Circulation of these bulletins, combined with the firsthand reports from returning escapees, made Warsaw (the ghetto in particular) among the first cities to learn what Treblinka *was*, and the evolution and spread of this knowledge grew apace. Just eight days after the first deportations, Szymanowski wrote on July 30, 1942, "What is going on in Treblinka? No one knows for sure. . . . In any case, the vast majority of Jews are killed there in some mass way."[10] Menachem Kon, whose writings were found in the Oyneg Shabes Archive, wrote on August 6, 1942 (just two weeks after deportations began), "[The Nazis] have already expelled thousands to the square from which these are to be transported in box-carts for *extermination in a place called Treblinka*."[11] And by October 1, 1942, any ambiguity about what Treblinka meant in the Warsaw ghetto had been erased. On that day, from his position eighty kilometers away in a "sealed off" ghetto, Kon wrote an astonishing description of a death camp he had never seen and was not even supposed to know about: "Between six and eight thousand were being killed there daily, the bodies thrown into pits dug by machines to the depth of 30 meters. People still alive were being thrown in together with the dead. The pits were slaked with lime. This work of burial was done by Jewish teams."[12]

From Warsaw, the information soon spread throughout occupied Poland and beyond.[13] Thanks in large part to the efforts of Jan Karski, who went to great lengths to smuggle a report of the Reinhard camps out of occupied Poland, the rest of the world soon learned about Treblinka.[14] By December 10, 1942, Poland's exiled Ministry of Foreign Affairs published the following detailed report from its London base: "As far as is known, the trains were dispatched to three localities—Tremblinka [*sic*], Belzec, and Sobibor . . . 'Extermination camps.' . . . It is reported that on arrival in camp the survivors were stripped naked and killed by various means, including poison gas and electrocution. The dead were interred in mass graves dug by machinery."[15] And by April 1943, similar reports had crossed the ocean to the United States. One, called *The Massacre of a People*, put out by the American Labor Zionist journal *Jewish Frontier Association*, notably had corrected the London report's misspelling of "Tremblinka" to "Treblinka," a detail highlighting an increasing familiarity with what was happening in rural Poland.[16]

However, this might not, in fact, have been the first information about Treblinka to travel abroad. A memo to American Jewish Committee head Morris D. Waldman dated September 8, 1942, includes the following excerpt: "The information about the massacre of a hundred thousand Jews in Warsaw was received in code by the State Department from one of its representatives in Switzerland. Dr. Jacob Rosenheim, leader of the Agudath Israel, learned about this from the State Department and transmitted the information to the Union of Orthodox Rabbis, which has called a meeting of the representatives of the various Jewish organizations, among them, The American Jewish Congress, the Jewish Labor Committee, B'nai B'rith, Federation of Polish Jews, Mizrachi, etc." Just forty-nine days after the killing started at Treblinka, these Jewish organizations from around the world had not only met to discuss this concerning news but offered the recommendation a few lines later "that President Roosevelt make a direct appeal to the German government to stop these massacres."[17] Hindsight of history notwithstanding, this is an eerie reminder about just how unisolated Treblinka's workings were, even from the beginning, and how quickly, even in 1942, information could travel. In our interconnected world of today, where people can interface across the globe within milliseconds, such a reminder is all too prescient—it has never been easier to witness, learn of, or be implicated in genocide and other atrocities.

While charting the speed and spread of information about Treblinka illustrates how different spatial interactions formed intricate and far-reaching webs of knowledge, it is also somewhat paradoxical, because just as quickly and widely as the world found out about Treblinka, the camp had ceased to exist. To finish this story of the spaces of Treblinka, then, is to return to the scene of the crime. When the Germans tore down the camp in late 1943, they relegated its physical space to history. Laying no memorial on the site, they instead leveled the area, planted some trees to disguise the human remains still mixed within the sandy soil, and built a small farmhouse (using bricks from the gas chambers), where they left a Ukrainian guard named "Strebel" to chase away anyone who wandered too close. No record of Strebel's fate exists, though we can assume he likely fled in early 1944 to escape retribution by the advancing Red Army for his clear collaboration with the Nazis.[18] Sweeping through the area, the Red Army further transformed the landscape, their battles with the retreating Germans devastating large swaths of the Polish countryside. "Throughout the Siedlce-Małkinia railway route, the length of over 60 kilometers, there was hardly a single station or bridge standing," local investigator Zdzisław Łukaszkiewicz wrote. "Even large sections of the tracks are torn off."[19] As for the empty field of Treblinka, "The entire area is currently riddled with pits and craters of different sizes. . . . Some craters are up to 7 meters deep and up to 25 meters in diameter. . . . The

FIG. 22. Polish soldiers stand in the scarred field of Treblinka after the war, surveying a landscape decimated by bomb craters and holes dug by human hands. Courtesy of Yad Vashem Photo Archive, 11A09.

pits were dug up by locals looking for gold and valuables, while the craters were made when the aerial bombs and shells were exploded by the soldiers from a Red Army unit."[20]

It was this pockmarked moonscape that greeted Grossman, whose 1944 report "The Treblinka Hell" shocked international readers with its graphic depictions of the horrors carried out at the former death camp—many confirming the ghastly rumors that had been spreading. Yet as seen in figure 22, the space had changed so drastically in just the first few months after the camp was torn down that even before Grossman penned his report, the historical spatial reality of Treblinka had already been relegated to memories dispersed as widely as the thousands of camp witnesses who had formed them.

Polish residents of the area around Treblinka sought to carry on their everyday lives in the former death camp's shadows—the remnants of which, by fate of geography, now lay forever in their backyard. Simultaneously, they had to contend with the destruction caused by the Red Army and the subsequent regime change—the third in the area since 1939—as

Soviet-influenced leaders took charge of Poland.[21] Amid the chaos, some Poles did the unthinkable—they dug through the remains of Treblinka, shoveling aside human remains as they sought the treasures they imagined lay buried in the sandy ground.[22] Evidence suggests this wave of plundering did not last long, and afterward, most Poles reestablished their prewar lives—ones that, according to filmmaker Claude Lanzmann, were defined even in 1978 by simplistic, "nineteenth-century" rural lifestyles "all but impossible to imagine" elsewhere in contemporary Western Europe.[23]

But the spatial monstrosity of Treblinka remained deeply embedded in local memory, unable to be replaced by anachronistic endeavors aimed at restoring a nostalgic past upon the landscape. "The persistence and disfigurement of places are the rhythm and measure of our lives," Lanzmann wrote. "I have seen as much in other, desperate circumstances during the filming of *Shoah*, when I encountered the landscape of extermination in Poland. This battle, this contrast between continuity and destruction, was for me an overwhelming shock, a veritable explosion, the source of everything."[24] When Lanzmann showed up in the middle of the night at the doorstep of Małkinia resident Henryk Gawkowski, who had driven trains to Treblinka, Lanzmann said, "[Gawkowski] seemed so surprised by my urgency that it was as though he shared it. He had neither forgotten nor recovered from the horrifying past in which he had played a role, and he found it entirely just that he should have to answer any demands made on him at any hour."[25] Here, then, within the recollections of the thousands of local witnesses (some of which were detailed in this book), the traces of Treblinka were carried forth into the postwar world (and to this day).

Certainly, traces also followed the same Germans and Ukrainians responsible for building the camp and murdering hundreds of thousands of people there. Since nearly all later deflected their guilt, pointed the finger at others, or simply never faced justice, we can assume their recollections of Treblinka carried forth differently, perhaps deeply repressed into the subconscious. Franz Stangl, who, like other guilty parties, fled to South America hoping to escape persecution, ultimately could not escape what he had done at Treblinka: "Once, years later in Brazil . . . my train stopped next to a slaughterhouse. The cattle in the pens, hearing the noise of the train, trotted up to the fence and stared at the train. They were very close to my window, one crowding the other, looking at me through that fence. I thought then

'Look at this; this reminds me of Poland; that's just how the people looked, trustingly, just before they went into the tins. . . . I couldn't eat tinned meat after that . . . those big eyes . . . which looked at me . . . not knowing that in no time at all they'd all be dead."[26] Whether he exaggerates here to make himself appear more sympathetic to readers or whether this statement, like select others he told interviewer Gitta Sereny, reveals some truth, we cannot know. But we do know that the German and Ukrainian killers were not (and could never be, as human beings and not the automatons of Nazi ideology) *immune* from the horrific crimes they inflicted, and what they witnessed as they murdered nearly a million innocent people in the span of sixteen months undoubtedly never left them.

Ultimately, though, it was the survivors of Treblinka whose lives perhaps carried forth the deepest traces of the camp they had once escaped. "In *those* camps," Lanzmann observed, "there was no question as to who would live or die: everyone was condemned to die and knew it; those few survivors, those I refer to in my film as the 'revenants,' having mordaciously survived, were themselves dead men granted a stay of execution."[27] Indeed, many survivors later demarcated the narrative arcs of their lives by this seminal event. As one survivor later introduced himself, "I, Saul Kuperhand, lived in Poland in the 1920s and 1930s. Now I do not live anywhere. I survive. I do it in a time and place I can only call 'after Treblinka.'"[28] For others, performing normal post-Treblinka tasks took on new meaning—forever altered. "Even now, when I pick up a glass of cold water," Abraham Krzepicki wrote, "this drink seems so valuable that my hands begin to tremble."[29]

In all the places they went afterward, these survivors spread the traces of Treblinka by telling their stories and sharing their memories. Samuel Willenberg put it this way: "All my life, I have tried to ensure the memory of what happened would not be lost. . . . I give interviews to anyone who wants to hear about the horrifying things I lived through during my 10-month stay in the camp." Yet Willenberg, too, acknowledged the ephemeral and fleeting nature of a space that no longer exists: "During the uprising, our main goal was destruction—so that it could no longer operate. We succeeded only partially, however the ss finished what we started in an attempt to hide the truth of what happened here. And thus, in order to understand what took place in Treblinka one must use one's imagination."[30]

Such has been the precise goal of this book and its endeavor to reimagine the spaces of Treblinka: preserving forever what no longer *is* but what future generations can never be allowed to forget. There is no more fitting coda than the words that an unnamed Treblinka survivor spoke to Rachel Auerbach: "Treblinka is not over yet. Treblinka hasn't ended. It follows us wherever we go, just as it has been following us up until now, in the woods, in the fields, in all the nooks and crannies we had to abandon for fear that someone might give us away. Now it's in the streets, in this restaurant where I'm still sitting with my Jewish nose, even though by right I should have been in the other world a long time ago."[31]

NOTES

Introduction

1. Lefebvre, *Production of Space*, 164.
2. Grossman, "Treblinka Hell," 47–48.
3. Donat, *Death Camp Treblinka*, 55.
4. Lanzmann, *Patagonian Hare*, 527.
5. I am intentional about word choice. I alternate between *Nazi* and *German* when referring to perpetrators. I generally use Nazi when speaking of higher-level ideology or government initiatives. I use German most often when referencing individuals. Most Germans in the book were also Nazis. Also noteworthy, several Treblinka guards were Austrian, but most, as members of the ss, readily identified as German.
6. Bergen, *War and Genocide*, 111–14. The largest ghettos were in Poland, as were all three Reinhard camps, though the latter each existed within the so-called General Government. Many Reinhard victims were Polish Jews, though others were deported there from across Europe.
7. Arad, *Belzec, Sobibor, Treblinka*, 14–17; Webb and Chocholatý, *Treblinka Death Camp*, 5–7. The 1.6 million figure is included within the total 3 million murdered.
8. Exact numbers of those killed at Treblinka may never be known because meticulous records were not kept there. Yitzhak Arad's best calculation is 875,000. Arad, "Jewish Prisoner Uprisings," 34.
9. Arendt, *Origins of Totalitarianism*, 447; Bryant, *Eyewitness to Genocide*, 6.
10. Young, *Texture of Memory*, 186–90.
11. Meng, *Shattered Spaces*, xii; Zelizer, *Remembering to Forget*, 3; Young, "Jewish Memory," 229; Sikorski, *Polish House*, 130; Hartman, "Introduction," 7; Heidemarie Uhl writes that these memorials are "seismographs of historical consciousness [providing] insights into the ongoing transformations of collective memory." Uhl, "From the Periphery," 222.
12. Father Patrick Desbois, who interviews witnesses to the "Holocaust by Bullets" in Eastern Europe, had a similar reaction when a Ukrainian woman he

was interviewing pointed out the location of a shooting. He wrote, "It seemed impossible to imagine that this bucolic landscape was the backdrop to such a massacre." Desbois, *Holocaust by Bullets*, 165.

13. The famous 1956 French film *Night and Fog* has particularly ingrained this concept. Andrew Charlesworth and Michael Addis write that today's visitors to camps and memorials *expect* to catch "sight of the Birkenau gatehouse either appearing out of the early morning mist or framed against a leaden sky." Charlesworth and Addis, "Memorialization," 231.

14. I am reminded of something specific survivor Thaddeus Stabholz wrote as he was being transferred out of Treblinka to Majdanek: "We ride through the woods, going back the way we came. Now we are in an open field. Above the forest, a large cloud of dense, black smoke rises." Stabholz, *Seven Hells*, 27.

15. Massey, *For Space*, 9.

16. A key book is Raul Hilberg's *Perpetrators, Victims, Bystanders*; see also Jan Gross's 2001 book, *Neighbors*, which explores how the Polish population of Jedwabne murdered their Jewish neighbors. Since then, the idea of "neighbors" has often been employed by those studying local witnesses. For more examples, see Charnysh and Finkel's "Death Camp Eldorado," Grabowski's *Hunt for the Jews*, and Gross's *Golden Harvest*.

17. Arad, *Belzec, Sobibor, Treblinka*, 14–17; Webb and Chocholatỳ, *Treblinka Death Camp*, 5–7; Chrostowski, *Extermination Camp Treblinka*. The benchmark work on the Reinhard camps is still Arad's *Belzec, Sobibor, Treblinka*, which was published over thirty years ago. Other work done since then, particularly Chrostowski's and Webb and Chocholatỳ's, has revised, updated, and clarified many of Arad's original observations—adding new sources and increasing our understanding of Treblinka. Yet these works still treat Treblinka as a relatively isolated space and do not update Arad's initial explorations into the areas surrounding the camps. Therefore, to date, we have a picture of Treblinka mainly from the viewpoints of "perpetrators" and "survivors," but the contemporaneous experiences connecting Jews, Germans, and Poles have remained discordant.

18. Heller, "Only 2 Survivors"; Samuel Willenberg writes, "Here, however, we face a problem I have encountered myself. There is a magnificent memorial in Treblinka but there are very few things that help understand how the camp operated. . . . And thus, in order to understand what took place in Treblinka one must use one's imagination." Willenberg, "Memory of Treblinka."

19. I found this pamphlet in the Harry Mazal Collection, once the world's largest privately held Holocaust archive, at the University of Colorado–Boulder, which now houses the material. The pamphlet's cover is striking for its depiction of Treblinka as a modern factory (see figure 8).

20. Nikolic-Dunlop, *Treblinka*.

21. Willenberg spares no details in his 1989 book *Surviving Treblinka*. He adds elsewhere, "We need to create a space where . . . they can talk about the horrors of this place." Willenberg, "Memory of Treblinka." Other survivors and witnesses outline the specific horrors they witnessed. One devastating example is found in Wiernik, *Year in Treblinka*, 20–36.

22. Didi-Huberman, *Images*, 3.

23. Lefebvre, *Production of Space*, 160.

24. Tyner, *Genocide*, 4.

25. Lefebvre, *Production of Space*, 85; see also Tyner, *Genocide*, 4–5; and Cresswell, *Place*, 8–9. Edward Said suggested that our ability to communicate with one another comes from how we imagine the spaces of our lives, which in turn "legitimates a vocabulary, a representative discourse peculiar to the understanding" of the world. Said, *Orientalism*, 71.

26. Tuan, *Space and Place*, 6, 138; see also Massey, *For Space*, 4. Another common term is *landscape*, which is different from place or space because landscapes are generally viewed by someone not residing in the space. See Cresswell, *Place*, 11; and Gregory, *Geographical Imaginations*, 298.

27. Massey, *For Space*, 140.

28. Brown, *Biography of No Place*, 236–37; see also Lefebvre, *Production of Space*, 164. Pierra Nora explains the dissonance created at "sites of memory" that are no longer "real environments of memory." Nora, "Between Memory and History," 7.

29. Schama, *Landscape and Memory*, 25.

30. Massey, *For Space*, 12.

31. Foucault, *Discipline and Punish*, 136–38; Porteous, *Landscapes*, 70; Abrams, *Spell of the Sensuous*, 37, 42.

32. Lefebvre, *Production of Space*, 162.

33. Rodaway, *Sensuous Geographies*, 3; see also Cresswell, *Place*, 85.

34. Gigliotti, *Train Journey*, 129. I expand upon Gigliotti's use of the term "sensory witnessing" in examining confined environments, like cattle cars, to show how it applies to larger unconfined spaces in and around Treblinka.

35. Felman, "Film as Witness," 91.

36. All translations from Polish, German, and Yiddish in the book are mine unless otherwise noted.

37. Oyneg Shabes was the code name given to the archive kept by Emmanuel Ringelblum and others in the Warsaw Ghetto. It is Yiddish for "Joy of the Sabbath." See Kassow, *Who Will Write?*

38. The Institute of National Remembrance website is https://www.zapisyterroru .pl/dlibra. Holdings include transcripts of the Ludwig Fischer case of 1945–46.

Fisher was a high-ranking Nazi in charge of occupied Warsaw who was tried, and ultimately executed, by the Polish Supreme National Tribunal. Evidence used in his trial included testimonies from Treblinka witnesses collected immediately after the war, and these testimonies provide contemporary accounts from survivors and Poles living near the death camp.

39. Roma and Sinti are ethnic groups within a larger ethnic minority population in Europe (often called Roma or Romani). There are no known Roma or Sinti survivors of Treblinka, so it is difficult to quote them directly. Yet we know that they shared the experiences of Treblinka's Jewish victims. To be sure, survivor Yankel Wiernik mentions them several times (though using the derogatory term *gypsy*, which is often considered a racial slur), including here: "The gate flew open and about 100 gypsies were marched in. About 20 of them were men, the rest women and children. . . . The gypsies were gassed just like all the others and cremated." Wiernik, *Year in Treblinka*, 38. Trying to cover Roma and Sinti experiences through Jewish voices is not representative because each individual's experience of Treblinka was unique. As Ari Joskowicz has pointed out, there was "great diversity of European Jewish and Romani communities and individuals." Joskowicz, "Separate Suffering," 115.

40. Yahad-in Unum documents Holocaust mass graves in Eastern Europe. Their website is here: http://www.yiu.ngo/en. Father Desbois, who leads the project, has published several books, including *The Holocaust by Bullets*. As Desbois observes on page 98 of *Holocaust by Bullets*, "The perpetrators of genocide used everything—cliffs, grain silos, beaches, irrigation wells, ditches. Everything that could be closed off was used as a prison. Schools, town halls, synagogues, wine cellars, police stations, shops, the kolkhoze [collective farm] pigsties, chicken houses, and stables, had become, one after the other, the antechambers of death. The landscapes, buildings, and children became, in the hands of the assassins, tools to exterminate."

41. Shneer, "Ghostly Landscapes," 235–37.

42. Stone, *Histories of the Holocaust*, 146; Paolo Giaccaria and Claudio Minca argue that Auschwitz represented a *spatial threshold*, which they define as "a spatial structure which, at first sight, seems to be the most extraordinary example of calculative rationality translated into space." Giaccaria and Minca, "Topographies/Topologies," 5. While Auschwitz certainly was a spatial threshold, I argue Treblinka more embodies Nazism's "calculative rationality translated into space" because the camp's sole mission was the production of death.

43. Sturdy Colls, "Holocaust Archaeology," 70–104; Abate and Sturdy Colls, "Multi-level and Multi-sensory," 129–35; Sturdy Colls, *Holocaust Archaeologies*.

44. Gross, *Neighbors*.

45. Gross, *Golden Harvest*. Volha Charnysh and Evgeny Finkel explore the same phenomenon but utilize a macrolevel approach to chart redistribution of property among local Poles. See Charnysh and Finkel, "Death Camp Eldorado," 801–18. My research here builds on that of Gross, Charnysh, and Finkel by defining the individual experiences of Polish witnesses, putting their voices in conversation with those of Jews and Germans *during* the camp's operation.

46. Lanzmann, *Patagonian Hare*, 475–76.

1. An Ideological Space

1. Desbois, *Holocaust by Bullets*.
2. Mommsen, *From Weimar to Auschwitz*, 239.
3. *Trial of the Major War Criminals*, 4:493–94.
4. Ley, "Auschwitz," 125.
5. Kershaw, *Hitler*, xxviii; Stone, *Histories of the Holocaust*, 196. Rejecting the Judeo-Christian morality of scholars and ethical philosophers, the Nazis felt their mission at Treblinka was beyond the world's ability to understand their "need" for industrialized murder.
6. Foucault, *History of Sexuality*, 137.
7. This chapter looks at the first three components: Poland's physical spaces, the intentionally manipulated spaces demarcating Treblinka, and the deceptive facades they built there. This examination spatially pinpoints the Nazis' ideological goals (the next chapter tackles the latter two components—Treblinka's mission and secrecy—as behavioral elements of how this ideology translated, or failed to translate, in practice versus theory).
8. Pachirat, *Every Twelve Seconds*, 2–4, 7. On page 11, Pachirat further explains that modern "power" is defined by creating "barriers to sight, by eradicating obstacles that create possibilities for darkness and concealment." Correspondingly, by placing Reinhard camps in "isolated" spaces and then camouflaging them, Nazi planners sought to exercise power to implement their ideological goals as they desired.
9. Hagen and Ostergren, *Building Nazi Germany*, xv, 5.
10. "Bauten des dritten Reiches," 878. Speer stated that Hitler's wish "was to pass on to posterity monuments of his own time . . . to make them immortal through buildings." Speer, "Manipulation des Menschen," 131.
11. Hagen and Ostergren, *Building Nazi Germany*, 3.
12. Troost, *Bauen im Neuen Reich*, 155.
13. Grossman, "Treblinka Hell," 28.
14. Ząbecki, *Wspomnienia*, 12. Treblinka here references the town of Treblinka.
15. Lefebvre, *Production of Space*, 110.

16. Lefebvre, *Production of Space*, 30. See also Blackbourn, *Conquest of Nature*, 303–6; and Cresswell, *Place*, 50. In modern Western conceptions, "wilderness" is associated with "virgin" or wild and "mysterious" spaces. Gregory, *Geographical Imaginations*, 129–32.

17. Hellpach, *Einführung in die Völkerpsychologie*, 43.

18. Hellpach, *Einführung in die Völkerpsychologie*, 40–41.

19. Sandler, "Here Too Lies," 148–49.

20. Maschke, "Wiedergewinnung des Deutschen Ostens," 114; see also Bassin, "Blood or Soil?," 216.

21. Maschke, "Wiedergewinnung des Deutschen Ostens," 116 (emphasis added).

22. Knapp, *Deutsche Dorfplanung*, 5.

23. Kenyon, "War Crimes," cou 1806:01:030:0009.

24. Maschke, "Wiedergewinnung des Deutschen Ostens," 106.

25. Maschke, "Wiedergewinnung des Deutschen Ostens," 109, 115. Maschke claims a fifteenth-century Prussian monarch ceded control of the region to the Jagiellonian crown. See also Blackbourn, *Conquest of Nature*, 252; and Hellpach, *Einführung in die Völkerpsychologie*, 5, 29.

26. Lillian Goldman Law Library, "Program of the National Socialist."

27. Barnes and Minca, "Nazi Spatial Theory," 673.

28. Kenyon, "War Crimes," cou 1806:01:030:0009.

29. Maschke, "Wiedergewinnung des Deutschen Ostens," 116.

30. Gregory, *Geographical Imaginations*, 130.

31. Snyder, *Black Earth*, 46; Lekan, *Imagining the Nation*, 202; Rieger, *Creator*, 105.

32. Hesse, "Annual Report," 333.

33. Republic of Poland Ministry of Foreign Affairs, *German Occupation of Poland*, 184.

34. Republic of Poland Ministry of Foreign Affairs, *German Occupation of Poland*, 181. Forster's speech occurred November 26, 1939.

35. Barnes and Minca, "Nazi Spatial Theory," 671.

36. "Defense Document #4," cou 1806:01:034:0023, 37.

37. Republic of Poland Ministry of Foreign Affairs, *German Occupation of Poland*, 180. Greiser's speech is from October 6, 1939.

38. Schama, *Landscape and Memory*, 70.

39. Aldor, *Germany's "Death Space*," 141.

40. After dividing Poland with the USSR in 1939, Germany incorporated some Polish territory into the Reich but left another portion, the General Government, outside the Reich, though still under German control.

41. Republic of Poland Ministry of Foreign Affairs, *German Occupation of Poland*, 182–83.

42. Snyder, *Black Earth*, 253–54.

43. Arendt, *Origins of Totalitarianism*, 451.

44. Named after the program's main office at Tiergartenstraße 4 in Berlin, "Aktion T4" was a planned euthanasia system whereby Nazi "doctors" murdered as many as 250,000 Germans with mental or physical disabilities, the elderly, and others deemed a "burden" to Germany's economy. The six killing sites were at Grafeneck, Hartheim, Hadamar, Sonnenstein, Brandenburg, and Bernburg. See Crowe, *Holocaust*, 145–53.

45. *Trial of the Major War Criminals*, 19:511.

46. Griech-Polelle, "Image," 50–51; see also Crowe, *Holocaust*, 153. The T4 program continued until the war's end in more secretive ways, including by starving victims to death, lethally injecting them with drugs, or transferring them to Reinhard camps.

47. *Trial of the Major War Criminals*, 19:510–14.

48. Donat, *Death Camp Treblinka*, 10.

49. Murawska-Gryń and Gryń, *Majdanek*, 9. See also Webb and Chocholatý, *Treblinka Death Camp*, 11–14, 19; Lasman, *Pięćdziesiąt kilometrów*, 14; and Schelvis, *Sobibor*, 25.

50. Sereny, *Into That Darkness*, 100; see also Webb and Chocholatý, *Treblinka Death Camp*, 5.

51. This border was established in 1939 after the invasion of Poland by Germany and the Soviet Union. Małkinia sits four kilometers from the town of Treblinka. See map 2 (chapter 6).

52. Łukaszkiewicz, *Obóz Straceń*, 6.

53. Ząbecki, *Wspomnienia*, 11–12.

54. Edward Sypko, KARTA AHM_V_0030, video 2, 14:45–16:15; Marian Łopuszyński, 16 November 1945, IPN GK 196/69. See also Eugeniusz Goska, USHMM RG-50.488.0027, tape 1, 6:00–6:40.

55. APS 1403/0/9.5/1527; Kopówka and Rytel-Andrianik, *Dam Im Imię*, 366, 384; Ząbecki, *Wspomnienia*, 11. This farm continued to operate during the war.

56. AAN 2134/0/45.

57. Kopówka, *Treblinka*, 77–78.

58. Ząbecki, *Wspomnienia*, 11.

59. Town background information comes from Kopówka and Rytel-Andrianik, *Dam Im Imię*, 16–17; see also ŻIH 209/38.

60. Kopówka and Rytel-Andrianik, *Dam Im Imię*, 416.

61. Kopówka and Rytel-Andrianik, *Dam Im Imię*, 20–21.

62. "Wspomnienia Antoniego Tomczuka," KARTA AW II/3490.

63. APS 62/718/0/-/55; Gumkowski and Rutkowski, *Treblinka*; Weinstein, *Quenched Steel*, 36; Ząbecki, *Wspomnienia*, 19.

64. Kopówka, *Treblinka*, 78–82. Barbara Goska mentions a Polish train driver who refused to take a trainload of Jews into the death camp and was sent to Treblinka I as punishment—he later died there of exhaustion; Kopówka and Rytel-Andrianik, *Dam Im Imię*, 412. Fred Kort, says local farmers were in Treblinka I for failing to hit grain or livestock quotas; Fred Kort, VHA 1753, tape 3, 21:15–22:00. See also "Wspomnienia Antoniego Tomczuka," KARTA AW II/3490.

65. Edward Sypko, KARTA AHM_V__0030, video 5, 35:05–35:45. Sypko says the rotation of Treblinka I prisoners had to be "crazy," since ten thousand died there in the span of three years.

66. "Wspomnienia Antoniego Tomczuka," KARTA AW II/3490. Jerzy Królikowski said that the arduous labor combined with poor nutrition led to "a total loss of strength and health." ŻIH 302/224, 4.

67. Kopówka and Rytel-Andrianik, *Dam Im Imię*, 392.

68. Gumkowski and Rutkowski, *Treblinka*.

69. ŻIH 302/224, 4.

70. Ząbecki, *Wspomnienia*, 36; see also *Justiz und NS-Verbrechen*, 34:755.

71. *To Live with Honor*, 43; Łukaszkiewicz, *Obóz Straceń*, 8.

72. ŻIH 301/1186.

73. Lucjan Puchała, 26 October 1945, IPN GK 196/69.

74. The Yad Vashem album notes, "Aus den Steinen sollen die neuen prösseren gaskammern in Treblinka im August/September 1942 erbaut wordensein" (The new, better gas chambers in Treblinka are thought to have been built from these bricks, August/September 1942). Yad Vashem Digital Photo Archive, sign. 1448, item 38353.

75. Edward Sypko, KARTA AHM_V_0030, video 2, 11:45–12:40. Oskar Strawczyński states that later, anything needed at Treblinka was taken from stolen Jewish goods at the camp or from the nearby town of Kosów Lacki (7 km). ŻIH 302/32, 27.

76. Donat, *Death Camp Treblinka*, 298. See also *Justiz und NS-Verbrechen*, 34:755; and ŻIH 209/38.

77. Łukaszkiewicz, *Obóz Straceń*, 7.

78. Stanisław Kucharek, Jechiel Rajchman, Samuel Rajzman, 6 November 1945, IPN GK 196/69; AAN 2134/0/45.

79. ŻIH 302/32, 25.

80. Bauer, *History of the Holocaust*, 333; Stone, *Histories of the Holocaust*, 196.

81. Tyner, *Genocide*, 12–13.

82. Arendt, *Eichmann in Jerusalem*, 150; see also Fritzsche, *Life and Death*, 202.

83. Donald Bloxham calls spaces where morality was inverted "zones of exception," and he lists extermination camps as such. Bloxham, *Final Solution*, 285. I amend the concept here to highlight how the "exception" in these zones was that Nazi morality dominated the space.

84. Early descriptions describe a quadrangle approximately 760 by 600 meters; Grossman, "Treblinka Hell," 31. Another report references 600 by 800 meters; ŻIH 230/63, Other research shows a somewhat smaller camp, around 400 by 600 meters; Arad, *Belzec, Sobibor, Treblinka*, 40. See also Webb and Chocholatý, *Treblinka Death Camp*, 22. A Treblinka museum pamphlet mentions 15 hectares (33–37 acres); Gumkowski and Rutkowski, *Treblinka*; and *Treblinka 1996*. For mention of the time to walk around the camp, see Feldman, *Understanding the Holocaust*, 2:228; for the Suchomel reference, see Lanzmann, *Shoah*, 110.

85. Willenberg, *Surviving Treblinka*, 110–11; for reference to 50 km of barbed wire, see ŻIH 301/26.

86. Wiernik, *Year in Treblinka*, 13; Arad, *Belzec, Sobibor, Treblinka*, 40; ŻIH 301/5089.

87. Lefebvre, *Production of Space*, 87.

88. Eugeniusz Goska, USHMM RG-50.488.0027, tape 1, 10:00–11:20.

89. Edward Sypko, KARTA AHM_V_0030, video 2, 43:40–45:10.

90. Weinstein, *Quenched Steel*, 51; Arad, *Belzec, Sobibor, Treblinka*, 110; Webb and Chocholatý, *Treblinka Death Camp*, 90–91; Samuel Rajzman, 9 October 1945, IPN GK 196/69.

91. Willenberg, *Surviving Treblinka*, 102.

92. ARG II 382 (Ring. II/299), 175.

93. ARG II 382 (Ring. II/299), 184.

94. Willenberg, *Surviving Treblinka*, 110.

95. Treblinka's appearance and layout did change over time, though the general internal divisions of the camp spaces stayed quite similar. Map 1 shows Treblinka by the time of the uprising in 1943. P. Laponder, who created this map, also created another map to show Treblinka in its earlier stages. See Webb and Lisciotto, "Mapping Treblinka."

96. Wiernik, *Year in Treblinka*, 28.

97. Wójcik, *Treblinka '43*.

98. Wacław Bednarczyk, 27 October 1945, IPN GK 196/70; see also Kopówka and Rytel-Andrianik, *Dam Im Imię*, 385.

99. ŻIH 230/63; Horwitz, "Places Far Away," 414. The Germans' attempt to further distance themselves within Treblinka suggests that psychological distancing was an ongoing process.

100. Wiernik, *Year in Treblinka*, 13.

101. Donat, *Death Camp Treblinka*, 47.

102. ŻIH 302/32, 25.

103. Sereny, *Into That Darkness*, 200. See also Arad, *Belzec, Sobibor, Treblinka*, 38–39; Glazar, *Trap*, x–xi; Cresswell, *Place*, 24; and Webb and Chocholatý, *Treblinka Death Camp*, 380. Edward Westermann writes, "Camp canteens at the killing centers at Bełżec, Sobibór, and Treblinka also were sites of bacchanalian excess involving alcohol, music, and sexual coercion." Westermann, *Drunk on Genocide*, 119.

104. Quoted portion from Arad, *Belzec, Sobibor, Treblinka*, 41, though Arad also gives more details on the camp layout on pages 38–41. See also Łukaszkiewicz, *Obóz Straceń*, 12; Webb and Chocholatý, *Treblinka Death Camp*, 59; Chrostowski, *Extermination Camp Treblinka*, 30; Glazar, *Trap*, 15; Krakowski, *War of the Doomed*, 238; and Roiter, *Voices*, 162.

105. Apenszlak et al., *Black Book*, 146. Original report from Oyneg Shabes noted as ARG II 432b (Ring. II/319). It can also be found as ŻIH 230/63.

106. Abraham Bomba, VHA 18061, tape 3, 12:50–13:20, 20:25–20:45.

107. ŻIH 301/5483, 4–5. *Lager* (Camp) 1 and 2 here refer to the internal divisions of Treblinka II, the death camp. Even though there existed two main camps, Treblinka I and II, those inside the death camp (Treblinka II) often referred to the Totenlager portion of it as "Camp II."

108. ŻIH 302/32, 28.

109. Aleksander Kudlik, 10 October 1945, IPN GK 196/69.

110. ARG II 382 (Ring. II/299), 172.

111. Chil Rajchman, USHMM RG-50.030.0185, 25:00–25:55.

112. Mark, *Extermination*, 9.

113. Wiernik, *Year in Treblinka*, 11; Krzepicki quote from ARG II 382 (Ring. II/299), 146.

114. Weinstein, *Quenched Steel*, 26–27.

115. *In Everlasting Remembrance*, 34. Adolf Eichmann referred to Treblinka's train station as a "perfect imitation" of a real one. Arendt, *Eichmann in Jerusalem*, 89.

116. Descriptions of Treblinka's station are found in many places, such as survivor Samuel Rajzman's Nuremberg testimony, *Trial of the Major War Criminals*, 8:326. See also Willenberg, *Surviving Treblinka*, 107; Sereny, *Into That Darkness*, 200; Grossman, "Treblinka Hell," 32; Łukaszkiewicz, *Obóz Straceń*, 26; and ŻIH 302/32, 26. Willenberg also remembers seeing 3 o'clock on the clock's face in his earlier postwar testimony; ŻIH 301/1134. Another witness testified that he worked at Treblinka's "cash registers"; JNSV, 8:269.

117. ŻIH 301/1134.

118. Ząbecki, *Wspomnienia*, 42.

119. Wiernik, *Year in Treblinka*, 13; Glazar, *Trap*, 13; Arad, *Belzec, Sobibor, Treblinka*, 122; Łukaszkiewicz, *Obóz Straceń*, 29.
120. Edward Westermann suggests that ritualistic humiliation served many purposes, including an expression of power dynamics and a manifestation of "performative masculinity" among perpetrators who bonded over the rituals. Westermann, *Drunk on Genocide*, 51–53.
121. ŻIH 302/32, 28; Arad, *Belzec, Sobibor, Treblinka*, 120; Wiernik, *Year in Treblinka*, 18; ŻIH 301/26.
122. Donat, *Death Camp Treblinka*, 228. The same testimony from the same person, Stanisław Kon, is included in Łukaszkiewicz, *Obóz Straceń*, 47.
123. Many victims likely saw through the deception, but the speed of the process meant they had little time to act. See chapter 3.
124. ŻIH 230/63.
125. *Trial of the Major War Criminals*, 4:485.

2. A Behavioral Space

1. Christopher Browning writes, "The behavior of any human being is, of course, a very complex phenomenon, and the historian who attempts to 'explain' it is indulging in a certain arrogance." Browning, *Ordinary Men*, 188; see also Goldhagen, *Hitler's Willing Executioners*.
2. While my research adds to the increasing understanding that behavioral categorizations in the Holocaust (perpetrator, bystander, victim, survivor, etc.) are hard to define, the perpetrators I refer to in this chapter are the Germans and Ukrainians willfully carrying out mass murder at Treblinka.
3. Cresswell, *In Place/Out*, 149–58; see also Lefebvre, *Production of Space*, 39.
4. Sara Berger has outlined 5 "types" of Reinhard ss men: I. "Violent, proactive perpetrators in authority positions" (23 total), II. "Proactive but only functionally-violent" authority figures (15), III. Excessive and undisciplined violent perpetrators (majority), IV. Criminals "by the book" (47), V. Transferred out at own request (16). Berger, *Experten der Vernichtung*, 346–67.
5. ARG II 382 (Ring. II/299), 145; Ringelblum, *Polish-Jewish Relations*, 255.
6. For examples, see the introduction's reference to Heller, "Only 2 Survivors"; and Nikolic-Dunlop, *Treblinka*.
7. JNSV, 8:272.
8. Bloxham, *Final Solution*, 285.
9. Arendt, *Origins of Totalitarianism*, 445.
10. JNSV, 8:268.
11. Westermann, *Drunk on Genocide*.
12. Koonz, *Nazi Conscience*, 1–2; Fritzsche, *Life and Death*, 202.

13. *Das Menschenschlachthaus Treblinka*.

14. Foucault explains how modern society adopted methods of "discipline and punishment" that occur "behind the walls," making it a matter between the state and individual and no longer a public spectacle. And although we are talking about neither specifically here, since the Jews were not guilty of anything, the model helps reveal how many processes of modern life are deemed acceptable when moved out of sight. Foucault, *Discipline and Punish*, 124–25. Timothy Pachirat writes that power in the contemporary era is defined by "*removing barriers to sight, by eradicating obstacles that create possibilities for darkness and concealment.*" Pachirat, *Every Twelve Seconds*, 11.

15. Łukaszkiewicz, *Obóz Straceń*, 30; Hannah Arendt calls the camps "corpse factories." Arendt, *Origins of Totalitarianism*, 454n.

16. Grossman, "Treblinka Hell," 39.

17. Later chapters distinctively show Treblinka's horrors and further deconstruct Nazi imagery.

18. Arendt, *Origins of Totalitarianism*, 445.

19. Donat, *Death Camp Treblinka*, 41.

20. *Trials of War Criminals*, 1:865–70.

21. Blatman, *Death Marches*, 28.

22. *Trial of the Major War Criminals*, 3:567. This is an official Polish Government Commission report investigating German crimes in Poland; the Frankfurt court stated in the 1951 Treblinka trial, "The Treblinka camp was set up for the sole purpose of killing as many Jews as possible." JNSV, 8:269; see also Katz, "On the Neutrality," 303.

23. Wiernik, *Year in Treblinka*, 11.

24. Blumental, *Dokumenty i Materiały*, 172.

25. Sereny, *Into That Darkness*, 202.

26. Sereny, *Into That Darkness*, 214 (emphasis added).

27. *Trial of the Major War Criminals*, 8:329.

28. Donat, *Death Camp Treblinka*, 228.

29. Hannah Arendt writes, "The real secret, the concentration camps, those laboratories in the experiment of total domination, is shielded by the totalitarian regimes from the eyes of their own people as well as from all others." Arendt, *Origins of Totalitarianism*, 436.

30. *Trial of the Major War Criminals*, 29:145.

31. Westermann states, "The glorification of martial virtues and violence as 'the highest manifestation of manhood' emerged as defining characteristics of the National Socialist ideal of hypermasculinity, especially within the ss." Westermann, *Drunk on Genocide*, 19–30.

32. *Trials of War Criminals*, 1:865–70.

33. Donat, *Death Camp Treblinka*, 273.

34. Republic of Poland Ministry of Foreign Affairs, *German Occupation of Poland*, 181 (emphasis added).

35. Arad, *Belzec, Sobibor, Treblinka*, 182–84; see also Rückerl, *NS Vernichtungslager*, 120.

36. Quoted section from Sereny, *Into That Darkness*, 80; nicknames given in this passage are from Donat, *Death Camp Treblinka*, 273.

37. Rieger, *Creator*, 134.

38. *Trials of War Criminals*, 1:866–67. Globočnik claimed this conversation occurred during Hitler's visit to the Reinhard camps, which never happened. Therefore, the context in which Gerstein quoted Globočnik was probably, according to Yitzhak Arad, "Globočnik's own invention, probably to stress his high status and the importance of his mission. There is, however, a possibility that such a conversation transpired with Himmler during his visit to Lublin in the middle of July 1942. Its veracity aside, this story is important as an insight to Globočnik's ideological approach to the extermination of the Jews." Arad, *Belzec, Sobibor, Treblinka*, 102–3.

39. Perz, "Austrian Connection," 401.

40. Berger, *Experten der Vernichtung*, 17.

41. As mentioned in chapter 1, T4 was "officially" shut down partly in response to protests from the German public, including the Catholic Church, though increases in planning for Operation Barbarossa also played a role. What extent the protests had on Nazi decision-making, though, is still debated. See Griech-Polelle, "Image," 41–57; see also Crowe, *Holocaust*, 153.

42. *Justiz und NS-Verbrechen*, 34:750.

43. Arad, "Jewish Prisoner Uprisings," 357. See also Arendt, *Eichmann in Jerusalem*, 108; and Stone, *Histories of the Holocaust*, 183–85.

44. De Mildt, *In the Name*, 239.

45. Lifton, *Nazi Doctors*, 157. There were also temporal differences—Auschwitz and Majdanek were erected before Barbarossa but were retroactively adapted to become killing centers after Operation Reinhard began. Thus, after the Reinhard camps became operational, T4-trained ss men also began appearing at these earlier-established camps.

46. Chrostowski, *Extermination Camp Treblinka*, 359; ARG II 382 (Ring. II/299), 188; ŻIH 301/26.

47. Sereny, *Into That Darkness*, 51; see also *Justiz und NS-Verbrechen*, 34:737.

48. Sereny, *Into That Darkness*, 164.

49. Hans Mommsen writes that the Holocaust functioned because of "the acceptance and toleration of it, [and] the approval and support for it, which came from the

leading officials in all areas of the regime." Mommsen, *From Weimar to Auschwitz*, 8. See also Kershaw, *Hitler*, 533, 539; and Childers, *Third Reich*, 505–6.

50. *Trial of the Major War Criminals*, 4:318, 327–28.

51. JNSV, 22:119.

52. *Justiz und NS-Verbrechen*, 34:749–50. The two "Treblinka trials" took place from 1964 to 1970 in Düsseldorf, though a 1951 Frankfurt court tried Josef Hirtreiter for his role at Treblinka.

53. *Justiz und NS-Verbrechen*, 34:776 (emphasis added). The court continued, "[Stangl] had never been officially promoted, he claimed, and was simply the highest-ranking person there after the reorganization" of the camp.

54. *Justiz und NS-Verbrechen*, 34:783. Sara Berger writes, "The decision to remain in the extermination camps was also driven by interests, and there were several motivating and compensatory incentives. On the one hand, good salaries were paid, and privileges and benefits granted, but on the other hand, freedom of action within the structure also offered advantages to the perpetrators. . . . Overall, the T4-Reinhard men were subject to very few rules." Berger, *Experten der Vernichtung*, 328.

55. *Justiz und NS-Verbrechen*, 34:776.

56. Sereny, *Into That Darkness*, 201–3 (emphasis added).

57. Sereny, *Into That Darkness*, 207–8 (emphasis on "did" in original; emphasis on "human relations" added).

58. Foucault, *"Society Must Be Defended,"* 240.

59. Tyner, *Genocide*, 25.

60. Sereny, *Into That Darkness*, 117–18. Stangl never disputed the outfit or having rode around in the uniform on horseback (he claimed that poor road conditions made such transport logical).

61. Sereny, *Into That Darkness*, 202.

62. *Justiz und NS-Verbrechen*, 34:784, 798.

63. Rieger, *Creator*, 101.

64. Donald Bloxham states that places of exception so thoroughly conditioned behavior that it "helps explain why, when soldiers and policeman returned from the places of exception" after the war, they "reintegrated relatively easily." Bloxham, *Final Solution*, 285.

65. JNSV, 8:269–70 (emphasis added).

66. JNSV, 22:119.

67. Donat, *Death Camp Treblinka*, 61.

68. JNSV, 22:49–50, 55 (emphasis added). The court added that "Franz 'particularly distinguished himself' in the sense of the Nationalist Socialist worldview of the time" regarding the mass killing of Jews in Treblinka.

69. The *Lalka* moniker appears in several places. See Krzepicki's testimony in Donat, *Death Camp Treblinka*, 93–94; and Klee, Dressen, and Riess, *"Good Old Days,"* 291–92.

70. Klee, Dressen, and Riess, *"Good Old Days,"* 226–27; Berger, *Experten der Vernichtung*, 328.

71. Lanzmann, *Shoah*, 105–6 (emphasis added). The song's text also appears in the 1965 Düsseldorf trial, JNSV, 22:105. The lyrics differ slightly in each source, but I've chosen to quote here Lanzmann's interview of Suchomel because the trial does not directly quote an SS person. Additionally, Suchomel twice repeats the lyrics to Lanzmann, each time identically.

72. JNSV, 8:261, 266, 270.

73. De Mildt, *In the Name*, 254–55. Although he is summarizing trial documents, specifically JNSV, 8:266–70, I cite here de Mildt's phrasing around Hirtreiter's "advancement."

74. JNSV, 8:270.

75. JNSV, 22:99–100.

76. JNSV, 22:105.

77. JNSV, 22:109, 110, 121, 122.

78. JNSV, 22:109. De Mildt uses the term "lifeless robot" instead of "Frankenstein." De Mildt, *In the Name*, 260–61.

79. JNSV, 22:189–90.

80. Weitz, "Modernity of Genocides," 58.

81. *Trial of the Major War Criminals*, 4:494.

82. Chrostowski, *Extermination Camp Treblinka*, 42; Arad, "Jewish Prisoner Uprisings," 359; ARG II 382 (Ring. II/299), 188; ŻIH 301/26.

83. ARG II 382 (Ring. II/299), 188; see also ŻIH 301/228. Peter Black writes, "Most common among their violations were taking unauthorized leave, drunkenness, theft, curfew violation, sleeping on guard duty, and corruption, all infractions for which the truant could receive up to three weeks in solitary or even a lashing." Black, "Foot Soldiers," 32–33.

84. Łukaszkiewicz, *Obóz Straceń*, 18. See also Blumental, *Dokumenty i Materiały*, 180; ŻIH 301/656; and ŻIH 301/26.

85. Black, "Foot Soldiers," 32.

86. Willenberg, *Surviving Treblinka*, 56–57.

87. Łukaszkiewicz, *Obóz Straceń*, 18; ARG II 382 (Ring. II/299), 188; Willenberg, *Surviving Treblinka*, 59; Chrostowski, *Extermination Camp Treblinka*, 43; Black, "Foot Soldiers," 22–23.

88. United States v. Demjanjuk (ND Ohio 1981), 518 F. Supp. 1362 (emphasis added). Demjanjuk was one of two Ukrainians who operated the gas chambers.

89. Browning, *Ordinary Men*, 188–89; Berger describes the social networks and friendships T4/Reinhard men formed, writing how in postwar trials many "were reluctant to comment too critically on the behavior of their accomplices, even describing violent criminals among them as decent." Berger, *Experten der Vernichtung*, 332.

90. Bauer, *History of the Holocaust*, 221; see also Bryant, *Eyewitness to Genocide*, 94.

91. Arendt, *Origins of Totalitarianism*, 403.

92. Grossman, "Treblinka Hell," 30; see also Berger, *Experten der Vernichtung*, 328.

93. Stefan Kucharek, USHMM RG-50.488.0006, cassette 3, tape 1, 31:00–35:32.

94. Wiernik, *Year in Treblinka*, 22–23.

95. Chersztein, *Ofiary Nikczemności*, 93.

96. Ząbecki, *Wspomnienia*, 83.

97. Burleigh and Wipperman, *Racial State*, 67–68.

98. Arad, *Belzec, Sobibor, Treblinka*, 125. Kurt Gerstein wrote, "At Belzec and Treblinka, nobody bothered to take anything approaching an exact count of the persons killed." *Trials of War Criminals*, 1:869. This contrasts with the "operation reports" kept by the *Einsatzgruppen*. For examples of these reports, see *Trials of War Criminals*, 4:140–200. Abraham Bomba writes about a man who escaped Treblinka, went to Warsaw, and sneaked back into the ghetto, but the Germans did not notice his absence at the camp. Abraham Bomba, VHA 18061, tape 4, 19:00–20:00. However, some type of broad record was kept, at least unofficially. There was a party to celebrate the one hundred thousandth victim from Warsaw. Westermann, *Drunk on Genocide*, 86.

99. Arad, Gutman, and Margaliot, *Documents*, 274–75; Rückerl, *NS Vernichtungslager*, 117–23; Arad, "Jewish Prisoner Uprisings," 361; *Justiz und NS-Verbrechen*, 34:750.

100. ŻIH 302/32, 8. The very existence of Kurt Franz's photo album shows restrictions were not rigidly self-policed; as Berger writes, "It was more important to them to do their job than to strictly observe the commandments." Berger, *Experten der Vernichtung*, 328.

101. Józef Kuźmiński, 16–23 October 1945, IPN GK 196/69.

102. Ząbecki, *Wspomnienia*, 43.

103. Ząbecki, *Wspomnienia*, 50.

104. Ząbecki, *Wspomnienia*, 38.

105. By then, also, Auschwitz's massive gas chambers, capable of further mass murder, had been built.

106. Chil Rajchman, USHMM RG-50.030.0185, 37:45–39:50.

107. Bauer, *History of the Holocaust*, 326; AAN 1333/0/3/212.III.1.

108. Łukaszkiewicz, *Obóz Straceń*, 30.

109. *Trial of the Major War Criminals*, 7:592–93.

110. AAN 2134/0/42.

111. Klee, Dressen, and Riess, *"Good Old Days,"* 247; Sereny, *Into That Darkness*, 249–50; Arad, *Belzec, Sobibor, Treblinka*, 371, 379; *Justiz und NS-Verbrechen*, 34:771. The Germans built a farmhouse on the leveled ground to further disguise the space, and two Ukrainians stayed there to stop looting and to prevent Russian access (neither was achieved).

112. Eugeniusz Goska, USHMM RG-50.488.0027, tape 1, 18:00–19:30; see also APS 1403/0/9.5/1527.

113. ŻIH 301/689.

114. AAN 2975/0/3.5.4.11/400.

115. Rieger, *Creator*, 101.

116. Wiernik, *Year in Treblinka*, 17.

117. ARG II 382 (Ring. II/299), 143.

118. Roiter, *Voices*, 154.

119. Wiernik, *Year in Treblinka*, 19.

120. Berger, *Experten der Vernichtung*, 358.

121. Lanzmann, *Shoah*, 55.

122. The court did not believe he acted "as intensively as one might have assumed," if, in fact, this was his reason for wanting to transfer. "He never went in person to any relevant office, nor did he take the most obvious and promising route of reporting to the front." JNSV, 8:271.

123. Berger writes, "Several times a year the men also received two weeks of home leave." She adds later, "Most did not experience any particular disadvantages resulting from their decision." Berger, *Experten der Vernichtung*, 329, 358.

124. *Archives of the Holocaust*, 22:424.

125. *Archives of the Holocaust*, 22:413–14.

126. *Justiz und NS-Verbrechen*, 34:782.

127. ŻIH 301/688.

128. AAN 1333/0/3/212.III.1.

129. Donat, *Death Camp Treblinka*, 40.

130. De Mildt, *In the Name*, 243. Eberl was an "extermination expert" at the T4 facilities in Brandenburg and Bernberg; Globočnik told Eberl upon arriving at Treblinka, "How dare you accept so many [people] every day when you can only process three thousand?" Lanzmann, *Shoah*, 65–66.

131. Suchomel admits as much in Lanzmann, *Shoah*, 52–56.

132. ŻIH 302/32, 24. See also Rieger, *Creator*, 120; and Arad, *Belzec, Sobibor, Treblinka*, 104.

133. Berger, *Experten der Vernichtung*, 329–30.

134. Ząbecki, *Wspomnienia*, 78.

135. Berger, *Experten der Vernichtung*, 358–61.

136. Aziz, *Doctors of Death*, 192.

137. Rieger, *Creator*, 135; Donat, *Death Camp Treblinka*, 275.

138. Donat, *Death Camp Treblinka*, 42–43.

139. JNSV, 22:120.

140. Sol Liber, VHA 58, tape 3, 18:15–18:30 (emphasis added). See also ŻIH 204/62; Chrostowski, *Extermination Camp Treblinka*, 33; Arad, *Belzec, Sobibor, Treblinka*, 352–56; and ŻIH 301/6080.

141. Wiernik, *Year in Treblinka*, 22. William Schneiderman recounted that the Ukrainians were "drinking all the time." USHMM RG-50.030.0288, tape 2, 18:30–19:45.

142. Westermann, *Drunk on Genocide*, 161.

143. Berger, *Experten der Vernichtung*, 332–33.

144. Sereny, *Into That Darkness*, 209. Similar examples abound. For one, a member of Police Battalion 101 explains, "Most of the other comrades drank so much solely because of the many shootings of Jews, for such a life was quite intolerable sober." Browning, *Ordinary Men*, 82.

145. ŻIH 204/62.

146. ŻIH 302/224, 30 (emphasis added).

147. ŻIH 302/321, 47; Berger, *Experten der Vernichtung*, 334. German guards also met with local prostitutes.

148. ŻIH 302/32, 16. Abraham Krzepicki stated, "Local peasants were well aware that they couldn't beat the prices they got at Treblinka for their products anywhere else." ARG II 382 (Ring. II/299), 190.

149. Stefan Kucharek, USHMM RG-50.488.0006, cassette 3, tape 2, 9:30–12:50; see also ŻIH 204/62.

150. Wiernik, *Year in Treblinka*, 26.

151. AAN 2725/0/-/242. In the 1950s several Ukrainian guards were accused of having raped local women near Treblinka. The guards countered (disturbingly) that because they subsequently married the women (sometimes through force) and raised children with them for years afterward, they were not guilty of crimes.

152. ŻIH 301/6080.

153. I use Grossman's own words here to contrast the *Menschenschlachthaus* imagery. Ironically enough, some of the *Menschenschlachthaus* pamphlet derives from Grossman's "Treblinka Hell" report.

154. ŻIH 301/4870.

155. Donat, *Death Camp Treblinka*, 64–65; see also ŻIH 301/6080.

156. In fact, a postwar trial against Ukrainian guards cited a Wólka Okrąglik resident named Irena Oleszczuk, who "could have been to some extent initiated

into the secrets of criminal activity" carried out at Treblinka because of her relationships with the guards. Although she was not tried for complicity, the level of knowledge insinuated by her relationship with people who were at the camp is telling. ŻIH 344/589, 5.

157. Sereny, *Into That Darkness*, 193.
158. Sereny, *Into That Darkness*, 365–66.

3. A Space of Life and Death

1. Bauer, *Rethinking the Holocaust*, 14.
2. Lefebvre, *Production of Space*, 35 (parentheses in original).
3. This is a reference to the previous chapter. The Nazi belief was that Reinhard camps offered a more distanced, "clean" way to kill people. Yet as this and each subsequent chapter shows, that was not the reality, and instead, Treblinka was a brutal, horrific space of mass murder.
4. ARG II 382 (Ring. II/299), 164–65.
5. The research conducted here suggests the real number is quite a bit higher. For one, as is shown in subsequent chapters, Jews were constantly escaping Treblinka, and while many were recaptured, unknown numbers also survived. Additionally, German record keeping at the camp was not meticulous (especially since so many people went straight to the gas chambers). Therefore, since we do not know everyone who ended up at Treblinka, we may never know for sure who or how many escaped the camp, but it is certainly higher than the documented number of survivors.
6. ARG II 382 (Ring. II/299), 139. This inability to escape the camp afterward was certainly not limited to Treblinka. Primo Levi's writings show the lasting impacts of surviving a camp, and he struggled to define what his survival meant until the day he died. When he heard about Levi's death, fellow survivor Elie Wiesel famously said, "Primo Levi died at Auschwitz forty years later." The insinuation is that physically escaping a camp does not necessarily mean completely surviving it. See Levi, *Drowned and the Saved* and *Survival in Auschwitz*.
7. Chaim Kwiatek escaped and used the familiar landscape to walk home to Stoczek (13 km). ŻIH 301/668.
8. Central Commission for Investigation of German Crimes in Poland, *German Crimes*, 104.
9. ŻIH 301/466.
10. ŻIH 301/1565.
11. Linda Penn, VHA 55144, tape 1, 16:00–17:00.
12. Kopówka and Rytel-Andrianik, *Dam Im Imię*, 421.

13. Józef Kuźmiński, 16–23 October 1945, IPN GK 196/69.
14. Wiernik, *Year in Treblinka*, 41.
15. Eugenia Samuel, USHMM RG-50.488.0008, tape 1, 1:08:50–1:10:15 (emphasis added).
16. Goldstein, *Stars Bear Witness*, 115–16.
17. Apenszlak et al., *Black Book*, 144–45. Original report from Oyneg Shabes noted as ARG II 432b (Ring. II/319). It can also be found as ŻIH 230/63.
18. "Holocaust Testimony of Jack Price," Gratz College Holocaust Oral History Archive.
19. Roiter, *Voices*, 147.
20. Grunspan, *Uprising*, 27; ŻIH 301/688.
21. ŻIH 230/72; ŻIH 230/91, 16.
22. ŻIH 301/688.
23. ARG II 382 (Ring. II/299), 154.
24. ŻIH 301/1049.
25. ŻIH 302/153.
26. Kuperhand and Kuperhand, *Shadows of Treblinka*, 108. For similar examples, see Willenberg, *Surviving Treblinka*, 39.
27. Wiernik, *Year in Treblinka*, 26.
28. ŻIH 230/63.
29. William Schneiderman, USHMM RG-50.030.0288, tape 1, 27:00–29:15.
30. ARG II 379 (Ring. II/296).
31. Donat, *Death Camp Treblinka*, 31.
32. *Trial of the Major War Criminals*, 8:328.
33. Not least was *when* someone arrived at Treblinka. Henryk Poswolski, who arrived on January 19, 1943, recalled that by then, the ticket booth "had already fallen into disuse." Indeed, the Germans relied less on these facades and deceptions as knowledge of Treblinka spread after the first massive waves of deportation. Henryk Poswolski, 9 October 1945, IPN GK 196/69.
34. Łukaszkiewicz, *Obóz Straceń*, 26.
35. ŻIH 204/62.
36. Donat, *Death Camp Treblinka*, 29.
37. ARG II 382 (Ring. II/299), 155.
38. *Trial of the Major War Criminals*, 8:326.
39. ŻIH 302/32, 3.
40. Abraham Bomba, VHA 18061, tape 3, 6:15–6:30.
41. Roiter, *Voices*, 126. Depending on when a specific transport arrived, the experience might have been different. For example, "a milder treatment based more on the principle of deception was only found on a few transports from western

countries. On the other hand, it was especially hard and brutal on transports from Warsaw in the later days, where people already knew or suspected what fate awaited them." *Justiz und NS-Verbrechen*, 34:762.

42. Donat, *Death Camp Treblinka*, 29.
43. Roiter, *Voices*, 125.
44. For Czechowicz, see ŻIH 301/688; for Bomba, see Abraham Bomba, VHA 18061, tape 3, 9:40–10:10.
45. ARG II 382 (Ring. II/299), 155.
46. ŻIH 230/63.
47. Leon Finkelsztein, 28 December 1945, IPN GK 196/70.
48. Abraham Bomba, VHA 18061, tape 4, 4:45–5:15.
49. ŻIH 301/228.
50. ŻIH 230/63.
51. Henryk Poswolski, 9 October 1945, IPN GK 196/69.
52. ARG II 382 (Ring. II/299), 180.
53. Abraham Bomba, vha 18061, tape 3, 9:20–9:35; żih 301/5089; *Justiz und NS-Verbrechen*, 34:764; Lanzmann, *Shoah*, 110. Samuel Rajzman called it *Himmelfahrt Strasse* (Ascension Street). *Trial of the Major War Criminals*, 8:325.
54. Willenberg, *Surviving Treblinka*, 10.
55. ŻIH 302/32, 2.
56. ARG II 382 (Ring. II/299), 170–71.
57. Roiter, *Voices*, 145.
58. Donat, *Death Camp Treblinka*, 34–35; see also żih 230/63.
59. Wiernik, *Year in Treblinka*, 19.
60. *Justiz und NS-Verbrechen*, 34:828.
61. Łukaszkiewicz, *Obóz Straceń*, 26. Rachel Auerbach states, "If they had any illusions left until then, they certainly lost them during the 'trip to Heaven.'" Donat, *Death Camp Treblinka*, 35.
62. *Justiz und NS-Verbrechen*, 34:765; ARG II 382 (Ring. II/299), 174.
63. ARG II 382 (Ring. II/299), 174.
64. Donat, *Death Camp Treblinka*, 34. Yankel Wiernik provides a similar description; see Wiernik, *Year in Treblinka*, 14.
65. ARG II 382 (Ring. II/299), 174; żih 302/32, 28; żih 301/688. Detail about doors with rubber seals found in Łukaszkiewicz, *Obóz Straceń*, 9. Caroline Sturdy Colls and Michael Branthwaite found these same reddish terra-cotta tiles (that once composed the gas chamber floors) in their archeological dig at Treblinka. Sturdy Colls and Branthwaite, "'This Is Proof?,'" 435–36.
66. ŻIH 301/688; see also żih 301/5483, 5.
67. Szyja Warszawski, 9 October 1945, IPN GK 196/69.

68. Donat, *Death Camp Treblinka*, 35. A witness from the Nuremberg trials corroborates this by stating, "Small children were simply thrown inside" the gas chambers; *Trial of the Major War Criminals*, 3:56. Łukaszkiewicz records a survivor who notes that those inside the gas chambers had to raise their arms to fit more people; Łukaszkiewicz. *Obóz Straceń*, 27.

69. ŻIH 230/63.

70. Donat, *Death Camp Treblinka*, 35–36.

71. Bour, Tutin, and Pasquier, "Central Nervous System," 2–4.

72. Forbes, "Carbon Monoxide Uptake," 75.

73. Wiernik, *Year in Treblinka*, 14–15; Abraham Kolski said that within twenty to twenty-five minutes, everyone was dead. USHMM RG-50.030.0113, tape 1, 24:20–24:40.

74. ŻIH 301/688.

75. ŻIH 301/852.

76. ŻIH 301/688.

77. Quoted portion from ŻIH 301/5089. For other details mentioned, see ŻIH 302/32, 7; Henryk Poswolski, 9 October 1945, IPN GK 196/69; and ŻIH 301/688.

78. ŻIH 302/153; ŻIH 301/1134.

79. ŻIH 301/5089.

80. Donat, *Death Camp Treblinka*, 58.

81. *Archives of the Holocaust*, 22:424; *Trial of the Major War Criminals*, 3:567; Arad, "Jewish Prisoner Uprisings," 359. William Schneiderman remembers there being about one thousand "work" Jews at Treblinka. William Schneiderman, USHMM RG-50.030.0288, tape 2, 20:00–20:30. Bomba, on the other hand, recalled that eight hundred workers in Treblinka was "a lot" at any one time. Abraham Bomba, VHA 18061, tape 3, 10:35–10:40.

82. Arad, "Jewish Prisoner Uprisings," 359; Łukaszkiewicz, *Obóz Straceń*, 19.

83. Samuel Rajzman, 9 October 1945, IPN GK 196/69.

84. ŻIH 301/852; Chrostowski, *Extermination Camp Treblinka*, 45–48; Willenberg, *Surviving Treblinka*, 55, 103–4; ŻIH 204/62; *Justiz und NS-Verbrechen*, 34:760; Łukaszkiewicz, *Obóz Straceń*, 20; ŻIH 302/32, 5–6; ŻIH 301/228.

85. Henryk Poswolski, 9 October 1945, IPN GK 196/69.

86. ŻIH 230/63.

87. Samuel Rajzman, 9 October 1945, IPN GK 196/69 (parentheses in original).

88. Wiernik, *Year in Treblinka*, 36.

89. ŻIH 301/5341.

90. Samuel Rajzman, 9 October 1945, IPN GK 196/69.

91. *Archives of the Holocaust*, 22:425.

92. Roiter, *Voices*, 160.

93. Willenberg, *Surviving Treblinka*, 93.

94. ARG II 382 (Ring. II/299), 193. Krzepicki uses the German phrase here in original.

95. ŻIH 302/32, 16–18.

96. Wiernik, *Year in Treblinka*, 26.

97. ŻIH 301/1049.

98. ARG II 382 (Ring. II/299), 184; Bomba recalls only seeing one or two women inside Treblinka. Abraham Bomba, VHA 18061, tape 3, 21:30–22:15.

99. ŻIH 302/32, 18; see also *Justiz und NS-Verbrechen*, 34:761.

100. Kopówka and Rytel-Andrianik, *Dam Im Imię*, 73–74.

101. ŻIH 301/5483, 6.

102. Person, "Sexual Violence," 115–16; Sommer, "Sexual Exploitation of Women," 53. Sommer and Person show the inaccuracy of early beliefs that Jewish women in death camps did not suffer sexual violence.

103. Wiernik, *Year in Treblinka*, 22.

104. Sereny, *Into That Darkness*, 204–5.

105. Westermann explains further that alcohol use also played a role in lowering inhibitions toward committing sexual violence, and individual perpetrators bragged about their "conquests" as a way to display "their own virility and masculinity" and to bond with others. Westermann, *Drunk on Genocide*, 89–96. Some studies suggest as many as 50 percent of all ss and German police "violated the 'ban on undesirable intercourse with ethnically alien women." Mühlhäuser, "Between 'Racial Awareness,'" 203.

106. Linda Penn, VHA 55144, tape 1, 20:00–23:35.

107. Roiter, *Voices*, 146.

108. Abraham Bomba, VHA 18061, tape 3, 7:40–8:10. The quote in the final sentence is taken from *Justiz und NS-Verbrechen*, 34:763.

109. ARG II 380 (Ring. II/297).

110. Leon Finkelsztein, 28 December 1945, IPN GK 196/70.

111. Isadore Helfing, USHMM RG-50.042.0014, tape 1, 1:15–2:30.

112. ŻIH 302/118, 19.

113. Roiter, *Voices*, 127.

114. Chil Rajchman, USHMM RG-50.030.0185, 20:50–21:30.

115. ŻIH 301/6795. This unnamed survivor's story was preserved by AK partisan Maria Krych.

116. Apenszlak and Polakiewicz, *Armed Resistance*, 27.

117. Donat, *Death Camp Treblinka*, 227–28.

118. Tim Cole suggests the idea of ghettoization was fluid because, according to the Nazis, it was a "step" toward genocide. Cole, *Holocaust City*, 30, 80.

119. Donat, *Death Camp Treblinka*, 36.

120. Willenberg, *Surviving Treblinka*, 60.

121. ŻIH 230/63; Leon Finkelsztein, 28 December 1945, IPN GK 196/70.

122. ARG II 382 (Ring. II/299), 157.

123. Edward Sypko, KARTA AHM_V_0030, video 3, 5:25–6:25.

124. *Justiz und NS-Verbrechen*, 34:766.

125. Jerzy Rajgrodzki never forgot that, as he wrote, "women burnt better than men." ŻIH 301/5483, 6.

126. Hejnoch Brener, 9 October 1945, IPN GK 196/69.

127. Roiter, *Voices*, 150.

128. Wiernik, *Year in Treblinka*, 14.

129. ŻIH 301/688.

130. Edward Sypko, KARTA AHM_V_0030, video 5, 30:25–31:20.

131. ARG II 382 (Ring. II/299), 167.

132. Hejnoch Brener, 9 October 1945, IPN GK 196/69.

133. ARG II 382 (Ring. II/299), 165.

134. Lanzmann, *Shoah*, 49.

135. Willenberg, *Surviving Treblinka*, 77.

136. Blumental, *Dokumenty i Materiały*, 177.

137. ARG II 382 (Ring. II/299), 166–67; see also Abraham Bomba, VHA 18061, tape 5, 4:30–5:00.

138. Edward Sypko, KARTA AHM_V_0030, video 2, 0:25–0:45; see also *Justiz und NS-Verbrechen*, 34:767.

139. Willenberg, *Surviving Treblinka*, 42.

140. Blumental, *Dokumenty i Materiały*, 177; see also Willenberg, *Surviving Treblinka*, 123.

141. Edward Sypko, KARTA AHM_V_0030, video 4, 34:30–36:20.

142. Willenberg, *Surviving Treblinka*, 123.

143. ŻIH 301/6795.

144. ARG II 382 (Ring. II/299), 183.

145. AAN 2975/0/3.5.4.11/400.

146. ŻIH 301/2226.

147. Roiter, *Voices*, 150.

148. ARG II 382 (Ring. II/299), 191.

149. Lanzmann, *Shoah*, 50.

150. ARG II 382 (Ring. II/299), 159.

151. ARG II 382 (Ring. II/299), 165–66.

152. Chil Rajchman, USHMM RG-50.030.0185, 36:30—37:15.

153. Isadore Helfing, USHMM RG-50.042.0014, tape 2, 10:00–10:45.

154. Donat, *Death Camp Treblinka*, 289.

155. ARG II 382 (Ring. II/299), 164.

156. Roiter, *Voices*, 130.

157. Willenberg, *Surviving Treblinka*, 53.

158. Willenberg, *Surviving Treblinka*, 53.

159. Levi, *Drowned and the Saved*, 25–56.

160. Roiter, *Voices*, 138.

161. ARG II 382 (Ring. II/299), 161–62.

162. Roiter, *Voices*, 138.

163. ARG II 382 (Ring. II/299), 185.

164. Willenberg, *Surviving Treblinka*, 67.

165. ARG II 382 (Ring. II/299), 155.

166. Willenberg, *Surviving Treblinka*, 139–40.

167. ARG II 382 (Ring. II/299), 179.

4. An Interactional Space

1. It is believed around half, roughly 300, of the Jews who revolted at Treblinka made it into the forests outside the camp, though only around 150 are believed to have survived the revolt beyond a day or two. Of this number, roughly half survived until the war's end. See Wójcik, *Treblinka '43*. Prior to the Treblinka Uprising, the Warsaw Ghetto Uprising saw thousands of Jews resist violently against SS and German soldiers sent in to deport them to Treblinka in April 1943. Upwards of three hundred SS were killed while putting down the resistance. Some of the Jewish survivors and witnesses of the uprising ended up at Treblinka and likely also helped inspire the revolt there.

2. ARG II 380 (Ring. II/297); see also ŻIH 302/32, 13.

3. Weiner Weber, "Life and Death," 35.

4. Pollefeyt, *Holocaust and Nature*, 9.

5. Bikont, *Crime and the Silence*, 267.

6. Sudilovsky, "Growing Up."

7. Jan Gross writes, "In prewar Poland, Hungary, and Romania, political anti-Semitism was even more entrenched. Complemented by the obscurantist anti-Semitism of Christian churches and the moral authority they wielded with their constituencies, it is hardly surprising that the elimination of Jews . . . was welcomed both by elites and the general public." Gross, *Golden Harvest*, 16. Anna Bikont writes that in Jedwabne and Radziłów, areas representative of other parts of Poland, more than 90 percent of Jews and Poles were poor. Yet "when Catholic neighbors were told that the Jews were the cause of their poverty, many had no trouble believing it." Bikont, *Crime and the Silence*, 24–25; see also Gilbert, *Righteous*, xix.

8. Grabowski, *Hunt for the Jews*, 7. Father Patrick Desbois wrestles with the fluid nature of behavioral responses he identified in non-Jewish witnesses to the mass shootings in Eastern Europe. Desbois, *Holocaust by Bullets*, 51–98.

9. Ringelblum, *Polish-Jewish Relations*, 137.

10. Gross, *Polish Society*, 163.

11. Zuckerman, *Surplus of Memory*, 486.

12. The Nazi colonial mission is discussed in chapter 1, specifically in relation to Blut und Boden. For further reading, the second part of Hannah Arendt's *Origins of Totalitarianism*, entitled "Imperialism," (pp. 123–304) details Germany's planned continental colonization. See also Lower, *Nazi Empire-Building*.

13. Tuan, *Landscapes of Fear*, 206.

14. Cresswell, *Place*, 24.

15. Far from seeking to apologize for Polish behavior that rightly merits condemnation, I instead build context by examining the spatial dynamics of Poland's colonization. If nothing else, it shows that a new morality dictated by the ethics of wartime occupation existed in the Polish spaces around Treblinka—one where the existential threats posed by the Germans affected the decision-making process for many Poles living there during the war.

16. "Natural" spaces around Treblinka included forests, crop fields, and meadows. The idea of natural spaces comes from ideas of wilderness, a word that has its roots in the Old English *weald* or *woeld*, which means "forest." Tuan, *Landscapes of Fear*, 80–81.

17. ŻIH 301/5483, 2.

18. ARG II 382 (Ring. II/299), 189.

19. Willenberg, *Surviving Treblinka*, 122–23.

20. AAN 2134/0/45.

21. ŻIH 301/26.

22. Donat, *Death Camp Treblinka*, 222.

23. ŻIH 301/688.

24. Wiernik, *Year in Treblinka*, 45–46.

25. ŻIH 302/32, 34–35.

26. *Justiz und NS-Verbrechen*, 34:805.

27. Isadore Helfing, USHMM RG-50.042.0014, tape 1, 24:30–26:10.

28. ŻIH 301/668.

29. William Schneiderman, USHMM RG-50.030.0288, tape 3, 17:30–19:00.

30. Glazar, *Trap*, 150.

31. Abraham Bomba, VHA 18061, tape 5, 12:00–13:15.

32. Abraham Kolski, USHMM RG-50.030.0113, tape 2, 2:00–5:00.

33. ARG II 382 (Ring. II/299), 203.

34. Kuperhand and Kuperhand, *Shadows of Treblinka*, 131.

35. ARG II 382 (Ring. II/299), 202.

36. Donat, *Death Camp Treblinka*, 28.

37. ARG 378 (Ring. II/295).

38. ŻIH 302/118.

39. Rajchman, *Last Jew of Treblinka*, 129.

40. ARG II 382 (Ring. II/299), 202.

41. Donat, *Death Camp Treblinka*, 223.

42. Weiner Weber, "Life and Death," 112.

43. Tenenbaum, *Underground*, 259; Roiter, *Voices*, 164–66.

44. Shmuel Krakowski mentions a group that spent over a year in the forests hiding. Krakowski, *War of the Doomed*, 244.

45. Weiner Weber, "Life and Death," 126–27, 135, 144, 154. She cites examples from her interviews with Holocaust survivors who lived in the forests, including Larry Gamulka, who revealed which types of branches burned different ways; Samuel Lato, who learned which water was drinkable based on which insects lived in it; and Arthur Silverberg, who learned from cows what foods were edible and natural remedies for lice. See also Cole, "'Nature Was Helping Us,'" 671–72; and Levin, *Under the Yellow*, 26–28.

46. Willenberg, *Surviving Treblinka*, 144.

47. Glazar, *Trap*, 150–51.

48. Greene and Kumar, *Witness*, 95.

49. Weinstein, *Quenched Steel*, 78.

50. Rajchman, *Last Jew of Treblinka*, 129.

51. Weinstein, *Quenched Steel*, 78.

52. Chil Rajchman, USHMM RG-50.030.0185, 1:05:45–1:06:15.

53. Uno Ingard wrote, "The audibility of sound by night should thus be better than in the daytime." Ingard, "Review of the Influence," 407–8.

54. ŻIH 301/85.

55. ŻIH 301/5483, 11–12. Chaim Grabel states similarly of his experience, "We hid in the forest during daytime and we traveled at night"; ŻIH 301/228.

56. ARG 378 (Ring. II/295).

57. Glazar, *Trap*, 150.

58. ARG II 382 (Ring. II/299), 203.

59. Apenszlak and Polakiewicz, *Armed Resistance*, 64. Treist here may refer to a group of Jews who hid in the forests around Treblinka to avoid deportation. These groups often merged with others who later escaped, and anyone hiding in the forests for long durations undoubtedly experienced similar deprivations.

60. Beorn and Knowles, "Killing on the Ground," 113.

61. Levin, *Under the Yellow*, 31.

62. Cole, "'Nature Was Helping Us,'" 675.

63. Glazar, *Trap*, 151.

64. Wiesel, *Gates*, 61.

65. Cole, "'Nature Was Helping Us,'" 678–79.

66. Pollefeyt, *Holocaust and Nature*, 9 (parentheses in original).

67. Tec, *Defiance*, 81.

68. Willenberg, *Surviving Treblinka*, 147–48.

69. ŻIH 301/5483, 11–12.

70. ARG II 382 (Ring. II/299), 202.

71. Apenszlak and Polakiewicz, *Armed Resistance*, 59–61.

72. AAN 2134/0/45; see also ŻIH 301/5089.

73. ŻIH 301/6080.

74. AAN 2134/0/45.

75. Gutman and Krakowski, *Unequal Victims*, 220, 242; Willenberg, *Surviving Treblinka*, 186. Sobibór survivor Toivi Blatt wrote, "I knew of cases in which the AK had killed innocent Jews." Blatt, *From the Ashes*, 200. Treblinka survivor Saul Kuperhand wrote similarly, "Instead of coordinating activities with Jewish partisans in the woods, [the AK] would attack Jewish groups at every opportunity." Kuperhand and Kuperhand, *Shadows of Treblinka*, xiii.

76. Edward Sypko, KARTA AHM_V_0030, video 3, 12:30–14:15.

77. AAN 2134/0/45.

78. Blumental, *Dokumenty i Materiały*, 181.

79. Chil Rajchman, USHMM RG-50.030.0185, video 1, 54:00–55:45.

80. ARG II 382 (Ring. II/299), 190.

81. William Schneiderman, USHMM RG-50.030.0288, tape 2, 16:20–17:20.

82. Donat, *Death Camp Treblinka*, 215.

83. ARG II 380 (Ring. II/297).

84. Sereny, *Into That Darkness*, 193; Arad, *Belzec, Sobibor, Treblinka*, 203–5; Kuperhand and Kuperhand, *Shadows of Treblinka*, 129.

85. AAN 2134/0/42.

86. ŻIH 301/5483, 12; Mosze Klajman employed a similar strategy. ŻIH 302/118, 49–50.

87. ŻIH 301/228.

88. ARG II 379 (Ring. II/296) (emphasis added).

89. Willenberg, *Surviving Treblinka*, 142–43.

90. Kopówka and Rytel-Andrianik, *Dam Im Imię*, 408.

91. Eugenia Samuel, USHMM RG-50.488.0008, tape 1, 24:00–24:30.

92. Henryk Slebzak, USHMM RG-50.488.0028, video 2, 3:30–7:00, 9:45–11:00.

93. Kopówka and Rytel-Andrianik, *Dam Im Imię*, 416 (emphasis added).

94. Czesław Borowi—Treblinka, USHMM RG-60.5032, film ID 3348, 1:14:00–1:17:00.

95. Kopówka and Rytel-Andrianik, *Dam Im Imię*, 309.

96. Kopówka and Rytel-Andrianik, *Dam Im Imię*, 318–19.

97. Kopówka and Rytel-Andrianik, *Dam Im Imię*, 416.

98. Kopówka and Rytel-Andrianik, *Dam Im Imię*, 253–57.

99. Kopówka and Rytel-Andrianik, *Dam Im Imię*, 225.

100. Eugeniusz Goska, USHMM RG-50.488.0027, tape 1, 12:00–12:45.

101. Henryk Slebzak, USHMM RG-50.488.0028, video 2, 31:00–33:00.

102. Kopówka and Rytel-Andrianik, *Dam Im Imię*, 401.

103. Chil Rajchman, USHMM RG-50.030.0185, 58:00–1:00:45.

104. ŻIH 301/1186.

105. Edward Sypko, KARTA AHM_V_0030, video 3, 8:20–10:30.

106. ARG II 379 (Ring. II/296).

107. Donat, *Death Camp Treblinka*, 65. Auerbach traveled postwar alongside an investigative team and survivors to Treblinka.

108. Abraham Kolski, USHMM RG-50.030.0113, tape 2, 11:00–16:30.

109. Isadore Helfing, USHMM RG-50.042.0014, tape 1, 24:30–26:10.

110. ARG II 382 (Ring. II/299), 198.

111. Tec, *When Light Pierced*, 91–92. Lieber was one of the only women to escape Treblinka in the August uprising. While at the camp, she worked in the laundry, probably passing herself off as Polish, since many other women working there long term were Poles. See chapter 3.

112. ŻIH 301/656. Goldberg recalled that they passed through Wólka Okrąglik (1 km), then Kosów Lacki (7 km), and then Lipki (9 km), an area he referred to as "all the villages around" Treblinka; see also Blumental, *Dokumenty i Materiały*, 181.

113. ŻIH 301/6795.

114. Chil Rajchman, USHMM RG-50.030.0185, 57:30–59:00.

115. Kopówka and Rytel-Andrianik, *Dam Im Imię*, 301–2.

116. Donat, *Death Camp Treblinka*, 247.

117. ŻIH 302/27, 147–48.

118. ŻIH 301/5483, 12.

119. ARG II 382 (Ring. II/299), 201.

120. ŻIH 301/688.

121. ŻIH 302/118, 49–50.

122. ŻIH 301/5483, 12.

123. Many Poles willingly gave help to Polish partisans, so disguising as one could work. Being on the run from Treblinka often meant ingenuity and scrapping for survival.

124. ŻIH 301/85.

125. ŻIH 301/228.

126. Tenenbaum, *Underground*, 259; Rajzman hiding near Węgrów (as found in Tenenbaum) is confirmed by Polish witnesses in Kopówka and Rytel-Andrianik, *Dam Im Imię*, 247.

127. Donat, *Death Camp Treblinka*, 64.

128. Willenberg, *Surviving Treblinka*, 55.

129. Central Commission for Investigation of German Crimes in Poland, *German Crimes*, 105; Łukaszkiewicz, *Obóz Straceń*, 42.

130. Kenyon, "War Crimes," COU 1806:01:030:0009.

131. Kenyon, "War Crimes," COU 1806:01:030:0009. It is noteworthy that while Polish Jews were targeted for racial reasons in ways non-Jewish Poles were not, this document includes Jews within the overall Polish population reduction plan.

132. The "General Plan East" suggested that in ethnically cleansing the new areas annexed by the Reich, some thirty million people between the Soviet Union and Germany would be declared "racially undesirable" and therefore "excess" population in need of "resettlement." Though final versions of the plan do not survive, leading historians have suggested that Nazi planners like Himmler envisioned the mass murder of this thirty million people, largely Poles, perhaps through starvation. See Gellately, "Third Reich," 254–59; see also Childers, *Third Reich*, 487–89.

133. ŻIH 230/5.

134. Ząbecki, *Wspomnienia*, 30. Ząbecki also states on page 95 that local Poles "suffered for hiding Jews." Many were beaten, sent to Treblinka I, or as often happened later in the war, shot.

135. Lucjan Puchała, 26 October 1945, IPN GK 196/69.

136. Ząbecki, *Wspomnienia*, 51.

137. *Justiz und NS-Verbrechen*, 34:787.

138. ŻIH 301/6080.

139. Kopówka and Rytel-Andrianik, *Dam Im Imię*, 140, 187.

140. Wiernik, *Year in Treblinka*, 23.

141. Eugenia Samuel, USHMM RG-50.488.0008, tape 1, 1:01:00–1:05:00; Stanisław Kucharek also mentions the murder of Podleś, though Kucharek believed it resulted from price gouging Ukrainian guards while trading for Treblinka goods. Stanisław Kucharek, 11 November 1945, IPN GK 196/69.

142. Jan Sułkowski, 20 December 1945, IPN GK 196/70.

143. Locals were executed for aiding Jews who escaped Treblinka or the trains leading there. One example is the Malickis, who worked in Warsaw forging documents

for Jews. When caught, they were sent to Treblinka, tortured, and murdered. Gilbert, *Righteous*, 114. For other examples, see pages 106–7, 121, 123, 128–30.

144. Ząbecki, *Wspomnienia*, 84.

145. Edward Sypko, KARTA AHM_V_0030, video 2, 27:20–28:00.

146. Kopówka and Rytel-Andrianik, *Dam Im Imię*, 368–69.

147. Ząbecki, *Wspomnienia*, 88.

148. ŻIH 302/224, 5.

149. Kopówka and Rytel-Andrianik, *Dam Im Imię*, 402. We should not overlook that many people still inexplicably offer justifications and apologies for Polish behavior in cases clearly warranting condemnation. My intervention here is only to suggest that we must recognize the complexity of individual experience in all its facets to be able to correctly categorize and evaluate behavior, and even then, blanket statements are less instructive than more nuanced, case-by-case explorations—especially when we take spatial considerations into account.

150. Levi, *Drowned and the Saved*, 25–56.

151. Ząbecki, *Wspomnienia*, 59.

5. A Sensory Space

1. Donat, *Death Camp Treblinka*, 52.

2. AAN 2975/0/3.5.4.11/400 (emphasis added).

3. Bergen, *War and Genocide*, 251.

4. Henri Lefebvre says spaces are defined by the meanings ascribed to them. Lefebvre, *Production of Space*, 92. See also Cresswell, *Place*, 12.

5. Rodaway, *Sensuous Geographies*, 3; see also Cresswell, *Place*, 85.

6. Gigliotti, *Train Journey*, 129.

7. Didi-Huberman, *Images*, 3.

8. Tuan, *Space and Place*, 13–15.

9. Porteous, *Landscapes*, 7, 196; see also Lefebvre, *Production of Space*, 113–14.

10. The camp itself is included in this space, and sources from within the camp often comment on the amount of sensory contamination spreading into the outside world.

11. Porteous, *Landscapes*, 7; see also Ackerman, *Natural History*, 10–11.

12. Porteous, *Landscapes*, 23–24, 37.

13. Lucjan Puchała, 26 October 1945, IPN GK 196/69.

14. APS 1403/0/9.5/1527; see also Kopówka and Rytel-Andrianik, *Dam Im Imię*, 366, 384.

15. ARG II 382 (Ring. II/299), 164.

16. ŻIH 301/688.

17. Wiernik, *Year in Treblinka*, 10.

18. Willenberg, *Surviving Treblinka*, 59.

19. Chersztein, *Ofiary Nikczemności*, 122.

20. ŻIH 302/224, 18.

21. Sereny, *Into That Darkness*, 155.

22. Levinson, *Pragmatics*, 150; see also Day, "Synesthesia."

23. ŻIH 302/224, 17.

24. Rodaway, *Sensuous Geographies*, 4.

25. ŻIH 302/224, 17–19 (emphasis added).

26. ŻIH 302/224, 17.

27. Stefan Kucharek, USHMM RG-50.488.0006, cassette 3, tape 1, 24:30–26:55.

28. Józef Pogorzelski, 18 October 1945, IPN GK 196/69.

29. ŻIH 302/224, 18 (parentheses in original).

30. Sereny, *Into That Darkness*, 157.

31. Łukaszkiewicz, *Obóz Straceń*, 30; *Archives of the Holocaust*, 22:429; Webb and Chocholatý, *Treblinka Death Camp*, 77; Willenberg, *Surviving Treblinka*, 107.

32. Edward Sypko, KARTA AHM_V_0030, video 5, 41:55–42:25.

33. Donat, *Death Camp Treblinka*, 30; ARG II 382 (Ring. II/299), 194.

34. ŻIH 302/32, 21.

35. Weinstein, *Quenched Steel*, 39.

36. Fred Kort, VHA 1753, tape 2, 29:30–30:10.

37. Abraham Bomba, VHA 18061, tape 5, 0:25–1:15.

38. Edward Sypko, KARTA AHM_V_0030, video 3, 3:40–5:20.

39. ŻIH 302/32, 2.

40. Central Commission for Investigation of German Crimes in Poland, *German Crimes*, 98. Willenberg recalled the "eternal flame" consuming "an endless supply of corpses." Willenberg, *Surviving Treblinka*, 43. Jerzy Rajgrodzki stated that during the winter of 1942, the stench "dispersed throughout the area." ŻIH 301/5483, 6.

41. Roiter, *Voices*, 145.

42. ŻIH 301/688.

43. Weinstein, *Quenched Steel*, 51 (emphasis added).

44. Stanisław Adamczyk, 26 October 1945, IPN GK 196/69 (emphasis added).

45. Kazimierz Gawkowski, 21 November 1945, IPN GK 196/69.

46. Łukaszkiewicz, *Obóz Straceń*, 26–27.

47. Kopówka and Rytel-Andrianik, *Dam Im Imię*, 414.

48. Czesław Borowi—Treblinka, USHMM RG-60.5032, film ID 3349, 2:00:20–2:11:25 (emphasis added); ŻIH 301/4870.

49. Bikont, *Crime and the Silence*, 429.

50. Eugenia Samuel, USHMM RG-50.488.0008, tape 1, 1:01:00–1:05:00.

51. Lanzmann, *Patagonian Hare*, 474.

52. Porteous, *Landscapes*, 23–24, 37.

53. Marian Pietrzak, USHMM RG-50.488.0074, tape 2, 14:45–16:20.

54. Ząbecki, *Wspomnienia*, 78.

55. Czesław Borowi—Treblinka, USHMM RG-60.5032, film ID 3349, 2:00:20–2:11:25.

56. Stefan Kucharek, USHMM RG-50.488.0006, cassette 3, tape 1, 8:30–9:30 (emphasis added).

57. ŻIH 204/62 (emphasis added).

58. Piotr Ferenc, USHMM RG-50.488.0169, tape 2, 3:22–6:58 (emphasis added).

59. AAN 2134/0/45 (emphasis added).

60. Edward Sypko, KARTA AHM_V_0030, video 3, 3:40–5:20 (emphasis added).

61. Berg, *Warsaw Ghetto*, 210.

62. Central Commission for Investigation of German Crimes in Poland, *German Crimes*, 97; *Justiz und NS-Verbrechen*, 34:767.

63. Kopówka and Rytel-Andrianik, *Dam Im Imię*, 414. Kadej claimed to have gone to Treblinka with a local memorial group whose goal was to bury bones still strewn about the camp's grounds. It is probable some of these human remains were unearthed by other locals who had dug through the site searching for valuables. See also Gross, *Golden Harvest*.

64. Wiernik, *Year in Treblinka*, 38.

65. Rodaway, *Sensuous Geographies*, 4; see also Abrams, *Spell of the Sensuous*, 125–30.

66. Kuperhand and Kuperhand, *Shadows of Treblinka*, 110.

67. Willenberg, *Surviving Treblinka*, 107. Krzepicki also mentioned "billows of smoke." ARG II 382 (Ring. II/299), 163. Survivor Thaddeus Stabholz recalled, "Above the forest, a large cloud of dense, black smoke rises." Stabholz, *Seven Hells*, 27.

68. Kopówka and Rytel-Andrianik, *Dam Im Imię*, 408. It is unlikely that Goska and Willenberg are referencing the same exact experience, but the consistency of clouds of smoke above Treblinka means their experiences are comparable.

69. ŻIH 301/6080 (emphasis added).

70. Kopówka and Rytel-Andrianik, *Dam Im Imię*, 332–33.

71. Kazimierz Gawkowski, 21 November 1945, IPN GK 196/69 (emphasis added).

72. ŻIH 204/62.

73. *Das Menschenschlachthaus Treblinka*, 41. Given the exaggerations the same report made in other areas—it listed three million dead at Treblinka—we can assume forty kilometers is somewhat overestimated.

74. Studies of the September 11, 2001, attack in New York City note that the smoke plume rising from the collapse of the World Trade Center towers was almost 1.5 miles high (2,400 m) and visible from space. Stenchikov et al., "Multiscale

Plume Transport," 425–50. While obviously created by different circumstances, the visibility of the smoke is made clear in this study, but beyond that, the sight is a staple of most witnesses' experiences and accounts of that day.

75. If we assume the Majdanek photo is potentially misdated, it may be from early November 1943, when Operation Erntefest (Harvest Festival) occurred, where tens of thousands of Jews were shot and then burned at the camp. Thus, if this indeed caused the plume, the number of burning bodies is probably quite similar in scale to the number burned daily at Treblinka (which often exceeded ten thousand). See Friedländer, *Years of Extermination*, 559; and Bergen, *War and Genocide*, 176–77.

76. ŻIH 301/689, 4.

77. Wiernik, *Year in Treblinka*, 30.

78. ŻIH 302/32, 4 (emphasis added).

79. Chil Rajchman, USHMM RG-50.030.0185, 39:30–44:00; see also Wiernik, *Year in Treblinka*, 29–30.

80. ŻIH 302/118, 13; for a similar example, see Edward Sypko, KARTA AHM_V_0030, video 3, 3:40–5:20.

81. Sereny, *Into That Darkness*, 193.

82. Donat, *Death Camp Treblinka*, 65.

83. Lanzmann, *Shoah*, 14.

84. Kopówka and Rytel-Andrianik, *Dam Im Imię*, 366.

85. Stanisław Adamczyk, 26 October 1945, IPN GK 196/69.

86. Czesław Borowi—Treblinka, USHMM RG-60.5032, film ID 3349, 2:00:20–2:11:20.

87. Roiter, *Voices*, 164. Rajzman's description is also found in Donat, *Death Camp Treblinka*, 245.

88. Donat, *Death Camp Treblinka*, 222. Though here he probably references fires started during the revolt, the phenomenon was likely similar to how skies in the area looked nightly while bodies burned at Treblinka for months on end.

89. ŻIH 302/32, 21.

90. Bewerunge, "Himmel," 7.

91. Garstang, "Brightness of Clouds," 1; see also Bogard, *End of Night*.

92. Apenszlak et al., *Black Book*, 141. See also Sereny, *Into That Darkness*, 171; and Wiernik, *Year in Treblinka*, 16.

93. ARG II 382 (Ring. II/299), 173.

94. *Justiz und NS-Verbrechen*, 34:757.

95. Henry Kruger, USHMM RG-50.447.1223, tape 1, 11:00–15:00.

96. APS 62/718/0/-/55. This file contains a German poster from Siedlce explaining that local farmers could end up at Treblinka for not making grain quotas; see also Ząbecki, *Wspomnienia*, 80.

97. Glazar, *Trap*, 8.

98. Abraham Bomba, VHA 18601, tape 5, 0:25–1:15.

99. ARG II 382 (Ring. II/299), 193.

100. Filipowicz also said a woman was shot simply for looking toward Treblinka. Kopówka and Rytel-Andrianik, *Dam Im Imię*, 406–7.

101. Sereny, *Into That Darkness*, 152.

102. Czesław Borowi—Treblinka, USHMM RG-60.5032, film ID 3351, 4:00:13–4:31:18.

103. Lanzmann, *Shoah*, 25–26.

104. Czesław Borowi—Treblinka, USHMM RG-60.5032, film ID 3348, 1:07:30–1:14:30.

105. Kopówka and Rytel-Andrianik, *Dam Im Imię*, 406.

106. Julian Leszczyński said that the gas chambers were "completely isolated" from the other spaces of Treblinka. ŻIH 301/5089.

107. Eugenia Samuel, USHMM RG-50.488.0008, tape 1, 1:01:00–1:08:30.

108. Stanisław Kucharek, 11 November 1945, IPN GK 196/69.

109. Henryk Slebzak, USHMM RG-50.488.0028, video 1, 1:16:00–1:17:00.

110. Wacław Bednarczyk, 27 October 1945, IPN GK 196/70.

111. Władysław Chomka, 16 November 1945, IPN GK 196/69.

112. Gawkowski, 21 November 1945, IPN GK 196/69.

113. Roiter, *Voices*, 126; Abraham Bomba, VHA 18601, tape 3, 9:40–10:10; ŻIH 301/688.

114. Kopówka and Rytel-Andrianik, *Dam Im Imię*, 389.

115. Kopówka and Rytel-Andrianik, *Dam Im Imię*, 405.

116. Kopówka and Rytel-Andrianik, *Dam Im Imię*, 417.

117. Lucjan Puchała, 16 October 1945, IPN GK 196/69.

118. Stefan Kucharek, USHMM RG-50.488.0006, cassette 3, tape 1, 15:38–19:16.

119. ŻIH 302/133.

120. Fred Kort, VHA 1753, tape 3, 22:15–23:40.

121. Brown, *Biography of No Place*, 212.

122. Ackerman, *Natural History*, 178.

123. Łukaszkiewicz, *Obóz Straceń*, 50 (emphasis added).

124. Kopówka and Rytel-Andrianik, *Dam Im Imię*, 425.

125. Czesław Borowi—Treblinka, USHMM RG-60.5032, film ID 3351, 4:00:10–4:31:20.

126. Stanisław Kucharek, 11 November 1945, IPN GK 196/69.

127. ŻIH 302/32, 5; see also Central Commission for Investigation of German Crimes in Poland, *German Crimes*, 101.

128. Ackerman, *Natural History*, 304.

129. Marian Łopuszyński, 16 November 1945, IPN GK 196/69.

130. Abraham Bomba, VHA 18601, tape 5, 2:00–2:30.

131. Isadore Helfing, USHMM RG-50.042.0014, tape 1, 7:00–7:30.

132. Abraham Kolski, USHMM RG-50.030.0113, tape 1, 26:00–27:20.

133. Stanisław Adamczyk, 26 October 1945, IPN GK 196/69.

134. Grossman, "Treblinka Hell," 39.

135. ŻIH 230/63 (emphasis added).

136. ARG II 382 (Ring. II/299), 192.

137. Ząbecki, *Wspomnienia*, 41.

138. Kopówka and Rytel-Andrianik, *Dam Im Imię*, 408.

139. ARG II 382 (Ring. II/299), 181.

140. Sol Liber, VHA 58, tape 3, 23:15–23:45.

141. Kopówka and Rytel-Andrianik, *Dam Im Imię*, 410.

142. ARG II 382 (Ring. II/299), 174–75; Blumental, *Dokumenty i Materiały*, 174; ŻIH 302/313.

143. ŻIH 302/32, 19.

144. Jerzy Skarżyński and Eugeniusz Wójcik, USHMM RG-50.488.0007, tape 2, 8:00–8:50.

145. Ehrenburg and Grossman, *Black Book*, 440.

146. ŻIH 302/153.

147. Donat, *Death Camp Treblinka*, 44; Blumental, *Dokumenty i Materiały*, 179.

148. Westermann, *Drunk on Genocide*, 138–43; Bergen, *War and Genocide*, 198.

149. Blumental, *Dokumenty i Materiały*, 186; see also ŻIH 301/852.

150. Donat, *Death Camp Treblinka*, 57; see also ŻIH 230/63.

151. Kopówka and Rytel-Andrianik, *Dam Im Imię*, 408.

152. ŻIH 301/688.

153. Willenberg, *Surviving Treblinka*, 111. Jerzy Rajgrodzki describes enforced singing at roll calls. ŻIH 301/5483, 7.

154. Łukaszkiewicz, *Obóz Straceń*, 27.

6. An Extended Space

1. Ząbecki, *Wspomnienia*, 41.

2. One immediately thinks of the Holocaust, but other examples include Stalin's forcible deportation of millions to either "special settlements" or gulags. See Snyder, *Bloodlands*, 26–29, 327–31. Another example is the partition of India in 1947. Historian Navdip Kaur writes, "As many as 673 refugee trains moved approximately 2,800,000 refugees within India and across the border. . . . No image of Partition, textual or in the mind's eye, photograph or film, escapes from the overloaded trains with men, women and children moving from one side of the border to the other. . . . They have become symbolic of the last journey of the masses." Kaur, "Violence and Migration," 947–54.

3. Some 265,040 Jews were sent to Treblinka within the first forty-six days of the camp becoming operational on July 22, 1942. In August 1942 alone, 135,120 Jews

were sent to Treblinka from Warsaw. See Feldman, *Understanding the Holocaust*, 2:238; Mierzewjewski, *Most Valuable Asset*, 2:127; Gutman, *Jews of Warsaw*, 213; and *To Live with Honor*, 43.

4. ŻIH 302/118, 12.

5. Gigliotti, *Train Journey*, 2; see also Foucault, *Discipline and Punish*, 25–30.

6. My estimation of one to two kilometers is how far on either side of the tracks most interactions happened.

7. ŻIH 301/6037; ŻIH 230/91, 26; Kazimierz Gawkowski, 21 November 1945, IPN GK 196/69; ŻIH 302/224, 3. The Warsaw line passed through several Warsaw substations at Zielonka, Kobyłka, and Url and thereafter the towns of Wołomin, Tłuszcz, and Łochów.

8. This chapter's structure is loosely based on how witnesses themselves might have encountered trains—first observing train cars before interacting with the people escaping or remnants left behind. Relatedly, the chapter examines more collective forms of witnessing before zooming in to focus on more personal and individual interactions.

9. Kuperhand and Kuperhand, *Shadows of Treblinka*, 106.

10. *Massacre of a People*, 43; see also Blumental, *Dokumenty i Materiały*, 176.

11. Gigliotti, *Train Journey*, 2; Sereny, *Into That Darkness*, 200–201; Bauman, *Modernity*, 102; Aly and Heim, *Architects of Annihilation*, 184. Jacob Freier recalls the use of the German word *Stücke* (pieces). Jacob Freier, USHMM RG-50.043.0003, 1:17:00–1:18:30.

12. Czesław Borowi—Treblinka, USHMM RG-60.5032, film ID 3350, 3:02:25–3:12:00. These transports were few, but they were striking for their stark contrast with the thousands of cattle cars.

13. Łukaszkiewicz, *Obóz Straceń*, 22–23; Abraham Bomba, VHA 18601, tape 2, 28:30–29:05; Donat, *Death Camp Treblinka*, 11.

14. Sol Liber, VHA 58, tape 3, 19:00–19:30. Gigliotti says anthropologists identify the body as the primary target for state and ethnic violence. Gigliotti, *Train Journey*, 28.

15. Ząbecki, *Wspomnienia*, 40.

16. ŻIH 302/313.

17. *Justiz und NS-Verbrechen*, 34:753. See also Fred Kort, VHA 1753, tape 3, 12:30–13:00; Roiter, *Voices*, 144; and Łukaszkiewicz, *Obóz Straceń*, 22.

18. ARG II 382 (Ring. II/299), 153.

19. Ząbecki, *Wspomnienia*, 40; Auerbach quoted from Donat, *Death Camp Treblinka*, 24. Mosze Klajman recalled how "mothers took saliva and gave it to children to moisten their dry lips." ŻIH 302/118, 12.

20. Lanzmann, *Shoah*, 28, 109.

21. Blumental, *Dokumenty i Materiały*, 178.
22. ARG II 382 (Ring. II/299), 159.
23. ŻIH 301/228.
24. Weinstein, *Quenched Steel*, 40.
25. Survivor estimate from Tenenbaum, *Underground*, 192; Suchomel quote from *Archives of the Holocaust*, 22:424. Fred Kort estimated that 30 percent of the four thousand people in his transport died. Fred Kort, VHA 1753, tape 3, 10:45–11:55.
26. ŻIH 301/2226.
27. Sereny, *Into That Darkness*, 159. The same account is found in Gilbert, *Final Journey*, 117.
28. Gigliotti, *Train Journey*, 101.
29. ARG II 382 (Ring. II/299), 152.
30. Kopówka and Rytel-Andrianik, *Dam Im Imię*, 426.
31. Sereny, *Into That Darkness*, 151.
32. ŻIH 301/3960.
33. ŻIH 302/224, 10–11.
34. Lasman, *Pięćdziesiąt kilometrów*, 23.
35. Kopówka and Rytel-Andrianik, *Dam Im Imię*, 401; Noach Lasman writes of a survivor who, even after escaping, could "unmistakably" hear another death train approaching while hiding in the forests a kilometer from the tracks. Lasman, *Pięćdziesiąt kilometrów*, 32.
36. Ząbecki, *Wspomnienia*, 40.
37. ŻIH 302/313.
38. ŻIH 302/118, 12.
39. Kopówka and Rytel-Andrianik, *Dam Im Imię*, 421 (emphasis added). Stefan Kucharek witnessed escape attempts from many Treblinka-bound trains from his vantage point in Małkinia (7 km). Stefan Kucharek, USHMM RG-50.488.0006, cassette 3, tape 1, 22:14–26:55.
40. Weinstein, *Quenched Steel*, 35.
41. Lanzmann, *Shoah*, 108.
42. Marian Pietrzak, USHMM RG-50.488.0074, tape 2, 12:50–14:45. Witness Jack Price said, "There was a Ukrainian guard on top of every car . . . to shoot anyone who escaped." "Holocaust Testimony of Jack Price," Gratz College Holocaust Oral History Archive; see also Lasman, *Pięćdziesiąt kilometrów*, 11.
43. Tenenbaum, *Underground*, 416.
44. ŻIH 301/1236 (emphasis added).
45. Marian Łopuszyński, 16 November 1945, IPN GK 196/69.
46. Sol Liber, VHA 58, tape 3, 20:50–21:10.

47. Seidman, *Warsaw Ghetto Diaries*, 103. Tanhum Grinberg recalled that his train *dragged* throughout the night. żih 302/153.

48. Fred Kort, vha 1753, tape 2, 27:45–28:30. Mosze Klajman recalled similarly, "For three days, we wandered from place to place until everyone lay dead at the bottom of the car." żih 302/118, 12.

49. żih 302/27, 143.

50. arg II 379 (Ring. II/296).

51. Szpilmana and Waldorff, *Śmierć Miasta*, 104.

52. żih 230/91, 8.

53. Łukaszkiewicz, *Obóz Straceń*, 5.

54. Szpilmana and Waldorff, *Śmierć Miasta*, 106, 111–12, 114.

55. arg II 382 (Ring. II/299), 152; see also żih 301/656.

56. żih 230/91, 7, 23. Especially in later roundup actions, as ghettos emptied, trains sat longer at their origin points before departure.

57. Blumental, *Dokumenty i Materiały*, 178.

58. żih 302/172.

59. Józefa Miros, ushmm RG-50.488.0298, 8:39–10:43.

60. *Justiz und NS-Verbrechen*, 34:753.

61. Mierzewjewski, *Most Valuable Asset*, 2:116.

62. Łukaszkiewicz, *Obóz Straceń*, 23; Zabecki quote from Ząbecki, *Wspomnienia*, 65. Ząbecki adds, "Passenger trains . . . could only stop at the semaphore, or on the route between the stations."

63. Henryk Gawkowski and Treblinka railway workers, ushmm RG-60.5036, film ID 3365, camera roll 15, 04:06:15–04:11:12.

64. żih 302/224, 8–10.

65. Ząbecki, *Wspomnienia*, 48.

66. Piotr Ferenc, ushmm RG-50.488.0169, tape 1, 32:23–34:24; see also Mierzewjewski, *Most Valuable Asset*, 2:121.

67. Ząbecki, *Wspomnienia*, 39–40. The seven thousand estimate was probably accurate for some trains, although later trains held around five thousand people. But Ząbecki could not have known exactly how many were inside each; see also Sereny, *Into That Darkness*, 152.

68. Henryk Slebzak, ushmm RG-50.488.0028, video 1, 1:19:45–1:21:15.

69. Piotr Ferenc, ushmm RG-50.488.0169, tape 1, 32:23–35:24.

70. "The most active period seems to have been from August to the middle of December, 1942. . . . After that, from the middle of January to the middle of May, 1943, the average was probably one a week. Some of the witnesses put the figure at three." Central Commission for Investigation of German Crimes in Poland, *German Crimes*, 103. Jerzy Królikowski said that the most trains he saw

in one day was four, though he also noted, "We only saw transports from the Małkinia side and we could not see any transports from the Siedlce side." ŻIH 302/224, 12. See also Łukaszkiewicz, *Obóz Straceń*, 34; and *Trial of the Major War Criminals*, 3:567.

71. Henry Kruger, USHMM RG-50.447.1223, tape 1, 11:00–15:00. Kruger was Jewish, hiding in plain sight as a railway worker; Krolikówski also recalled seeing these Pullman cars with "decently dressed gentlemen and ladies." ŻIH 302/224, 20.

72. AAN 2134/0/42; Ząbecki, *Wspomnienia*, 43.

73. AAN 2134/0/42 (emphasis added).

74. Roiter, *Voices*, 124. See also ŻIH 302/224, 9; and "Holocaust Testimony of Jack Price," Gratz College Holocaust Oral History Archive. Price notes that Polish railway men from Warsaw even started to venture out to investigate what happened to these trains.

75. Donat, *Death Camp Treblinka*, 32; Łukaszkiewicz, *Obóz Straceń*, 22–23; ŻIH 302/224, 12; Ząbecki, *Wspomnienia*, 47.

76. ARG II 380 (Ring. II/297); Isadore Helfing, USHMM RG-50.042.0014, tape 1, 6:15–7:00; Blumental, *Dokumenty i Materiały*, 184.

77. Ząbecki, *Wspomnienia*, 46, 73.

78. USHMM RG-50.488.0006, cassette 3, tape 1, 13:30–15:30.

79. ARG II 382 (Ring. II/299), 153.

80. "Wspomnienia Antoniego Tomczuka," KARTA AW II/3490; see also Berenstein and Rutkowski, *Assistance to the Jews*, 37.

81. Kopówka and Rytel-Andrianik, *Dam Im Imię*, 420.

82. Edward Sypko, KARTA AHM_V_0030, video 2, 34:50–36:10.

83. Ząbecki, *Wspomnienia*, 69.

84. Sereny, *Into That Darkness*, 158–59. The same account is found in Gilbert, *Final Journey*, 116.

85. Henryk Slebzak, USHMM RG-50.488.0028, video 1, 1:24:00–1:25:00 (emphasis added).

86. Marian Pietrzak, USHMM RG-50.488.0074, tape 2, 12:50–14:45.

87. ŻIH 301/4147.

88. Grossman, "Treblinka Hell," 30–31. He added that only on rare days did no trains pass by.

89. Henry Kruger, USHMM RG-50.447.0217, part 1, 34:30–35:15. Kruger was in the Jewish ghetto of Wołomin. He later survived the war using a fake identity as a Polish train worker.

90. Lanzmann, *Shoah*, 34 (parentheses in original). Zdzisław Goldstein recalled how Poles walking amid the trains "showed us that we were going to death." ŻIH 301/1049.

91. ARG II 379 (Ring. II/296). German and Ukrainian guards tightly regulated initial interactions, but their attention waned over time, and later some accepted bribes or actively took part.

92. Willenberg, *Surviving Treblinka*, 39.

93. Piotr Ferenc, USHMM RG-50.488.0169, tape 1, 32:23–35:24.

94. Wiernik, *Year in Treblinka*, 8. See also Weinstein, *Quenched Steel*, 37; and Ząbecki, *Wspomnienia*, 40.

95. ARG II 380 (Ring. II/297).

96. Kopówka and Rytel-Andrianik, *Dam Im Imię*, 408.

97. Czesław Borowi—Treblinka, USHMM RG-60.5032, film ID 3348, 1:00:30–1:02:30; and film ID 3349, 2:00:20–2:11:25.

98. Ząbecki, *Wspomnienia*, 48.

99. ŻIH 302/224, 12–13.

100. Abraham Bomba, VHA 18061, tape 3, 3:15–4:15.

101. ŻIH 302/224, 15 (emphasis added). Vasily Grossman met a local witness who described how sixty people escaped from one train, but most were shot or recaptured before reaching safety. Grossman, "Treblinka Hell," 34.

102. One thinks back to Slebzak watching from his living room as Jews crossed through his yard after escaping Treblinka (see chapter 5).

103. Lanzmann, *Shoah*, 29. The man described people jumping from the trains: "There was a mother and a child. . . . She tried to run away, and they shot her in the heart."

104. Kopówka and Rytel-Andrianik, *Dam Im Imię*, 423.

105. Czesław Borowi—Treblinka, USHMM RG-60.5032, film ID 3350, 3:12:10–3:17:45.

106. Ząbecki, *Wspomnienia*, 48.

107. Henryk Slebzak, USHMM RG-50.488.0028, tape 1, 1:27:00–1:28:00.

108. Stefan Kucharek, USHMM RG-50.488.0006, cassette 3, tape 1, 26:55–31:00.

109. Kopówka and Rytel-Andrianik, *Dam Im Imię*, 421 (emphasis added).

110. Sol Liber, VHA 58, tape 3, 19:40–20:15. Liber says "roads" here but clearly means tracks.

111. Kuperhand and Kuperhand, *Shadows of Treblinka*, 107. Knowledge of Treblinka was unclear for the first deportation trains. Yet after a certain date, it seems most knew much more about their destination in advance.

112. Piotr Ferenc, USHMM RG-50.488.0169, tape 2, 6:58–10:30.

113. ŻIH 301/1460.

114. "Holocaust Testimony of Jack Price," Gratz College Holocaust Oral History Archive.

115. ŻIH 301/1049.

116. ŻIH 301/2019.

117. ŻIH 301/1261.

118. Jacob Freier, USHMM RG-50.043.0003, 1:17:00–1:18:30.

119. Luba Olenski, USHMM RG-50.407.0035, 1:19–1:20. Luba Frank later became Luba Olenski, and the two testimonies—the USHMM interview and ŻIH 301/1261 file—match in many details despite being recorded years apart.

120. *To Live with Honor*, 212–13.

121. Lasman, *Pięćdziesiąt kilometrów*, 27.

122. Ząbecki, *Wspomnienia*, 47; Piotr Ferenc witnessed how German gendarmes searched after a train passed to "finish off" any injured person. That this extended all the way to Sokołów shows how far along the railway corridors bodies lay. Piotr Ferenc, USHMM RG-50.488.0169, tape 2, 6:58–10:30. Mieczysław Laskowski noted, "The German Gendarmerie from Sokołów . . . went on patrol along the tracks *especially* for that purpose." Mieczysław Laskowski, 18 October 1945, IPN GK 196/69.

123. Nuchem Perlman writes, "Many people [who] jumped out of the cars . . . came back . . . with their legs broken," referring to injuries he witnessed from the Polish town of Parczew. ŻIH 301/608.

124. Willenberg, *Surviving Treblinka*, 38.

125. Seidman, *Warsaw Ghetto Diaries*, 102. Having seen the gray, confined spaces of the ghetto and now being trapped in the sensory horrors of the cattle car, Rabinowitz reflects on how the natural world continues despite his plight.

126. ŻIH 302/77, 21.

127. Stabholz, *Seven Hells*, 19.

128. Lasman, *Pięćdziesiąt kilometrów*, 26, 31 (emphasis added). Lasman is recounting a survivor's story.

129. Weinstein, *Quenched Steel*, 66.

130. AAN 2134/0/45.

131. Luba Olenski, USHMM RG-50.407.0035, 1:20:00–1:21:00, 1:23:20–1:25:30; ŻIH 301/1261.

132. Eugeniusz Goska, USHMM RG-50.488.0027, tape 1, 12:00–14:30.

133. ŻIH 301/1261.

134. Reder, *Bełżec*, 105–6. Rost edited and published Bełżec survivor Rudolf Reder's original account in Polish in 1946. Though referring to Bełżec, the description quoted here was also probably accurate for the spaces around Treblinka and the railway lines leading there.

135. Jacob Freier, USHMM RG-50.043.0003, 1:18:30–1:21:15; see also ARG II 382 (Ring. II/299), 198.

136. Luba Olenski, USHMM RG-50.407.0035, 1:23:20–1:25:30.

137. Kopówka and Rytel-Andrianik, *Dam Im Imię*, 179–80, 223–24, 283.

138. *To Live with Honor*, 593.

139. ŻIH 302/30.

140. Krakowski, *War of the Doomed*, 121.

141. Luba Olenski, USHMM RG-50.407.0035, 1:22:30–1:23:20.

142. AAN 2134/0/45.

143. ŻIH 301/3960. At the Stangl trial, the transcripts note, "Outside the camps, on both sides of the railway line leading from Treblinka lay the corpses of Jews who had been shot in escape attempts." *Justiz und NS-Verbrechen*, 34:756.

144. ŻIH 301/1236. Presumably this action was taken to make room within the overcrowded cattle car and/or to eliminate the smells coming from the rotting corpses.

145. Weinstein, *Quenched Steel*, 42; see also Lasman, *Pięćdziesiąt kilometrów*, 11.

146. Wacław Sawicki, "Wierzyć i Trwać," KARTA AW II/3185 (emphasis added).

147. ŻIH 302/224, 16.

148. Donat, *Death Camp Treblinka*, 64 (emphasis added).

149. Józef Sobolewski, 17 June 1969, IPN Ds. 54/71 zastepcze t.1.

150. Łukaszkiewicz, *Obóz Straceń*, 50. Stangl trial transcripts note that there were "corpses scattered everywhere from the Treblinka station." *Justiz und NS-Verbrechen*, 34:779. Similarly, Józef Pogorzelski stated, "*Whenever* a transport departed, there were many corpses lying at the station." Józef Pogorzelski, 18 October 1945, IPN GK 196/69 (emphasis added).

151. Kazimierz Gawkowski, 21 November 1945, IPN GK 196/69.

152. Sereny, *Into That Darkness*, 159. The same account is found in Gilbert, *Final Journey*, 116–17.

153. Wacław Wołosz, 18 October 1945, IPN GK 196/69.

154. ŻIH 301/55.

155. Czesław Borowi—Treblinka, USHMM RG-60.5032, film ID 3350, 3:12:10–3:17:45.

156. Eugenia Samuel, USHMM RG-50.488.0008, tape 1, 1:05:00–1:06:30; Kalembasiak's statement found at ŻIH 301/4870.

157. Józef Sobolewski, 17 June 1969, IPN Ds. 54/71 zastepcze t.1.

158. Wacław Wołosz, 18 October 1945, IPN GK 196/69.

159. ŻIH 302/224, 14; see also Czesław Borowi—Treblinka, USHMM RG-60.5032, film ID 3350, 3:17:40–3:22:00.

160. Ząbecki, *Wspomnienia*, 49.

161. Henry Kruger, USHMM RG-50.447.0217, part 1, 33:30–34:00.

162. *Oświęcim Camp of Death*, 16. While this report is ostensibly on Auschwitz, the example cited appears to be from a witness near Warsaw, from which trains were sent to Treblinka. Thus, it likely references a Treblinka-bound train.

163. Massey, *For Space*, 9. Contemporaneous plurality is a concept in which distinct trajectories of perception from multiple witness groups coalesce to compose "space." See the introduction.

164. Łukaszkiewicz, *Obóz Straceń*, 51.

165. Document No. NO-060, "Abrelieferte Werte," COU 1806:01:001:006. Survivor Samuel Rajzman gives numbers of train cars in Blumental, *Dokumenty i Materiały*, 187. See also Donat, *Death Camp Treblinka*, 57; Ząbecki, *Wspomnienia*, 72; and *Justiz und NS-Verbrechen*, 34:754.

166. Mitch Ciegielski, KARTA AWII/3094. Ciegielski quotes his sister Zosia's Warsaw ghetto diary; see also Central Commission for Investigation of German Crimes in Poland, *German Crimes*, 167.

167. AAN 2134/0/42.

168. Łukaszkiewicz, *Obóz Straceń*, 43. Łukaszkiewicz references the same file found today here: Józef Pogorzelski, 18 October 1945, IPN GK 196/69.

169. The potential scale of those implicated in the occupied territories and in greater Germany who ultimately received these items is vast but, unfortunately, outside the scope of this study. However, for reference to the sheer quantity of the materials stolen and transported, consider what one Treblinka survivor told Auerbach: "I spent about six months going through gold pens—ten hours a day, for six months, just sorting pens." Donat, *Death Camp Treblinka*, 56.

170. Roiter, *Voices*, 133. William Schneiderman notes, "A lot of people went in hiding between the clothes, and they jumped off the train on the way out." William Schneiderman, USHMM RG-50.030.0288, tape 2, 28:00–29:30. Józef Gutman was one person who escaped hiding "nestled in the rags" within the car. ŻIH 301/2226; see also ŻIH 302/316.

171. Weinstein, *Quenched Steel*, 66, 68; *Justiz und NS-Verbrechen*, 34:754. Poles breaking into cattle cars to steal goods raises an interesting comparison to instances of grave digging at Treblinka as outlined by Jan Gross in *Golden Harvest* and Volha Charnysh and Evgeny Finkel in "The Death Camp Eldorado." At Treblinka, Poles operated under the assumption that Jews had discarded any wealth directly on the grounds of the camp, whereas the provenance of goods within cattle cars was somewhat more diffuse. After all, these were Jewish goods stolen by Germans that were then stolen by Poles. In both cases (at Treblinka and in trains), though, Poles sought to acquire household goods for personal use in addition to valuables to be sold for financial gain. For an example of the latter (regarding a large diamond dug up from the camp), see APS 1569/0/9.3/580.

172. ŻIH 301/466 (emphasis added).

Conclusion

1. ŻIH 302/224, 9. Witness Władysław Chomka states, "According to the telegram, the train was to transport residents of Warsaw, who, because of overpopulation in the city, would settle in Treblinka. Being aware of the local conditions, we

were surprised as to the purpose of sending people to Treblinka, since there was no proper accommodation for them." Władysław Chomka, 16 November 1945, IPN GK 196/69.

2. *Archives of the Holocaust*, 16:105.
3. Ehrenburg and Grossman, *Black Book*, 403.
4. See chapters 2 and 4.
5. Łukaszkiewicz, *Obóz Straceń*, 27.
6. Mitch Ciegielski, KARTA AWII/3094. Ciegielski quotes his sister Zosia's Warsaw ghetto diary.
7. ŻIH 230/91, 22; Jack Price states, "After July 22 . . . they started every day to take 10,000 people to send them to Treblinka. So, on the way some of them succeeded in escaping and they came back to the ghetto and told them what's happening to them." "Holocaust Testimony of Jack Price," Gratz College Holocaust Oral History Archive; see also ŻIH 230/63.
8. Ząbecki, *Wspomnienia*, 53.
9. ŻIH 230/72.
10. ŻIH 230/91, 12.
11. *To Live with Honor*, 80 (emphasis added).
12. *To Live with Honor*, 83, 85.
13. Tenenbaum, *Underground*, 81.
14. Karski, *Story of a Secret*.
15. Republic of Poland Ministry of Foreign Affairs, *Mass Extermination*, 9.
16. *Massacre of a People*, 6, 43. The report includes sections on page 6 taken from the December 1942 London report by the Polish government, which noted that Jews of Poland were "gradually and methodically exterminated in groups of several thousands daily by machine-guns, or in lethal gas chambers, or by electrocution."
17. *Archives of the Holocaust*, 17:122.
18. Sereny, *Into That Darkness*, 249–50; Eugeniusz Goska, USHMM RG-50.488.0027, tape 1, 18:00–19:30.
19. Łukaszkiewicz, *Obóz Straceń*, 14.
20. Stanisław Kucharek, Jechiel Rajchman, Samuel Rajzman, 6 November 1945, IPN GK 196/69.
21. The area was Polish until September 1939, when the Germans occupied the territory and held it until the Soviets overran it in 1944. After this time, Poland became a Communist puppet state, not truly democratic and independent again until 1989.
22. Donat, *Death Camp Treblinka*, 67; ŻIH 301/6237. One Polish man from Kiełczew (8 km from Treblinka) was arrested for digging up a diamond from the Treblinka

grounds, which he then sold for two hundred thousand złotys, a large amount of money; APS 1569/0/9.3/580. Another report states, "[Treblinka] had been excavated by the local population seeking gold and valuables"; ŻIH 301/1095. A different report notes that other people sought "items for daily use," like spoons, forks, and combs; ŻIH 303XX.280, 2. Local witness Barbara Kadej recalls that those digging in Treblinka's graves encountered skulls, shins, thigh bones, and other human remains; Kopówka and Rytel-Andrianik, *Dam Im Imię*, 412.

23. Lanzmann, *Patagonian Hare*, 156.
24. Lanzmann, *Patagonian Hare*, 156.
25. Lanzmann, *Patagonian Hare*, 475–77.
26. Sereny, *Into That Darkness*, 201.
27. Lanzmann, *Patagonian Hare*, 515–16.
28. Kuperhand and Kuperhand, *Shadows of Treblinka*, 87.
29. ARG II 382 (Ring. II/299), 164.
30. Willenberg, "Memory of Treblinka."
31. Donat, *Death Camp Treblinka*, 28. Rachel Auerbach documents this conversation, though she leaves the survivor anonymous.

BIBLIOGRAPHY

Archives

AAN. Archiwum Akt Nowych w Warszawie, Warsaw, Poland
1333/0/3/212.III.1. Janina Buchholcowa. "Obóz śmierci w Treblince."
2134/0/42. "Treblinka."
2134/0/45. "Treblinka."
2725/0/-/242. Archiwum Władysława Siła-Nowickiego.
2975/0/3.5.4.11/400. "Akta Ryszarda Nazarewicza."

APS. Archiwum Państwowe w Siedlcach, Siedlce, Poland
62/718/0/-/55.
1403/0/9.5/1527. "Treblinka."
1569/0/9.3/580.

COU. Harry Mazal Collection, University of Colorado, Boulder, Colorado
"Defense Document #4: Hans Frank." N.d. COU 1806:01:034:0023.
Document No. NO-060. "Abrelieferte Werte aus der Aktion Reinhard, 27 February 1943." Office of U.S. Chief of Counsel, Subsequent Proceedings Divisions, U.S. Army. July 10, 1946. COU 1806:01:001:006.
Kenyon, Edward H. "War Crimes and Crimes against Humanity, Part IV: Germanisation of Occupied Territories." Nuremberg, Germany: International Military Tribunal, n.d. COU 1806:01:030:0009.

Gratz College Holocaust Oral History Archive
"Holocaust Testimony of Jack Price." Interviewed by Gayle Kammerman and Josey G. Fisher. May 16, 1989; January 20, 22, 1993. Transcript of Audiotaped Interview, published 2009. Sent to author by Josey G. Fisher, Archive Director.

IPN. Institute of National Remembrance, https://www.zapisyterroru.pl/
Ds. 54/71 zastepcze t1. Józef Sobolewski testimony. June 17, 1969.
IPN GK 196/69. Fischer's trial, vol. 18. Stanisław Adamczyk testimony. October 26, 1945.
IPN GK 196/69. Fischer's trial, vol. 18. Hejnoch Brener testimony. October 9, 1945.

IPN GK 196/69. Fischer's trial, vol. 18. Władysław Chomka testimony. November 16, 1945.

IPN GK 196/69. Fischer's trial, vol. 18. Kazimierz Gawkowski testimony. November 21, 1945.

IPN GK 196/69. Fischer's trial, vol. 18. Stanisław Kucharek, Jechiel Rajchman, Samuel Rajzman testimonies. November 6, 1945.

IPN GK 196/69. Fischer's trial, vol. 18. Stanisław Kucharek testimony. November 11, 1945.

IPN GK 196/69. Fischer's trial, vol. 18. Aleksander Kudlik testimony. October 10, 1945.

IPN GK 196/69. Fischer's trial, vol. 18. Józef Kuźmiński testimony. October 16–23, 1945.

IPN GK 196/69. Fischer's trial, vol. 18. Mieczysław Laskowski testimony. October 18, 1945.

IPN GK 196/69. Fischer's trial, vol. 18. Marian Łopuszyński testimony. November 16, 1945.

IPN GK 196/69. Fischer's trial, vol. 18. Józef Pogorzelski testimony. October 18, 1945.

IPN GK 196/69. Fischer's trial, vol. 18. Henryk Poswolski testimony. October 9, 1945.

IPN GK 196/69. Fischer's trial, vol. 18. Lucjan Puchała testimony. October 26, 1945.

IPN GK 196/69. Fischer's trial, vol. 18. Samuel Rajzman testimony. October 9, 1945.

IPN GK 196/69. Fischer's trial, vol. 18. Szyja Warszawski testimony. October 9, 1945.

IPN GK 196/69. Fischer's trial, vol. 18. Wacław Wołosz testimony. October 18, 1945.

IPN GK 196/70. The shorthand record of the trial of Fischer and others, vol. 19. Wacław Bednarczyk testimony. October 27, 1945.

IPN GK 196/70. The shorthand record of the trial of Fischer and others, vol. 19. Leon Finkelsztein testimony. December 28, 1945.

IPN GK 196/70. The shorthand record of the trial of Fischer and others, vol. 19. Jan Sułkowski testimony. December 20, 1945.

JNSV. Justiz und NS-Verbrechen, https://junsv.nl/westdeutsche-gerichtsentscheidungen
Lfd. Nr. 270a. LG Frankfurt/M. March 2, 1951. Bd. 8.

Lfd. Nr. 596a. LG Düsseldorf. September 3, 1965. Bd. 22.

KARTA Foundation, Warsaw, Poland

AHM_V_0030. Sypko, Edward. Interview from the collections of the KARTA Center and History Meeting House.

AW II/3094. Mitch Ciegielski.

AW II/3185. Wacław Sawicki. "Wierzyć i Trwać." 1974.

AW II/3490. Wspomnienia Antoniego Tomczuka. Zbiory Archiwum Ośrodka KARTA.

USHMM. United States Holocaust Memorial Museum, https://collections.ushmm.org/

RG-50.030.0113. Oral history interview with Abraham Kolski. Interviewed by Linda G. Kizmack. March 29, 1990.

RG-50.030.0185. Oral history interview with Chil Rajchman. Interviewed by Herman Taube. December 7, 1988.

RG-50.030.0288. Oral history interview with William Schneiderman. Interviewed by Randy M. Goldman. September 21, 1994.

RG-50.043.0014. Oral history interview with Isadore Helfing. Interviewed by Sandra Brandley. March 9, 1992.

RG-50.043.0003. Oral history interview with Jacob Freier. June 1892.

RG-50.407.0035. Oral history interview with Luba Olenski. Interviewed by Geri Kras. March 6, 1996.

RG-50.447.0217. Oral history interview with Henry Kruger. Interviewed by Ann Feibelman, Walter Partos, Lisa William-Zigmund. August 12, 1993.

RG-50.447.1223. Oral history interview with Henry Kruger. Interviewed by Ann Feibelman, Claude Marger, Walter Partos, Lisa William-Zigmund. May 1, 1987.

RG-50.488.0006. Oral history interview with Stefan Kucharek. Interviewed by Michał Sobelman and Edward Kopówka. March 1998.

RG-50.488.0007. Oral history interview with Jerry Skarżyński and Eugeniusz Wójcik. Interviewed by Eugeniusz Wójcik, Edward Kopówka, and Michał Sobelman. March 12, 1998.

RG-50.488.0008. Oral history interview with Eugenia Samuel. Interviewed by Edward Kopówka and Michał Sobelman. March 12, 1998.

RG-50.488.0027. Oral history interview with Eugeniusz Goska. July 7, 1998.

RG-50.488.0028. Oral history interview with Henryk Slebzak. Interviewed by Edward Kopówka. July 7, 1998.

RG-50.488.0074. Oral history interview with Marian Pietrzak. July 7, 1999.

RG-50.488.0169. Oral history interview with Piotr Ferenc. July 17, 2002.

RG-50.488.0298. Oral history interview with Józefa Miros. Interviewed by Patrycja Bukalska. May 1, 2010.

RG-60.5032. Czeslaw Borowi [Borowy]—Treblinka. Claude Lanzmann Shoah Collection. Film ID: 3348, 3349, 3350, 3351. July 1978.

RG-60.5036. Henryk Gawkowski and Treblinka railway workers. Film ID 3365, Camera Roll 15.

VHA. USC Shoah Foundation Visual History Archive

58. Sol Liber. Interviewed by Merle Goldberg. August 11, 1994.

1753. Fred Kort. Interviewed by Dana Schwartz. March 29, 1995.

18061. Abraham Bomba. Interviewed by Louise Bobrow. August 14, 1996.

55144. Linda Penn. Interviewed by Ann Estus. January 24, 1992.

Yad Vashem Digital Photo Archive
 Signature 1448. Item 38353. April 4, 1984. https://photos.yadvashem.org
żih. Żydowski Instytut Historyczny, Warsaw, Poland
 204/62. "Treblinka—obóz śmierci." 1943.
 209/38. "Treblinka." Kopia raportu opartego na relacjach naocznych świadków
  dot. obozu śmierci podczas jego funkcjonowania (25.03.1943).
 230/5. Builetyn Informacyjny, December 16, 1943.
 230/63. "Obóz śmierci w Treblince. Wydawnictwo 'Głosu Warszawy.' Opis
  funkcjownowania obozu zagłady na podstawie felacji świadków." 1943.
 230/72. *Informacja Bieżąca.* Number 30/55. August 17, 1942.
 230/91. Antoni Szymanowski. "Likwidacja ghetta warszawskiego. Reportaz." 1942.
 301/26. Stanisław Kon.
 301/55. Abram Finkler.
 301/85. Mojżesz Mydło.
 301/228. Chaim Grabel.
 301/446. Gedali Rydlewicz.
 301/608. Nuchem Perlman.
 301/656. Szymon Goldberg.
 301/668. Chaim Kwiatek.
 301/688. Aron Czechowicz.
 301/689. N.N. "Treblinka Fabryka Smierci."
 301/852. Nachman Diament.
 301/1049. Zdzisław Goldstein.
 301/1095. Z. Łukaszkiewicz i J. Maciejewski.
 301/1134. Samuel Willenberg.
 301/1186. Szmuel Miedziński.
 301/1236. Adolf Lewin.
 301/1261. Luba Frank.
 301/1460. Nochem Babikier.
 301/1565. Blanka Goldhurst.
 301/2019. Elias Magid.
 301/2226. Józef Gutman.
 301/3960. Nachemiasz Szulklaper.
 301/4147. Henryk Mściwój Radziszewski.
 301/4870. Michał Kalembasiak.
 301/5089. Julian Leszczyński.
 301/5341. Karol Tajgman.
 301/5483. Jerzy Rajgrodzki. "Wspomnienia z Treblinki."
 301/6037. Stanisław Borkowski.

301/6080. Celina Kalembaziak.

301/6237. Bogumił Nowacki.

301/6795. Maria Krych.

302/27. Samuel Puterman.

302/30. Stanisław Zeminski.

302/32. Oskar Strawczyński. "Wspomnienia: Dziesięć miesięcy Treblinki. 5 października 1942–2 sierpnia 1943."

302/77. N.N. (Unknown Author)

302/118. Mosze Klajman.

302/133. Noemi Wajnkrano-Szac.

302/153. Tanchem [Tanhum] Grinberg.

302/172. Jan Przedborski.

302/224. Jerzy Królikowski. "Wspomnienia z okolic Treblinki w czasie okapacji."

302/313. Cypora Jabłoń-Zonszajn.

302/316. Irena Smiegielska. "The Stolen Years." "Wspomniena z czasów Zagłady."

302/321. Mieczysław Chodźko.

303XX.280. Josef Kermisz. "W Treblince poraz drugi."

344/589. "Wachman w Treblince."

ARG 378 (Ring. II/295).

ARG II 379 (Ring. II/296). David Nowodworski. "Relacja z pobytu w obozie zagłady w Treblince. (28.08.[1942 r.])."

ARG II 380 (Ring. II/297). "Relacja Uciekiniera z Treblinki."

ARG II 382 (Ring. II/299). Original Ring. II/299 is in Yiddish. I consulted the Polish translation in the ŻIH published record of the Ringelblum Archive. Citation is here: Żydowski Instytut Historyczny im. Emanuela Ringelblaum. *Archiwum Ringelbluma: Konspiracyjne Archiwum Getta Warszawy, Tom 13: Ostatnim etapem przesidlenia jest śmierć, Pomiechówek, Chełmo and Nerem, Treblinka.* Warsaw: Wydawnictwa Uniwersytetu Warszawskiego, 2013. Physical copy available at ŻIH.

ARG II 432b (Ring. II/319).

Published Works

Abate, Dante, and Caroline Sturdy Colls. "A Multi-level and Multi-sensory Documentation Approach of the Treblinka Extermination and Labor Camps." *Journal of Cultural Heritage* 34 (2018): 129–35.

Abrams, David. *The Spell of the Sensuous: Perception and Language in a More-Than-Human World.* New York: Vintage, 1996.

Ackerman, Diane. *A Natural History of the Senses.* New York: Vintage, 1991.

Aldor, Francis. *Germany's "Death Space": The Polish Tragedy.* London: Francis Aldor, 1940.

Aly, Götz, and Susanne Heim. *Architects of Annihilation: Auschwitz and the Logic of Destruction.* Translated by A. G. Blunden. Princeton: Princeton University Press, 2002.

Apenszlak, Jacob, Jacob Kenner, Isaac Lewin, and Moses Polakiewicz, eds. *The Black Book of Polish Jewry: An Account of Martyrdom of Polish Jewry under the Nazi Occupation.* New York: Roy, 1943.

Apenszlak, Jacob, and Moshe Polakiewicz. *Armed Resistance of the Jews in Poland.* New York: American Federation for Polish Jews, 1944.

Arad, Yitzhak. *Belzec, Sobibor, Treblinka: The Operation Reinhard Death Camps.* Bloomington: Indiana University Press, 1987.

———. "Jewish Prisoner Uprisings in the Treblinka and Sobibor Extermination Camps." In *The Nazi Concentration Camps: Proceedings of the Fourth Yad Vashem International Historical Conference*, edited by Yisrael Gutman and Avital Saf, 357–400. Jerusalem: Daf Chen, 1984.

Arad, Yitzhak, Israel Gutman, and Abraham Margaliot, eds. *Documents on the Holocaust: Selected Sources on the Destruction of the Jews of Germany and Austria, Poland, and the Soviet Union.* 8th ed. Translated by Lea Ben Dor. Lincoln: University of Nebraska Press, 1999.

Archives of the Holocaust: An International Collection of Selected Documents. Vol. 16, *United Nations Archives, New York: United Nations War Crimes Commission.* Edited by George J. Lankevich. New York: Garland, 1990.

Archives of the Holocaust: An International Collection of Selected Documents. Vol. 17, *American Jewish Committee, New York.* Edited by Henry Friedlander, Sybil Milton, and Frederick D. Bogin. New York: Garland, 1993.

Archives of the Holocaust: An International Collection of Selected Documents. Vol. 22, *Zentrale Stelle der Landesjustizverwaltungen Ludwigsburg.* Edited by Henry Friedlander and Sybil Milton. New York: Garland, 1993.

Arendt, Hannah. *Eichmann in Jerusalem: A Report on the Banality of Evil.* New York: Penguin Classics, 1963. Reprint, 2006.

———. *The Origins of Totalitarianism.* New York: Meridian, 1960.

Aziz, Philippe. *Doctors of Death.* Geneva: Ferni, 1976.

Barnes, Trevor J., and Claudio Minca. "Nazi Spatial Theory: The Dark Geographies of Carl Schmitt and Walter Christaller." *Annals of the Association of American Geographers* 103, no 3 (2013): 669–87.

Bassin, Mark. "Blood or Soil? The Völkisch Movement, the Nazis, and the Legacy of Geopolitik." In *How Green Were the Nazis? Nature, Environment, and Nation in the Third Reich*, edited by Franz-Josef Brüggemeier, Mark Cioc, and Thomas Zeller, 204–42. Athens: Ohio University Press, 2005.

Bauer, Yehuda. *A History of the Holocaust.* New York: Franklin Watts, 1982.

———. *Rethinking the Holocaust.* New Haven: Yale University Press, 2001.

Bauman, Zygmunt. *Modernity and the Holocaust.* Ithaca NY: Cornell University Press, 1989.

"Die Bauten des dritten Reiches." *Baugilde* 19, no. 26 (1937): 877–78.

Beorn, Waitman, and Anne Kelly Knowles. "Killing on the Ground and in the Mind: The Spatialities of Genocide in the East." In *Geographies of the Holocaust*, edited by Anne Kelly Knowles, Tim Cole, and Alberto Giordano, 88–119. Bloomington: Indiana University Press, 2014.

Berenstein, Tatiana, and Adam Rutkowski. *Assistance to the Jews in Poland, 1939–1945.* Warsaw: Polonia Publishing House, 1963.

Berg, Mary. *Warsaw Ghetto: A Diary by Mary Berg.* Edited by S. L. Shneiderman. New York: L. B. Fischer, 1945.

Bergen, Doris L. *War and Genocide: A Concise History of the Holocaust.* 3rd ed. Lanham MD: Rowman and Littlefield, 2016.

Berger, Sara. *Experten der Vernichtung: das T4-Reinhardt-Netzwerk in den Lagern Belzec, Sobibor und Treblinka.* Hamburg: Hamburger Edition, 2013.

Bewerunge, Lothar. "'Der Himmel war rot über Treblinka:' Die Angeklagten bestreiten alle Zeugenaussagen/Der Düsseldorfer Prozess weitet sich aus." *Frankfurter Allgemeine Zeitung* no. 286, p. 7. December 9, 1964.

Bikont, Anna. *The Crime and the Silence: Confronting the Massacre of Jews in Wartime Jedwabne.* Translated by Alissa Valles. New York: Farrar, Straus and Giroux, 2015.

Black, Peter. "Foot Soldiers of the Final Solution: The Trawniki Training Camp and Operation Reinhard." *Holocaust and Genocide Studies* 25, no. 1 (Spring 2011): 1–99.

Blackbourn, David. *The Conquest of Nature: Water, Landscape, and the Making of Modern Germany.* New York: W. W. Norton, 2006.

Blatman, Daniel. *The Death Marches: The Final Phase of Nazi Genocide.* Translated by Chaya Galai. Cambridge MA: Belknap Press of Harvard University Press, 2011.

Blatt, Toivi. *From the Ashes of Sobibor: A Story of Survival.* Evanston: Northwestern University Press, 1997.

Bloxham, Donald. *The Final Solution: A Genocide.* Oxford: Oxford University Press, 2009.

Blumental, N. *Dokumenty i Materiały, Tom 1: Obozy.* Łódź: Wydawnictwa Centralnej Żydowskiej Komisji Historycznej w Polsce 1946.

Bogard, Paul. *The End of Night: Searching for Natural Darkness in an Age of Artificial Light.* New York: Back Bay Books, 2013.

Bour, H., Tutin, M., and P. Pasquier. "The Central Nervous System and Carbon Monoxide Poisoning I. Clinical Data with References to 20 Fatal Cases." In *Carbon Monoxide Poisoning*, edited by H. Bour and I. McA. Ledingham. Amsterdam: Elsevier, 1967.

Brown, Kate. *A Biography of No Place: From Ethnic Borderland to Soviet Heartland.* Cambridge MA: Harvard University Press, 2004.

Browning, Christopher. *Ordinary Men: Reserve Police Battalion 101 and the Final Solution in Poland.* New York: Harper Perennial, 1998.

Bryant, Michael S. *Eyewitness to Genocide: The Operation Reinhard Death Camp Trials, 1955–1966.* Knoxville: University of Tennessee Press, 2014.

Burleigh, Michael, and Wolfgang Wipperman. *The Racial State: Germany 1933–1945.* Cambridge: Cambridge University Press, 1991.

Central Commission for Investigation of German Crimes in Poland. *German Crimes in Poland.* Vol. 1. Warsaw: Drukarni św. Wojciecha pod Zarządem Państwowym, 1946.

Charlesworth, Andrew, and Michael Addis. "Memorialization and the Ecological Landscapes of Holocaust Sites: The Cases of Plaszow and Auschwitz-Birkenau." *Landscape Research* 27, no. 3 (2002): 229–52.

Charnysh, Volha, and Evgeny Finkel. "The Death Camp Eldorado: Political and Economic Effects of Mass Violence." *American Political Science Review* 111, no. 4 (2017): 801–18.

Chersztein, M. *Ofiary Nikczemności.* Stuttgart: Rządu Wojskowego Württemberg—Baden, 1945.

Childers, Thomas. *The Third Reich: A History of Nazi Germany.* New York: Simon & Schuster Paperbacks, 2018.

Chrostowski, Witold. *Extermination Camp Treblinka.* London: Vallentine Mitchell, 2004.

Cole, Tim. *Holocaust City: The Making of a Jewish Ghetto.* New York: Routledge, 2003.

———. "'Nature Was Helping Us': Forests, Trees, and Environmental Histories of the Holocaust." *Environmental History* 19, no. 4 (Oct. 2014): 665–86.

Cresswell, Tim. *In Place/Out of Place: Geography, Ideology, and Transgression.* Minneapolis: University of Minnesota Press, 1996.

———. *Place: A Short Introduction.* Malden MA: Blackwell, 2004.

Crowe, David. M. *The Holocaust: Roots, History, and Aftermath.* 2nd ed. New York: Routledge, 2022.

Das Menschenschlachthaus Treblinka: Dokumente Der Nazi-Barbarei. Wien: Stern Verlag, 1946.

Day, Sean. "Synesthesia and Synesthetic Metaphors." *Psyche* 2, no. 32 (July 1996).

De Mildt, Dick. *In the Name of the People: Perpetrators of Genocide in the Reflection of Their Post-war Prosecution in West Germany, the "Euthanasia" and "Aktion Reinhard" Trial Cases.* The Hague: Martinus Nijhoff, 1996.

Desbois, Patrick. *The Holocaust by Bullets: A Priest's Journey to Uncover the Truth behind the Murder of 1.5 Million Jews.* New York: Palgrave Macmillan, 2008.

Didi-Huberman, Georges. *Images in Spite of All: Four Photographs from Auschwitz*. Chicago: University of Chicago Press, 2008.

Donat, Alexander, ed. *The Death Camp Treblinka: A Documentary*. New York: Holocaust Library, 1979.

Ehrenburg, Ilya, and Vasily Grossman. *The Black Book: The Ruthless Murder of Jews by German-Fascist Invaders Throughout the Temporarily Occupied Regions of the Soviet Union and in the Death Camps of Poland during the War of 1941–1945*. Translated by John Glad and James S. Levine. New York: Holocaust Library, 1981.

Feldman, George. *Understanding the Holocaust*. Vol. 2. Detroit: UXL, 1998.

Felman, Shoshana. "Film as Witness: Claude Lanzmann's *Shoah*." In *Holocaust Remembrance: The Shapes of Memory*, edited by Geoffrey Hartman, 90–103. Cambridge MA: Blackwell, 1995.

Forbes, W. H. "Carbon Monoxide Uptake via the Lungs." *Annals of the New York Academy of Sciences* 174, no. 1 (October 5, 1970): 72–76.

Foucault, Michel. *Discipline and Punish: The Birth of the Prison*. New York: Pantheon, 1977.

———. *The History of Sexuality*. Vol. 1, *An Introduction*. Translated by Robert Hurley. New York: Pantheon, 1978.

———. *"Society Must Be Defended": Lectures at the College de France, 1975–1976*. Edited by Mauro Bertani and Alessandro Fontana. Translated by David Macey. New York: Picador, 1997.

Friedländer, Saul. *The Years of Extermination: Nazi Germany and the Jews, 1939–1945*. New York: Harper Perennial, 2008.

Fritzsche, Peter. *Life and Death in the Third Reich*. Cambridge MA: Belknap Press of Harvard University Press, 2009.

Garstang, R. H. "Brightness of Clouds at Night over a City." *Observatory* 127, no. 1 (2007): 1–12.

Gellately, Robert. "The Third Reich, the Holocaust, and Visions of Serial Genocide." In *The Specter of Genocide: Mass Murder in Historical Perspective*, edited by Robert Gellately and Ben Kiernan, 241–64. Cambridge: Cambridge University Press, 2003.

Giaccaria, Paolo, and Claudio Minca. "Topographies/Topologies of the Camp: Auschwitz as a Spatial Threshold." *Political Geography* 30, no. 1 (2011): 3–12.

Gigliotti, Simone. *The Train Journey: Transit, Captivity, and Witnessing in the Holocaust*. New York: Berghahn, 2009.

Gilbert, Martin. *Final Journey: The Fate of the Jews in Nazi Europe*. New York: Mayflower, 1979.

———. *The Righteous: The Unsung Heroes of the Holocaust*. New York: Henry Holt, 2003.

Glazar, Richard. *Trap with a Green Fence: Survival in Treblinka*. Translated by Roslyn Theobald. Evanston: Northwestern University Press, 1995.

Goldhagen, Daniel Jonah. *Hitler's Willing Executioners: Ordinary Germans and the Holocaust*. New York: Knopf, 1996.

Goldstein, Bernard. *The Stars Bear Witness*. Edited and Translated by Leonard Shatzkin. New York: Viking, 1949.

Grabowski, Jan. *Hunt for the Jews: Betrayal and Murder in German-Occupied Poland* Bloomington: Indiana University Press, 2013.

Greene, Joshua, and Shiva Kumar, eds. *Witness: Voices from the Holocaust*. New York: Free Press, 2000.

Gregory, Derek. *Geographical Imaginations*. Cambridge MA: Blackwell, 1994.

Griech-Polelle, Beth. "Image of a Churchman-Resister: Bishop von Galen, the Euthanasia Project and the Sermons of Summer 1941." *Journal of Contemporary History* 36, no. (2001): 41–57.

Gross, Jan. *Golden Harvest: Events at the Periphery of the Holocaust*. Oxford: Oxford University Press, 2012.

——. *Neighbors: The Destruction of the Jewish Community in Jedwabne, Poland*. Princeton: Princeton University Press, 2001.

——. *Polish Society under German Occupation: The Generalgouvernement, 1939–1944*. Princeton: Princeton University Press, 1979.

Grossman, Vasily. *Life and Fate*. London: Vintage, 2006.

——. *A Writer at War: A Soviet Journalist with the Red Army, 1941–45*. Edited by Antony Beevor and Luba Vinogradova. New York: Vintage, 2007.

Grossman, Vassili. "The Treblinka Hell: The Story of a Concentration Camp." *International Literature* 12, no. 6 (1945): 28–48.

Grunspan, Roman. *The Uprising of the Death Box of Warsaw: A Documentary Book about Jewish and Christian Lives under Nazi Rule in the Warsaw Ghetto and in the Non-Jewish Region of Warsaw*. New York: Vantage, 1978.

Gumkowski, J., and A. Rutkowski. *Treblinka*. Warsaw: DSP, 1961.

Gutman, Yisrael. *The Jews of Warsaw, 1939–1943: Ghetto, Underground, Revolt*. Translated by Ina Friedman. Bloomington: Indiana University Press, 1982. Reprint, 1989.

Gutman, Yisrael, and Shmuel Krakowski. *Unequal Victims: Poles and Jews during World War Two*. New York: Holocaust Library, 1986.

Hagen, Joshua, and Robert Ostergren. *Building Nazi Germany: Place, Space, Architecture, and Ideology*. Lanham MD: Rowman and Littlefield, 2019.

Hartman, Geoffrey. "Introduction: Darkness Visible." In *Holocaust Remembrance: The Shapes of Memory*, edited by Geoffrey Hartman, 1–22. Cambridge MA: Blackwell, 1995.

Heller, Aron. "Only 2 Survivors Remain from Nazi Camp Treblinka." Associated Press. October 31, 2010. https://www.nbcnews.com/id/wbna39939248.

Hellpach, Willy. *Einführung in die Völkerpsychologie*. Stuttgart: Ferdinand Enke Verlag, 1944.

Hesse, K. "Annual Report on Military Economics, 1936." *Friends of Europe: Monthly Survey of German Publications*, no. 42 (October 1937): 332–34.

Hilberg, Raul. *Perpetrators, Victims, Bystanders: The Jewish Catastrophe, 1933–1945*. New York: HarperCollins, 1992.

Horwitz, Gordon J. "Places Far Away, Places Very Near: Mauthausen, the Camps of the Shoah, and the Bystanders." In *The Holocaust and History: The Known, the Unknown, the Disputed, and the Reexamined*, edited by Michael Berenbaum and Abraham J. Peck, 409–20. Bloomington: Indiana University Press, 1998.

In Everlasting Remembrance: A Guide to Memorials and Monuments Honoring the Six Million. New York: American Jewish Congress, 1969.

Ingard, Uno. "A Review of the Influence of Meteorological Conditions on Sound Propagation." *Journal of the Acoustical Society of America* 24, no. 3 (May 1953): 405–11.

Joskowicz, Ari. "Separate Suffering, Shared Archives: Jewish and Romani Histories of Nazi Persecution." *History and Memory* 28, no. 1 (Spring/Summer 2016): 110–40.

Justiz und NS-Verbrechen: Sammlung Deutscher Strafurteile Wegen Nationalsozialistischer Tötungsverbrechen 1945–1999. Band 34. Amsterdam: Amsterdam University Press, 2005.

Karski, Jan. *Story of a Secret State: My Report to the World*. Foreword by Madeleine Albright. Washington DC: Georgetown University Press, 2013. Originally published by Houghton Mifflin, 1944.

Kassow, Samuel D. *Who Will Write Our History? Rediscovering a Hidden Archive from the Warsaw Ghetto*. London: Penguin, 2009.

Katz, Eric. "On the Neutrality of Technology: The Holocaust Death Camps as a Counterexample." In *Death by Design: Science, Technology, and Engineering in Nazi Germany*, edited by Eric Katz, 291–308. New York: Pearson Longman, 2006.

Kaur, Navdip. "Violence and Migration: A Study of Killing in the Trains during the Partition of Punjab in 1947." *Proceedings of the Indian History Congress* 72, part 1 (2011): 947–54.

Kershaw, Ian. *Hitler, 1889–1936: Hubris*. London: Allen Lane, Penguin Press, 1998.

Klee, Ernst, Dressen, Willi, and Volker Riess, eds. *"The Good Old Days": The Holocaust as Seen by Its Perpetrators and Bystanders*. Translated by Deborah Burnstone. New York: Konecky & Konecky, 1991.

Knapp, Werner. *Deutsche Dorfplanung: Gestalterische Grundlagen, 1. Bauen und Planen der Gegenwart*. Stuttgart: Karl Krämer Verlag, 1942.

Koonz, Claudia. *The Nazi Conscience*. Cambridge MA: Belknap Press of Harvard University Press, 2005.

Kopówka, Edward. *Treblinka: Nigdy Więcej*. Siedlce: Muzeum Walki i Męczeństwa w Treblince, 2002.

Kopówka, Edward, and Pawel Rytel-Andrianik. *Dam Im Imię na Wieki (Księga Izajasza 56,5): Polacy z okolic Treblinki ratujący Żydów*. Warsaw-Rembertów: Drukarnia Loretańska, 2011.

Krakowski, Shmuel. *The War of the Doomed: Jewish Armed Resistance in Poland, 1942–1944*. New York: Holmes & Meier, 1984.

Kuperhand, Miriam, and Saul Kuperhand. *Shadows of Treblinka*. Introduction by Alan Adelson. Urbana: University of Illinois Press, 1998.

Lanzmann, Claude. *The Patagonian Hare: A Memoir*. Translated by Frank Wynne. New York: Farrar, Straus and Giroux, 2012.

———. *Shoah: An Oral History of the Holocaust; The Complete Text of the Film*. New York: Pantheon, 1985.

Lasman, Noach. *Pięćdziesiąt kilometrów od Treblinki*. Warsaw: Borgis, 1994.

Lefebvre, Henri. *The Production of Space*. Translated by Donald Nicholson-Smith. Malden MA: Blackwell, 1991.

Lekan, Thomas M. *Imagining the Nation in Nature: Landscape Preservation and German Identity, 1885–1945*. Cambridge MA: Harvard University Press, 2004.

Levi, Primo. *The Drowned and the Saved*. Translated by Raymond Rosenthal. New York: Simon & Schuster, 1988.

———. *Survival in Auschwitz*. New York: Touchstone, 1996.

Levin, Alex. *Under the Yellow & Red Stars*. Toronto: Azrieli Foundation, 2012.

Levinson, S. C. *Pragmatics*. Cambridge: Cambridge University Press, 1983.

Ley, Michael. "Auschwitz—Ein historischer Essay." In *Auschwitz: Versuche einer Annäherung*, edited by Charlotte Kohn-Ley and Michael Ley, 55–136. Vienna: Verlag Für Gesellschaftskritik, 1996.

Lifton, Robert Jay. *The Nazi Doctors: Medical Killing and the Psychology of Genocide*. New York: Basic Books, 1986.

Lillian Goldman Law Library. "Program of the National Socialists Workers' Party." *The Avalon Project: Documents in Law, History and Diplomacy*. Yale Law School, 2008. https://avalon.law.yale.edu/imt/nsdappro.asp.

Lower, Wendy. *Nazi Empire-Building and the Holocaust in Ukraine*. Chapel Hill: University of North Carolina Press, 2005.

Łukaszkiewicz, Zdzisław. *Obóz Straceń w Treblince*. Warsaw: Państwowy Instytut Wydawniczy, 1946.

Mark, B. *The Extermination and the Resistance of the Polish Jews during the Period 1939–1944*. Translated and edited by A. Rutkowski. Warsaw: Jewish Historical Institute, 1955.

Maschke, Erich. "Die Wiedergewinnung des Deutschen Ostens." In *Europas Schicksal im Osten: 12 Vorträge*, edited by Hans Hagemeyer, 104–16. Breslau: NS-Druckerei, 1939.

The Massacre of a People: What the Democracies Can Do. New York: Jewish Frontier Association, 1943.

Massey, Doreen. *For Space*. London: Sage, 2005.

Meng, Michael. *Shattered Spaces: Encountering Jewish Ruins in Postwar Germany and Poland*. Cambridge MA: Harvard University Press, 2011.

Mierzewjewski, Alfred C. *The Most Valuable Asset of the Reich: A History of the German National Railway*. Vol. 2, *1933–1945*. Chapel Hill: University of North Carolina Press, 2000.

Mommsen, Hans. *From Weimar to Auschwitz: Essays on German History*. Princeton: Princeton University Press, 1991.

Mühlhäuser, Regina. "Between 'Racial Awareness' and Fantasies of Potency: Nazi Sexual Politics in the Occupied Territories of the Soviet Union, 1942–1945." In *Brutality and Desire: War and Sexuality in Europe's Twentieth Century*, edited by Dagmar Herzog, 197–220. New York: Palgrave Macmillan, 2009.

Murawska-Gryń, Zofia, and Edward Gryń. *Majdanek*. Lublin, Poland: Państwowe Muzeum na Majdanku, 1984.

Nikolic-Dunlop, Alex, dir. *Treblinka: Hitler's Killing Machine*. Watford: Furneaux & Edgar Productions, 2013. Documentary.

Nora, Pierre. "Between Memory and History: *Les Lieux de Mémoire*." *Representations* 26 (Spring 1989): 7–24.

Oświęcim Camp of Death (Underground Report). Foreword by Florence J. Harriman. New York: "Poland Fights" Polish Labor Group, 1944.

Pachirat, Timothy. *Every Twelve Seconds: Industrialized Slaughter and the Politics of Sight*. New Haven: Yale University Press, 2011.

Person, Katarzyna. "Sexual Violence during the Holocaust: The Case of Forced Prostitution in the Warsaw Ghetto." *Shofar* 33, no. 2 (Winter 2015): 103–21.

Perz, Bertrand. "The Austrian Connection: SS and Police Leader Odilo Globocnik and His Staff in the Lublin District." *Holocaust and Genocide Studies* 29, no. 3 (Winter 2015): 400–430.

Pollefeyt, Didier, ed. *Holocaust and Nature*. Münster: LIT Verlag, 2013.

Porteous, J. Douglas. *Landscapes of the Mind: Worlds of Sense and Metaphor*. Toronto: University of Toronto Press, 1990.

Rajchman, Chil. *The Last Jew of Treblinka: A Survivor's Memory, 1942–1943*. Translated by Solon Beinfeld. New York: Pegasus, 2001.

Reder, Rudolf. *Bełżec*. Edited by Franciszek Piper, Joachim S. Russek, and Teresa Świebocka. Kraków: Drukarnia Uniwersytetu Jagiellońskiego w Krakowie, 1999.

Republic of Poland Ministry of Foreign Affairs. *German Occupation of Poland: Extra of Note Addressed to the Governments of the Allied and Neutral Powers: [Polish White Book]*. New York: Greystone, 1941.

Republic of Poland Ministry of Foreign Affairs. *Mass Extermination of Jews in German Occupied Poland, Addressed to the Governments of the United Nations on December 10th, 1942, and Other Documents*. London: Hutchinson, n.d.

Rieger, Berndt. *Creator of Nazi Death Camps: The Life of Odilo Globocnik*. London: Vallentine Mitchell, 2007.

Ringelblum, Emmanuel. *Polish-Jewish Relations during the Second World War*. New York: Fertig, 1976.

Rodaway, Paul. *Sensuous Geographies: Body, Sense and Place*. London: Routledge, 1994.

Roiter, Howard. *Voices from the Holocaust: Asurno Holocaust Documentation Series*. Vol. 1. Givataim, Israel: Asurno Press, 1975.

Rückerl, Adalbert. *NS Vernichtungslager im Spiegel deutscher Strafprozesse*. München: Deutscher Taschenbuch Verlag, 1977.

Said, Edward W. *Orientalism*. New York: Vintage, 1979.

Sandler, Willeke. "'Here Too Lies Our *Lebensraum*:' Colonial Space as German Space." In *Heimat, Region, and Empire: Spatial Identities under National Socialism*, edited by Claus-Christian W. Szejnmann and Maiken Umbach, 148–65. New York: Palgrave Macmillan, 2012.

Schama, Simon. *Landscape and Memory*. New York: Alfred A. Knopf, 1995.

Schelvis, Jules. *Sobibor: A History of a Nazi Death Camp*. Oxford: Berg, 2007.

Seidman, Hillel. *The Warsaw Ghetto Diaries*. Translated by Yosef Israel. New York: Feldheim, 1997.

Sereny, Gitta. *Into That Darkness: An Examination of Conscience*. New York: Vintage, 1983.

Shneer, David. "Ghostly Landscapes: Soviet Liberators Photograph the Holocaust." *Humanity* 5, no. 2 (2014): 235–46.

Sikorski, Radek. *The Polish House: An Intimate History of Poland*. London: Phoenix, 1997.

Snyder, Timothy. *Black Earth: Holocaust as History and Warning*. New York: Tim Duggan, 2015.

———. *Bloodlands: Europe between Hitler and Stalin*. New York: Basic Books, 2012.

Sommer, Robert. "Sexual Exploitation of Women in Nazi Concentration Camp Brothels." In *Sexual Violence against Jewish Women during the Holocaust*, edited by Sonja Hedgepeth and Rochelle Saidel, 45–60. Waltham MA: Brandeis University Press, 2010.

Speer, Albert. "Die Manipulation des Menschen: Albert Speer im Gespräch." In *Die Erfindung der Geschichte: Aufsätze und Gespräche zur Architektur unseres Jahrhunderts*, edited by Wolfgang Pehnt. Munich: Prestel, 1989.

Stabholz, Thaddeus. *Seven Hells.* Translated by Jacques Grunblatt and Hilda R. Grunblatt. New York: Holocaust Library, 1990.

Stenchikov, Georgiy, Nilesh Lahoti, David J. Diner, Ralph Kahn, Paul J. Lioy, and Panos G. Georgopoulos. "Multiscale Plume Transport from the Collapse of the World Trade Center on September 11, 2001." *Environmental Fluid Mechanics* 6, no. 5 (2006): 425–50.

Stone, Dan. *Histories of the Holocaust.* Oxford: Oxford University Press, 2010.

Sturdy Colls, Caroline. *Holocaust Archaeologies: Approaches and Future Directions.* London: Springer, 2015.

———. "Holocaust Archaeology: Archaeological Approaches to Landscapes of Nazi Genocide and Persecution." *Journal of Conflict Archaeology* 7, no. 2 (2012): 70–104.

Sturdy Colls, Caroline, and Michael Branthwaite. "'This Is Proof?' Forensic Evidence and Material Culture at Treblinka Extermination Camp." *International Journal of Historical Archaeology* 22 (2018): 430–53.

Sudilovsky, Judith. "Growing Up near Treblinka Inspired Priest's Holocaust Research." Catholic News Service. April 28, 2014. https://www.catholicsun.org/2014/04/28/growing-up-near-treblinka-inspired-priests-holocaust-research/.

Szpilmana, Władysława, and Jerzy Waldorff. *Śmierć Miasta: Pamiętniki Władysława Szpilmana, 1939–1945.* Warsaw: Spółdzielnia Wydawnicza, 1946.

Tec, Nechama. *Defiance: The Bielski Partisans.* Oxford: Oxford University Press, 1993.

———. *When Light Pierced the Darkness.* New York: Oxford University Press, 1986.

Tenenbaum, Joseph. *Underground: The Story of a People.* New York: Philosophical Library, 1952.

To Live with Honor and Die with Honor! . . . Selected Documents from the Warsaw Ghetto Underground Archives "O.S." ("Oneg Shabbath"). Edited by Joseph Kermish. Jerusalem: Yad Vashem, 1986.

Treblinka 1996. Siedlce: Muzeum Walki i Męczeństwa w Treblince Oddział Muzeum Okręgowego w Siedlcach, 1996.

The Trial of the Major War Criminals before the International Military Tribunal. Vol. 3, *Proceedings 1 December 1945–14 December 1945.* Nuremberg, Germany, 1947.

The Trial of the Major War Criminals before the International Military Tribunal. Vol. 4, *Proceedings 17 December 1945–8 January 1946.* Nuremberg, Germany, 1947.

The Trial of the Major War Criminals before the International Military Tribunal. Vol. 7, *Proceedings 5 Feb. 1946–19 Feb. 1946.* Nuremberg, Germany, 1947.

The Trial of the Major War Criminals before the International Military Tribunal. Vol. 8, *Proceedings 20 February 1946–7 March 1946.* Nuremberg, Germany, 1947.

The Trial of the Major War Criminals before the International Military Tribunal. Vol. 19, *Proceedings 19 July 1946–29 July 1946.* Nuremberg, Germany, 1948.

The Trial of the Major War Criminals before the International Military Tribunal. Vol. 29, *Documents and Other Material in Evidence, Numbers 1850-PS to 2233-PS.* Nuremberg, Germany, 1948.

Trials of War Criminals before the Nuernberg Military Tribunals under Control Council Law No. 10. Vol. 1, *The Medical Case.* Washington DC: U.S. Government Printing Office, 1949.

Trials of War Criminals before the Nuernberg Military Tribunals under Control Council Law No. 10. Vol. 4, *The Einsatzgruppen Case* and *The Rusha Case.* Washington DC: U.S. Government Printing Office, n.d.

Troost, Gerdy. *Das Bauen im Neuen Reich.* Vol. 1. Bayreuth, Germany: Gauverlag Bayreuth, 1938.

Tuan, Yi-Fu. *Landscapes of Fear.* Minneapolis: University of Minnesota Press, 1979.

———. *Space and Place: The Perspective of Experience.* Minneapolis: University of Minnesota Press, 2001.

Tyner, James A. *Genocide and the Geographical Imagination: Life and Death in Germany, China, and Cambodia.* Lanham MD: Rowman and Littlefield, 2012.

Uhl, Heidemarie. "From the Periphery to the Center of Memory: Holocaust Memorials in Vienna." *Dapim: Studies on the Holocaust* 30, no. 3 (2016): 221–42.

United States v. Demjanjuk. 518 F. Supp. 1362 (ND Ohio 1981). https://law.justia.com/cases/federal/district-courts/FSupp/518/1362/2128864/.

Webb, Chris, and Michal Chocholatý. *The Treblinka Death Camp: History, Biographies, Remembrance.* Stuttgart: ibidem-Verlag, 2014.

Webb, Chris, and Carmelo Lisciotto. "Mapping Treblinka." Aktion Reinhard Camps. 2006. http://www.deathcamps.org/treblinka/maps.html.

Weiner Weber, Suzanne. "Life and Death in the Forest: Landscape Agency during the Holocaust." PhD dissertation. Florida International University, 2007.

Weinstein, Edi. *Quenched Steel: The Story of an Escape from Treblinka.* Jerusalem: Yad Vashem, 2002.

Weitz, Eric D. "The Modernity of Genocides: War, Race, and Revolution in the Twentieth Century." In *The Specter of Genocide: Mass Murder in Historical Perspective,* edited by Robert Gellately and Ben Kiernan, 53–74. Cambridge: Cambridge University Press, 2003.

Westermann, Edward B. *Drunk on Genocide: Alcohol and Mass Murder in Nazi Germany.* Ithaca NY: Cornell University Press, 2021.

Wiernik, Yankel. *A Year in Treblinka.* New York: American Representation of the General Jewish Workers' Union of Poland, 1945.

Wiesel, Elie. *The Gates of the Forest.* New York: Schocken Books, 1982.

Willenberg, Samuel. "Memory of Treblinka." The Memory of Treblinka Foundation. 2015–22. https://memoryoftreblinka.org/about-the-memory-of-treblinka
-foundation/samuel-willenberg/.

——. *Surviving Treblinka*. Edited by Władysław T. Bartoszewski. Oxford: Basil
Blackwell, 1989.

Wójcik, Michał. *Treblinka '43: Bunt w fabryce śmierci*. Kraków: Znak literna nova, 2018.

Young, James E. "Jewish Memory in Poland." In *Holocaust Remembrance: The Shapes
of Memory*, edited by Geoffrey Hartman, 215–31. Cambridge MA: Blackwell, 1995.

——. *The Texture of Memory: Holocaust Memorials and Meaning*. New Haven: Yale
University Press, 1993.

Ząbecki, Franciszek. *Wspomnienia dawne i nowe*. Warsaw: Instytut Wydawniczy
Pax, 1977.

Zelizer, Barbie. *Remembering to Forget: Holocaust Memory through the Camera's Eye*.
Chicago: University of Chicago Press, 1998.

Zuckerman, Yitzhak. *A Surplus of Memory: Chronicle of the Warsaw Ghetto Uprising*.
Translated and edited by Barbara Harshav. Berkeley: University of California
Press, 1993.

INDEX

Page numbers in *italics* refer to figures.

sounds, 153; and spatial arrangements, 22, 26–27; and Treblinka's conceptual mission, 38

The Gates of the Forest (Wiesel), 109–10

Gawkowski, Henryk, 173, 200

Gawkowski, Kazimierz, 137, 142, 150, 189

gendered nature of Treblinka's spatial layout, 85

General Directorate of the Eastern Railway, 172–73

General Government, 8–11, 172, 175, 203n6, 208n40

General Plan East, 232n132

Generalplan Ost (General Plan East), 232n132

German guards, 243n91; behavior of, 57–63, 213n4; bribing of, 83; and command structures, 42–43; in forests near Treblinka, 112; and the gas chambers, 77–79; and information, 196; in local Polish spaces, 117; and Nazi ideology, 39; and sensory witnessing, 149; and traces of Treblinka, 200–201. *See also* Ukrainian guards

German living area (*Wohnlager*), 22

German *Reichsbahn* (Imperial Railway), 172

Germans and Germany, 9–10, 208n40, 232n132, 246n169; and *Bahnschutz* formations, 183–84; and *Blut und Boden* (Blood and Soil) ideology, 3, 5–9, 228n12; and bodies of murdered Jews, 133, 136–46; and cattle cars, 165–66; and covering up the sounds of mass murder, 156; and displaced Polish farmers, 147; and the end of the war, xvii, 55; and invasion of Poland, 41, 99–100,

124–29, 209n51; and Jewish workers, 81–83; and the junction town of Małkinia-Górna, 162, *164*; and notes dropped from transports, 192; and occupied Poland, 125–28; and Polish-Jewish interactions, 99–100; and Polish railway workers, 177; property stolen and redistributed throughout, 192–93; and railway corridors, 162–63; rebuilding of, 3–6; and remains of Jews along railway corridors, 191; and singing of Polish songs, 158; and traces of Treblinka, 198–200; and train movements, 172–73; and women, 85

Gerstein, Kurt, 37–39, 61, 215n38, 218n98

Giaccaria, Paolo, 206n42

Gigliotti, Simone, xxiii, 131, 161, 163–64, 166–67, 205n34, 239n14

Głąbiński, Stanisław, 56

Glazar, Richard, 38, 63, 90, 92, 102–4, 107–9, 145–47, 178–79

Globočnik, Odilo, 39–40, 42–43, 47, 49–50, 52, 61, 192, 215n38, 219n130

Goebbels, Joseph, 42

Gold, Artur, 156–57

Goldberg, Szymon, 112, 120, 166, 231n112

Golden Harvest (Gross), xxviii, 246n171

Goldhurst, Blanka, 69

Goldjuden (gold Jews), 82

Goldstein, Bernard, 70

Goldstein, Zdzisław, 71–72, 84, 182, 242n90

Göring, Hermann, 42

Goska, Barbara, 115, 141, 155, 157, 179, 210n64, 235n68

Goska, Eugeniusz, 21, 117, 186

Ingard, Uno, 229n53
insanity, 89–90
interactions / interactional space,
    xxiv, 97–129; and forests, 100–110;
    and German invasion of Poland,
    124–28; of humans with Jews who
    escaped Treblinka, 110–24; and the
    leaving behind of material objects,
    191–93; with Polish railway work-
    ers, 173–77; and railway corridors,
    162–63; between those who escaped
    trains and local populations, 180,
    185–88
isolation, 19–28, 34, 130

Jabłoń-Zonszajn, Cypora, 165, 167–68
Jakubik, Bronisława, 138, 156
Jewish Frontier Association (journal),
    197
Jewish Labor Committee, 198
Jewish organizations, 198
Jewish workers ("work Jews"), 29,
    66–68, 81–85, 92, 97, 224n81
Jews from outside of Poland, 69
Joskowicz, Ari, 206n39
Judenfrei (Jew-free) worldview, 2, 30.
    See also Nazi ideology
jumping from cattle cars, 181–91,
    240n39, 244n123
juxtaposition: between attempts at
    escape and observation from homes,
    180–81; between fear of hiding and
    harmony with nature, 110; and gas
    chambers, 78–79; between interior
    of cattle cars and rural landscapes,
    184–85; between nature and spaces
    of death, 95; between safety of
    homes and uncertainty of escapees,
    114–15; between sound and silence,

155–56; and sympathetic speeches,
    73. *See also* deception / deceptive
    components

Kadej, Barbara, 140, 235n63, 248n22
Kaina, Erwin, 60–61
Kalembasiak, Michał, 62, 138, 191
Kalembaziak, Celina, 111, 126, 141
Kapos (barrack leaders), 84, 87
Karczmarczyk family, 116–17
Karski, Jan, 197
Kaur, Navdip, 238n2
Kazierodek, Anna, 13, 115–16
Kielce, Poland, 69
Kiełczew, Poland, 247–48n22
Kisiel, Piotr, 92
Klajman, Mosze, 87, 104, 122, 145, 168,
    239n19, 241n48
Klein, Heniek, 117
Klinzmann, Willi, 55
Knajp, Jan, 123
Knapp, Werner, 6
knowledge, 158–59, 195–98
Knowles, Anne Kelly, 108–9
Kobus, Jan, 92
Kohn, Shalom, 88
Kolasiński, 116
Kolski, Abraham, 103, 119–20, 154,
    224n73
Kon, Menachem, 197
Kopachke (digging machine), 157–58
Kort, Fred, 137, 152, 169, 210n64,
    240n25
Korytnicki, Zelek, 13
Kosów Lacki, Poland, 11–12, 62, 113–14,
    121–22, 183, 231n112
Kosów-Małkinia road, 16
Kostki, Poland, 135
Kristallnacht, 10

Królikowski, Jerzy: and behavior of camp personnel, 62; and conditions in cattle cars, 167; and health, 210n66; and the leaving behind of material objects, 191; and local Poles, 195; after release from Treblinka, 128; and remains of Jews along railway corridors, 189; and sensory witnessing, 133–35; and stops near villages or towns, 173–74, 180, 241–42n70; before Treblinka, 14–15

Kruger, Henry, 175, 178, 191, 242n71, 242n89

Krych, Maria, 120, 225n115

Krzepicki, Abraham, 220n148; and adaptation to life in Treblinka, 93; and behavior of camp personnel, 57; and conditions in cattle cars, 165–67; and deception / deceptive components, 74; and emotions, 95–96; escape of, 103–4, 108, 111; on the gas chambers, 78; and industrial imagery, 33; and interaction with death, 68, 89; and loading of cattle cars, 171; photograph of, 67; and Polish-Jewish interactions in the areas around Treblinka, 112–13, 120–21; and Polish railway workers, 176; and power dynamics, 51; and psychological effects, 90–92; and resettlement narrative, 71; and sensory witnessing, 133, 136, 146–47, 155, 235n67; and spatial arrangements, 22, 28; and traces of Treblinka, 201; in the *Waldkommando* (Forest Brigade), 100; and women, 84

Kucharek, Stanisław, 149, 153, 232n141

Kucharek, Stefan, 53, 62, 135, 139–40, 152, 176, 181, 240n39

Kudlik, Aleksander, 28

Kuperhand, Saul, 72, 103, 141, 163, 181, 201, 230n75

Kurczewsky forest, 103

Kurtzebie, Józef, 187

Küttner, Fritz, 60–61

Kuźmiński, Józef, 55, 69

Kwiatek, Chaim, 102, 221n7

Lambert, Erwin, 58

landscape agency, 105

landscapes, 128–29, 161–62, 184–85

Lanzmann, Claude, xvi, xxiii, xxviii, 138, 148, 180, 200–201, 217n71

Laskowski, Mieczysław, 244n122

Lasman, Noach, 183, 240n35, 244n128

Lato, Samuel, 229n45

Lazarett (hospital), 29, 49, 80–81

leaves taken from the camp, 58

Lefebvre, Henri, xv, xxi–xxiii, 4, 20, 65, 233n4

Leszczyński, Julian, 81, 237n106

Levi, Primo, 94, 128, 221n6

Levin, Alex, 109

Lewin, Adolf, 168, 188

Ley, Michael, 2

Liber, Sol, 61, 155–56, 165, 168, 181, 243n110

Lieber, Sonia, 120, 231n111

life and death, spaces of, 65–96; and adaptations, 87–96; and death at Treblinka, 68–81; and Jewish workers, 81–84; and reprieve from spaces of death, 59, 95; and women, 84–86

light pollution, 145–46

liminal spaces, 98, 100, 128

Lipki, Poland, 231n112

livestock, 107

living Jews of Treblinka. *See* Jewish workers ("work Jews")

loading platform (*Umschlagplatz*), 70–76, 83, 169–73, 176
local materials in building Treblinka, 16–17
local Poles: and behavioral responses to Jews, 98–99; and heavy machinery, 157; and interactions with cattle cars, 173, 192–93; and interactions with those who escaped trains, 180, 184–88; and invasion of Poland, 124–29; and knowledge, 195–96; living near train stations or tracks, 177–81; and Polish-Jewish interactions in the areas around Treblinka, 98–99, 110–24; and remains of Jews along railway corridors, 191; and Ukrainians, 62–63. *See also* sensory witnessing
Łochów-Tłuszcz section of railway corridor, 189
Łopuszyński, Marian, 11–12, 153, 168
lower class, 84
Lublin, Poland, 40–41, 109, 142–44, 182
luck, 86, 90
Łukaszkiewicz, Zdzisław: on behavioral responses of locals, 137–38; and creating knowledge, 159; and the dismantling of Treblinka, 55–56; on the gas chambers, 78, 224n68; and the natural landscape, 16; and Nazi planners, 11; and power dynamics, 51; and resettlement narrative, 73; and roundup actions, 170
Łuków, Poland, 183, 188

machinery, 37–38
Magid, Elias, 182–83
Majdanek death camp, xvi, xvii, 41, 86, 142, 144, 204n14, 215n45, 236n75

Malicki family, 232–33n143
Małkinia, Poland: and backlogs of trains, 176; and conditions in cattle cars, 167; and escape from cattle cars, 181–82; and local materials in building Treblinka, 16–17; and the Małkinia-Górna railway junction, 11–12, 162–63, *164*; and notes dropped from transports, 192; and occupied Poland, 126, 209n51; and remains of Jews along railway corridors, 191; and residents near train stations or tracks, 179; and sensory witnessing, 135, 139–40, 150; and the Wilków Military Organization (WMO), 111–12; and witnessing sites, 174–75; and workers from Treblinka, 152
Marchenko, Nikolaj, 51
Maschke, Erich, 5–7, 208n25
The Massacre of a People, 197
Massey, Doreen, xix, xxii
mass graves, 21–22, 24, 55–56, 97, 151–52, 191, 197, 206n40, 248n22
mass shootings, xxvii, 1, 8, 10, 23, 38, 54, 228n8
material objects, 123–24, 191–93, 246n169, 246n171, 247–48n22
Matthes, Heinrich, 49–50
Mauthausen, 41
Menschenschlachthaus ideology, 59, 63
Das Menschenschlachthaus Treblinka (The Human Slaughterhouse Treblinka) (pamphlet), xxi, 35–36, 57, 142, 204n19, 220n153
Mentz, Willi, 42, 48, 50, 61
middle class, 84
Miedziński, Szmuel, 15, 118–19

silence, 155–56

Silverberg, Arthur, 229n45

Sinakowska, Henryka, 121

Sinti, 206n39

situational reality, 128

Skarżyński, Jerzy, 156

Skarżyński, Kazimierz, 178

Slebzak, Henryk, 115, 117, 149, 174–75, 177, 181, 243n102

smells, 132–40, 166–69

smoke, 140–46, 235–36n74, 235nn67–68

Snyder, Timothy, 9

Sobibór death camp, xvi–xvii, 1, 39, 41, 61, 136, 156, 197, 212n103, 230n75

Sobolewski, Józef, 189, 191

Socha, Karol, 116

Sokołów Podlaski, Poland: and *Bahnschutz* formations, 183; and escape by jumping from cattle cars, 181; and gunfire, 168; and interactions with Polish railway workers, 176; and Jews sent to Treblinka, 69; and observations of transports, 177–78; and Polish-Jewish interactions in the areas around Treblinka, 119; and remains of Jews along railway corridors, 189–91; and sensory witnessing, 139; before Treblinka, 14–15

Sonderkommando (special unit), 76–79, 82, 88–89, 133–34, 144, 149

Sonnenstein, 209n44

sounds, 152–58, 167–69

sovereignty, 45, 99–100

Soviet Union, 1, 11, 124, 200, 209n51, 232n132

spatiality: and contemporaneous plurality, xix–xx, xxvii, 128–29, 256n163; and intrusion, 126–28; and spatial freedom, 33–34, 75, 83–84; and spatial layout of the Umschlagplatz, 169–73; and spatial layout of Treblinka, 19–30, 26–27; and spatial layouts of small Polish towns, 177–78; and Treblinka's spatial threshold, 33, 206n42

Speer, Albert, 42, 207n10

Sperling, Heniek, 57

Srebnik, Haim, 187

Srulek, Jabłkowski, 13

ss guards. *See* German guards

Stabholz, Thaddeus, 184, 204n14, 235n67

Stangl, Franz: behavior of, 44–47, 57, 61; and command structures, 43; and conditions in cattle cars, 165; and the efficiency narrative, 59; on the gas chambers, 77; and guilt, 63–64; and leaves taken from the camp, 58; and lighting in gas chambers, 146; and masking of smells, 139; and occupied Poland, 126–27; and personality types, 52; photograph of, 46; and secrecy, 53–54; and sensory witnessing, 136; and spatial arrangements, 23–26; and the T4 euthanasia program, 41–42; and traces of Treblinka, 200–201; and Treblinka's conceptual mission, 38; trial of, 245n143, 245n150

State Department, 197–98

stat sheets, 54

Stefańczuka, Stanisława, 113

Stern Publishers, Vienna, 35

Stoczek, Poland, 13, 15, 102, 119, 121, 187, 221n7

stolen property, 192–93

Willenberg, Samuel: and burning of bodies, 137, 141; escape of, 95, 105–7, 114–15; and experiences with death shared outside the Totenlager, 93–94; on the gas chambers, 76–77; and interaction with death, 88; and material objects, 123; and the natural world, 110; photograph of, *106*; and psychological effects, 90–91; and sensory witnessing, 133, 234n40, 235n68; and singing of Polish songs, 158; and spatial arrangements, 22, 27–29; and spatial contradictions, 184; and stops near villages or towns, 179; and traces of Treblinka, xx–xxi, 201, 204n18, 205n21; and Treblinka's town station, 212n116; and Ukrainian guards, 51; and the visual narrative, 21; in the *Waldkommando* (Forest Brigade), 100

Wirth, Christian, 39–40, 43, 49–50, 52

witnesses, xix–xxi, xxii–xxiv, 195, 198–201; and people living up and down the railway corridors, 193–94; and Polish railway workers, 173–77; and residents near train stations or tracks, 177–81; and spatial layout of the Umschlagplatz, 169–73; to train journeys, 161–63. *See also* sensory witnessing

WMO (Wilków Military Organization), 111–12

Wólka Okrąglik, Poland, xviii–xix, 11–13, 231n112; and backlogs at village stations, 177; and the natural landscape, 16–19; and occupied Poland, 125–27; and Polish-Jewish interactions in the areas around Treblinka, 115, 117; and propaganda, 70; and remains of Jews along railway corridors, 191; and sensory witnessing, 133, 138, 141, 149, 153, 157; and stops near

villages or towns, 179–80; before Treblinka, 15; and witnesses to passing Treblinka-bound trains, 174–75

Wołkowysk, Poland (today Vawkavysk, Belarus), 69

Wołomin, Poland, 123, 178

Wołosz, Wacław, 189–91

women, 84–86, 225n98, 231n111

work details, 150–52

work Jews. *See* Jewish workers ("work Jews")

Yad Vashem, 98, 210n74

Yahad-in Unum, xxvii–xxviii, 206n40

Yugoslavia, 69

Ząbecki, Franciszek, 241n62; and backlogs of trains, 177; and *Bahnschutz* formations, 183; and code used to organize and disguise trains, 54–55, 175; and conditions in cattle cars, 165, 167, 241n67; and contemporaneous plurality, 128–29; and the dismantling of Treblinka, 56; and the General Directorate of the Eastern Railway, 173; and the leaving behind of material objects, 191; and local Poles, 147–48; and occupied Poland, 125–26; and passing trains, 160; and Polish railway workers, 174, 176; and residents near train stations or tracks, 180–81; and secrecy, 53–55; and sensory witnessing, 134, 142–43, 155, 167; and transports with belongings of victims, 193; before Treblinka, 4, 11, 15

Zeminski, Stanisław, 187–88

Złotki, Poland, 13, 126

zones of exception, 211n83

zoos, 23, 26–27

Zuckerman, Yitzhak, 99